Fundamentals of the Theory of Computation

of the Theory

of Computation

Principles and Practice

Fundamentals of the Theory of Computation

Principles and Practice

Raymond Greenlaw

University of New Hampshire

H. James Hoover

University of Alberta

 Morgan Kaufmann Publishers, Inc.
San Francisco, California

Sponsoring Editor   Michael B. Morgan
Director of Production and Manufacturing   Yonie Overton
Production Editor   Cheri Palmer
Assistant Editor   Marilyn Alan
Cover Design   Carrie English, canary studios
Text Design   Detta Penna, Penna Design & Production
Additional Design   Windfall Software
Composition and Illustrations   Windfall Software, using ZzTEX
Copyeditor   Ken DellaPenta
Proofreader   Jennifer McClain
Printer   Courier Corporation

Morgan Kaufmann Publishers, Inc.
Editorial and Sales Office
340 Pine Street, Sixth Floor
San Francisco, CA 94104-3205
USA
Telephone   415 / 392-2665
Facsimile   415 / 982-2665
Email   mkp@mkp.com
WWW   www.mkp.com
Order toll free   800 / 745-7323

Library of Congress Cataloging-in-Publication Data
Greenlaw, Raymond,
     Fundamentals of the theory of computation : principles and
practice / Raymond Greenlaw, H. James Hoover.
        p.   cm.
     Includes bibliographical references and index.
     ISBN 1-55860-474-X (cloth). — ISBN 1-55860-547-9 (paper)
     1. Computer science.   2. Computer algorithms.   I. Hoover, H.
James.   II. Title.
QA76.G715   1998
004—dc21   98-12048
                                                                  CIP

This book is dedicated to our parents.
Thanks for bringing us into this exciting world.

Contents

Preface

What is this book? It is an introduction to the *theory of computation*—the concepts and mathematics that we use to model and predict the behavior of algorithmic computations. By "algorithmic," we mean applications like parsing and compiling, communication protocols, operating systems, optimization, databases, and all those computing activities that involve the manipulation of symbols. The theory of computation does not tell us much about nonalgorithmic activities, such as the dynamics of human–machine interactions, or the social aspects of computing. But even there the theory can contribute—for example, by providing the theory behind the strong encryption technology essential to privacy.

What is in this book? This book is not intended to be a comprehensive presentation of the field of computability theory. Rather it contains what we feel is the most fundamental material that sophomores and juniors should know and can digest in a one-semester course, including the basic machine types (tape-based machines for sequential computation and Boolean circuits for parallel computation), formal languages and grammars, the notions of resource consumption, and the classification of feasible and intractable problems. We, of course, point you to fundamental references for additional subject areas and more advanced material.

Why was this book written? We have been teaching theory of computation courses for many years, using all of the classics and standards, and having read many more. We decided to write another book for two reasons. The theory of computation is very elegant and deep and can be studied on its own without any connection to the practice of computing. But we wanted a text that had a greater connection to reality, showing how the theory is motivated by and applied in practice. Second, we wanted a text that covered essential computation theory ideas that every computing science major should know after one semester. Thus we dropped many important (to theoreticians) subjects and added a few that do not normally appear in such a text (such as Boolean circuits and P-completeness). We, of course, did not cover all the topics that form the core.

How is this book written? The stereotypical scholarly presentation of a subject begins with simple ideas and linearly builds up to the climax of the grand theory. Naturally, clean linear presentations are an illusion, and trying to follow this illusion often results in a rather long, boring, incremental development that loses its audience before the exciting results are reached. To counter this and get you excited about the power of theory, we show our hand early with the important notions of languages, state, pumping, and the Halting problem all in the introduction. Only then do we begin a systematic incremental development.

We are unconventional at times. For example, we present all tape machines (i.e., finite–state, pushdown, and Turing) as just variations on the same finite–control tape machine. Unfortunately, this generality comes at the expense of some notational baggage, thus providing an example of the real–life trade–off between generality and simplicity. As another example, before introducing *NP*–completeness, we present a chapter on feasible problems. The chapter deals with *P*–completeness theory—a theory analogous to *NP*–completeness theory but one where the reductions are often less complex and the underlying machine model is deterministic. It is debatable, but we think this makes the concept of *NP*–completeness more accessible.

The mathematical rigor and level of our presentation varies according to the topic at hand. Like all subject areas of substance, some ideas must appear and be applied informally before they can be treated rigorously. Sometimes a rigorous treatment clarifies our understanding, but often it merely clothes a simple idea in impenetrable notation.

Finally, this book does not contain any review of discrete mathematics. Our experience is that the discrete mathematics backgrounds of students varies wildly. There is no point consuming 10 to 20 percent of a book as review for such an unpredictable audience. We leave the discrete mathematics to others who do it well and thoroughly.

To the Student

The theory of computation is a challenging subject. It takes hard work to master and can be very frustrating. Our best advice is to remember that almost all of the key ideas are programming problems in disguise: the machines and languages may be a bit weird, but the techniques are essentially the same ones you use in the design and implementation of real applications.

When you master this material, it will forever change the way you practice computing.

Corrections and Suggestions

Undoubtedly, the text still contains a few errors, and certain topics may have been omitted that you feel are especially relevant for inclusion. In anticipation of possible future printings, we would like to correct our mistakes and incorporate as many suggestions as possible. Please send your comments via email to us at *greenlaw@cs.unh.edu* or *hoover@cs.ualberta.ca*. Corrigenda and additions to this work can by found in the directory *pub/hoover/Computability* at *ftp.cs.ualberta.ca* and via the World Wide Web at *www.cs.unh.edu/~greenlaw /research/COMPUTABILITY/newbook.html*. We especially welcome input from students.

Research Support

We gratefully acknowledge financial support from the following organizations:

Ray Greenlaw's research was supported in part by the National Science Foundation grant CCR-9209184, a Senior Research Fulbright Scholarship, and a fellowship from the Ministry of Scientific and Technical Investigations of Spain.

Jim Hoover's research was supported by the Natural Sciences and Engineering Research Council of Canada grant OGP 38937.

Acknowledgments

Ray gratefully acknowledges the hospitality of the Universitat Politènica de Catalunya in Barcelona, Spain, where a portion of this text was written.

A special thanks to Larry Ruzzo for allowing us to include some of the material from our joint book. Thanks to Kevin Charter and Erin Cruess for carefully reading the book and providing us with very valuable comments from a TA and student perspective.

We wish to thank the reviewers who provided us with general comments about the organization of the book. We have tried to incorporate as many of their suggestions as possible, although not all of them were feasible for us. A special thanks to David Barrington, whose insightful and thorough remarks helped to significantly improve this work.

Thanks to Mona Lisa Agrawal, Dan Lipsa, Derek Rhode, Anu Subramanian, and Vassili Sukharev. A very special thanks to our students who weathered being taught from early drafts of this book.

Authors' Addresses

RAYMOND GREENLAW
Department of Computer Science
University of New Hampshire
Durham, NH 03824
email address: *greenlaw@cs.unh.edu*
World Wide Web personal page: *www.cs.unh.edu/~greenlaw*

H. James Hoover
Department of Computing Science
University of Alberta
Edmonton, Alberta, Canada T6G 2H1
email address: *hoover@cs.ualberta.ca*
World Wide Web personal page: *www.cs.ualberta.ca/~hoover*

Book's Uniform Resource Locator

You should always be able to access the online information about the text by visiting our Web pages. Since World Wide Web addresses do change occasionally, another option would be to locate the online material through Morgan Kaufmann's Web site: *www.mkp.com*.

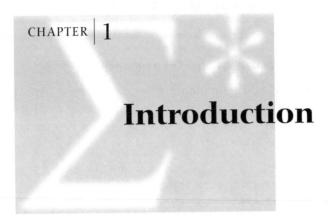

CHAPTER | 1

Introduction

If only there were a computability book that appealed to my intuition about programming.

      —*Former computability student*

Let's begin with an informal look at the subject of computability, a discussion of some related works, and an overview of this book.

1.1 Some Computing Puzzles

Computability—what computers can and cannot do—is often the subject of almost mystical philosophical diatribes. Our goal in this book is to convince you that, far from being unearthly, understanding the power and limitations of computing is well within the grasp of anyone with a sound computer science intuition. Thus we begin with four puzzles in computing. The first two are easy to solve, and the third is harder but accessible once you see the trick. Resolving the fourth on your own is a definite sign of brilliance. Most people have trouble following the arguments in full detail the first time through, so do not attempt to understand everything.

    The process of working through these puzzles exposes four fundamental concepts in the theory of computation: the notion of a *language*,[1] the concept of *configuration* or *state*, the idea of *structural constraints* limiting what a computation can do, and the astonishing fact that certain computations are *intrinsically impossible*. In later chapters these ideas will be presented in more detail and in different settings.

---

1. Our convention is to put technical words in *italics* upon their first use. (Italics are also used for emphasis.) When we define a concept, the term is put in **boldface**.

1.1.1   A Restricted Version of the C Language

One of the challenges of computing is to do the most with your available resources. Our study of computation begins with a very restricted subset of the C programming language, which we will call C--.[2] A C-- program always has the following basic structure (or *syntax*):

```
void main() {
    int s = 0;  /* initialize integer s to 0 */
    while (1) { /* loop until an exit occurs */
        <body>
    }
}
```

There is only one variable, named s, in a C-- program.

The <body> of the program can contain only two kinds of statements: assignments to s and control flow.

The only operation on s is an assignment of an integer constant as follows:

```
s = <integer constant>;
```

where the notation <integer constant> stands for *any* integer from the set $\{\ldots, -2, -1, 0, 1, 2, \ldots\}$. For convenience, you can also use character constants (any symbol from a standard keyboard enclosed in quotes, like 'b'), instead of their integer representations (in ASCII, 'b' is 98).

Execution of the program is controlled by statements of the following forms. Controlling flow on the basis of s takes this form:

```
switch(s) {
    case <integer constant>:
            .
            .
            .
        break;

    case <integer constant>:
            .
            .
            .
        break;

        .
        .
        .

    default:
}
```

---

2. There is nothing special about using a restriction of C; a similar restriction on Pascal or Ada or any other language would do as well. The main point is to use a real language so that you can compile and test your programs.

Reading a character from the input and controlling flow on the value of the character just read takes the following form:

```
switch(getchar()) {
    case <integer constant>:
          .
          .
          .
        break;

    case <integer constant>:
          .
          .
          .
        break;

          .
          .
          .
    default:
}
```

Input to a C-- program comes from the standard input stream via the getchar function, which returns an integer that is either a character or EOF (*end of file*). All input streams end with EOF. The input stream is read-only and one-way: you cannot look ahead, and once a character is read, it is removed from the stream.

The program stops via

```
exit(Yes);
```

or

```
exit(No);
```

A C-- program does not write any output. Instead, it sets the exit code using the conventions that exit(Yes) means YES or okay, and exit(No) means NO or not okay. Yes and No are predefined constants with logical values 1 (TRUE) and 0 (FALSE), respectively.[3]

In the next few sections we study a number of C-- programs.

1.1.2 Problem 1—Detecting Strings in a Language

Suppose there is a large collection of text files for a mathematics book that is about to be published. We need to search the files and locate all of those that contain the word "onto" so that it can be replaced by the more verbose word "surjective." Can we write a program, call it Detect, in C-- that will take as input a file and tell us whether that file requires editing?

---

3. A source of confusion among novice programmers is that in many operating systems, the logical value TRUE is represented by an exit code of 0, and FALSE by a nonzero exit code. Thus, in the event of failure, the exit code also contains some hint as to the kind of failure.

Since a file is simply one long string of characters, the general purpose of our program is to detect any string (i.e., file) that contains "onto" as a substring. The idea is to feed a string into Detect that then processes the string and eventually answers YES or NO depending on whether it found the substring or not. We call the set of all the strings on which Detect says YES its *language*.

Here is one attempt at writing Detect:

```
void main() {
    int s = 0;
    while (1) {
        s = getchar();  // Oops, not a valid C-- statement
           .
           .
           .
    }
}
```

We see that in C-- we cannot even save the input in a variable. Even worse, there is only one variable, namely s. So Figure 1.1 is another try at Detect.

It is easy to see that this version of Detect does the job. Either Detect finds the string "onto" in the input and exits answering YES, or it runs out of input and exits answering NO. The language accepted by Detect consists of all strings having the substring "onto." Of course, we are not done yet. Just because a string contains "onto" does not mean that we want to replace every "onto" with "surjective." Consider what would happen to the word "ontology."

If you want to match a different string, say, "polymorphism," the details will change, but the structure of the matching program will follow that of Detect. So C-- is not a totally useless programming language. In fact, C-- is powerful enough to do some very general pattern matching of strings in a file, as we will see later. Several other pattern–matching problems appear in the exercises.

1.1.3   Problem 2—Execution Configuration

When an operating system runs many programs simultaneously, it does so by running a program for a small amount of time, interrupting it, running another program, and then eventually resuming execution of the original program. Suppose that we want to interrupt the execution of a C-- program and then resume it later. What information do we need to save in order to be able to restart the program later in exactly the same place? That is, what is the *configuration* of the program? We need to know what statement was about to be executed, the value of s, and the characters still to be read in the input stream. If we assume that the interruption always occurs at the top of the while loop, then all we need is the value of s and the remaining characters in the input (or the

```
void main() {
   int s = 0;
   while (1) {
      switch(s) {
         // s == 0 means we are looking for a leading 'o'
         case 0:
             switch(getchar()) {
                case 'o': s = 1; break;
                case EOF: exit(No); break;
                default: break;
             }
             break;
         // s == 1 means previous char was an 'o'
         case 1:
             switch(getchar()) {
                case 'o': s = 1; break;
                case 'n': s = 2; break;
                case EOF: exit(No); break;
                default: s = 0; break; // restart
             }
             break;
         // s == 2 means previous characters were 'on'
         case 2:
             switch(getchar()) {
                case 'o': s = 1; break;
                case 't': s = 3; break;
                case EOF: exit(No); break;
                default: s = 0; break; // restart
             }
             break;
         // s == 3 means previous characters were 'ont'
         case 3:
             switch(getchar()) {
                case 'o': exit(Yes); break;
                case EOF: exit(No); break;
                default: s = 0; break; // restart
             }
      } // no default needed, s is only 0, 1, 2, or 3
   } // end while
} // end main
```

Figure 1.1

The second C-- program for Detect.

position of the file pointer). This type of "snapshot" of a program is usually called a configuration.

We illustrate with another simple problem. Suppose we are given a bunch of binary strings—that is, strings containing only the characters 0 and 1—and we need to compute the *parity* of each string. The parity of a string is a statement about the number of 1's in the string. The parity is even if there is an even number of 1's, and odd if there is an odd number.

Our task is to write a C-- program, `Parity`, whose language consists of all the binary strings with an even number of occurrences of the character 1. The program in Figure 1.2 does this by implementing a mod 2 counter that is incremented every time a 1 is read.

Suppose that the input to `Parity` is the string 01101. We start the program and let it read 011, stopping it just as it is about to execute the `switch(s)` at the top of the `while` loop. To restart `Parity` later, we need to know that we are just about to execute the `switch(s)` statement, that s has value 0, and that 01 remains to be read from the input. We do not need any more information.

1.1.4   Problem 3—Deducing Behavior from Structure

By now you should have noticed that the syntax of C-- forces all programs to have the same global structure: a single `while` loop containing code that determines the next value of s given the current value of s and zero or more input characters. We do not have a lot of creative room when writing C-- programs. Does this affect the kinds of programs that we can write?

For example, can you write a program in C-- that determines if the input contains equal numbers of "a" and "b" characters? That is, the program returns YES if the number of a's and b's are equal, and NO otherwise. We guarantee that you will find this an impossible task. In this section we prove why.

Suppose someone comes along and claims that they have such a C-- program, called `Count`, which does what we claim is impossible—determines if the input has an equal number of a's and b's for any possible input. The rub is that the person refuses to let us see their[4] source code. Can we reverse-engineer such a program? Can we determine if their claim is correct?

Even though we do not know what the code of program `Count` looks like, we can deduce a surprising amount of information about the behavior of `Count` by exploiting the structural properties of C-- programs.

---

4. We are attempting to revive the old gender-free singular use of "their" as an alternative to "his/her."

```
void main() {
  int s = 0;
  while (1) {
    switch (s) {
      // s == 0 means even number of 1's
      case 0:
        switch(getchar()) {
          case '1':
            s = 1;
            break;
          case EOF:
            // DONE: have even number
            exit(Yes);
            break;
          default:
            s = 0;   // included for emphasis
            break;
        }
        break;
      // s == 1 means odd number of 1's
      case 1:
        switch(getchar()) {
          case '1':
            s = 0;
            break;
          case EOF:
            // DONE: have odd number
            exit(No);
            break;
          default:
            s = 1;   // included for emphasis
            break;
        }
    }  // no default needed, s is only 0 or 1
  }  // end while
}  // end main
```

Figure 1.2

A C-- program for Parity.

Consider the basic form of C-- programs:

```
void main() {
    int s = 0;
    while (1) {
        // inspection point for s
        <body>
    }
}
```

We have marked the position immediately at the top of the while(1) loop and called it the *inspection point*. We will only look at the configuration of the program at this point. Thus we need only remember the value of s and the remaining unread input.

Now let's deduce some properties of Count.

Fact 1: Suppose we inspect the value of s at the top of the while loop. What are the possible values of s at this point? Since the program is a fixed length, there are only a finite number of assignment statements to s, and each can only assign a constant value (no expressions are allowed in C--). Thus s can only have a fixed–size set of possible values, and this set must come from the set of right–hand–side values in assignments to s. Let $n \in \{1, 2, 3, \ldots\}$ be an *upper bound* on the number of possible values that s can have. By "upper bound" we mean the number of possible distinct values assigned to s is less than or equal to n.

Fact 2: We know that Count must read all of the input before it stops and gives an answer. Why? If it did not read all of its input, Count might miss some incoming a or b characters. The only way Count can guarantee that it does not miss any input is to read until it obtains an EOF on a getchar operation. When we say all the input has been read, we mean EOF has been read, too.

Fact 3: After all the input has been read, if the value of s repeats at the inspection point, then Count is in an infinite loop. Why is this? Suppose that Count has processed all of the input, and then executes for some number of steps, during which time the value s repeats itself. When executing the body of the while loop, the next value of s at the inspection point is a function of its current value and the input characters read during that pass. If there is no more input to read, then only the current value of s affects its next value. If some future value is the same as the current value, then when that future value is reached, the program is in exactly the same configuration. This means that Count is now in a cycle, repeating the same sequence of values of s forever. Clearly, we will not be getting the required YES or NO answer back from Count in this case.

Fact 4: After exhausting the input, if `Count` makes more than n additional iterations of the `while` loop, it will never exit. Why? Since there are at most n possible values of s, this means that after more than n passes of the inspection point, the same value of s must have appeared twice, and we can apply Fact 3.

Fact 5: Fact 4 can be generalized. Between any two reads of the input, `Count` cannot make more than n iterations of the `while` loop. Why? Not reading an input is essentially the same as running out of input—only the current value of s can affect its next value. Thus the same value of s cannot appear twice without reading at least one input character.

Now let's do a thought experiment. Our goal is to show that `Count` must accept a string of the wrong form—that is, the number of a's does not equal the number of b's. Suppose we feed a string into `Count` and look at the value of s at the inspection point every time we reach it. In general, the value of s can change without actually reading a character from the input stream (but it cannot change more than $n - 1$ times by Fact 5). In addition, during one cycle of the `while` loop, `Count` could read more than one character by having multiple `getchar`'s, but only a fixed number more (why?). Let k be the maximum possible number of characters read on one pass through the loop. Recall, we know that all characters must be read, including `EOF`, before `Count` stops (Fact 2).

On any input string of length at least kn, the inspection point has been reached at least n times. Let's feed in the specific string t consisting of kn occurrences of a followed by kn occurrences of b. So,

$$t = \underbrace{a \ldots a}_{kn} \underbrace{b \ldots b}_{kn}.$$

`Count` should say YES on this input since there are an equal number of a's and b's.

Now consider the sequence of values that s takes, as observed at the inspection point, as the a characters in the input are fully processed:

$$s_0, s_1, s_2, \ldots, s_m,$$

where s_i denotes the value of s after passing through the `while` loop i times. Since $n \leq m$ and there are $m + 1$ values in the sequence, two of the values of s, say s_i and s_j, with $i < j$, are the same (by the *Pigeonhole Principle*).[5] Let p be the number of a characters read prior to pass i, and let l be the number of input characters read between pass i and pass j. Observe that l is greater than or equal to 1, because if it

---

5. Informally, the Pigeonhole Principle states that if there are p pigeons and h holes, with $p > h$, then two pigeons will share the same hole.

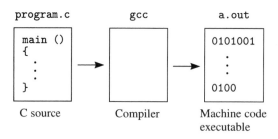

Figure 1.3

The compilation process for a C program.

were not, the program would repeat a configuration and go into an infinite loop. Thus the same value of s occurs after reading p or $p + l$ a characters. Therefore, we can delete l occurrences of a from the input, and Count will not know the difference. That is, Count will still answer YES on the shortened input. But this shortened input does not have an equal number of a and b characters. So we have managed to fool Count into giving the wrong answer.

Our argument did not use any information other than that Count was a C-- program. Thus no C-- program can answer YES on exactly those strings with equal numbers of a and b characters. The C-- programming language is not powerful enough to recognize the language consisting of such strings. Therefore, the person that claimed to have such a program was in error. Perhaps this is the reason our unnamed programmer refused to show us their source code.

1.1.5   Problem 4—The Halting Problem

The programming language C-- is an example of a *computational model*. Problems 1 and 2 are examples of things that are possible to compute in the model, and Problem 3 is an example of something provably impossible to compute in the model. What do we have to add to C-- to make a new model in which the impossible problems (for the C-- model at least) can be solved, or perhaps the feasible ones solved better—for example, faster or using less memory? Maybe all problems can be solved in C. At least it is easy to write a C program for the language consisting of an equal number of a and b characters.

All compilers for C take as input a source program and produce as output executable code. This process is depicted in Figure 1.3. Compilers can be quite sophisticated. They can detect *syntax* errors, they can indicate possible *semantic* errors (such as using "=" in a situation that normally calls for "=="), they can optimize the resulting code for time or memory, and they can even introduce errors.

How clever can a compiler be? For example, could it detect that on all negative input values the following program goes into an infinite loop?

```
void main () {
   int i = 0;
   int a;
   scanf("%d", &a);   // read in the value of a
   while ( i > a ) {
      i = a + 1;
   }
}
```

Recall that & is the *unary* address operator and scanf reads characters from the standard input, interprets them based on the given format, and saves the result(s) in the pointer(s) that are specified.

Perhaps the compiler is not quite that sophisticated, but still could answer a general question, such as "Does a program P halt when given a particular input I?" If the compiler were able to, we could extract out the program text for the part of it that answers this question and encapsulate the code segment into a function called Halts. Since both a program and its input are simply text strings, Halts could be specified as follows:

```
// Halts(P, I) == 1  if string P is a valid C program
//                    that eventually halts when reading
//                    input I.
//
//               == 0  otherwise.
```

```
int Halts(char *P; char *I);
```

We assume that Halts works for any pair of strings. So, for example, if we have

```
char *prog = "void main () { int i = 0; int a; scanf("%d", &a);
            while ( i > a ) { i = a + 1; } }";
```

then we have that Halts(prog, "1") returns 1, and Halts(prog, "-1") returns 0. Next let's write a somewhat strange, new program that looks like this:

```
<insert C source for the Halts program here>

void main() {
   char *program;
   // read all of the input stream, allocating as
   // much memory as is required to hold it.  mscanf is
   // guaranteed to return.
   mscanf("%s", &program);

   if ( Halts(program, program) == 1 ) {
      // call this location point *
      // loop forever
      while(1) { }
   }
}
```

Now place the source code for the above program into a file called `diagonal.c` and compile it. Then run `diagonal` on its own source, as in

```
diagonal < diagonal.c
```

What is the result returned by `diagonal` on input `diagonal.c`? During execution, this results in the call

```
Halts(program, program)
```

where the string `program` contains the text of `diagonal.c`. So what happens when we do this and feed `diagonal` its own source code as input? Remember regardless of what program is fed into it, `Halts` is supposed to return either 1 or 0, telling us whether that program halts or not, respectively. To answer our question, let's consider `Halts` on input `diagonal`. There are two cases.

> *Case 0*: If `Halts(diagonal, diagonal)` returns 0, then this means that `diagonal` on input `diagonal` loops forever. Note that `diagonal` is a legal C program. But since `Halts` is supposed to always return, the infinite loop can only happen if the `while` loop at point * is reached. This can only happen if the evaluation of `Halts` returns 1. However, since the contents of `program` is the same as `diagonal`, this means that `Halts(diagonal, diagonal)` is 1. This is a contradiction, and so `Halts(diagonal, diagonal)` cannot return 0.
>
> *Case 1*: If `Halts(diagonal, diagonal)` returns 1, then this means that `diagonal` on input `diagonal` halts. But this can only happen if the `while` loop at point * is never reached. This can only happen if the evaluation of `Halts` returns 0. However, since the contents of `program` is the same as `diagonal`, this means that `Halts(diagonal, diagonal)` is 0. This is also a contradiction, and so `Halts(diagonal, diagonal)` cannot return 1.

This is strange indeed. Both possible return values for `Halts` lead to a contradiction. This can mean one of two things. One possibility is that `Halts` never returns on such a call, but this contradicts the assumption that `Halts` works for all possible inputs. The other situation is that it is impossible to actually write down the text of `diagonal`, and so we could not perform `Halts(diagonal, diagonal)`. If that is the case, since we certainly can write the `main` part of `diagonal`, it must mean that we cannot write down the code for `Halts`. This leads us to conclude that there is no possible C code for computing the function `Halts`.

So `Halts` is not programmable in C. Is it programmable in any other language? To attempt any kind of mathematical or logical treatment of this flavor of question, we will have to use the more precise models of computation we develop in later chapters. In fact, it turns out that the answer to this question is NO.

In summary, we have argued that the *Halting problem*—the problem of determining whether a program halts on a given input—is *undecidable*. This is to say that no program (in our case C program, but in general any type of program could be used by an analogous argument) can correctly code Halts. Intuitively, by equating the concept of "algorithm" with that of "program," this says that there is no algorithm for deciding the Halting problem. So, regardless of how clever someone is, they cannot devise an algorithm for solving the Halting problem; the Halting problem is simply not solvable. This result proves that not all problems are solvable by computers—something that may be counterintuitive to you. The proof technique we used in proving this undecidability result is known as *diagonalization*, and we will encounter it again in Chapter 2. There are entire classes of undecidable problems; in fact, most properties of programs cannot be decided by a general method.

1.2   *What Is Computability?*

In the previous section we appealed to your intuition and knowledge of programming to introduce a number of important concepts in computability. We continue this theme by defining *computability* and the key notion of *problem*.

Computability deals with the following kinds of questions: Given a specific problem, can its solution be computed? Can it be computed on a particular kind of machine? If it can be computed on one kind of machine, can another kind of machine be used instead? If it can be computed, what amounts of resources (e.g., time or memory) are consumed? What are the minimum amounts of resources needed to solve a problem? Are there trade-offs between resources (e.g., does more speed require more memory)? Are the resources required to solve a problem so great that it is impossible in practice to solve? What are the practical amounts of resources that we can apply to solving problems? Can feasible and intractable classes of problems be defined? If so, is there a clean breakpoint between the two categories?

Before we begin to look at these questions, we need a more precise idea of what we mean by "problem." We begin with a simple illustrative example, leaving the actual definitions to Chapter 2.

A problem you typically encounter in an introductory computing course is to write a program that determines an average value of its inputs. Let $\mathbb{N} = \{0, 1, 2, \ldots\}$ denote the **natural numbers**. Suppose you are given n numbers $x_1, \ldots, x_n$, where each x_i is a natural number. You would like to compute the average of these values.

We will adopt the convention of systematically specifying our computational problems in terms of a *given part* and a *problem part*. The given part describes the information supplied to the problem solver. The problem part specifies the question to be solved. Each problem is given a name, such as Average for this example.

Average

Given: A natural number n, with $n > 0$, and a list of n natural numbers $l = \langle x_1, \ldots, x_n \rangle$.

Problem: Compute the average value, $\frac{1}{n} \sum_{i=1}^{n} x_i$.

An *instance* of Average is a specific set of values for the given part. For example, $n = 4, l = \langle 1, 2, 7, -1 \rangle$.

It is easy to write a program that runs on a personal computer and quickly outputs the answer to any instance of Average. Once your program is compiled and tested so that it produces a value based on the formula given above, you would feel that the problem had been solved. Furthermore, you would notice that even for large values of n (for example, 10^7) the answer gets printed very quickly, within minutes say, by your code. This indicates that the problem has a *feasible* solution.

In this book we will study problems having a flavor similar to Average. One hurdle we must overcome in addressing such problems is that our computational models are severely limited in the type of input they can handle. Most theoretical machines are not allowed to input natural numbers directly. The numbers might have to be encoded into some other data type, such as bits (0's and 1's), that the machine can accept. Similarly, a machine may not be able to directly output a natural number; instead its output must *encode* it. For example, suppose a particular machine can only output bits. Then to produce a value of 33, it could print the bit string 100001—an encoding of 33 in binary. So associated with a problem description is always an encoding into a form that a machine can handle. What kinds of encodings are possible and reasonable is another question that must be addressed when solving a problem.

The other kind of issue that the theory of computation addresses is the relationships between the different kinds of machines we use to solve a problem. Suppose a solution to Average on a machine M requires n^2 steps of computation, where n is the number of x_i's. How long will it take to solve Average on a different variety of machine, say M'? Perhaps M is a four–processor Unix™ workstation and M' is a Mac. Can M' mimic M's behavior somehow? If so, what is the cost of the simulation? For example, if each step of M can be simulated using only n steps of M', then Average can be solved on M' using n^3 steps. Can any program that is run on M, not just the one to solve Average, be simulated by a program on M'?

Computability plays an important role in a number of different fields, including biology, operations research, and physics. The theory is applicable to subjects such as algorithms, compilers, networks, operating systems, and even software engineering. You cannot do computer science without understanding the basics of computability.

1.3   *Related Works*

The goal of this book is to provide an introduction to computability theory. There are many topics in this theory, each with an interesting history. Since it is impossible to cover all the important aspects of computability in an introductory text, we can cover only the basic principles. So here are some references to some of the more advanced topics. Our intention is not to be complete, but simply to note a few that we are familiar with. We also list a number of discrete mathematics texts.

The book *Introduction to Automata Theory, Languages, and Computation* by Hopcroft and Ullman is the classic text in the field [26], published in 1979. We used this text in our first computability course many years ago. The text covers a great deal of advanced material that is not appropriate for inclusion here.

The text *Elements of the Theory of Computation* is another classic [33]. Written by Lewis and Papadimitriou in 1981, it includes material about the propositional calculus and the predicate calculus that is not contained in our text.

In addition to the two classics, we mention several other texts that might be appropriate at both the undergraduate and graduate level: *Computability, Complexity, and Languages* by Davis, Sigal, and Weyuker [12]; *Languages and Machines* by Sudkamp [42]; *The Language of Machines* by Floyd and Beigel [15]; and *Theory of Computation* by Wood [46]. These books can supplement the material described in this book and offer you another perspective.

The two-book series *Structural Complexity I* and *Structural Complexity II* by Balcázar, Díaz, and Gabarró provides a more advanced treatment of the material contained in Chapters 8, 10, and 11 [3, 4]. The books address many other recent topics in complexity theory as well. If you are interested in pursuing research in this area, these two books would be an excellent place to continue your studies.

Papadimitriou's book *Computational Complexity* provides a more recent discussion of many key ideas in complexity theory [35]. This book is more advanced and would be suitable as a follow-up to the current text.

There are two books that deal in depth with the subject matter contained in Chapters 10 and 11: *Limits to Parallel Computation: P-Completeness Theory* by Greenlaw, Hoover, and Ruzzo [23], covering the material in Chapter 10, and *Computers and Intractability: A Guide to the Theory of NP-Completeness* by Garey and Johnson [17], covering the material in Chapter 11. Each book provides expanded coverage of one of these subjects and includes extensive problem lists. Both books contain extensive reference lists.

Lastly, we mention several texts on discrete mathematics that we are familiar with. This list is meant to give you a starting point for review or additional information: *Concrete Mathematics: A Foundation for Computer Science* by Graham, Knuth, and Patashnik [20]; *Discrete Mathematics* by Ross and Wright [40]; *Discrete Mathematics and Its Applications* by Rosen [39]; and *Mathematical Structures for Computer Science* by Gersting [18].

1.4   *Overview of This Book*

In Chapter 2 we examine languages and problems—the fundamental objects in the theory of computation. We introduce languages, using examples of calculators and forms on the World Wide Web. Different problem types are described in terms of language recognition questions, and numerous important languages are presented. The diagonalization technique introduced in Section 1.1 is applied again in this chapter.

A concise method for representing languages, namely via regular expressions, is presented in Chapter 3. In this chapter the relationship between regular expressions and regular languages is explored. Applications of regular expressions to compilers, networks, and operating systems are described.

The basic computational models of interest in computability are described in Chapters 4 and 6. We define the finite automata, pushdown automata, and Turing machines. Several simulation results relating the computing power of the deterministic versions of the models to the nondeterministic versions are also presented.

Properties of finite-state languages are explored in Chapter 5. Numerous machine simulations are presented. We show the equivalence of regular expressions and finite automata. In addition, we explain a method for proving that certain languages are not regular.

Regular and context-free grammars are discussed in Chapter 7. The relationship between context-free grammars and pushdown automata is also explained. Applications of grammars to programming languages and parsing are described.

Chapter 8 develops a framework to study resource-bounded computations. It examines the resources of time and space. A number of important complexity classes are defined. Basic simulations are presented, as is the notion of reducibility. Other fundamental points from complexity theory are also described.

The elegant Boolean circuit model is the highlight of Chapter 9. This model is defined, and several examples are provided to illustrate it. A number of basic results are described, and the parallel complexity class NC is defined in terms of the circuit model. This class consists of those problems that can be solved "very fast" in parallel while using a "reasonable" number of processors.

In Chapter 10 the focus is on the class of problems that can be solved in feasible sequential time. This class is called P, standing for *polynomial*. P contains problems for which there are efficient algorithms. A number of examples of problems that are P-complete are given.

Chapter 11 introduces the concept of intractability in the form of the NP-complete problems. NP stands for *nondeterministic polynomial*. The NP-complete problems, in contrast to those in the complexity class P, do not have efficient solution algorithms. They are problems whose solutions can be verified efficiently but not found efficiently.

Appendix A contains a list of the notation used throughout the book; Appendix B lists the Greek alphabet.

1.5   *Exercises*

This is the first set of exercises. Words like "show" mean write a mathematically rigorous proof for your solution. Always give an explanation of your answer, and try to prove that your solution is correct. When asked to provide examples, justify with proofs why your examples are correct. We have tried to present problems that you will find enlightening as well as interesting and practical.

Section 1.1   *Some Computing Puzzles*

1. Write C-- programs to recognize the following patterns in a string:

   (a) 01
   (b) *hey*
   (c) *ababa*

   Implement these C-- programs as C programs, and test them on a number of positive and negative examples.

2. In each case write a C-- program to recognize strings that do *not* contain the specified pattern:

   (a) 01
   (b) 1101
   (c) *toto*

   Implement these C-- programs as C programs, and test them on a number of positive and negative examples.

3. Prove that in a C-- program it is impossible to increment s forever.

 4. What if you restricted C-- further to allow only one occurrence of a switch statement? How powerful is this version of C--?

5. Suppose that you restrict the range of the integer constants that can be used in a C-- program. Does this limit what can be computed by a C-- program?

6. Write a C-- program that detects input strings that contain either the words "ontop" or "toronto".

7. A string of 0's and 1's has k-parity if the number of 1's it contains is 0 modulo k. For example, even parity is 2-parity. The string 1101 has 3-parity but not 2-parity. Given a constant k, describe how to construct a C-- program that computes the k-parity of its input.

8. How do you construct a longest running program? That is, given n different possible values for s, and an input of length m, how long can a C-- program run and still eventually stop?

9. Write a program in C (or any other language) that takes no input, does no file I/O other than writing to standard output, and writes its own source text to standard output. That is, when the program is run, it prints itself out.

CHAPTER | 2

Languages and Problems

The computer says it's a binary code.
It's just a pity I can't understand it.
—*Flock of Seagulls*

2.1 Introduction

The purpose of computation is to solve problems. However, before we can attempt to solve a problem, we must communicate it to another person, a computer, or just ourselves. We do this with a *language*. In very general terms, a language is a system of signs used to communicate information between one or more parties. In this book the language we use to talk *about* computation is a combination of English and mathematics. But what about the language *of* computation? That is, what language do we use to communicate problems to, and get answers from, our computing machines? Answering this question is the goal of this chapter.

Even equipped with a fancy graphical user interface, a computer remains fundamentally a symbol manipulator. Unlike the natural languages of humans, each symbol is precise and unambiguous. A computer takes sequences of precisely defined symbols as inputs, manipulates them according to its program, and outputs sequences of similarly precise symbols. If a problem cannot be expressed symbolically in some language, then it cannot be studied using the tools of computation theory.

Thus the first step of understanding a problem is to design a language for communicating that problem to a machine. In this sense, a *language* is the fundamental object of computability. Let's begin with some informal discussion and examples of this abstract concept of language before proceeding with the technical details.

Consider the following very general "problem": develop a graphical user interface for evaluating arithmetic expressions that has the same look and feel as a

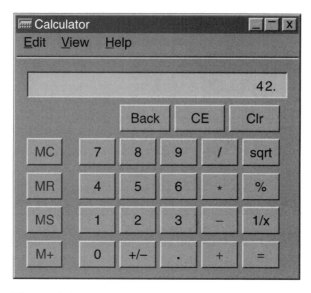

Figure 2.1

An online calculator program. The buttons represent inputs to the calculator. An input is triggered or sent to the calculator program by clicking on the = key. Using the Clr key resets the entire input.

physical calculator. What exactly is the problem here? At a high level, the problem faced by the programmer is to actually build such an application. This kind of problem belongs to the realm of algorithm design and software engineering.

We use the term "problem" in a much narrower sense. The problem in the calculator case is to evaluate arithmetic expressions. The problem consists of many *instances*, where each instance provides an input (in some suitable language) that gives a specific arithmetic formula to be evaluated. The value of the formula, which is the solution of the instance, is then output (again in some suitable language).

For example, if we run a calculator program online, the input is generated by clicking on the calculator's buttons, as shown in Figure 2.1. We could create a legal input by clicking on the 4, 0, 6, ÷, 5, 0, and =. The solution to the problem would then appear in the display as the sequence of symbols 8.12. Of course, not all sequences of input symbols are legitimate instances of the problem, and only certain combinations of mouse clicks should be allowed by the input language. For example, clicking × first and then = would probably cause the calculator to complain that the input was invalid. Exactly how the valid and invalid combinations can be concisely specified is an interesting topic in itself that we discuss in Chapter 7.

Intuitively, we as experienced calculator users know what is allowed in the language of expression evaluation. Arithmetic combinations such as $37.4 + 12.8 + 100.78$ are okay; expressions such as $73.2 + +1$ are not. But to talk about this problem in an exact mathematical sense requires us to precisely describe this language. In general, we will describe a problem as a task to be performed on a specific input. Inputs will consist of sequences of symbols, and outputs will be produced as sequences of symbols. Thus the arithmetic expression evaluation problem is to take as input an arithmetic expression, and to output its value.

Now consider the "problem" of correctly addressing email. Suppose you are submitting a form on the World Wide Web and one field asks for your email address. Figure 2.2 provides a typical scenario, and we see one field is labeled "email address." What type of inputs would be syntactically correct here? You would probably expect things like *jallen@aol.com* or *LeahDenellio@pharm.uri.edu* to be legal. That is, a user's name followed by an @ symbol and then a domain name with each subdomain separated by a "dot." Note that just because an address is syntactically correct does not mean that it actually corresponds to a real person.

The problem in this case is for the script that processes the Web screen to check the input for proper form. The script should verify that the email address entered has the correct layout; that is, it contains only one @, contains tokens separated by dots, and so on. We can think of all the possible inputs of the correct format as the language of properly formatted email addresses. The form processing script should only allow the user to submit a form if the data specified by the user in the email field is, in fact, in the language of valid email addresses. This ensures that the user has correctly filled out the form. If someone types an email address like "hello world", a string that is not in the language representing email addresses, the program should recognize this as an invalid address and reply "Sorry, invalid email address format." All field validation problems are essentially checking if the supplied input is a legitimate string in some language. So, for example, we have the language of email addresses, the language of signed integer numbers, the language of monetary dollar amounts, and so on.

It is important to note that there is something fundamentally different about the languages associated with the calculator and Web problems. In the calculator case, the problem was to actually evaluate the input expression, so the language of the arithmetic expression problem has to handle both input and output communication. In the Web form case, the language simply described all the legitimate inputs to the field. In this case, there is no output to communicate other than the binary value of YES or NO, depending on whether the input was in the language or not. We will be dealing with both kinds of problems: those *computation problems* that have both an input and an output language, and those *recognition problems* that have only an input language. What is interesting is that from a theory–of–computation perspective, almost all problems can be expressed just in terms of language recognition.

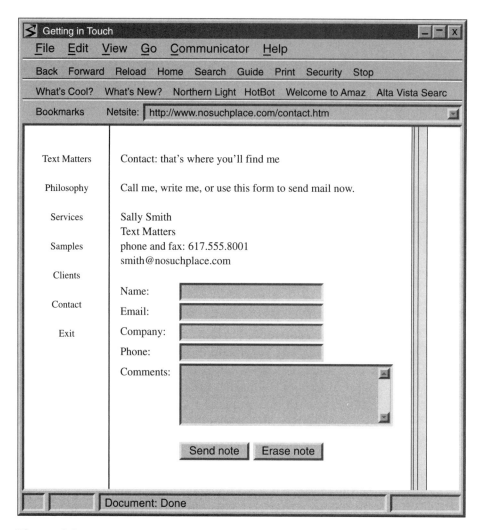

Figure 2.2

An example of a form on the World Wide Web. What types of inputs are allowed in each field? The set of all possible inputs for a given field represents a language.

The theory of computation deals with the essence of problems and abstracts away many of the details. The goal of computation theory is to take a real–life problem, with all of its ugly implementation details and ambiguous behavior, and distill the core aspects: Is the problem solvable? How much time does a given instance take? How much memory does it use? How do time and memory requirements grow as the size of the instance gets bigger?

The problem with real–life computing can be described as the following:

1. There are many types of computers.

2. The details involving specific machines and circumstances (such as instruction set, processor speed, programming language installed, and so on) get rather involved and vary widely.

So one of the main goals of computation theory is to define abstract machines that hide many of the details of reality, yet capture the important factors. Designing these simple abstract machines is the goal of Chapters 4 and 6. But first we must be able to express our problems using symbols that can be manipulated in a computation.

2.2   *Symbols, Alphabets, and Strings*

Since we use languages to communicate, we usually must give the language some meaning (its *semantics*). However, much of the manipulation of *symbols*, *strings*, and languages can be done without understanding their semantics. Such *syntactic* manipulation is the subject of this section.

The most primitive notion we have is that of a symbol. Symbols are the atoms of the world of languages. A **symbol** is any single object such as #, 0, 1, *a*, or *b*. Any object can be considered to be a symbol—for example, the keywords **begin**, **else**, or **while**. Usually, we will use only the characters from a typical keyboard as symbols.

We need at least one symbol to communicate; we normally need more, but never more than a fixed number. An **alphabet** is any finite, nonempty set of symbols. Let's consider a few sample alphabets.

Example 2.2.1   Alphabets

1. Binary alphabet: $\{0, 1\}$

2. Lowercase English alphabet:
   $\{a, b, c, d, e, f, g, h, i, j, k, l, m, n, o, p, q, r, s, t, u, v, w, x, y, z\}$

3. First five letters of the uppercase English alphabet: $\{A, B, C, D, E\}$

4. Portion of a calculator: $\{0, 1, 2, 3, 4, 5, 6, 7, 8, 9, \div, =, -, +, \times, (,)\}$

5. Several alphabets having two symbols: $\{T, F\}$, $\{!, ?\}$, and $\{a, b\}$

6. Alphabet containing some symbols normally used to denote set operations: $\{-, \cap, \cup\}$

7. Binary alphabet with a delimiter: $\{0, 1, \diamond\}$ ∎

Remember that an alphabet is simply a finite, nonempty set[1] and thus has no intrinsic order to the way its elements are written. Nevertheless, when we list the members of an alphabet, we usually do so in "alphabetical" order if there is a commonly accepted order. Such an ordered listing makes it easier to check that all the symbols are included. For example, in part 2 of Example 2.2.1, the ordering simplifies the verification that all lowercase letters are present. The capital Greek letters Γ (pronounced "gamma") and Σ (pronounced "sigma") will often be used to denote alphabets.

2.2.1 Strings

We combine the symbols from an alphabet into words or strings. A **string** is a finite sequence of symbols over an alphabet. The **length** of a string is defined as the number of symbols in the string. The length of string x is denoted by $|x|$, by overloading[2] the normal mathematical "absolute value notation."

For example, 0011 and 11010 are two strings over the binary alphabet. These strings have lengths four and five, respectively. That is, $|0011| = 4$ and $|11010| = 5$. How short can a string be? A single character such as 0 is a string of length one. However, we can also consider a string of length zero—that is, a string containing no characters. We use the Greek letter Λ (pronounced "lambda") to denote the **empty string**. Note that $|\Lambda| = 0$. To avoid confusion, and sticking with our convention that symbols usually appear on typical keyboards, the letter Λ will *not* be allowed in the alphabets considered in this book.[3]

As a mathematical object, a string x of length n over alphabet Σ is a function from the set $\{1, \ldots, n\}$ to the set Σ. When we write $x(i)$, or alternatively x_i, we are "evaluating" x and getting the value of the ith character of x. This, of course, only makes sense if $1 \leq i \leq n$. If x is the empty string, its length is 0, so the set $\{1, \ldots, 0\}$ is empty and there are no values in the domain of x.

---

1. Recall that the order of elements is not important in sets. The sets $\{0, 1\}$ and $\{1, 0\}$ are equal. Elements can be repeated inside a set, although we usually list each element just once. For example, $\{0, 1\} = \{0, 0, 1, 1, 1\}$.

2. When a symbol is used with more than one meaning we say that the symbol is *overloaded*. The notation $|\cdot|$ is overloaded to mean both the cardinality of a set (the number of elements) and the length of a string. This is usually not confusing.

3. We often use the letters u, v, w, x, y, and z to denote strings. The letters i, j, k, l, m, and n will be used to denote natural numbers.

For example, suppose Σ is the lowercase English alphabet and $x = jogger$. Then $|x| = 6$ and $x(1) = j$, $x(2) = o$, $x(3) = x(4) = g$, $x(5) = e$, and $x(6) = r$. Using the subscript notation, we have $x_1 = j$, $x_2 = o$, and so on. We say that symbol $\sigma \in \Sigma$ **occurs** in the ith position of a string x if $x(i) = \sigma$.

It is often useful to test if a particular character occurs in a specific position of a string. This is done with the **occurrence test**, given by

$$x_c(i) = \begin{cases} 1 & \text{if } x(i) = c \\ 0 & \text{otherwise} \end{cases}$$

The symbol g is repeated twice in the string $jogger$. We use the notation $\#_c(x)$ (x's number of c's) to denote the number of times the symbol c occurs in the string x. That is,

$$\#_c(x) = \sum_{i=1}^{|x|} x_c(i)$$

$\#_g(jogger) = 2$ because $jogger(3)$ and $jogger(4)$ are equal to g, and no other letters of $jogger$ are. We distinguish between the first and second g's in $jogger$ by calling the one in position three the first occurrence of g and the one in position four the second occurrence. More precisely, position k is the jth **occurrence** of c in a string x if $x(k) = c$ and $j = \sum_{i=1}^{k} x_c(i)$. For example, if $x = ultrarunner$, then $x(6)$ is the second occurrence of r in x. Observe that in this case $\#_r(x) = 3$.

2.2.2   Lexicographical and Enumeration Ordering

When an alphabet has an ordering among its symbols, we can sort the strings over that alphabet. We do that by taking the ordering of the symbols and using it to define an ordering over the strings. This ordering of the strings is called an alphabetical or *lexicographical* order.

Let Σ be an alphabet with an ordering $<$ over its symbols. The order $<$ can be extended to a lexicographical order, $<_{\text{lex}}$, of strings over Σ as follows: Let x and y be strings over Σ. Let j, $0 \leq j \leq \min \{|x|, |y|\}$, be the largest position such that for every i, $1 \leq i \leq j$, we have $x(i) = y(i)$. That is, x and y match up to position j but no further. We say that x is **lexicographically less than** y, and write $x <_{\text{lex}} y$, if and only if

1. $j = |x|$ and $|x| < |y|$, or
2. $j < \min \{|x|, |y|\}$ and $x(j+1) < y(j+1)$.

For example, over the usual keyboard alphabet, with the usual ordering of characters, $apple <_{\text{lex}} dog$, $dog <_{\text{lex}} doggie$, and $dog <_{\text{lex}} dot$.

Frequently, for algorithmic reasons, we want to manipulate strings in increasing length—that is, handle all the length zero strings, then the length one, then the length two, and so on. In these cases, it is useful to have an *enumeration ordering* on strings.

Let x and y be strings over an alphabet Σ with lexicographical ordering $<_{\text{lex}}$. We say that x is **enumerated before** y, and write $x <_{\text{enum}} y$, if and only if

1. $|x| < |y|$, or
2. $|x| = |y|$ and $x <_{\text{lex}} y$.

For example, *dog* $<_{\text{enum}}$ *apple*, *dog* $<_{\text{enum}}$ *doggie*, *dog* $<_{\text{enum}}$ *dot*.

2.2.3   String Concatenation

There are a number of basic operations on strings. In this section we investigate one of them called *concatenation*.

Instead of writing 00000, it is easier to write and read 0^5 ("zero to the fifth" versus "zero, zero, zero, zero, zero"). We can view this string of length five as consisting of five 0's "glued" together or, alternatively, say, as a string of two 0's glued together with a string of three 0's. The notion of gluing strings together, placing them adjacent to each other in order to form a new string, is known as concatenation of strings.

Concatenation lets us assemble more complex strings from simpler ones. A form is just the concatenation of all its fields, a program is the concatenation of individual statements, and so on. For example, U.S. social security numbers consist of three digits, concatenated together with a −, concatenated together with two digits, concatenated together with another −, and finally concatenated together with four digits (at least as of this writing). Canadian social insurance numbers consist of eight digits, followed by a check digit.

Suppose x and y are two strings over an alphabet Σ. The **concatenation** of x and y, denoted $x \circ y$, is defined as the string z, where

1. $|z| = |x| + |y|$,
2. $z(i) = x(i)$ for $1 \le i \le |x|$, and
3. $z(|x| + j) = y(j)$ for $1 \le j \le |y|$.

That is, the leading part of z comes from x and the trailing part from y. All we are doing here is gluing two strings together and saying where one leaves off the other continues.

Example 2.2.2   Concatenation of strings

1. $NC \circ SA = NCSA$.
2. $cook \circ ing = cooking$.
3. Let $x = 01010$ and $y = 1111$, then $x \circ y = 010101111$.

4. $abab \circ \Lambda = abab$. Here, using the definition of $x \circ y$, $|y| = |\Lambda| = 0$, so there is no j such that $1 \leq j \leq 0$. Thus, $z(i) = x(i)$ for $1 \leq i \leq 4$.

5. Let z be any string. $z \circ \Lambda = \Lambda \circ z = z$.

6. Associativity. Let x, y, and z be any three strings. Then $(x \circ y) \circ z = x \circ (y \circ z)$.

∎

Sometimes, it will be convenient to drop the $\circ$ symbol. Instead of writing $x \circ y$, we simply write xy. We can now give an *inductive definition* for our shorthand notation to represent multiple copies of a string. Let x be any string over an alphabet Σ. Then

$$x^0 = \Lambda$$
$$x^{i+1} = x^i \circ x, \qquad i \in \mathbb{N} \tag{2.1}$$

where $\mathbb{N}$ is the set of nonnegative integers $\{0, 1, 2, 3, \ldots\}$.

This kind of inductive definition is very common in computer science. It has a base case (here $x^0 = \Lambda$), and then an inductive step that defines the next term by reference only to earlier terms. Inside every recursive program or **for** loop is lurking some inductive definition. Inductive definitions are sometimes called *recursive definitions*.

2.2.4   Parts of Strings

We have seen how to produce many copies of a string using a shorthand notation. It will also be important for us to talk about various parts of a string—for example, a leading part, a middle segment, or a trailing part. These concepts are known as *prefix*, *substring*, and *suffix*, respectively. If u is a string and $u = vw$ for some w, then v is a **prefix** of u. If there exist strings v and x such that $u = vwx$, then w is a **substring** of u. If x is a string and $x = yz$ for some y, then z is a **suffix** of x. The following example should aid in making these definitions clear.

Example 2.2.3   Parts of strings

1. Let $u = javascript$. Then *java* is a prefix of u. This is because we can let $v = java$, $w = script$, and then $u = vw$, fitting the definition of prefix. Analogous reasoning shows *script* is a suffix of *javascript*.

2. Let $u = gymnastics$. Then *nasti* is a substring of u, since we can let $v = gym$ and $x = cs$ in the definition.

3. Let $x = roses$. The prefixes of x are Λ, r, ro, ros, $rose$, and $roses$. In fact, if u is a string and $|u| = n$, then there exists exactly one prefix of u for each m, where $0 \leq m \leq n$. Similar observations can be made pertaining to suffixes.

4. Here x, y, and z are strings and the alphabet over which they will be defined is $\{e, n, r, s, t, w\}$. Let $x = western$, $y = west$, and $z = ern$. Then y is a

prefix of x, and z is a suffix of x. Also, z is neither a prefix, substring, nor suffix of y.

5. Let $x = coffee$. Then taking $y = \Lambda$, we see $z = coffee$ is a suffix of x. That is, *coffee* is a suffix of itself.

6. Let $x = 001$ and $y = x^3$. It is apparent that y contains the substring x three times, that x is a prefix of y, and that x is a suffix of y. y also contains two occurrences of the substring x^2, namely, $y(1) \cdots y(6)$ and $y(4) \cdots y(9)$. Notice that occurrences can overlap.   ■

2.2.5   String Reversal

Next we consider a string operation known as *reversal*. Intuitively, when we reverse a string x, denoted x^R, we simply "flip it over to the left." Let x be a string of length $n = |x|$ over Σ. The **reversal of string** x, denoted x^R, is the string of length n that satisfies

$$x^R(i) = x(n + 1 - i), \quad \text{for } 1 \le i \le n$$

Example 2.2.4   Reversal of strings

1. Let $x = butter$. Then $x^R = rettub$ and $(x^R)^R = butter$.

2. Let x be a string over an alphabet Γ. Then $(x^R)^R = x$.

3. Let $x = ylf$ and $z = rettub$. Then

$$(xz)^R = (ylfrettub)^R = butterfly = butter \circ fly = z^R x^R.$$

4. Let x and y be strings over an alphabet Γ.
   Then $(xy)^R = y^R x^R$.   ■

2.3   *Languages*

Armed with a good sense of strings and basic operations on them, we are now ready to present the definition of a language. Suppose we have fixed an alphabet Σ. A **language**[4] L over Σ is any finite or infinite set of strings over Σ. The elements in L are strings—that is, finite sequences of symbols.

Example 2.3.1   Languages over the alphabet $\{0, 1\}$

1. All strings of length two or less: $\{\Lambda, 0, 1, 00, 01, 10, 11\}$. Note Λ is in the language of strings of length two or less since it has length zero, but observe $\Lambda \notin \{0, 1\}$. We repeat again for emphasis that Λ is not in any alphabet.

---

4. We usually use the letter L for representing a language.

2. All strings consisting only of 0's: $\{\Lambda, 0, 00, 000, \ldots\}$.

3. All strings that consist of only 0's or only 1's, and have an odd length: $\{0, 1, 000, 111, 00000, 11111, \ldots\}$.

4. Empty language: $\{\} = \emptyset$.

5. Language consisting of the empty string: $\{\Lambda\}$.

We often use the convention of listing the strings in the language in enumeration order; that is, ordered in increasing length, and ordered lexicographically within the same length.

A language is just a set, and so need not contain any elements, in which case it is called the **empty language**. It is important not to confuse the empty language with the empty string. Remember that $\{\} \neq \{\Lambda\}$. This is easy to see since $|\{\}| = 0$, whereas $|\{\Lambda\}| = 1$.

Once we have fixed a particular alphabet, we frequently need to talk about the set of all strings over that alphabet. We denote the set of all strings over an alphabet Σ by Σ^* (pronounced "sigma star"). Therefore, any language L defined over an alphabet Σ satisfies $L \subseteq \Sigma^*$.

Example 2.3.2   All strings over an alphabet

1. Let $\Sigma = \{a\}$. Then $\Sigma^* = \{\Lambda, a, aa, \ldots\}$.

2. Let $\Sigma = \{0, 1\}$. Then $\Sigma^* = \{\Lambda, 0, 1, 00, 01, 10, 11, \ldots\}$.

3. Let $\Sigma = \{\$, \%, \#\}$. Then $\Sigma^* = \{\Lambda, \$, \%, \#, \$\$, \$\%, \$\#, \%\$, \%\%, \%\#, \#\$, \#\%, \#\#, \ldots\}$.

Observe that the empty string is always contained in the set of all strings over an alphabet.

In Example 2.3.1 we listed all strings over an alphabet of length less than or equal to two. Using sets of strings with a maximum length is so common that there is a general notation for the strings of length less than or equal to n over an alphabet Σ. It is $\Sigma^{\leq n}$. For example,

$$\{a, b\}^{\leq 3} = \{\Lambda, a, b, aa, ab, ba, bb, aaa, aab, aba, abb, baa, bab, bba, bbb\}$$

The notation $\Sigma^{=n}$ denotes all strings of length equal to n over the alphabet Σ. For example,

$$\{a, b\}^{=2} = \{aa, ab, ba, bb\}$$

Instead of $\Sigma^{=n}$, we sometimes write Σ^n when this won't be confused with the n-fold Cartesian product of Σ.

In the next section we will examine ways in which languages can be manipulated and combined to generate additional languages.

2.4 *Operations on Languages*

Let $\Sigma = \{0, 1\}$. We have already seen several languages defined over this alphabet. It is often convenient to express a language in terms of a property possessed by its strings, especially when there is no obvious pattern to follow when listing the strings of the language. Additionally, the description of a language presented via a property is usually more concise.

For example, instead of listing all of the strings in the following language L, it is easier to define

$$L = \{x \mid x \in \Sigma^* \text{ and } 81 \le |x| \le 89\}$$

This can be read "the set of strings x such that x is an element of sigma star, and the length of x is between eighty and ninety."

In general, if P is a property or predicate[5] mapping strings over Σ^* to $\{0, 1\}$, then

$$L = \{x \mid x \in \Sigma^* \text{ and } P(x)\}$$

defines the language consisting of strings satisfying property P. That is, the strings in L have $P(x)$ being TRUE or equaling 1. Frequently we drop the "$\in \Sigma^*$" part of the set definition because it is understood what alphabet the strings are over.

Since languages are just sets, the usual set operations of complement, union, intersection, and symmetric difference can be applied directly to generate new languages. Also the usual set relationships hold, such as DeMorgan's Laws.

Other language operations, such as length subsetting and reversal, depend on the fact that a language is a set of strings.

2.4.1 Union

Certainly one of the simplest operations on two languages is *union*. Languages are sets of strings, so the **union** of two languages L_1 and L_2 is the usual set union, denoted $L_1 \cup L_2$. That is, a string $x \in L_1 \cup L_2$ if and only if $x \in L_1$ or $x \in L_2$. When we say let L_1 and L_2 be languages, you may wonder whether the languages are defined over the same alphabet. We can assume without loss of generality that they are. Why? Let's suppose L_1 were defined over Γ_1, and L_2 were defined over Γ_2, with Γ_1 and Γ_2 possibly different. We could view each language as being defined over a new alphabet $\Gamma = \Gamma_1 \cup \Gamma_2$. Unless otherwise noted, when specifying multiple languages, we assume they are over the same alphabet.

---

5. By convention we identify a value of 1 as meaning TRUE, and a value of 0 meaning FALSE. Then we can use either logical predicates or numerical properties equivalently.

Example 2.4.1   Union of languages

1. Let $L_1 = \{0, 01, 001\}$ and $L_2 = \{\Lambda, 001, 1^9\}$. Then $L_1 \cup L_2 = \{\Lambda, 0, 01, 001, 1^9\}$.

2. Let $L_1 = \{0, 000, 00000, \ldots\}$ and $L_2 = \{\Lambda, 00, 0000, \ldots\}$. Then $L_1 \cup L_2 = \{0\}^*$.

3. In terms of properties, the previous statement becomes: Let $L_1 = \{x \mid x$ has an odd number of 0's and $x \in \{0\}^*\}$ and $L_2 = \{x \mid x$ has an even number of 0's and $x \in \{0\}^*\}$. Then $L_1 \cup L_2 = \{x \mid x \in \{0\}^*\}$.

4. Let $L_i = \{1^i\}$. Then

$$\bigcup_{i=0}^{9} L_i = L_0 \cup L_1 \cup \cdots \cup L_9 = \{\Lambda, 1, 11, \ldots, 1^9\}$$

Also,

$$\bigcup_{i=0}^{\infty} L_i = \{\Lambda, 1, 11, \ldots\} = \{1\}^*$$

■

2.4.2   Complementation

The next operation on languages we consider is *complementation*. Suppose L is a language over an alphabet Γ. The **complement** of L, denoted $\bar{L}$ or L^c, is the language consisting of all those strings that are not in L over the alphabet Γ. In terms of the usual set difference operator $-$, this would mean $\bar{L} = \Gamma^* - L$. Let's consider an example.

Example 2.4.2   Complement of languages

1. Let $L = \{\Lambda, 1, 11, \ldots\}$ be a language over $\{0, 1\}$. Then $\bar{L}$ consists of all strings containing at least one 0.

2. Let $L = \{0, 000, 00000, \ldots\}$ be a language over $\{0, 1\}$. Then $\bar{L} = \{\Lambda, 0, 1, 00, 01, 10, 11, \ldots\} - L$.

3. Let $L = \{0^2, 0^3, 0^5\}$ be a language over $\{0, 1\}$. It is tempting to say $\bar{L}$ consists of all strings of 0's representing prime numbers greater than five; however, $\bar{L}$ also contains many other types of strings. For example, any string containing a 1 would be in $\bar{L}$. In fact, $\bar{L} = \{0, 1\}^* - \{0^2, 0^3, 0^5\}$.

4. Let L be any language over Γ^*. Then $\Gamma^* = L \cup \bar{L}$.

5. Let $L = \{x \mid x$ represents a prime number in binary with no leading 0's$\}$. Then $\bar{L} = L_1 \cup L_2 \cup L_3$, where $L_1 = \{y \mid y$ represents a composite number in binary with no leading 0's$\}$, $L_2 = \{z \mid z$ is any string with $z(1) = 0\}$, and $L_3 = \{\Lambda\}$.

6. Let $L = \{x \mid \#_0(x) = \#_1(x)\}$. Then $\bar{L} = \{x \mid \#_0(x) \neq \#_1(x)\}$.

■

2.4.3   Intersection

The next language operation we consider is *intersection*. Let L_1 and L_2 be two languages over an alphabet Γ. Then the **intersection** of L_1 and L_2, denoted $L_1 \cap L_2$, is the set of strings x such that $x \in L_1$ and $x \in L_2$. Let's consider an example.

Example 2.4.3   Intersection of languages

1. Let $L_1 = \{\Lambda, 00, 0000, 000000, \ldots\}$ and $L_2 = \{\Lambda, 0^3, 0^6, 0^9, \ldots\}$. Then $L_1 \cap L_2 = \{x \mid \#_0(x) \bmod 6 = 0 \text{ and } x \in \{0\}^*\}$.

2. Let $L = \{\Lambda\}$ and $L' = \emptyset$. Then $L \cap L' = \emptyset$.

3. Let L be any language. Then $L \cap \overline{L} = \emptyset$.

4. Let $L_1 = \{x \mid \#_0(x) = \#_1(x)\}$ and $L_2 = \{0^i 1^i \mid i \geq 0\}$. Then $L_1 \cap L_2 = L_2$. ◼

2.4.4   Symmetric Difference

Another important but perhaps less familiar operation is *symmetric difference*. Suppose L_1 and L_2 are two languages. The **symmetric difference** of L_1 and L_2, denoted $L_1 \oplus L_2$, is defined to be the language $(L_1 - L_2) \cup (L_2 - L_1)$. That is, $L_1 \oplus L_2$ consists of all those elements that are contained in L_1 or L_2 but not both. This is why the *exclusive or* symbol, $\oplus$, is used to denote the symmetric difference.

Example 2.4.4   Symmetric difference of languages

1. $\Sigma^{\leq 2} \oplus \{\Lambda, 0, 00, 101\} = \{1, 01, 10, 11, 101\}$.

2. Let $L_1 = \{0, 000, 00000, \ldots\}$ and $L_2 = \{1, 111, 11111, \ldots\}$. Then $L_1 \oplus L_2 = \{0, 1, 000, 111, 00000, 11111, \ldots\} = L_1 \cup L_2$.

3. Let $L_1 = \{x \mid \#_0(x) = \#_1(x)\}$ and $L_2 = \{0^i 1^i \mid i \geq 1\}$. Then $L_1 \oplus L_2 = L_1 - L_2 = \{x \mid \#_0(x) = \#_1(x) \text{ and not all of the 0's come before the first 1}\}$.

4. Let L and L' be two languages. Then $L \oplus L' = (L \cup L') - (L \cap L')$.

5. Let L be a language over an alphabet Γ. Then $L \oplus \emptyset = L$, $L \oplus L = \emptyset$, $L \oplus \Gamma^* = \overline{L}$, and $L \oplus \overline{L} = \Gamma^*$. ◼

2.4.5   DeMorgan's Laws

The following two equations are known as DeMorgan's Laws. Let L_1, L_2, and L_3 be any three languages.

$$L_1 - (L_2 \cup L_3) = (L_1 - L_2) \cap (L_1 - L_3) \tag{2.2}$$

$$L_1 - (L_2 \cap L_3) = (L_1 - L_2) \cup (L_1 - L_3) \tag{2.3}$$

DeMorgan's Laws let you express the intersection of two languages over Γ in terms of the operations of union and complementation. That is,

$$L_1 \cap L_2 = (L_1^c \cup L_2^c)^c \qquad\qquad (2.4)$$

or equivalently

$$= \Gamma^* - ((\Gamma^* - L_1) \cup (\Gamma^* - L_2))$$

2.4.6   Length Subsetting

For a fixed alphabet Σ and a particular language $L \subseteq \Sigma^*$, it is also useful to describe the strings in L of length less than or equal to a certain fixed size. The notations $L^{\leq n}$ and $L^{=n}$ are used to denote all strings in L of length less than or equal to n and all strings of length equal to n, respectively. In these terms, notice the notation $\Sigma^{\leq n}$ for a fixed alphabet Σ is really just an abbreviation for $(\Sigma^*)^{\leq n}$ and similarly $\Sigma^{=n} = (\Sigma^*)^{=n}$. Let's consider an example.

Example 2.4.5   Length subsetting of a language

1. Let $L = \{0, 00, 000, \ldots\}$. Then $L^{=3} = \{000\}$ and $L^{\leq 5} = \{0, 00, 000, 0000, 00000\}$.

2. Let $L = \{0, 1\}$. Then $L^{=0} = \emptyset$, $L^{=1} = L$, and $L^{\leq 1} = L$. Also, $L^{=i} = \emptyset$ and $L^{\leq i} = L$ for $i \in \mathbb{N}$, $i > 2$.

3. Let $L = \{0, 1\}^*$. Then $L^{=2} = \{00, 01, 10, 11\}$, $L^{\leq 2} = \{\Lambda, 0, 1, 00, 01, 10, 11\}$, and $|L^{=i}| = 2^i$ for $i \in \mathbb{N}$.

4. Let $L_1 = \{\Lambda, 101, 0^9\}$ and $L_2 = \{0, 1\}^{\leq 8}$. Then $L_1 \cap L_2 = \{\Lambda, 101\}$.   ■

2.4.7   Concatenation

Previously we defined what it means to concatenate two strings together. Here we examine the *concatenation of two languages*. The idea is to group all possible strings that are formed by taking any string from the first language and concatenating to it any string from the second language. Think in terms of grabbing one string from the first language and then separately gluing every other string from the second language to it, and then repeating this process for each string in the first language. More formally, the **concatenation** of two languages L_1 and L_2, denoted $L_1 \circ L_2$ or $L_1 L_2$ for short, is the language

$$L = \{x \circ y \mid x \in L_1 \text{ and } y \in L_2\}$$

Let's consider an example.

Example 2.4.6   Concatenation of languages

1. Let $L_1 = \{ab, abb, bb\}$ and $L_2 = \{bb, bbb\}$. Then $L_1 \circ L_2 = \{abbb, abbbb, abbbbb, bbbb, bbbbb\}$. Note that $L_1 \times L_2 = \{(ab, bb), (ab, bbb), (abb, bb), (abb, bbb), (bb, bb), (bb, bbb)\}$, which is something very different. In this case $|L_1 \circ L_2| = 5$

and $|L_1 \times L_2| = 6$. This is because the ordered pairs (ab, bbb) and (abb, bb) represent the same element in the concatenation, i.e., $ab \circ bbb = abb \circ bb$. Of course, strings and ordered pairs are two different types of structures.

2. Let L be any language. Then $L\emptyset = \emptyset L = \emptyset$.

3. Let $L_1 = \{0\}^*$ and $L_2 = \{1\}^*$. Then $L_1 L_2 = \{x \mid x$ consists of zero or more 0's followed by zero or more 1's$\}$.

4. Let $L_1 = \{0, 1\}^*$ and $L_2 = \{0, 1\}$. Then $L_1 L_2 = \{0, 1\}^* - \{\Lambda\}$.   ∎

Analogous to the notation x^i for representing i concatenations of a string x, we use the notation L^i to denote i concatenations of the language L. We define it recursively by

$$L^0 = \{\Lambda\} \tag{2.5}$$

$$L^{i+1} = L^i \circ L \tag{2.6}$$

2.4.8   Reversal

The *reversal of a language* is an operation that is very helpful in illustrating how various machines work. Earlier we defined what it means to *reverse a string*. The **reversal of a language** L is the language $L^R = \{x \mid x^R \in L\}$. Equivalently, we could have expressed L^R as $\{x^R \mid x \in L\}$. L^R is obtained by reversing each string in L. We illustrate this operation below.

Example 2.4.7   Reversals of languages

1. Let $L = \{0, 01, 001, 0001\}$. Then $L^R = \{0, 10, 100, 1000\}$.
2. Let $L = \{0^i 1^i \mid i \geq 1\}$. Then $L^R = \{1^i 0^i \mid i \geq 1\}$.
3. Let $L = \{0, 1\}^*$. Then $L^R = \{0, 1\}^*$.   ∎

2.4.9   Kleene Star

The final operation on languages we consider is called *Kleene star*. The **Kleene star** of a language L is the language L^* consisting of all the strings obtained by concatenating any finite number (including zero) of strings from L together. That is,

$$L^* = \{x \mid x = \Lambda \circ x_1 \circ \cdots \circ x_k, \text{ where } k \geq 0 \text{ and } x_1, \ldots, x_k \in L\}$$

The Λ appearing at the head of the concatenation is to ensure that L^* contains the empty string. Notice if L is a language over alphabet Γ, then $L^* \subseteq \Gamma^*$. Let's consider an example.

Example 2.4.8   Kleene star of languages

1. $\emptyset^* = \{\Lambda\}$.
2. Let $L = \{0, 1\}$. Then L^* is the set of all strings over the alphabet $\{0, 1\}$. This agrees with our previously introduced use of Σ^* to denote the set of all possible strings over an alphabet Σ.
3. $\{00000\}^* = \{\Lambda, 0^5, 0^{10}, \ldots\}$.
4. Let $L = \{\Lambda\}$. Then $L^* = \{\Lambda\}^* = \{\Lambda\}$.   ∎

An equivalent way of thinking about the Kleene star of a language L is as the infinite union of the powers of L; that is,

$$L^* = L^0 \cup L^1 \cup L^2 \cup \cdots = \bigcup_{i \geq 0} L^i$$

Often we want to concatenate at least one instance of L, and thus define

$$L^+ = L \circ L^*$$

2.5   *Alphabet Encodings*

In general, when we invent a language to be used in some problem domain, we choose our alphabet to be convenient for humans to use. For example, normal written English has 52 upper- and lowercase alphabetic character symbols, 10 numerals, plus additional punctuation marks. When we write mathematics, we have an even richer alphabet that contains Greek letters, special symbols like the summation and integration operators, and many diacritical marks (dots, superscripts, subscripts, and so on) that we can use to mark the basic symbols.

On the other hand, we like to keep our computing devices as simple as possible, and so we try to keep the size of the alphabet of symbols manipulated by the machine as small as possible. So how do we translate from our symbolically rich problem domain to the symbolically impoverished world of a machine? We do this by *encoding* the richer alphabet in terms of the machine alphabet. This process is so natural that we tend to forget that it must be done. We speak quite naturally of ASCII[6] characters, forgetting that the ASCII character set is a way of encoding the alphabet of written English into the binary alphabet of machines.

The basic idea of alphabet encodings is simple. Each symbol in the larger alphabet must be translated into a string of one or more symbols in the smaller alphabet. The translation should be reversible, so that you can translate back and forth between strings in the two alphabets.

---

6. American Standard Code for Information Interchange.

Suppose that our problem domain alphabet Γ contains the symbols $\{a, b, c\}$, and our machine alphabet Σ is the binary alphabet $\{0, 1\}$. We could perform the following encoding of Γ in terms of strings over Σ:

$s \in \Gamma$	$h_1(s) \in \Sigma^*$
a	0
b	1
c	01

Using this encoding we could translate the string *abc* into the encoding 0101. But there is a problem. Suppose that you need to translate the encoding 0101 back into the original string. Does 0101 encode *abc*, or does it encode *cab*, or even *cc*? This particular encoding is not reversible: when given a binary string, we do not know where to break it into the substrings that map back to the original symbols from Γ. We can solve this problem in exactly the same way as for ASCII characters by ensuring that the encoding of any symbol in Γ always results in the same length string over Σ, as follows:

$s \in \Gamma$	$h_2(s) \in \Sigma^*$
a	00
b	11
c	01

Then *abc* is uniquely encoded as the binary string 001101. Given a binary encoding like 010011, we can easily decode it back unambiguously to *cab*. Note that not all blocks of two binary symbols encode a character, so for example 1010 is not the encoding of any string over Γ. In general, if $\Gamma = \{\gamma_1, \ldots, \gamma_k\}$ contains k symbols, we can encode each symbol γ_i by a binary string that represents the value of $i - 1$. Each symbol of Γ will be encoded into a bit string of length $\lceil \lg k \rceil$.[7] For example, we could revise the previous code to

$s \in \Gamma$	$h_3(s) \in \Sigma^*$
a	00
b	01
c	10

We can also be a bit more clever, and notice that instead of implicitly marking the boundaries between encoded characters by using equal-length blocks over Σ, we could alternatively pick an encoding that explicitly marks the transition

---

7. All logarithms in this text are base two unless noted otherwise. We use the now quite common notation $\lg x$ instead of $\log_2 x$. The ceiling notation, $\lceil x \rceil$, denotes the least integer not less than x.

between encoded characters. For example, suppose that you had the following encoding:

$s \in \Gamma$	$h_4(s) \in \Sigma^*$
a	10
b	110
c	1110

Notice how the symbol 0 is reserved as a delimiter between encoded symbols. Then the binary string 11101011011010 can be decoded uniquely as *cabba*.

Technically, an **encoding scheme** is a one-to-one function f from Γ^* to Σ^*, where Γ and Σ are alphabets. The strings of Γ^* are said to be *encoded* over Σ. A string $x \in \Gamma^*$ is encoded as $f(x)$ over Σ. Usually, we will take Σ equal to $\{0, 1\}$. In general, an encoding scheme can be completely arbitrary. Two similar strings might have completely unrelated encodings.

All of the encodings presented above, including the one that does not work (h_1), have an interesting property that relates the encoding of a string to the encoding of its substrings. This is the property of being a *homomorphism*.

Definition 2.5.1   *Let Γ and Σ be alphabets. A* **homomorphism** *from Γ^* to Σ^* is a function h such that*

$$h(x \circ y) = h(x) \circ h(y)$$

We can uniquely specify a homomorphism by defining how it maps the characters of Γ into Σ^*. The mapping can then be extended to strings in Γ^* by the following equations:

$$h(\Lambda) = \Lambda \tag{2.7}$$

$$h(\gamma \circ x) = h(\gamma) \circ h(x), \quad \text{for any } \gamma \in \Gamma, x \in \Gamma^* \tag{2.8}$$

giving the full homomorphism. Note in Equation 2.8 we arbitrarily wrote γ on the left of x. $h(x \circ y) = h(x) \circ h(y)$ defines the same mapping when γ is written on the right of x. We show below that this extension is indeed a homomorphism and then show how this can be used to our advantage in coding problems.

Lemma 2.5.2   *Let $\Gamma = \{\gamma_1, \ldots, \gamma_k\}$ and $\Sigma = \{\sigma_1, \ldots, \sigma_l\}$. Suppose $h(\gamma_i) = x_i$, where $1 \leq i \leq k$ and $x_i \in \Sigma^*$. If h is extended using Equations 2.7 and 2.8, then h is a homomorphism from Γ^* to Σ^*.*

Proof: We need to show that for $x, y \in \Gamma^*$ that $h(x \circ y) = h(x) \circ h(y)$. The proof is by induction on the length of x.

Suppose $|x| = 0$, then $x = \Lambda$. By Equation 2.7, $h(\Lambda) = \Lambda$, so $h(x \circ y) = h(\Lambda \circ y) = h(y) = \Lambda \circ h(y) = h(\Lambda) \circ h(y) = h(x) \circ h(y)$. This proves the base case.

For the inductive step, assume that $h(x \circ y) = h(x) \circ h(y)$ for all x of length n. Now consider $h(x' \circ y)$ for some $x' \in \Gamma^*$ of length $n + 1$. We have

$$
\begin{aligned}
h(x' \circ y) &= h((\gamma_i \circ x'') \circ y) && \text{where } x' = \gamma_i \circ x'' \text{ for some } \gamma_i \in \Gamma \\
&= h(\gamma_i \circ z) && \text{for } z = x'' \circ y, \text{ using the associativity of } \circ \\
&= h(\gamma_i) \circ h(z) && \text{using Equation 2.8} \\
&= h(\gamma_i) \circ h(x'' \circ y) && \text{substitution} \\
&= h(\gamma_i) \circ (h(x'') \circ h(y)) && \text{by the induction hypothesis} \\
&= h(\gamma_i \circ x'') \circ h(y) && \text{using Equation 2.8 and associativity of } \circ \\
&= h(x') \circ h(y) && \text{since } x' = \gamma_i \circ x''
\end{aligned}
$$

This completes the proof that h is a homomorphism.   ■

It is important to note that just because a function f is a homomorphism does not mean that it is an encoding. For example, the function $f(x) = \Lambda$ for all x is a homomorphism, yet is not an encoding function. To get an encoding, you need a *one-to-one homomorphism*.

Suppose Γ and Σ are two alphabets. What is the easiest way to produce an encoding from Γ^* to Σ^* that is a one-to-one homomorphism? If $|\Sigma| \geq |\Gamma|$ then any one-to-one map from Γ into Σ can be used to encode strings of Γ^* in Σ^*. On the other hand, if $|\Sigma| < |\Gamma|$, as is typically the situation, then let n be the smallest value such that $|\Gamma| \leq |\Sigma|^n$ (that is, $n = \lceil \log_{|\Sigma|} |\Gamma| \rceil$). Any one-to-one map from Γ into strings of Σ^* of length n can be used to encode strings of Γ^* in Σ^*. A string x over Γ when encoded becomes a string of length $|x| \times n$. In the case where $|\Gamma| < |\Sigma|^n$, some length n strings over Σ will not encode any character, as in our earlier example involving the encoding of a, b, and c. Using such a homomorphism as an encoding scheme makes encoding and decoding easy in the sense that these processes can be accomplished by the weakest computer models we will study in Chapter 4. We can call these *nice encoding homomorphisms*.

If we ultimately always encode into the binary alphabet—that is, take $\Sigma = \{0, 1\}$—then the length of a string from Γ^* is increased by a multiplicative factor of $\lceil \lg |\Gamma| \rceil$ by encoding it over Σ. Since any alphabet consists of a finite number of symbols, this is only a multiplicative constant factor increase. Therefore, any string in Γ^* can be encoded over the alphabet $\{0, 1\}$ with only a constant factor increase in length.

Let's revisit the situation with alphabets $\Gamma = \{0, 1, \Diamond\}$ and $\Sigma = \{0, 1\}$. This will show us how we can eliminate a delimiter from an alphabet. Here $3 = |\Gamma| \leq |\Sigma|^2 = 4$. In this case each character in Γ is encoded by a string of length two. We choose a mapping with $h(0) = 00$, $h(1) = 11$, and $h(\Diamond) = 01$ that can be extended to a homomorphism using Equations 2.7 and 2.8. Each string $x \in \Gamma^*$ is encoded by a string of length $2|x|$ in Σ^*, and there is no longer a need for an explicit delimiter.

2.6   *Some Test Languages*

The following languages have proven to be useful test languages for evaluating the power of various machines and illustrating various theorems. Keep them in mind when doing the exercises.

Example 2.6.1   Languages over the alphabet $\{\diamond, 0, 1, 2, 3\}$

1. $\{0^i 1^i \mid i \geq 0\}$
2. $\{0^i \mid$ where i is a prime number $\}$
3. $\{x \diamond x \mid x \in \{0, 1\}^*\}$
4. $\{xx \mid x \in \{0, 1\}^*\}$
5. $\{x \diamond x^R \mid x \in \{0, 1\}^*\}$
6. $\{xx^R \mid x \in \{0, 1\}^*\}$
7. $\{0^i 1^j 2^j 3^i \mid i, j \geq 0\}$
8. $\{0^i 1^i 2^i \mid i \geq 0\}$ ∎

All of the languages above have been defined over the alphabet $\{\diamond, 0, 1, 2, 3\}$ for consistency. However, we could have easily defined equivalent languages over other alphabets. For example, the language $\{0^i 1^i 2^i \mid i \geq 0\}$ has the same structural characteristics as the language $\{a^i b^i c^i \mid i \geq 0\}$. It is tempting to say that they are the same language, although they are not. We also could have used the encoding techniques developed in Section 2.5 to view the languages over the binary alphabet $\{0, 1\}$. You may want to think about how some of these languages might be encoded.

2.7   *How Many Languages Are There?*

In Section 2.4 we described a number of important operations on languages. We saw how to construct new languages from existing ones. There seemed to be many different ways to combine languages. Here we consider the question of how many languages there are over a given alphabet. In answering this question, we will describe an important proof technique in computability and complexity theory called *diagonalization*. As our intuition suggests, there are in fact an incredibly large number of languages. Prior to tackling this, it makes sense to consider the question of how many *strings* there can be over a given alphabet.

The smallest possible alphabet has only one symbol. It is natural to begin by looking at this case. Let $\Gamma = \{a\}$. Then $\Gamma^* = \{\Lambda, a, aa, \ldots\}$, so there are an infinite number of strings over even the simplest alphabet. How do we count these strings? The simplest way is to order them lexicographically and then begin counting with the first in the order. This ensures that there is exactly one string of Γ^* associated with each natural number from $\mathbb{N}$. Specifically, string a^i is associated with natural number i. That is, there is a bijection[8] f from Γ^* to $\mathbb{N}$, where $f(a^i) = i$. Whenever there is a bijection from a set S to $\mathbb{N}$, we say that S is **countably infinite**. So Γ^* is a countably infinite set.

Now what about counting the strings in Γ^* when alphabet Γ contains more than one symbol? We cannot simply order the strings of Γ^* lexicographically prior to counting them. To see this, consider the alphabet $\Gamma = \{a, b\}$. There are an infinite number of strings in Γ^* that begin with a that come lexicographically before the first string that begins with b. So we need some other way to arrange them for counting. The easiest way is to begin by counting the shortest strings first (those of length 0, 1, 2, and so on). Within each group of strings of the same length, count them lexicographically. Using this idea, it is relatively easy to show the following:

Lemma 2.7.1   *Let Γ be any alphabet. Then Γ^* is a countably infinite set.*

Proof: The proof is left as an exercise.   ∎

This fact has an important consequence. Since any language L over Γ is a subset of Γ^*, we can use the same basic counting idea (order by length, lexicographically within equal length) to count the strings in L. Thus every language L over Γ is countable in the sense that either there are a fixed number of strings in L or L is countably infinite.

How many languages are there over Γ? It is certainly an infinite number. For example, for any alphabet Γ, you can construct a countably infinite set of languages by picking any symbol γ from Γ and forming the set of languages

$$\{\{\Lambda\}, \{\gamma\}, \{\gamma\gamma\}, \ldots\}$$

But what about the set of all languages over Γ?

Since every language is a subset of Γ^*, the set of all languages over Γ is the power set[9] 2^{Γ^*}. How many languages is this? Unlike Γ^*, it turns out that the set 2^{Γ^*} is *uncountable*. That is, the number of languages is infinite and cannot be put into a one–to–one correspondence with the natural numbers.

How do we go about showing this? We begin by showing how to generate a new language from a countably infinite set of existing languages.

Lemma 2.7.2   *Let Γ be an alphabet, and let $S \subseteq 2^{\Gamma^*}$ be any countably infinite set of languages over Γ. Then there exists a language L over Γ such that L is not in S.*

---

8. A bijection from set A to set B is a function from A to B that is one–to–one and onto.

9. The **power set** of a set L, denoted 2^L, is defined to be all possible subsets of L. For example, if $L = \{a, b\}$, then $2^L = \{\emptyset, \{a\}, \{b\}, \{a, b\}\}$. The elements in this power set are languages.

Proof: The goal is to construct a new language L that is different from every language in S. How? Pick any language L' from S. Suppose string x is in L'. Then we can make sure that L is different from L' by keeping string x out of L. On the other hand, if x is not in L', we then add x to L to keep it different from L'. In general, it is sufficient to make L different from L' by finding a string x such that $x \in L$ if and only if $x \notin L'$.

Now we must make every language in S different from L. Since S is countably infinite, there is a bijection from S to $\mathbb{N}$, and we can thus write the elements of S in order as

$$S = \{L_0, L_1, L_2, \ldots\}$$

and our goal is to ensure that $L \neq L_i$ for every natural i. We can use the technique above, provided that for each language of S we use a string x not used previously.

Since Γ^* is countably infinite, we can similarly write the elements of Γ^* in some order as

$$\Gamma^* = \{x_0, x_1, x_2, \ldots\}$$

Now we define L as the subset of Γ^* that satisfies for all $i \in \mathbb{N}$

$$x_i \in L \text{ if and only if } x_i \notin L_i$$

Thus $L \neq L_i$ for all i, and thus $L \notin S$ as required.   ■

Lemma 2.7.2 now lets us show that we cannot count all the languages over an alphabet.

Theorem 2.7.3 *Let Γ be an alphabet. Then 2^{Γ^*} is uncountable.*

Proof: Let $S = 2^{\Gamma^*}$. S is certainly infinite. Suppose for contradiction that $S = 2^{\Gamma^*}$ is countably infinite. Then by Lemma 2.7.2 there is a new language L not in S. But S contains every possible language over Γ, so L must be in S. This is impossible; thus S must not be countable.   ■

The proof of Lemma 2.7.2 uses a technique called *diagonalization* to construct the new language L, so named because the feature that distinguishes the new language from every other is specified on the diagonal of the diagram in Figure 2.3. The diagonalization technique was first introduced by Cantor in his proof that the real numbers are uncountable.

2.7.1   Most Languages Do Not Have Compilers

Theorem 2.7.3 has a very important consequence: there are s~
in fact) for which we cannot write a compiler.

Pick your favorite programming language. We can thir.
contains all syntactically correct program texts for your langu

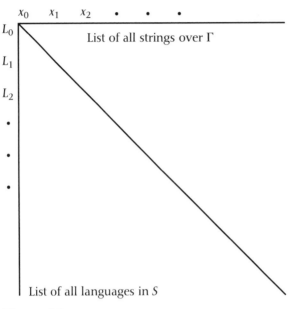

Figure 2.3

The framework for the diagonalization argument given in Lemma 2.7.2.

some alphabet Σ. So L is a language in the sense of this chapter. For the sake of argument, imagine that L contains all syntactically correct C programs written in ASCII.

Now consider some new programming language P. To use it, you need to write a compiler in your favorite programming language L. So that compiler will be some string y that is a program in language L. But L, being a language, contains only a countable number of strings. That is, there are only a countable number of compilers.

But the number of possible programming languages is uncountable, by Theorem 2.7.3. Thus there must be some languages for which there is no compiler.

This is a specific example of the general phenomenon that any *finite representation scheme* for languages, a means of describing languages using strings over an alphabet, will not be able to denote all languages. Every programming language is a finite representation scheme, as are the *regular expressions* of Chapter 3.

2.8   *Problem Representations*

The first step towards solving a problem is to express it using some language or notation, usually mathematical, that is especially suited to the problem. That is, we want to use a language that aids our understanding of the problem rather than obfuscating it. This process of expressing our problem in suitable language is called *problem representation*. Let's begin with a simple example.

Since we are primarily interested in problems solvable by a computing machine, we will consistently state our problems in two parts: a *given part* and a *problem part*. Consider the Average problem discussed earlier in Chapter 1:

Average

Given: A natural number n, with $n > 0$, and a list l of n natural numbers $\langle x_1, \ldots, x_n \rangle$.

Problem: Compute the average value, $\frac{1}{n} \sum_{i=1}^{n} x_i$.

At first glance, this problem has a very simple representation. The given part of Average could be supplied explicitly, as for example,

$$n = 4, l = \langle 29, 31, 64, 26 \rangle$$

We can easily imagine feeding this exact input into a machine after some suitable alphabet encoding. The first thing that the machine would have to do is parse the input to determine n (by converting from decimal to binary perhaps), and then extract out the natural numbers to be averaged. Alternatively, if we wanted to make things a bit easier for the machine (at the expense of more difficulty for the human) we could provide the inputs already converted into binary and simply separated by a character like #. For example:

100#11101#11111#1000000#11010

In the latter case, our input alphabet is smaller than before, but reading the representation is much harder for humans. So, in general, we will opt for representations that are much more natural and appealing to humans, so long as they can be converted reasonably easily by a machine. However, some machines have very limited computational power, and in those cases we will have to choose a representation that the machine can cope with.

A more difficult issue is how to represent the solution to the Average problem. We have two scenarios to deal with. The first, common to all problems, is what should the solution be when the input does not obey the problem constraints or is otherwise garbage? For example, the input could be $n = 0, l = \langle 1, 2 \rangle$ (a case of a bad n), or it could be $n = \langle -- \rangle$ (a case of simple garbage). For these kinds of given instances, the "solution" should probably be an error message such as "Bad Input," or perhaps a solution of Λ, using the empty string to indicate no solution because of bad input. How this is ultimately handled is problem–specific. As a general rule we want to choose our representations so that it is easy to check for legitimate inputs.

The second scenario involves the nature of the solution. The average of a list of natural numbers could be a *rational number*,[10] that is, a number a/b where $a \in \mathbb{N}$ and $b \in \mathbb{N} - \{0\}$. We should mention in the problem part that we expect a rational number as output, leaving the representation up to the problem solver. If we wanted to be more precise, we might say how we want the rational number to be represented and describe the problem as follows:

Average

Given: A natural number n, with $n > 0$, and a list l of n natural numbers $\langle x_1, \ldots, x_n \rangle$.

Problem: Compute natural numbers a and b such that $\frac{a}{b} = \frac{1}{n} \sum_{i=1}^{n} x_i$.

The machines we study in computation theory take strings as input and produce strings as output. They do not directly manipulate more general objects such as natural numbers, lists, graphs, or logical expressions. Instead they operate on encodings of representations of these objects. But since every alphabet can be encoded in terms of the binary alphabet, every problem representation can be translated into a binary string. This lets us give a very general abstract definition of the notion of problem:

Definition 2.8.1 *A **problem** Π is a total relation on $\{0, 1\}^* \times \{0, 1\}^*$. If $(G, S) \in \Pi$, then $G \in \{0, 1\}^*$ is called the **given part** of Π, and $S \in \{0, 1\}^*$ is called the **solution part** of Π. Associated with Π is the **problem part**, which consists of a question to resolve or a request to compute some object.*

A few remarks are in order regarding this definition. The given part G may be thought of as the input to Π (pronounced "pie"); it describes a particular *instance* of the problem. The problem part consists of the question to resolve or a request to compute some object. The solution part S is the answer to the problem part for a specific problem input; S may be considered as the output. Π is required to be a **total relation**. This means that each string in $\{0, 1\}^*$ appears as a first component of some ordered pair in Π. Thus every possible instance must have some associated solution part. Of course, some strings over $\{0, 1\}^*$ will not encode "legal" given instances of Π. That is, they will be degenerate or bad inputs; for example, in a problem involving graphs, they will not correspond to a valid representation of a graph. As we mentioned above, these issues must be dealt with in the problem specification.

---

10. The rational numbers are denoted $\mathbb{Q}$.

2.9   *Types of Problems*

The theory of computation deals with three key kinds of problems: *decision*, *function*, and *search*. Decision problems can be translated directly and naturally into language recognition problems, allowing us to relate groups of what would appear to be rather diverse and incompatible problems. Function problems are those where every input has a single output, and so have the property that machines that solve them always produce the same solution for the same instance. In general, problems can have more than one solution. If we just want an answer, we can search for any of the possible solutions. Since each instance of a search problem can have many possible solutions, every time we solve the same instance we could get a different answer than before. We might also wish to find all possible solutions, in which case we want to enumerate (or list) the possible solutions in some order.

We illustrate these three kinds of problems by a series of examples about *minimum cost spanning trees*. The first task is to decide on how to represent the graph that is part of the problem input.

2.9.1   Representing Graphs

An undirected graph $G = (V, E)$ has a set of vertices V and a set of edges E. How should we represent such an object? That is, what information do we actually write down in order to specify the set of vertices V and edges E that describe the graph? For a broad class of graphs, we can consider V as a set

$$V = \{v_1, \dots, v_n\}$$

of individual vertices, and E as a set of 2–vertex sets

$$E = \{\{v_i, v_j\} \mid \text{there is an edge between } v_i \text{ and } v_j\}$$

Note that this representation is insufficient for directed graphs, or graphs with self–loops (an edge from a vertex to itself) or parallel edges (multiple edges between the same pair of vertices).

Using the above representation directly gives us the *edge list* representation of the graph. In this case a natural number specifying the number of vertices in the graph is followed by a list of the edges of the graph. For example, an edge list representation of the graph in Figure 2.4 is

$$6 \ \{2, 5\} \ \{1, 2\} \ \{4, 5\} \ \{2, 3\} \ \{2, 4\} \ \{1, 4\}$$

Notice that the edges are listed in an arbitrary order. This string can easily be converted into a bit string using the techniques of Section 2.5. The number of vertices needs to be written out explicitly in this case because some vertices, like 6, may not be connected to any nodes. We can use other representations,

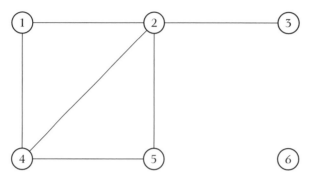

Figure 2.4

A sample undirected graph used to help illustrate various representation schemes.

provided that the information supplied in the given part of a problem lets us reconstruct V and E.

Another way of representing the graph is via an *adjacency matrix*. Given a graph $G = (\{v_1, \ldots, v_n\}, E)$, an $n \times n$ matrix A is formed to represent the graph. Entry $(a_{ij}) = 1, 1 \le i, j \le n$, if and only if $\{i, j\} \in E$. The entire matrix A can then be written as a bit string of length n^2. The number of vertices is provided implicitly, although for convenience may also be supplied. For example, the graph in Figure 2.4 is represented by

010100 100110 010000 110010 010100 000000

Here we have used *row major order* in our listing of A. This means that the entries are given from left to right within a row and the rows are listed from top to bottom; that is,

$$a_{11} \cdots a_{1n} a_{21} \cdots a_{2n} \cdots a_{n1} \cdots a_{nn}$$

Row major order is the convention most frequently used for adjacency matrix encoding, although *column major order* is also a possibility.

The third representation is known as the *adjacency list* coding scheme. In this case, for each vertex, a list of neighboring vertices is provided. A representation for the graph shown in Figure 2.4 is

1 : 2, 4 # 2 : 4, 5, 1 # 3 : 2 # 4 : 2, 1, 5 # 5 : 4, 2 # 6 : Λ

Observe that the vertices appear in an arbitrary order on the lists. Additionally, note that the number of vertices is stored implicitly in this representation. Again this string can easily be converted to a string over the alphabet {0, 1} by using the methods of Section 2.5.

All three graph representations are easy to use, and they are easy to code and decode. Furthermore, it is a simple task to convert from any one of these represen-

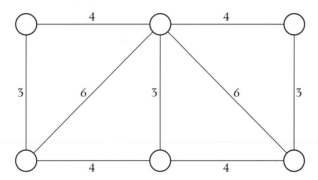

Figure 2.5

An example of a weighted, undirected graph used to illustrate concepts relating to spanning trees.

tations to any other. There are some trade-offs in terms of storage requirements needed by each scheme and in terms of access time of the information, but generally such issues will not concern us; our study of time bounds in Chapters 8, 10, and 11 concentrates on broad complexity classes and not so much on exact running times required for solving individual problems. We remark though, that when comparing the running times of algorithms for solving the same problem, it is important to make sure instances are represented in the same fashion (or at least "fairly").

Any one of the three representations described (or for that matter any "reasonable" representation scheme—intuitively, one that is compact and contains only the information relevant to the description of the problem) can be used in the definition of the graph problems that follow. Depending on which scheme is chosen, we will get a slightly different version of the problem. However, since it is easy to convert between the schemes, the problems based on different representations will have essentially the same difficulty. But this is not always the case. Sometimes the choice of representation can make the problem much easier or harder to solve.

For these kinds of reasons, most problem representations are not specified in great detail. It is left up to the solver to decide on a reasonable representation given the constraints of the problem and of the machine solving it. Let's now focus on spanning trees, which present a convenient framework for illustrating the three most important problem types in computability theory.

2.9.2 Spanning Trees

Let $G = (V, E)$ be an undirected graph with edge weights from $\mathbb{N}$ specified by the weighting function $w : E \mapsto \mathbb{N}$. V represents the set of vertices, and E the set of edges. An example of such a weighted graph is shown in Figure 2.5. The graph has six vertices and nine edges.

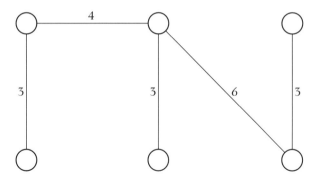

Figure 2.6

A spanning tree of the graph shown in Figure 2.5. The cost of this spanning tree is 19.

A **spanning tree** is a subgraph T of G that contains all the vertices of G, and just enough edges from E so that it connects all the vertices together but does not have any cycles.[11] Figure 2.6 illustrates a spanning tree of the graph shown in Figure 2.5. The **cost** of a spanning tree T is equal to the sum of the weights on the edges in the tree. The cost of the tree shown in Figure 2.6 is 19. A **minimum cost spanning tree** is a spanning tree with least cost among all possible spanning trees. There are many well-known algorithms for efficiently computing minimum cost spanning trees. The minimum cost spanning tree of the graph shown in Figure 2.5 has a cost of 17. It should be clear that this is indeed a minimum, since any spanning tree of this graph will contain five edges and the five least–cost edges sum to 17.

To actually talk about minimum cost spanning trees, we also need to augment the graph representation to include the edge weighting function w. We could supply it as a table that maps each edge (set of two vertices) to its corresponding weight. Or we could modify the representation to incorporate edge weights directly. For example, the adjacency matrix might be defined by

$(a_{ij}) = w$ if there is an edge of weight w between vertex v_i and v_j

and thus directly supply the weights as entries in the adjacency matrix. Any similar approach will work, and the details are left as an exercise.

With graph representation schemes and spanning trees in our toolkit, we can now proceed to define decision, function, and search problems. We start with the simplest of these—the decision problem.

---

11. A **cycle** is a path that returns back to its starting point without reusing any edges.

2.9.3   Decision Problems

The first type of problem we consider is a *decision problem*.

Definition 2.9.1   *A **decision problem** Π_D is a problem such that for each given part $G \in \{0, 1\}^*$ there exists a single solution part $S \in \{0, 1\}$.*

The given G states the input to the problem, and the solution part S specifies the answer. That is, the solution to a decision problem corresponding to a given part is unique and is either 1 (YES) or 0 (NO). A decision problem whose solution is 1 is called a YES instance, and one whose solution is 0 is called a NO instance.

Consider the following sample decision problem involving spanning trees. We assign the problem the acronym ST–D, standing for Spanning Tree Decision problem.

Definition 2.9.2   Spanning Tree Decision (ST–D)

Given: *An undirected graph $G = (V, E)$ with weights from $\mathbb{N}$ labeling the edges in E and a natural number k.*

Problem: *Is there a spanning tree of G with cost less than or equal to k?*

The first thing to notice is that the solution of the Spanning Tree Decision problem is simply a YES or NO answer represented by 1 or 0, respectively. Consider the graph shown in Figure 2.5 and a value of k equal to 18 as given. This instance of ST–D has a YES answer since there is a tree of cost less than or equal to 18, namely 17. If k had a value of 16 or less, the answer would be NO.

We specified one decision problem for spanning trees, but there may be several "natural" decision problems associated with a particular problem. Another natural decision problem for spanning trees has the following associated problem part: "Does the minimum cost spanning tree have value k?" Intuitively, it seems that to resolve decision questions such as these we must be able to actually compute spanning trees with low cost. Decision problems can usually be defined in a way that captures the important computational aspects of a problem. For example, ST–D only requires a YES or NO answer, but if we could provide an efficient solution to ST–D using a procedure SpanningTree, we could use SpanningTree to actually compute the value of the minimum cost spanning tree. This could be performed as described below.

First, compute an upper bound, W, on the weight of a minimum cost spanning tree by, for example, summing the $n - 1$ highest weights. Next use a *binary search* to zoom in quickly on the correct value. Say W, equal to 127, was an upper bound on the value of a minimum cost spanning tree; we could use SpanningTree to solve the question with k equal to 64. If SpanningTree returned YES, we cᵒᵘˡ ˡ solve ST–D with k equal to 32. If the answer were NO, we could ask S

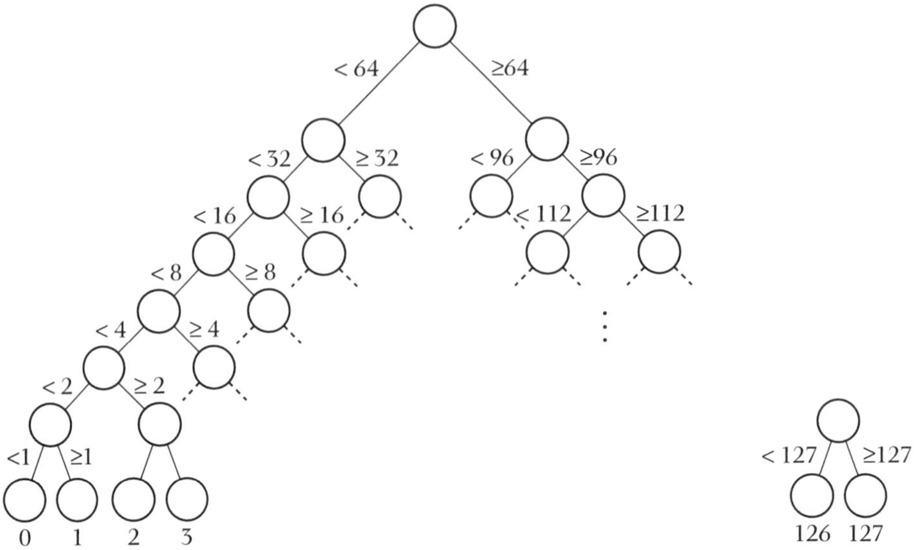

Figure 2.7

The binary search technique can be used to zoom in quickly on a value if we know an upper bound. For example, using the routine SpanningTree discussed in the text and supposing an upper bound of 127, this picture shows all possible comparisons that could be involved using binary search. The height of this tree is $7 = \lceil \lg 127 \rceil$, so after only at most seven calls to SpanningTree, we could pin down the exact weight of the minimum cost spanning tree.

k equal to 96. By continuing in this manner, it is clear that we could pin down the actual value of the minimum cost spanning tree. As described, this process would take $\lceil \lg W \rceil$ calls to SpanningTree, where W represents our upper bound on the cost of a minimum spanning tree. Figure 2.7 represents the binary search process pictorially. Since binary search is very efficient, the decision problem is not as restricted as it may have first seemed.

Decision problems are the preferred type of problem to work with in the theoretical framework because they translate easily into language recognition questions, as we will see later in this section. Some of the issues raised here will be addressed further in Chapters 10 and 11, where we examine a number of important decision problems. We note that although the binary search method works well for zooming in on a solution to some problems, in complexity classes that are not closed under complement, it cannot be used in this way.

2.9.4   Function Problems

In this section we consider our second class of problems, *function problems*.

Definition 2.9.3 *A* **function problem** Π_F *is a problem such that for each given part* $G \in \{0, 1\}^*$ *there exists a single solution part S, which is a string in* $\{0, 1\}^*$.

The given segment is similar to that for a decision problem; however, the solution part can be any string from $\{0, 1\}^*$. Thus, any type of coded object can be returned as an answer, but the solution corresponding to a specific input must be unique.

Let's define a function problem based on spanning trees in order to illustrate the definition.

Definition 2.9.4   Spanning Tree Function (ST–F)

Given: *An undirected graph* $G = (V, E)$ *with weights from* $\mathbb{N}$ *labeling the edges in E.*

Problem: *Compute the weight of a minimum cost spanning tree.*

Notice that we need to produce a value rather than just a YES or NO to answer ST–F. In this case the range from which the value must be produced is the natural numbers. For the graph shown in Figure 2.5, the answer to ST–F is 17 (or 10001 in binary). We saw earlier how a decision problem could be used in conjunction with binary search to solve a function problem in the case of spanning trees. Such techniques can often be used for other decision problems of this nature as well.

2.9.5   Search Problems

Search problems are the third and most general variety of problems we consider.

Definition 2.9.5 *A* **search problem** Π_S *is a problem such that for each given part* $G \in \{0, 1\}^*$ *there exists at least one solution part* $S \in \{0, 1\}^*$.

Since a search problem is any total binary relation over $\{0, 1\}^* \times \{0, 1\}^*$, it is in fact the same thing as a general problem. But the term "search problem" is often used in the literature to emphasize the general nature of the problem to be solved. Of course, any decision problem can be viewed as a function problem, and any function problem can be viewed as a search problem. However, the reverse of either of these statements does not hold in general.

Let's consider an example of a search problem involving spanning trees.

Definition 2.9.6   Spanning Tree Search (ST–S)

Given: *An undirected graph* $G = (V, E)$ *with weights from* $\mathbb{N}$ *labeling the edges in E.*

Problem: *Find a minimum cost spanning tree.*

Since there may be several minimum cost spanning trees associated with a specific input, this problem is not a function problem. A solution to the problem is any minimum cost spanning tree—that is, a bit string encoding a minimum cost spanning tree. For the graph shown in Figure 2.5, the solution happens to be unique and consists of the six vertices along with the five edges having weights three or four. Of course, this tree needs to be represented in such a way that it can be encoded as a bit string.

It may be that we actually want to find *all* minimum cost spanning trees—in which case we have an *enumeration problem*. The nature of the problem determines how we phrase the enumeration request. If there are a finite number of possible solutions, then we can express the enumeration as a search problem: the solution part S contains a list of all possible solutions. Since this list may not have any particular order, and two different lists can contain the same solutions but in different order, we cannot necessarily express the enumeration as a function problem. If there are an infinite (or even a very large) number of possible solutions, it is impossible to put all the solutions into one list. In this case we must phrase the enumeration in such a way that we can incrementally examine the possible solutions (or some subset of them). For example, we might give an ordering for spanning trees, and then phrase the enumeration as a function problem that given an index n returns the nth minimum cost spanning tree.

A search problem can also be viewed as a combined enumeration and decision problem. The idea is to enumerate all potential solutions, and to inspect each potential solution to decide if it is actually a solution.

2.10   *Casting Problems into Languages*

Each of the three types of problems studied in this section can be viewed as *language recognition problems*. A **language recognition problem** is the decision problem of determining whether a given string is in a particular language. In terms of classifying problems regarding their computational difficulty, it is important to view decision problems as language recognition problems, and to be able to translate function problems into decision problems. We explain how to do this below in each of these two cases. Language recognition for search problems does not play as important a role in computability theory.

Given a decision problem Π_D, we can form a language L_{Π_D} consisting of all the YES instances of the problem. For each G such that $(G, 1) \in \Pi_D$ include G in L_{Π_D}. That is, $L_{\Pi_D} = \{G \mid (G, 1) \in \Pi\}$. We obtain the following equivalence:

G is a YES instance of Π_D if and only if $G \in L_{\Pi_D}$

By answering the language recognition problem for L_{Π_D}, we can solve the decision problem for Π_D, and vice versa.

How can we represent a function problem Π_F as a language recognition problem? Function problems do not map to language recognition problems quite as easily as decision problems do. Suppose $(G, S) \in \Pi_F$. If we knew all the bits of S

and the positions their values occurred in, we could determine the value of S by concatenating the bits together in order. This leads us to consider the following language:

$$L_{\Pi_F} = \{G \Diamond i \Diamond j \mid (G, S) \in \Pi_F \text{ and bit } i \text{ of } S \text{ has value } j, j \in \{0, 1\}\}$$

Thus if we can compute the solution to a function problem, we can recognize its corresponding language, and vice versa. The proofs of these statements are left to the exercises.

This relationship between languages, decision problems, and function problems means that we can use language recognition as the common link between different kinds of problems and computation models. We can compare machines by comparing the languages they recognize, and we can compare problems by translating one problem's language into another's. The words "problem" and "language" will often be used synonymously due to this close connection.

2.11   *Decision, Search, and Enumeration*

Given some particular language L and a string x, we can ask the decision question of whether the string x belongs to L (see Figure 2.8). In this case we say we are testing for membership in L. Conceptually, when we test for membership, we imagine that we have the entire set of strings L at our disposal and that we check to see if L contains x. In practice we do something different. We look at how L was defined and then examine x to see if it meets the conditions for a string to be in L. If L is a simple language, such as 0^*, then testing for membership is very easy—just make sure the string x only contains 0's or is Λ. However, if L is more complex, say, $\{0^i \mid$ where i is a prime number$\}$, then in order to recognize whether a string x is in L, we need to determine if the number of 0's it contains is a prime number. Intuitively, this seems like a much more complex task than merely recognizing if the string does not contain any 1's. After all, it is difficult to recognize whether a large number is prime. For example, is 1,328,746,351 prime?

The Rolling Stones = {Mick Jagger, Keith Richards, Bill Wyman, Charlie Watts,
                              Ron Wood}
   Is Brian Jones in The Rolling Stones?   No

$L = \{0, 01, 000, 0001, 00001, 000001, 000\}$
   Is $0^{25}1 \in L$?   Yes

Figure 2.8

An illustration of two membership tests.

Rather than asking if a given string is in a particular language, we could ask for all the strings in the language. That is, we could ask if there is a program that can print out exactly the strings in *L*. Of course, if *L* is infinite, that program would never stop. When we ask for a language to be enumerated, we are in effect asking if there is a printer that, when given any *n*, will in a finite time eventually print out every string with length $\leq n$ in a given language *L*, and no others.

To measure the complexity of the language being enumerated, we could measure the "complexity of the printer." Languages such as 0* that you could imagine training your little sister to enumerate (obviating the need for a baby-sitter) are less complex than languages like {0^i | where *i* is a prime number}, which she might have more trouble with. Exactly how we measure the complexity of the printer will be clear when we study finite-state machines in Chapter 4. However, the general idea is that we measure the complexity of a problem by measuring the complexity of its associated language.

How do membership tests and enumeration relate? Suppose we are given a language *L* over an alphabet Σ and a string *x*. If we can solve the membership question for *L*, say, using an algorithm *A*, then we can answer with a YES or NO whether *x* is in *L*. Simply run *A* with input *x* and we get back an answer. Does this mean we can enumerate *L*? If we take a shotgun approach and start guessing *x*'s at random, applying algorithm *A*, and then printing the strings that produced YES's, what could go wrong? Well, we might not guess all possible strings, so we might not enumerate a string that we should. We should point out that we could also run into a problem with algorithm *A*. What we need is that *A* always returns a YES or NO answer (our usual meaning of algorithm). This procedure could not possibly work if *A* went into an infinite loop on some string not in *L*; we would never be able to continue the enumeration. So, in principle, if we were able to perform the following items:

1. Systematically list all strings over Σ.
2. Run *A* on them one by one.
3. Always have *A* return an answer and print out the strings corresponding to YES's as they came back.

then we could enumerate *L* using the membership testing algorithm *A*. It turns out that it is not too difficult to systematically list all strings over a given alphabet; we ask you to do this for the alphabet {0, 1} in the exercises.

What about in the other direction? Suppose we have a way of enumerating all of *L*. That is, we have a printer that prints out every value in the language *L* (at some time). Could we then test membership of *x* in *L*? Let's try it. One idea is simply to run the printer, and each time it prints a new string *y*, compare *x* to *y*. If they are equal, then we know *x* is in *L*. What happens if they are not equal?

This is unfortunate, since then we must continue this process. If L is an infinite language and $x \notin L$, then we would never be able to produce a NO answer. We would keep checking and never find our string.

Suppose we had a method of enumerating L in which we printed strings out in order of increasing size. If we did this and did not find x before the strings got larger than x, we would know that x could not be in L. If it were, we would have already printed it. Thus, using this special type of enumeration with shorter strings coming first, we could answer the membership question. Fortunately, printing the strings of bounded length over a fixed alphabet in enumeration order is not that difficult to do.

The above discussion indicates a very close correspondence between membership questions and enumeration of languages. The references contain additional information about this correspondence. As an aside, we should mention that the word *generate* is sometimes used in this context instead of *enumerate*.

2.12 *Language Operations and Enumeration*

Consider the language represented by $\{0\}^*$, that is, $\{\Lambda, 0, 00, \ldots\}$. We can view the expression $\{0\}^*$ as enumerating or generating the language as follows: think of the $*$ as meaning generate no 0's, then one 0, then two 0's, and so on forever. It is helpful in viewing this process to consider an order on the strings. In terms of high–level program code, we can view this process as a **for** loop and impose a natural order on the enumeration:

> **for** $i \leftarrow 0$ **to** ∞ **do**
>> print i 0's;   **comment:** when $i = 0$, print Λ

The language represented by $\{0\}^*$ is enumerated from shorter strings to longer strings. Notice the code will enumerate all of the language represented by $\{0\}^*$. Consider any string 0^m for some $m \in \mathbb{N}$. When i equals m, the **for** loop will output 0^m.

Let's look at another example. Consider the language $\{0, 1\}^* \circ \{101\}$. How can we view this representation as an enumerator? The starred expression can be viewed in a similar manner as we used to think about $\{0\}^*$ above. So $\{0, 1\}^*$ produces Λ, the shortest string in the language represented by this particular part of our expression, and then 101 is concatenated onto Λ to yield 101. The next string enumerated by $\{0, 1\}^*$ is 0. To the 0 we concatenate 101 to obtain 0101. This process continues forever. In terms of high–level program code, we can view this process as the following **for** loop:

> **for** $l \leftarrow 0$ **to** ∞ **do**
>> **for** $i \leftarrow 0$ **to** 2^l **do**
>>> print the ith string from $\{0, 1\}^l$ concatenated with 101;

Let L_1 and L_2 be arbitrary languages. We think of a union such as $L_1 \cup L_2$ as enumerating the strings that appear in L_1 or L_2; we think of a concatenation such as $L_1 \circ L_2$ as enumerating every combination of a string in L_1 followed by one from L_2; and we think of a Kleene star such as L_1^* as a **for** loop with an index i going from 0 to ∞ while enumerating a string in L_1 and concatenating it to the currently built–up string. The way of visualizing language operations through enumeration can also provide insight into the language represented by a *regular expression*. Regular expressions are the topic of the next chapter.

2.13 Exercises

Section 2.1   Introduction

1. Design C-- code to check whether a given input is a valid email address as discussed in the text (see page 21).

2. Can you find a form on the World Wide Web that validates the format of the date you enter into the fields?

3. In the spirit of this section, give three examples of applications in computer science where languages play an important role.

4. Build a table that compares five different types of computers. Include as many attributes as possible in the comparison: processor speed, memory capacity, price, and so on.

Section 2.2   Symbols, Alphabets, and Strings

5. Is the empty set, Ø, considered an alphabet?

6. Give four examples of sets that are not alphabets.

7. Are the alphabets $\{a, b\}$ and $\{A, B\}$ the same?

8. What are the lengths of the following strings *abba*, Λ, $0\diamond10000$, and *abbb* $\circ$ *bb*?

9. What is $\#_j(x)$ if $x = jumpingjacks$?

10. How many occurrences of *e* are there in *bookkeeper*? Where do they occur?

11. Let $x = bab$. Write out all the steps involved in determining x^3 using Equation 2.1.

12. Prove that concatenation of strings is associative. That is, let Σ be any alphabet and let x, y, and z be any strings over Σ. Show that $(x \circ y) \circ z = x \circ (y \circ z)$.

13. When can a string x simultaneously be a prefix, a substring, and a suffix of a string y?

14. Let $\Sigma = \{a, b\}$. List in lexicographic order the first 10 strings of Σ^* and the first 10 strings of $\Sigma^{=4}$, where $a < b$. Using properties of alphabetical ordering, can you develop a *bijection f* from Σ^* to $\mathbb{N}$? Recall, a **bijection** is a function that is *one-to-one* and *onto*.

15. Let Σ be an alphabet. How many prefixes does the string $x = \sigma_1 \cdots \sigma_n$ have? Here $\sigma_i \in \Sigma$ for $1 \le i \le n$.

16. Let Σ be an alphabet. What is the maximum number of possible distinct substrings of the string $x = \sigma_1 \cdots \sigma_n$, where $\sigma_i \in \Sigma$ for $1 \le i \le n$?

17. Are the number of suffixes of a string always equal to the number of prefixes? Prove your answer.

18. Give an inductive (or recursive) definition of string reversal.

19. Let x be a string over an alphabet Γ. Prove that $(x^R)^R = x$.

20. Let x and y be strings over an alphabet Γ. Prove that $(xy)^R = y^R x^R$.

21. A **palindrome** is a string x such that $x = x^R$. Give five English words of length four or more that are palindromes.

22. Search on the World Wide Web for palindromes using your favorite search engine. What is the longest sentence you found that is a palindrome? What is the uniform resource locator (URL) of the most interesting palindrome page you found?

Section 2.3   Languages

23. Is an alphabet a language?

24. Is $\emptyset$ a language?

25. Let $\Sigma = \{0, 1\}$. How many strings are there in the following languages?
    (a) $\Sigma^{\le 0}$
    (b) $\Sigma^{=0}$
    (c) $\Sigma^{\le 1}$
    (d) $\Sigma^{\le 2}$
    (e) $\Sigma^{\le 3}$
    (f) $\Sigma^{\le 4}$

26. Let $\Sigma = \{a, b, c\}$. How many strings are there in the following languages?
    (a) $\Sigma^{\le 0}$
    (b) $\Sigma^{=0}$
    (c) $\Sigma^{\le 1}$
    (d) $\Sigma^{\le 2}$
    (e) $\Sigma^{\le 3}$
    (f) $\Sigma^{\le 4}$

27. If $|\Sigma| = k$, how many strings are there in the languages $\Sigma^{=n}$ and $\Sigma^{\leq n}$ for a natural number n? Are the languages ever equal?

Section 2.4   *Operations on Languages*

28. Let $L = \{x \mid x \in \{0, 1\}^* \text{ and } \#_1(x) \geq 3\}$. What are $L^{=0}$, $L^{=4}$, $L^{\leq 2}$, and $L^{\leq 4}$?

29. Let $L = \{x \mid x \in \{0, 1\}^* \text{ and } x \text{ has } 001 \text{ as a prefix}\}$. What are $L^{=0}$, $L^{=3}$, $L^{=5}$, $L^{\leq 2}$, $L^{\leq 4}$, and $L^{\leq 5}$?

30. What is $\{\Lambda, 01, 001\} \cup \{\Lambda, 00, 10\}$?

31. Let $L_1 \cup L_2$ be languages. Prove that $L_1 \cup L_1 = L_1$ and $L_1 \cup L_2 = L_2 \cup L_1$.

32. Prove union is associative, that is, $(L_1 \cup L_2) \cup L_3 = L_1 \cup (L_2 \cup L_3)$ for any languages L_1, L_2, and L_3.

33. Let $L = \{\Lambda, 00, 01, 10, 11, 0^4, \ldots, 1111, \ldots\}$. What is $\overline{L}$ over the alphabet $\{0, 1\}$?

34. What is the complement of $\emptyset$ over the alphabet $\{0, 1\}$?

35. Let L be any language over an alphabet Γ. Prove that $\Gamma^* = L \cup \overline{L}$.

36. Informally describe the complement of the following language:

$$\{x \mid x \in \{0, 1\}^* \text{ and } \#_0(x) = 5\}$$

37. Let Γ be any alphabet and L a language over Γ. Prove $L = \overline{\overline{L}}$.

38. What is $\emptyset \cap \{\Lambda\}$?

39. Let L be any language. Prove $L \cap \overline{L} = \emptyset$.

40. Let L_1 and L_2 be any two languages over Γ. Prove the following properties:

$$L_1 \cap L_2 = L_2 \cap L_1, L_1 \cap L_1 = L_1, \text{ and } L_1 \cap \emptyset = \emptyset$$

41. Prove intersection is associative, that is, $(L_1 \cap L_2) \cap L_3 = L_1 \cap (L_2 \cap L_3)$ for any languages L_1, L_2, and L_3.

42. Prove DeMorgan's Laws.

43. What is the concatenation of $\{0, 11, 010\}$ and $\{\Lambda, 10, 010\}$?

44. Prove concatenation is not a commutative operation on languages.

45. Is there a language L such that $LL = L$?

46. Let $L = \{\Lambda, 0, 010, 1100\}$. What is L^R?

47. Specify an infinite language L, different from the one given in Example 2.4.7, such that $L = L^R$.

48. Does $\emptyset = \emptyset^R$?

49. Let $L_1 = \{ab, bb, bbb\}$ and $L_2 = \{b, ab, bb\}$. What is $L_1 \oplus L_2$?

50. Let L and L' be two languages. Prove $L \oplus L' = (L \cup L') - (L \cap L')$.

51. Let L be a language over an alphabet Γ. Prove $L \oplus \emptyset = L$, $L \oplus L = \emptyset$, $L \oplus \Gamma^* = \bar{L}$, and $L \oplus \bar{L} = \Gamma^*$.

52. When is L^* a finite language?

53. Let $L = \{0, 01, 001, \ldots\}$. Describe L^*.

54. Does the Kleene star of a language always result in a "larger" language?

55. Does $L^* = (L^*)^*$? Prove your answer.

56. Can L^+ ever equal L^*?

Section 2.5   Alphabet Encodings

57. Define a five–bit block encoding f of the lowercase English alphabet over the binary alphabet. What are $f(taco)$ and $f(burrito)$?

58. How would you encode the alphabet $\{0, 1, 2, 3, 4\}$ over the alphabet $\{a, b, c\}$?

59. Extend the mapping of the lowercase English alphabet to blocks of five bits to a homomorphism h using Equations 2.7 and 2.8. What are $h(taco)$ and $h(burrito)$?

60. Specify a mapping from $\{0, 1, \diamond\}^*$ to $\{0, 1\}^*$ that is *not* a homomorphism.

61. The next couple of problems deal with the *dyadic numbers*. Dyadic numbers are represented over the alphabet $\{1, 2\}$. They map to the natural numbers as follows:

$$\Lambda \to 0, \ \ 1 \to 1, \ \ 2 \to 2, \ \ 11 \to 3, \ \ 12 \to 4, \ \ 21 \to 5, \ldots$$

Present a formal definition for the dyadic numbers. Define a bijection f between the dyadic numbers and the natural numbers.

62. The dyadic numbers have an advantage over binary numbers in that representations are unique; that is, there are no "leading 0's." Define a homomorphism mapping $\{0, 1, \diamond\}^*$ into $\{1, 2\}^*$ and show how to code $00111\diamond11011\diamond10011\diamond111100$ using your homomorphism.

Section 2.6   Some Test Languages

63. For each language given below, list its five shortest strings.
    (a) $\{0^i 1^i \mid i \geq 0\}$
    (b) $\{xx \mid x \in \{0, 1\}^*\}$
    (c) $\{x \diamond x^R \mid x \in \{0, 1\}^*\}$
    (d) $\{0^i 1^j 2^j 3^i \mid i, j \geq 0\}$
    (e) $\{0^i 1^i 2^i \mid i \geq 0\}$

Section 2.7   How Many Languages Are There?

64. What are the power sets of $\emptyset$, $\{\Lambda\}$, and $\{a, b, ab\}$?

65. Define a bijection f from $\{0, 1\}^*$ to $\mathbb{N}$. What is $f(101111)$?

66. Prove that the set of even integers, $\{\ldots, -2, 0, 2, \ldots\}$, is countably infinite.

67. Is the set $\{0, 2, 4, \ldots, \}$ countably infinite?

68. Is there a bijection from the set $\{1, 2, 3, \ldots\}$ to $\{1, 3, 5, \ldots\}$?

69. Let $\Sigma = \{0, 1\}$. Specify a bijection from $\mathbb{N}$ to Σ^*.

70. Let $\Sigma = \{a, b, c\}$. Specify a bijection from $\mathbb{N}$ to Σ^*.

71. Let Σ be an alphabet. Prove that Σ^* is a countably infinite set.

72. Let $\Sigma = \{0, 1\}$. In this specific case, carry out the proof of Theorem 2.7.3.

73. Do Lemma 2.7.1 and Theorem 2.7.3 hold for all sets, that is, not just alphabets?

74. Prove that the set of real numbers in the interval $[0, 1]$ is uncountable. Do a proof using the diagonalization technique.

Section 2.8   Problem Representations

75. Define and give a representation for a problem, called *Minimum*, that finds the minimum value of some numbers.

76. Define and give a representation for a problem, called *Perfect Square*, that tests to see if its input is n^2 for some $n \in \mathbb{N}$.

77. Define and give a representation for a problem, called *Parity*, that checks to see if the input has even parity (see Section 1.1.3).

Section 2.9   Types of Problems

78. What is the solution to the instance of ST–D shown in Figure 2.9 with k equal to 25?

79. Construct three YES instances and three NO instances of ST–D.

80. What is the solution to the instance of ST–F shown in Figure 2.9?

81. What is a solution to the instance of ST–S shown in Figure 2.9? Is the solution unique?

82. Write out adjacency matrix, adjacency list, and edge list encodings of the graph shown in Figure 2.10. For the adjacency and edge list encodings, first do this at a high level and then as bit strings.

83. Informally, a *sparse graph* $G = (\{v_1, \ldots, v_n\}, E)$ is one containing few edges. For this exercise consider a sparse graph having exactly n edges. Compare the representation schemes listed in Section 2.9.1 in terms of their storage

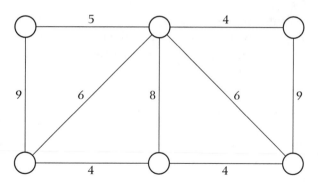

Figure 2.9

A weighted, undirected graph used in several of the exercises.

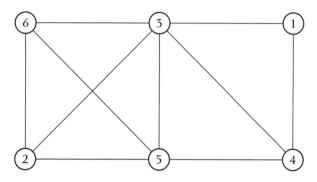

Figure 2.10

An undirected graph used in the exercises to examine encodings.

usage regarding sparse graphs. That is, how many bits does it take for representing an n-edge graph when the representation scheme is encoded into binary in the obvious way?

84. Informally, a *dense graph* $G = (\{v_1, \ldots, v_n\}, E)$ is one containing many edges. For this exercise consider a graph having exactly $n^2/4$ edges. Compare the representation schemes listed in Section 2.9.1 in terms of their storage usage regarding dense graphs. Do the comparison in the same way as required in Exercise 83.

85. Define your own decision problem about spanning trees.

86. Define a new function problem involving spanning trees.

87. Define an additional search problem that uses spanning trees.

88. A **matching** of an undirected graph $G = (V, E)$ is a subset of the edges, M, with the property that if m_1 and m_2 are in M, then $m_1 \cap m_2 = \emptyset$. Note that an undirected edge is expressed as a set consisting of its two endpoints. Develop a natural decision problem based on matchings. What is the solution to your problem for the underlying graph shown in Figure 2.10?

89. A **maximum weight matching** is a matching M in a weighted, undirected graph such that the sum of the weights of the edges in M is a maximum over all matchings. Develop a natural decision problem based on matchings. What is the solution to your problem for the graph shown in Figure 2.9?

90. Develop a natural function problem based on maximum weight matchings. What is the solution to your problem for the graph shown in Figure 2.9?

91. Develop a natural search problem based on maximum weight matchings. What is a solution to your problem for the graph shown in Figure 2.9? Is the solution unique?

92. Draw an instance of the maximum weight matching problem that has 8 vertices and 12 edges, has a maximum weight matching of size 25 that includes 3 edges, and has a unique solution.

93. Formulate language recognition problems corresponding to ST-D and ST-F.

Section 2.10   Casting Problems into Languages

94. Let Π_F be a function problem. Show that if we can solve the language recognition problem

$$L_{\Pi_F} = \{G \diamond i \diamond j \mid (G, S) \in \Pi_F \text{ and bit } i \text{ of } S \text{ has value } j, j \in \{0, 1\}\}$$

then we can compute Π_F, and vice versa.

95. Define a function problem that represents the function $f(n) = n^2 + 5$. Define a corresponding language recognition problem. For small values of n, illustrate the relationship between the two problems.

96. Derive a language recognition problem that can be used to represent a search problem. Show how the two concepts correspond to each other.

Section 2.11   Decision, Search, and Enumeration

97. Write C programs that take a user-entered input string x (perhaps from a file) and test membership in the following languages:
   (a) $\{0^2, 0^4, 0^6, \ldots\}$
   (b) $\{0, 1\}^*$

(c) $\{x \mid x \in \{0, 1\}^*$ and x has an even number of 0's$\}$

(d) $\{0^i \mid$ where i is a prime number$\}$

98. For each program in Exercise 97, enter the input 0^{23}. Is the response time noticeably faster for any of the programs? How about on input 0^{1123}? Can you devise an experiment that suggests a ranking in terms of the "complexity" of the languages based on your programs?

Section 2.12   *Language Operations and Enumeration*

99. Write C programs that run forever (bet you were never asked to do that in a programming class) to enumerate (print) the following languages:

(a) $\{\Lambda, 0, 00, \ldots\}$

(b) $\{0, 1\}^*$

(c) $\{x \mid x \in \{0, 1\}^*$ and x has exactly five 0's$\}$

(d) $\{0^i \mid$ where i is a prime number$\}$

100. For each program in Exercise 99, after five minutes (scale appropriately if this is too long or too short) of running time, how many values have been printed? Based on this experiment, how do you rank the languages in terms of their "complexities"?

101. Write C programs to enumerate the strings in the following languages. Design the programs within the spirit of the discussion from Section 2.11.

(a) 0^*

(b) $\{0, 1\}^*$

(c) $\{0, 1\}^* \circ \{0, 1\}^*$

CHAPTER 3

Regular Expressions and Languages

Regular expressions are one of the five greatest discoveries in theoretical computer science. Don't ask me what the other three are.

—*Famous theoretician*

3.1 Introduction

The power of computers is not in their speed or storage capacity. Computers are powerful because they take our programs of thousands or millions of lines of code and amplify them into millions or billions of actual processing operations. This amplification is possible because we write our programs using simple patterns that, in turn, specify very broad and generalizable behavior. Patterns let us express our wishes economically and let us communicate them to others without having to go into enormous tedious detail. Let's illustrate this idea with a simple example.

Suppose you have a directory called `public-html` that contains *all* of your personal World Wide Web files, and that this directory currently has no subdirectories. Suppose your `public-html` has grown out of control (like ours) and you now have hundreds of files in it. You know it contains some gif (graphics interchange format), html (hypertext markup language), Java, jpg (Joint Photographic Experts Group), midi (music instrument digital interface) files, and some others whose types you have completely forgotten. You decide that it is definitely time to reorganize your directory and to create subdirectories for each type of file. How do you proceed?

Probably the most time-consuming approach is to produce a listing of all the files in your directory and move each file individually into the appropriate subdirectory. Every file requires you to type (or mouse) a move command.

The least time-consuming approach is to recognize that there is a pattern to your actions. However, instead of doing the moving yourself, you instruct your assistant, if you are lucky enough to have one, to go and reorganize your directory structure so that there is a subdirectory for each possible file extension. You indicate that all files are to be moved into their corresponding subdirectory. That is, you give your assistant a reorganizational pattern to follow, which they then amplify into actual work.[1]

The reorganization performed by your assistant most likely also uses patterns to identify files with common extensions. That is, the pattern is used to extract (or *filter*) out some subset of objects from a larger collection. Identifying subsets of files by patterns is so useful that almost every command interpreter (or shell) has some form of pattern matching on file names. For example, a pattern such as `*.jpg` on our troublesome directory above might generate the following subset of files:

```
cs-alaska.jpg      larrym.jpg        people.jpg
cs-beaver.jpg      lbrick.jpg        robert.jpg
cs-eddieh.jpg      lightdot.jpg      toast.jpg
freebird.jpg       misslan.jpg
```

Thus your assistant, instead of entering 11 different move commands, simply types the command `mv *.jpg jpg-dir` instead. One simple move command is amplified to generate 11 moves. That one command works whether there are 11 or 11,000 `.jpg` files.

In some command shells, the filtering can be quite sophisticated. For example, the Unix shell lets you specify the pattern `cs-*.jpg`, which extracts out all files that begin with `cs-` and end with the `.jpg` extension:

```
cs-alaska.jpg       cs-beaver.jpg       cs-eddieh.jpg
```

You might use such a pattern if your course-related jpg files are all identified with a common prefix, and you would like to put them into their own directory.

Just how sophisticated can we make this pattern-matching mechanism while still preserving its compact representation and simplicity? Let's continue with this filtering problem and investigate the general problem we are trying to solve.

Our goal is to develop a way of specifying a filter that extracts out a desired subset of file names from a larger collection. How will this work? Since we are manipulating sets of file names, and a file name is just a string over some alphabet, we can express the filtering problem in terms of languages. Suppose that L_{dir} is the language that contains the names of all the files in your directory. How do we filter out the ones that begin with 1 and end with `.jpg`?

The filter defines a set, L_{filter}, that consists of all the file names accepted by the filter. So, by using the language operations we defined in Chapter 2, the set

---

1. An incompetent assistant needs explicit instructions for everything, thus creating so much extra work that you do the job yourself instead.

$L_{dir} \cap L_{filter}$

is exactly the files in our directory that match the filter pattern.

How can we generate L_{filter}? We can again use the same language operations. Suppose Σ is the alphabet of possible characters that can appear in file names. Then all the file names that begin with 1 can be described by the expression

$\{1\} \circ \Sigma^*$

All the files that end in .jpg can be described by the expression

$\Sigma^* \circ \{.jpg\}$

If we intersect these two, we get

$L_{filter} = \{1\} \circ \Sigma^* \circ \{.jpg\}$

This is indeed the set of strings that start with 1 and end in .jpg.

Thus the basic set operations on languages provide us with a mathematical way of specifying a filter. In fact, so many of the filters that we construct use just the simple set operations of union, concatenation, and Kleene star that we call the languages constructed in this way the *regular languages*.

Can we provide our command shell with the capability of defining regular language filters? If so, what kinds of filters can and cannot be constructed as regular languages?

3.2 *Regular Languages and Constructions*

The regular languages are those languages that can be constructed from the "big three" set operations of union, concatenation, and Kleene star.

Definition 3.2.1 *Let Σ be an alphabet. The class of* **regular languages** *over Σ is defined inductively as follows:*

1. *$\emptyset$ is a regular language.*

2. *For each $\sigma \in \Sigma$, $\{\sigma\}$ is a regular language.*

3. *For any natural number $n \geq 2$, if $L_1, L_2, \ldots, L_n$ are regular languages, then so is $L_1 \cup L_2 \cup \cdots \cup L_n$.*

4. *For any natural number $n \geq 2$, if $L_1, L_2, \ldots, L_n$ are regular languages, then so is $L_1 \circ L_2 \circ \cdots \circ L_n$.*

5. *If L is a regular language, then so is L^*.*

6. *Nothing else is a regular language unless its construction follows from rules 1 through 5.*

Thus every regular language can be written as an expression (or formula) using the operations of set union, concatenation, and Kleene star. To simplify the writing of these formulas, we adopt the following conventions:

1. Writing a symbol, say a, by itself is shorthand for $\{a\}$. That is, we promote a symbol to the singleton set containing it.

2. The concatenation symbol, $\circ$, can be dropped, as in xy instead of $x \circ y$.

3. Parentheses need be used only when it is necessary to override the normal precedence of $*$ over $\circ$ over $\cup$.

Each of these formulas is called a *regular construction*, and by definition the regular languages are exactly those languages that are generated by regular constructions.

Here are some examples of regular languages. We prove that they are regular by providing a regular construction for generating the language.

Example 3.2.2   Regular languages

1. $\emptyset$ is a regular language via rule 1, which is one of the base cases of the definition.

2. Let $\Gamma = \{\gamma_1, \ldots, \gamma_k\}$ be an alphabet. By rule 2, $\{\gamma_i\}$ is a regular language for $1 \leq i \leq k$. Applying rule 3 to these singleton sets, we see that Γ is a regular language.

3. $L = \{a, ab\}$ is a language over $\Sigma = \{a, b\}$. By rule 2, both $\{a\}$ and $\{b\}$ are regular languages. It follows from rule 4 that $\{a\} \circ \{b\} = \{ab\}$ is a regular language. Using rule 3, we see that $\{a\} \cup \{ab\} = L$ is a regular language.

4. $\{\Lambda\}$ is a regular language. By rule 1, $\emptyset$ is a regular language. Applying rule 5, we get $\emptyset^* = \{\Lambda\}$ is a regular language.

5. Let $L = \{\Lambda, 0^2, 0^4, 0^6, \ldots\}$. By rules 1 and 2, $\{00\}$ is regular, and by rule 5, $\{00\}^*$ is a regular language. Since L equals $\{00\}^*$, L is a regular language. ∎

Since the regular constructions are composed of set operations, we can use set properties to produce equivalent constructions, and prove that two constructions produce the same language. We list some of these in the following observation, whose proof we leave to you.

Observation 3.2.3   *Let Σ be an alphabet. Let R_1, R_2, and R_3 be any regular constructions over Σ. Then the following equivalences hold:*

1. $R_1 \circ \emptyset = \emptyset \circ R_1 = \emptyset$
   Concatenation with the empty language yields the empty language.

2. $R_1 \circ \emptyset^* = \emptyset^* \circ R_1 = R_1$
   The identity for language concatenation is $\emptyset^* = \{\Lambda\}$.

3. $R_1 \cup R_2 = R_2 \cup R_1$
   Commutativity of $\cup$.

4. $R_1 \cup (R_2 \cup R_3) = (R_1 \cup R_2) \cup R_3$
   Associativity of $\cup$.

5. $R_1 \circ (R_2 \circ R_3) = (R_1 \circ R_2) \circ R_3$
   Associativity of $\circ$.

6. $R_1 \circ (R_2 \cup R_3) = (R_1 \circ R_2) \cup (R_1 \circ R_3)$
   Left distribution of $\circ$ over $\cup$.

7. $(R_1 \cup R_2) \circ R_3 = (R_1 \circ R_3) \cup (R_2 \circ R_3)$
   Right distribution of $\circ$ over $\cup$.

Let's consider a few more examples.

Example 3.2.4   More regular languages

1. The language $\{\Lambda, a, aa, \ldots\}$ is constructed by a^*.

2. The language

   $$\{\Lambda, 0, 1, 00, 01, \ldots\} \cup \{\Lambda, 1, 11, \ldots\}$$

   can be constructed by $(0 \cup 1)^* \cup 1^*$. But note that this is also the same as $(0 \cup 1)^*$.

3. The language over the alphabet $\{0, 1\}$ that consists of all strings having the pattern 01 as a substring can be constructed simply by

   $$(0 \cup 1)^* 01 (0 \cup 1)^*$$

4. The language over the alphabet $\{0, 1\}$ whose strings contain an even number of 0's can be constructed by

   $$(1^*((01^*)(01^*))^*)$$

   or simply $1^*(01^*01^*)^*$. Notice that Λ is included in this language. We leave it to you to verify that this regular expression does in fact represent the language we claim.   ∎

In general, we try to pick our constructions so that it is obvious that they construct the language we desire. However, this is not always easy to do, nor is it always clear if the construction does in fact do what we want.

3.3   *Regular Expressions*

How do we take the notion of a regular language and turn it into a useful tool? One of the issues is syntactical. Typing in a mathematical expression like $\{1\} \circ \Sigma^* \circ \{.\mathtt{jpg}\}$ is a bit awkward, and so we would like to have a notation that is a bit easier to use at the keyboard.

In other words, we would like to define an easy-to-use notation for describing the construction of sets of strings using the basic language operations. This notation is, in fact, a tiny programming language, so we will have to specify its *grammar* (or *syntax*). We will also have to specify how it is interpreted (its *semantics*) as describing languages constructed by the set operations.

3.3.1   The Grammar of Standard Regular Expressions

A **grammar** is a set of rules for writing properly formed sentences in a language. Regular constructions are recursive, in the sense that larger ones are built from smaller ones constructed with the same rules. Thus the grammar of regular expressions can be presented inductively as follows:

Definition 3.3.1   *Let Σ be an alphabet. The* **standard regular expressions**[2] **(regular expressions** *for short) over the alphabet Σ are defined inductively as follows: each regular expression is a string over the alphabet $\Sigma \cup \{(,), |, *\}$.*

1. *The string* ( ) *is a regular expression.*
2. *For each $\sigma \in \Sigma$, the string symbol σ is a regular expression.*
3. *If R is a regular expression, then so is* (R).
4. *If R_1 and R_2 are regular expressions, then so is* $(R_1 | R_2)$.
5. *If R_1 and R_2 are regular expressions, then so is* $(R_1 R_2)$.
6. *If R is a regular expression, then so is* R*.
7. *Nothing else is a regular expression unless it follows from rules 1 through 6.*

Each regular expression is merely a string of symbols assembled using the syntactic rules of Definition 3.3.1. Note how within parts 3 through 6 of the inductive definition we mix specific symbols typeset in a typewriter font (like |) with grammatical variables typeset in italics (like R_1). A grammatical variable indicates a point where the definition is expanded recursively. We have a grammatically correct regular expression exactly when all of the grammatical variables have been expanded.

But what does a regular expression *mean*? That is, what is its semantics? The meaning we give to a regular expression depends on our perspective. In one sense, the meaning of the expression is the particular regular construction that it describes. For example (a|b)* describes the construction $(\{a\} \cup \{b\})^*$. But it is more useful to take a broader sense of meaning, in which the meaning of a

---

2. As contrasted to the extended regular expressions used in the Perl and Awk programming languages.

regular expression is the language it constructs. This way we can talk about two different regular expressions meaning the same thing.

Let's now define the language that each regular expression represents. To do this we establish the correspondence between the syntax of each regular expression and its associated language.

Definition 3.3.2 *Let R be a standard regular expression over alphabet Σ. Then $L(R)$ denotes the* **language associated with** *R, defined as follows:*

1. *If $R = (\ )$, then $L(R) = \emptyset$.*
2. *If $R = \sigma$ for some $\sigma \in \Sigma$, then $L(R) = \{\sigma\}$.*
3. *If $R = (R_1)$ for some regular expression R_1, then $L(R) = L(R_1)$.*
4. *If $R = (R_1 | R_2)$ for some regular expressions R_1 and R_2, then $L(R) = L(R_1) \cup L(R_2)$.*
5. *If $R = (R_1 R_2)$ for some regular expressions R_1 and R_2, then $L(R) = L(R_1) \circ L(R_2)$.*
6. *If $R = R_1*$ for some regular expression R_1, then $L(R) = L(R_1)^*$.*

When writing down complex regular expressions, the parentheses often clutter things up. To simplify matters we assign priorities to the operators just as we do in algebra (think of your favorite programming language and the precedence on the arithmetic operators). From highest to lowest precedence, we have $*$, concatenation, and $|$. That is, apply $*$ first, followed by concatenation, and then $|$. So, for example,

```
ba*
```

represents the language $\{b\} \circ (\{a\}^*)$ consisting of strings that contain a single b followed by zero or more a's, and not the language consisting of any number of ba's.

When it does not create confusion, we will often omit the $L(\cdot)$ notation, and simply identify a regular expression with its associated language. For example, when we say the language $0*$ is infinite, we actually mean the language $L(0*)$ is infinite. Or we might write something like "Does $(a|b)* = \{a, b\}^*$?"

3.3.2 Examples of Standard Regular Expressions

Let's look at some regular expressions and the languages they represent. Keep in mind that a regular expression is nothing more than a concise description of a set of strings.

Example 3.3.3 Regular expressions over the alphabet $\Sigma = \{0, 1, a, b\}$ and their associated languages

1. $(\ )$ is a regular expression (via rule 1, Definition 3.3.1) representing the empty language, that is, $L((\ )) = \emptyset$.

2. 0, 1, a, and b are regular expressions (via rule 2) and represent the languages {0}, {1}, {a}, and {b}, respectively.

3. (0|1) is a regular expression. This follows from the fact that 0 and 1 are regular expressions, and then by applying rule 4 in the definition of regular expressions. $L((0|1))$ is the language {0, 1}.

4. (01) is a regular expression. This follows from the fact that 0 and 1 are regular expressions, and then by applying rule 5 in the definition of regular expressions. (01) represents the language {01}.

5. 0* is a regular expression. This follows from the fact that 0 is a regular expression, and then by applying rule 6 in the definition of regular expressions. $L(0*)$ is the language {0}*.

6. ( )* is a regular expression. This follows from rules 1 and 6. Its associated language is {Λ} since $L((\ )*) = L((\ ))^* = \emptyset^* = \{Λ\}$.

7. ((((0|1)*(ab))a)(0|1)) is easily checked to be a regular expression using rules 2 through 6 of the definition of regular expressions. This regular expression represents the language that consists of strings having the following form: any string of 0's and 1's, concatenated with *aba*, and finally concatenated with either a 0 or a 1. So, 0101*aba*0 and *aba*1 are strings in this language. We would normally write this expression as (0|1)*aba(0|1).

8. Consider the language *L* over the alphabet {*a*, *b*} in which each string has exactly three occurrences of *b* and ends in an *a*. How can we produce a regular expression for this language? Somehow we need to "hard code" the fact the string has exactly three *b*'s and that the last character is an *a*. Since there is no other restriction on the *a*'s, any number of them including zero could come between any of the *b*'s. Consider the following regular expression:

   a*ba*ba*ba*a

   Notice any string in the language represented by this regular expression contains exactly three *b*'s and ends in an *a*. Furthermore, it is intuitively clear that any number of *a*'s can occur anywhere "inside" the string. Thus this expression correctly represents *L*. We leave a more formal proof of this fact to the exercises (see Exercise 10). ∎

3.3.3 Consistency and Completeness of Standard Regular Expressions

Regular expressions are *consistent* with respect to the regular languages. That is, it is clear from the definition of the language associated with a regular expression (see Definition 3.3.2) that every regular expression actually defines a regular language.

But it is not so clear that regular expressions are also *complete*. If a language is regular, is there at least one regular expression that represents it? If not, the regular expressions are not a complete description of the regular languages.

To determine that the regular expressions are complete, we need to show at least one way of translating every regular construction of Definition 3.2.1 into a regular expression of Definition 3.3.1 whose associated language is that of the regular construction. It is clear that the only difficult translation involves union and concatenation, which are defined for two or more regular languages in Definition 3.2.1, and only two in Definition 3.3.1. Using the associative properties of union and concatenation, we can "compile" the n–ary union or concatenation into a nested regular expression with parentheses. For example, $R_1 \cup R_2 \cup R_3 \cup R_4$ can be generated by the regular expression $(R_1 | (R_2 | (R_3 | R_4)))$.

Thus the regular expressions are a consistent and complete representation of the regular languages, and so are equivalent:

Observation 3.3.4   *A language is a regular language if and only if it can be represented by a regular expression.*

Let's close this section by introducing some notation that will prove useful later on in the text. Let Σ be a fixed alphabet. $\mathcal{L}_{\textbf{RE}}$ denotes the set of all languages over Σ that can be represented by regular expressions. $\mathcal{L}_{\textbf{RL}}$ denotes the set of all regular languages over Σ. By Observation 3.3.4 we have that $\mathcal{L}_{\textbf{RE}} = \mathcal{L}_{\textbf{RL}}$.

3.4   *Not All Languages Are Regular*

You might think that all languages are expressible using regular expressions, but this is not so. Recall Theorem 2.7.3, which states the number of languages over a given alphabet is uncountable. That is, for any alphabet Σ, 2^{Σ^*} is an uncountable set. But each regular language can be represented by a regular expression. Since each regular expression is a string, there are only a countable number of regular expressions over a given alphabet. That is, for a given alphabet Σ, the set of regular expressions over Σ is a countably infinite set. Even if all regular expressions represented different languages, there would still be an uncountable number of languages that are not represented. Thus there is certainly at least one nonregular language. This is an example of a nonconstructive argument. That is, it shows that there is at least one nonregular language, but does not give us a specific example of a nonregular language.

How do we go about finding a specific example of a nonregular language? We prove that a language is regular by giving a construction that starts from the base cases and builds from the rules. But to show that a language L is not regular, we need to show that no matter how anyone attempts to construct the language, they will fail. That is, every possible method of forming L using regular constructions or expressions will fail. This is a much more difficult proposition to prove since there are an infinite number of different methods for going about the construction. Our proof will have to say something about the way all regular constructions behave and give a meta–argument that these constructions cannot possibly work for *L*. In Chapter 5, we will prove that the class of regular languages is the same as the class of languages decided by C–– programs. Thus the language of Problem 3 in Chapter 1 (all strings with equal numbers of a and b characters) is not regular.

3.5   *Applications of Regular Expressions*

Once you are exposed to regular expressions and begin to use a computing environment where they are ubiquitous, you wonder how you could have ever gotten along without them. The purpose of this section is to illustrate just how broad their range of uses is.

We have already seen how regular expressions can be used to generate arguments to commands like cp, ls, mv, and rm. In general, the application of regular expressions can be loosely classified as follows:

1. Validation—determining that a string complies with a set of formatting constraints

2. Search and selection—identifying a subset of items from a larger set on the basis of a pattern match

3. Tokenization—converting a string of characters into a sequence of words for later interpretation

We explore each of these three applications below.

3.5.1   Validation

A typical shortcoming with users of computing systems is that they make mistakes in input. For example, if your program expects the user to enter in a positive integer, then sure enough someone will eventually enter "−1" or "fred." In order to program defensively, you need to validate the input before you send it off for processing. Many programmers do this by some ad hoc method that is directly programmed into the input routine. A better approach is to use routines such as regex that take the input string and a regular expression, and then return TRUE if the input string matches the regular expression. That is, the routine tests if the input string is in the language generated by the regular expression.

For example, if the input is supposed to be either "yes" or "no," then any input string should belong to the language

$(yes \cup no)$

and so we want to test all inputs against the regular expression

(yes|no)

If the input is supposed to be a single decimal digit, then any input string should belong to the language

$L_d = (0 \cup 1 \cup 2 \cup 3 \cup 4 \cup 5 \cup 6 \cup 7 \cup 8 \cup 9)$

A standard regular expression for this language would be

(0|(1|(2|(3|(4|(5|(6|(7|(8|9)))))))))

If the input is supposed to be a natural number, then any input string should belong to the language

$L_d(L_d)^*$

That is, a single digit followed by zero or more digits. Note that in this form leading 0's would be okay.

Certain forms of input, like having to specify the digits of L_d, are so common that many regular expression processing routines augment the usual standard regular expressions into the *extended regular expressions*. There are many varieties of extended regular expressions, but they typically allow things like omitting parentheses:

(0|1|2|3|4|5|6|7|8|9)

and directly expressing a range of characters:

[0-9]

They also handle the very common situation where we want at least one instance of something. For example, instead of having to write

(0|1)(0|1)*

for the language of strings of 0's and 1's with length at least one, they have the equivalent + operator:

(0|1)+

We have used the + sign in this spirit in several places already. In addition, special symbols are often used to name common sublanguages, such as . (dot) for any character in the alphabet, \s for whitespace (a blank or tab), \d for a decimal digit, or \w for an alphanumeric (any letter, digit, or the underscore character).

The extended regular expressions do not let us express more than the regular languages, but since they are more concise, they are much more convenient to use. On the other hand, it is easier to prove theorems about the standard regular expressions. As usual, you should pick the tool appropriate for the task.

An extended regular expression for validating that an input contains a positive integer, possibly surrounded by whitespace, is

```
\s*\d+\s*
```

Making a simple procedure call with this as an argument is certainly preferable to writing your own validation routine.

3.5.2   Search and Selection

Here we will explore how regular expressions can be used to locate files and lines within files using the grep[3] command. This section is not intended to be comprehensive but simply to give you a feel for some additional applications of regular expressions.

One use of the grep command is for searching a file for a pattern specified by a regular expression. Simplifying somewhat, the general form of the grep command is

```
grep <Unix-regular-expression> <filenames>
```

The <Unix-regular-expression> component of the command denotes a legal Unix regular expression (a flavor of extended regular expression), and <filenames> specifies the files to search (using the usual shell file name matching conventions). Each line in the file where the pattern is found is printed to standard output.

We examine a series of examples to demonstrate the utility of regular expressions in the grep command. In the commands below, the | denotes a pipe, where

```
prog1 | prog2
```

sends the output from command prog1 to command prog2.

The Unix program wc (word count) provides a count of the number of lines, words, and characters in a file. The command line entry

```
man grep | grep 'regular expression' | wc
```

yields (on our system) the Unix response

```
28      219      1888
```

---

3. grep stands for "global regular expression print." Although usually associated with Unix–like operating systems, there are implementations of grep for other PC environments. Searching the World Wide Web is the best way to locate these other versions.

indicating in the manual for `grep` there are 28 lines where the phrase "regular expression" occurs. (For implementation reasons it is often necessary to single quote regular expressions that are input to `grep`.) From the word count we can guess that regular expressions are the focus of this command.

The command

```
grep ^The REM.tex
```

prints all lines in the file `REM.tex` that begin with the word "The." Here the caret (`^`) indicates that the match must start at the first character of the line. `grep` is case sensitive, so this expression would not match the pattern "the." That is, the sentence

```
The end of the world as we know it.
```

would be printed by `grep`, whereas the sentence

```
the end of the world as we know it.
```

would not. Note the `grep` command normally prints *all* matching lines. It has options to print lines that *do not* match the pattern, or to only print the names of the files in which a match occurs.

The command

```
grep '.*a.*e.*i.*o.*u' /usr/dict/words
```

prints

```
adventitious
facetious
sacrilegious
```

as output. That is, all words containing at least one occurrence of each of the five vowels with the occurrences in alphabetical order. For example, in "adventitious," we have *adventitious*. Thus the pattern `.*a.*e.*i.*o.*u` can be read "match any character any number of times, then match 'a', match any character any number of times, then match 'e', . . . , and . . . match 'u'." Three lines in the dictionary word list file `/usr/dict/words` have this pattern.

Suppose you have a directory with a large number of files and in one of the files in the directory you refer to "Brownies." You have no idea which file this word occurs in, but you badly need this information in order to retrieve your daughter's email to you about her next meeting. The command

```
grep Brownies *
```

would yield the file name and lines where the word occurs. In this case the pattern we are looking for is `Brownies`, and the `*` is not the Kleene star. It is interpreted by the command line shell as the file wildcard matching character, and expands to a list of all files in the current directory.

The exercises provide some additional practice with grep. When you run the experiments, notice how amazingly fast grep responds.

3.5.3   Tokenization

Let's now turn our attention to the lex command. The first step of compilation, called *lexical analysis*, is to convert the input from a simple sequence of characters into a list of *tokens* of different kinds, such as numerical and string constants, variable identifiers, and programming language keywords. The purpose of lex is to generate *lexical analyzers*.

Regular expressions can be used to specify exactly what values are legal for the tokens to assume. Some tokens are simply keywords, like if, else, and for. Others, like identifiers, can be any sequence of letters and digits provided that they do not match a keyword and do not start with a digit. Typically, an identifier is a variable name such as current, flag2, or windowStatus. In general, an identifier is a *letter* followed by any combination of *digits* and *letters*.

We can build up the (extended) regular expression for an identifier as follows. Define *letter* to be an element of the language represented by the regular expression ([a-z]|[A-Z]). Define *digit* to be an element of the language represented by the regular expression [0-9]. Then an *identifier* can be represented as

letter(*digit*|*letter*)∗

That is, an identifier begins with a letter and that letter is followed by any combination of digits and letters. *Keywords* can also be represented by regular expressions. For example,

```
begin|else|function|if|procedure|then
```

is a regular expression representing some common keywords.

The lex utility generates a C program that is a **lexical analyzer**, a program that performs lexical processing of its character input. The source code for a lex program is a table of regular expressions coupled with corresponding actions, which are expressed as C code fragments. So, for example, if an identifier is found in the program, then the action corresponding to the identifier is taken. Perhaps some information would be added to the *symbol table* in this case. If a keyword such as if is recognized, a different action would be taken.

From this table of regular expressions and corresponding actions, lex builds a lexical analyzer that is then incorporated into your program. This analyzer is then responsible for reading the input and passing tokens back to your program. This allows you to concentrate on processing the meaning of the input, and avoid dealing with the individual characters that form it. For example, a simple lexical analyzer could return tokens that are properly formatted numbers. Your application would then not have to worry about validating the input before attempting to convert it.

3.6   *Exercises*

Section 3.2   *Regular Languages and Constructions*

1. Suppose the current directory has a large (over 50) number of C files, that is, files ending in the `.c` extension. Write a Unix command to list all and only the C files. Write a Unix command to copy all C files from the current directory to a subdirectory. Now write a Unix command to delete all C files from the current directory.

2. Prove $((\emptyset \circ a) \cup (a^* \circ b))$ is a regular language using Definition 3.2.1.

3. Justify your answers to the following true or false questions:

   (a) $\emptyset^* = \emptyset$
   (b) $(0^*1^*)^k = \{0, 1\}^*$
   (c) $0^* \cap 1^* = \emptyset$
   (d) $0^* \cup 1^* = \{0, 1\}^*$
   (e) $0^*(0^* \cup 1^*) = \{0, 1\}^*0^*$

4. Prove Observation 3.2.3.

Section 3.3   *Regular Expressions*

5. Write a standard regular expression that represents each of the following languages. Is your expression as short as possible? Can the expression be shortened further if you use extended regular expressions?

   (a) $\emptyset^*$
   (b) $(0 \cup 1)^* \cup (1 \cup 0)^* \cup 1^*$
   (c) $(0^*1^*)^*$
   (d) $0^* \cup 1^* \cup (0 \cup 1)^*$
   (e) $(0 \cup 1)^*1(0 \cup 1)^*0(0 \cup 1)^*$

6. Explain in words the languages that are represented by the regular expressions in Exercise 5.

7. Let $\Sigma = \{0, 1\}$. Write the shortest regular expression (in terms of number of symbols) possible for each of the following languages:

   (a) The empty language
   (b) The language that just contains the empty string
   (c) The language consisting of all strings of length three or more
   (d) The language consisting of all strings containing the pattern 000
   (e) The language consisting of all strings containing the pattern 000 exactly once
   (f) The language consisting of all strings where only 0's may occur in the even positions

8. Write a regular expression for the language consisting of those strings over {0, 1} that have an odd number of 0's and an even number of 1's.

9. Let Σ be an alphabet. Prove that the set of all standard regular expressions over the alphabet Σ is countably infinite.

10. Prove that the language

$$L = \{x \mid \#_b(x) = 3 \text{ and } x(k) = a \text{ where } k = |x|\}$$

over the alphabet $\{a, b\}$ is represented by the regular expression

```
a*ba*ba*ba*a
```

That is, each string $x \in L$ has three occurrences of b in it, and the last character of x must be an a. (Hint: use a proof by induction.)

Section 3.4   Not All Languages Are Regular

11. Prove $\{\Lambda, a, aab\}$ is a regular language.

12. Is the set of file names contained in a given Unix directory regular? Justify your answer.

13. Prove any finite language is a regular language.

14. Without using *, can an infinite language be proven regular by using Definition 3.3.1?

15. Prove the language consisting of all strings over a fixed alphabet is a regular language.

16. Define a language that you suspect is not regular. Argue informally why you think the language is not regular.

17. List an infinite set of regular languages over the alphabet {0}.

Section 3.5   Applications of Regular Expressions

18. Write an extended regular expression to validate an input that contains exactly three decimal integers, the first of which must be positive.

19. Write an extended regular expression to validate an input that contains a floating point number, possibly with an exponent.

20. Write a `grep` expression to print all words in the file `/usr/dict/words` that contain the letters e, l, n, and t in alphabetical order.

21. Write a `grep` expression to print all words in the file `/usr/dict/words` that contain the letters e, l, n, and t in any order.

22. Write a `grep` expression that prints all lines in a given file that end in any capital letter followed by a period. For example, the line containing the end of this sentence would be PRINTED.

23. Write a `grep` expression to print out all occurrences of the single quote symbol (') in the `grep` man page.

24. How many times does the word "Unix" appear in the `grep` man page?

25. What word in `/usr/dict/words` contains the most consecutive pairs of double letters?

26. Write a `grep` expression to search all `.html` files in the directory `public-html` for the pattern `house.gif`.

27. Write a program using `lex` that takes a file of letters (as defined in Section 3.5) and converts it to all lowercase letters.

CHAPTER | 4

Fundamental Machines Part I: Finite–State Control Machines

Welcome my friend.
Welcome to the machine.
   —*Pink Floyd*

4.1 *Introduction*

The real world of computation is messy. Actual computing machines suffer from all sorts of constraints caused by physical reality, engineering trade-offs, and marketing hype. So to fully understand the power and limitations of real machines, we must understand all of their ugly details. But the goal of real machines is to perform computations, and computation is a concept that is somehow common among all computing machines regardless of the messy details of actual hardware implementation. You could say that computation even transcends reality in the sense that no physical machine can embody more than a small fraction of what computation means.

There is no single universal notion of computation, and a large part of the-oretical computer science is dedicated to inventing and studying *computational models*—also known as idealized computers. The purpose of a computational model is to capture those aspects of computation that are relevant to the particu-lar problem you wish to solve, while hiding the other aspects that are unimpor-tant. You can think of a computational model as a custom machine designed for your particular needs. The details of the custom machine are irrelevant so long as it has the required main features.

Our computational models and sense of reality are interdependent. Reality gives us some idea of what is actually possible, so that we do not inadvertently provide our models abilities that violate physical laws. Conversely, models that are theoretically useful give us ideas about what capabilities and features we might want to build into our actual machines. The designer of a computational model is constantly aware of the following question: Is this feature good for my problem and could we, in principle, build this feature in hardware?

Many computational models have been invented. Some of the most important are the *deterministic finite automaton*, the *nondeterministic finite automaton*, the *deterministic pushdown automaton*, the *nondeterministic pushdown automaton*, the *deterministic Turing machine*, and the *nondeterministic Turing machine*. Each of these models is very significant in the theory of computation. The traditional textbook approach is to introduce these models individually, and then compare their relative abilities to perform computations.

We will do much the same, except that we will take a somewhat unconventional approach, and at the expense of a bit more notation and complexity in some definitions, we will present all of these models as variations on a single basic architecture: the *finite-state control, tape-memory machine*.

We begin by defining the most basic computational models first—the deterministic finite automaton and its nondeterministic variant. The other models, such as the deterministic pushdown automaton, nondeterministic pushdown automaton, deterministic Turing machine, and nondeterministic Turing machine, can easily be described as enhanced versions of either the deterministic or nondeterministic finite automaton. This will be done in Chapter 6, the second part of our description of fundamental machines, in which we extend these with machines with additional memory.

Alternatively, the various fundamental machines can be viewed as instances of Turing machines with restrictions on the amount and behavior of their memory resource (tapes). Thus it is perfectly natural to explore restrictions or enhancements on other resources. In Chapters 8, 10, and 11 we present numerous results in computational complexity along these lines.

4.1.1   The Church–Turing Thesis

There are many other important models whose architecture is significantly different from the finite–state control, tape–memory machines. For example, another model that behaves very much like a traditional (yet oversimplified) desktop computer is called the *random access machine* (RAM). How do we compare these different architectures? Is it possible that two radically different architectures could have fundamentally different computing ability? How different do two architectures have to be before they begin to vary in the kinds of problems they can solve with given resources?

The main technique for comparing various models of computation is simulation. For example, RAMs can simulate Turing machines in the sense that we can write a RAM program that takes a description of a Turing machine M and an input x to M, and then, step by step, simulates the actions of M on x. Thus the RAM program can produce the same output as M would. This is also true in reverse. We can write a Turing machine program that simulates an arbitrary RAM program. So RAMs and Turing machines have the same computational power. As another example, deterministic finite automata[1] and nondeterministic finite automata can simulate each other in the sense that they accept the same class of languages, and thus they have equivalent computational power.

On the other hand, Turing machines can simulate deterministic finite automata, but the reverse is not true. Thus Turing machines are computationally more powerful.

At some point, all models of computation hit the roadblock of unsolvable problems such as the Halting problem of Chapter 1. There are problems that simply cannot be solved by any model of computation that operates "algorithmically" using a finite set of symbols and rules for manipulating them. Furthermore, no general model of algorithmic computation is more powerful than the Turing machine (at least none have been found yet, and informed opinion believes none ever will be). That is, whatever these other models can "compute," so can Turing machines. This is true for *recursive functions* and *grammars*—two very different computing models.

The belief that all general models of algorithmic computation are no more powerful than Turing machines is called the *Church-Turing Thesis*. Although we cannot prove or disprove the Church–Turing Thesis, since it is not a formal mathematical statement, all models of general algorithmic computation proposed to date have been shown to be no more powerful than Turing machines. Thus the thesis is generally accepted among theoreticians.

Be wary of applying the Church–Turing Thesis to inappropriate domains. A typical such example would be the line of reasoning that the brain is a computer, thus the brain is predictable, and thus free will is an illusion. We simply do not understand enough about the basic physics, physiology, and psychology of the human brain to claim that it is an algorithmic computer. There is no doubt that the brain can perform algorithmic computations, but that does not mean that its underlying computational mechanism is algorithmic. It is quite possible that the brain can perform computations not expressible with Turing machines.

4.2   *Basic Machine Notions*

Consider the language generated by the regular construction $(00)^*$ over the alphabet $\{0, 1\}$. What would a C program look like that accepts this language? By "accept," we mean that if a user inputs a given string x over the alphabet $\{0, 1\}$ to the program, then the program should respond YES if $x \in (00)^*$, and NO otherwise. This is really just answering a membership question as discussed in Chapter 2.

---

1. Automata is the plural form of automaton.

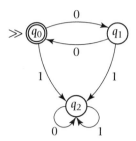

Figure 4.1

A sample state transition diagram useful for representing a deterministic finite automation that accepts the language $(00)^*$.

Since the language $(00)^*$ consists of all strings that contain an even number of 0's and no 1's, we can imagine a C program that keeps track of whether an even number of 0's have been encountered in the input and also whether or not a 1 has been seen. When the end of the input is reached, if an even number of 0's have been read and no 1 has been detected, then the program should respond YES; otherwise it should respond NO.

There is a useful way of diagraming such a program, shown in Figure 4.1; the picture is called a *(state) transition diagram*. The transition diagram is a directed graph enhanced with the special symbol $\gg$ and some labeling on the nodes and edges. The $\gg$ symbol indicates the state that the machine starts from, called the *initial state*. The transition diagram consists of three nodes, called *states*, labeled q_0, q_1, and q_2; and six edges, called *transitions*. Notice the edges are labeled by 0 and 1, symbols from the alphabet in consideration. The node with two circles, q_0, represents an *accepting state*, which coincidentally in this case is also the initial state.

Consider an "input" to the transition diagram such as 0000. If we trace through the figure on this input starting from state q_0, we go to state q_1 using up one 0, back to q_0 using up another 0, back to q_1 using the third 0, and finally back to q_0, at which point we have no more input remaining. The state we ended up in, q_0, is an accepting state, so the input 0000 is *accepted*. That is, $0000 \in (00)^*$. Let's trace the machine on input 10. From state q_0 we go to state q_2 using up the 1, and then stay in state q_2 using up the last symbol 0. Because q_2 does not have a double circle, it is not an accepting state; therefore, the machine does not stop in an accepting state. The input 10 is *rejected*, as it should be, because $10 \notin (00)^*$. Our task is to formalize these ideas.

4.2.1   Tapes

In the example just sketched, we did not say how the input was going to be represented. Let's address that now. All of our machines store information as strings on tapes. These tapes are divided into *tape cells* or *tape squares*, or just *cells* or

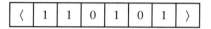

Figure 4.2

An illustration of an input tape. ⟨ and ⟩ are left and right end markers, respectively.

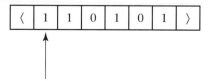

Figure 4.3

An illustration of the initial position of the input tape head. At this point the machine could read a 1 from the input tape.

squares for short. Each tape square holds a single symbol. The tape has a special organization. By convention the tape always contains two special symbols, called the *left* and *right end markers*, and denoted by the ⟨ and ⟩ symbols, respectively. A tape begins with the left end marker, and ends with the right end marker. Between these two markers, all symbols present on the tape must come from the *data alphabet*. The end markers are never part of the data alphabet. The data alphabet plus the end markers constitute the *tape alphabet*. If the data alphabet is Σ, then we denote the tape alphabet (that is, $\Sigma \cup \{\langle, \rangle\}$) by Σ_T. The *contents of a tape* is the string over the data alphabet that appears between the end markers. Thus a tape can contain the empty string if all it has is the left end marker followed immediately by the right end marker.

The input to a machine is a string, usually denoted x, over the data alphabet. The input is placed on an *input tape*. The individual characters comprising x appear in adjacent cells of the tape; the entire input is between end markers. The input tape is special in that it is *read-only*, as far as the machine is concerned. Since the machine cannot write to the tape, nothing can ever be stored on the tape except the original input. Figure 4.2 provides an illustration of a sample input tape. In this case the input x is the string 110101. The length of x is six.

Machines access a tape via a *tape head*. When the machine starts up, the tape head is always positioned to the first square immediately to the right of the left end marker. Thus, if $x \neq \Lambda$, the tape head is over $x(1)$, so that the first symbol of x can be read. If x is the empty string, Λ, then the tape head will be positioned over the right end marker. Figure 4.3 illustrates the tape head for the input tape and its initial positioning.

Further constraints can apply to the motion of the tape head. For example, some machines can only read the input once, while others can go over the input as many times as desired; we will specify each input access method as required.

When we describe an ongoing computation of a machine, we must be able to describe the contents of the tape and the current position of the tape head. These two pieces of information constitute the *tape configuration*.

Definition 4.2.1   *A* **tape configuration** *is a pair* $[p, x]$. *The head position* p, *with* $0 \leq p \leq |x| + 1$, *is a natural number indicating the position of the tape head on a tape with contents* x.

1. *When* $p = 0$, *the tape head is over the* $\langle$ *marker,*
2. *when* $p = |x| + 1$, *the tape head is over the* $\rangle$ *marker, and*
3. *otherwise the tape head is over symbol* $x(p)$.

The **current tape symbol** *in a tape configuration is the symbol under the tape head and is denoted* $\sigma[p, x]$. *The* **remaining tape** *in a tape configuration* $[p, x]$ *is the contents of the tape from under the tape head up to but not including the right end marker. The remaining tape, denoted by* $\rho([p, x])$, *is the string*

1. $\langle x$ *if* $p = 0$,
2. Λ *if* $p = |x| + 1$, *and*
3. $x(p)x(p + 1) \cdots x(|x|)$ *otherwise.*

The **initial tape configuration** *is* $[1, x]$, *also denoted by* $\tau^{Initial}(x)$. *The* **final tape configuration** *is* $[|x| + 1, x]$, *also denoted by* $\tau^{Final}(x)$.

In general, machines can also have *work tapes*. These are tapes that can be written and read, and so are used to store the intermediate results of a computation. All work tapes are initially blank. When the machine writes to a work tape, it writes a new symbol onto the tape square under the tape head, replacing the old contents of the square. If the tape square under the tape head is an end marker, the writing of a symbol also extends the tape by one cell, effectively moving the tape marker to the left or right depending on what end of the tape the head is at. If the tape head is somewhere between the end markers when the write of an end marker occurs, the result is that the tape is truncated so that the new contents of the tape are the squares between the new end marker and its match. Overwriting $\rangle$ with $\langle$ or vice versa is not permitted. Figure 4.4 illustrates the behavior of writes to the tape.

Finally, machines can also have an *output tape*. This is simply a work tape that is write–only; that is, you can write to the tape and move the head around, but not read from the tape. Usually the output tape has the additional restriction that after every write the head advances one square to the right, and the head can never move left. What this means is that the one–way output tape of a machine

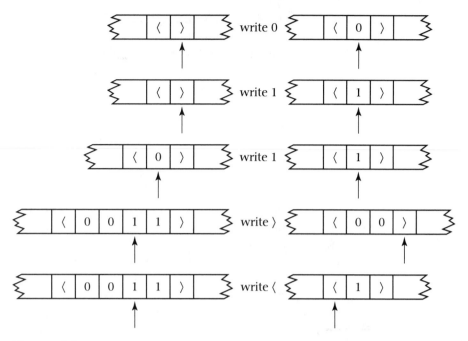

Figure 4.4

An illustration of the various effects of writing to a work tape.

can be used as the one-way input tape of another machine. This is important when you have to combine two machines so that the second one processes the output of the first—it enables you to eliminate the intermediate tape by making the output tape of the first the input tape of the second.

Tapes correspond to linked list data structures. The end markers indicate the head and tail of the list, and the tape head corresponds to the list cursor. Thus, like a linked list, the elements of the tape can only be accessed sequentially. Tapes are different from lists in one respect. Additions and deletions (including truncations) from the tape can only occur at the ends, unlike a list, where additions and deletions can occur at any cursor position. Of course, since the input tape is read-only, additions and deletions on it are forbidden.

4.2.2   Finite Controls

Tapes provide us with a model of how we present a machine with input, store intermediate data, and generate output. Now we have to consider the machine itself. How do we program it? What are the instructions of the machine? How do we know what instruction to execute next? What is the syntax of an instruction? What are the semantics of an instruction—that is, what happens when you execute an instruction? These are questions worth thinking about *before* we present their formal definitions below.

The *finite control* or *state transition function* is the key mechanism for defining all of our models. It is the machine's program and defines how the machine computes. One of the most important features of the finite control is the fact that it must be *finite*. This limits the machine to a finite set of instructions, and this fixed number of instructions is independent of the input.

Just like the program counter on a real machine, the current *state* of a finite control helps determine the next instruction to be executed by the machine. When an instruction is executed, the machine does one or more of the following, depending on the type of machine: reads a symbol under a tape head, writes a symbol to the tape cell under a tape head, and moves a tape head. The instruction then determines the next state or states of the program and changes the current state.

If the next state of a particular machine is always unambiguous (there is either a unique next state, or none at all), then the machine is said to be *deterministic*. If there are circumstances during the execution of the machine in which the next state is ambiguous (there are two or more possible next states), then the machine is said to be *nondeterministic*. The finite control of a deterministic machine is usually denoted δ (pronounced "delta"). The finite control of a nondeterministic machine is usually denoted by Δ (pronounced "cap delta"). The precise details of the state transition function for a machine depend on other specifications of the machine, such as how many tapes it has, and their input/output capabilities.

In general, finite–state control, tape–memory machines can be configured according to the following feature axes:

1. Is the machine deterministic or nondeterministic?

2. Labeling of transitions—are state transitions labeled with a single symbol from Σ_T, or a string from Σ_T^*, and is Λ allowed as a label? Must there be a transition for every possible symbol for every possible state?

3. Tape properties—how many tapes are there, how do the heads move on the tapes, what are their read and write restrictions, and are there limits on the length of the tapes?

We will now examine a particular machine model as a way of making these general notions concrete.

4.3   *Deterministic Finite Automata*

Let's now turn our discussion to a specific model: the deterministic finite automaton (DFA). A DFA is a very simple machine. It has one read–only input tape, with the restriction that the tape head can only move from left to right and can never change direction. The DFA has no other tapes. The finite control allows a DFA to read one input symbol from the input tape, and then based on the machine's current state, it may change state. As part of each computational step of a DFA,

Transition Number	State	Input Symbol	New State
1	q_0	0	q_1
2	q_0	1	q_2
3	q_1	0	q_0
4	q_1	1	q_2
5	q_2	0	q_2
6	q_2	1	q_2

Table 4.1

The transition table for the DFA presented in Figure 4.1. A transition table is a convenient method for representing the transition function of a DFA. The transitions are numbered for convenience, but this numbering is not part of the finite control.

the input tape head is automatically repositioned one square further to the right and is ready for reading the next input symbol.

For example, in Figure 4.1 the states are represented by the nodes. One part of the finite control corresponding to Figure 4.1 is the *transition*

$$\delta(q_0, 0) = q_1$$

That is, when in state q_0 and reading a 0, the machine transfers to state q_1. The input head is then automatically moved one square to the right (assuming not all of the input has been read). The transition

$$\delta(q_0, 1) = q_2$$

specifies that while in state q_0 and reading a 1, transfer to state q_2. Again the input head is automatically moved one square to the right. You should have no trouble specifying the remainder of the finite control for the transition diagram shown in Figure 4.1. The finite control is shown in its entirety in tabular form in Table 4.1. Note that there are no entries in the table to indicate what the next state should be when the input head is over an end marker. In such a case where there is no next state the machine simply stops.

At this point we are ready to present the formal definition of a DFA. The description of the DFA is presented as a five–tuple so that the order of the components is fixed; that is, each time someone shows you a DFA, the states come first, the input tape alphabet second, and so on.

Definition 4.3.1   *A **deterministic finite automaton (DFA)** is a five-tuple*

$$M = (Q, \Sigma, \delta, q_0, F)$$

with the components specified as follows:

1. *Q—a finite, nonempty set of* **states**
2. *Σ—the* **data alphabet** *(which induces the* **tape alphabet** $\Sigma_T = \Sigma \cup \{\langle, \rangle\}$*)*
3. *δ—the* **transition function** *or* **finite control**

$$\delta : Q \times \Sigma_T \mapsto Q$$

4. *q_0—the* **initial state** *or* **start state**, $q_0 \in Q$
5. *F—the set of* **accepting states**, $F \subseteq Q$

The *M* stands for "machine." We will usually use the symbols M, M', M_1, and so on to denote a machine. Let's examine each component of this definition in turn.

The set of states is denoted Q. Typically, we represent individual states by the symbols q_0, q_1, and so on, but keep in mind that other names would work as well. Note Q is nonempty and finite. Since $q_0 \in Q$, it follows that Q is nonempty; however, we prefer to write this condition explicitly in the definition.

The data alphabet is denoted Σ. These are the symbols that can occur on the input tape between $\langle$ and $\rangle$. End markers are not allowed as data symbols for obvious reasons. The tape alphabet Σ_T is the set of all possible symbols that appear on the tape, and so it is Σ plus $\{\langle, \rangle\}$.

We defer the description of δ for the moment.

The initial state is denoted q_0. This is a special state in Q and is the state that M begins executing from. Note the initial state is *not* expressed as a set like the other components in the definition.

F is the set of accepting states. Accepting states are typically denoted by f, f_1, f_2, and so on. These special states are used by a DFA to "signal" when it accepts its input, if in fact it does. When the machine stops in a nonaccepting state, this signifies the input is rejected. The formal notion of *acceptance* will be presented in Definition 4.3.6.

Where does the input tape appear in the definition? The tape is utilized in the transition function δ. The domain of δ is $Q \times \Sigma_T$, so elements in the domain of δ are ordered pairs. That is, δ takes a state and a symbol from the input tape (possibly an end marker). A typical argument to δ would be $(0, 1)$. Using standard function notation, we would write $\delta((0, 1))$ to signify δ being applied to its arguments. To simplify notation, we drop the "extra" set of parentheses, keeping in mind that the arguments to δ are really ordered pairs. So, we write $\delta(0, 1)$, for example (as we did earlier). The range of δ is Q.

Suppose $q \in Q$, $a \in \Sigma_T$, and $\delta(q, a) = q'$, where $q' \in Q$. This specifies a *transition* of M. This transition moves M from state q into state q' on reading an a, and the input head is then moved one square to the right. In Figure 4.1, transitions were represented by edges between states and labeled with input tape symbols.

Since δ is a function, DFAs behave deterministically. Another way of saying this is that the machine has only one "choice" for its next transition, just as a typical C program must execute a unique next instruction. The finite control is perhaps most easily understood and presented via a table, where each row represents one possible transition of M. In Table 4.1, the transitions of the DFA represented in Figure 4.1 are shown. This table is called the *transition table* of M.

Also important to note is that even though δ is a function, we do not require it to be total. That is, it need not be defined for all possible state and tape alphabet symbol pairs. However, in order to simplify certain constructions and proofs, we will sometimes require δ to be total, so that for each ordered pair in $Q \times \Sigma$, δ has a value. In this case, the transition table corresponding to a given DFA will always have $|Q| \times |\Sigma|$ rows. Note that we do not need δ of a DFA to be defined on $\{\langle, \rangle\}$, since the DFA can never see a beginning of tape mark, and it is not necessary to detect end of input.

Let's now look at the complete specification for the DFA shown in Figure 4.1.

Example 4.3.2   The complete formal specification of a DFA

The five–tuple for the DFA M shown in Figure 4.1 is

$$M = (\{q_0, q_1, q_2\}, \{0, 1\}, \delta, q_0, \{q_0\})$$

where δ is defined as in the transition table shown in Table 4.1, or equivalently expressed as

$$\{(q_0, 0, q_1), (q_0, 1, q_2), (q_1, 0, q_0), (q_1, 1, q_2), (q_2, 0, q_2), (q_2, 1, q_2)\}$$

Here we have written the function $\delta : Q \times \Sigma_T \mapsto Q$ as triples in $Q \times \Sigma_T \times Q$ using the obvious translation. Notice $|Q| \times |\Sigma| = 6$, and there are six transitions. ∎

In order to describe a computation of a DFA, we need to be able to specify "snapshots" of the machine detailing where the machine is currently at in its computation. What are the important ingredients in these snapshots? They are the contents and head position of the input tape and the current state of M. Think back to Chapter 1 and the examples involving C-- programs. Such a snapshot is called a *configuration*.

Definition 4.3.3   *A **configuration** of a DFA $M = (Q, \Sigma, \delta, q_0, F)$, on input $x \in \Sigma^*$, is a two-tuple $(q, [p, x])$, where*

1. *$q \in Q$, and*

2. *$[p, x]$ is a configuration of the input tape.*

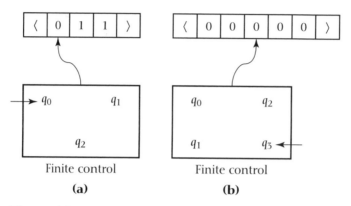

Figure 4.5

Another way of viewing a DFA's configurations: (a) The finite control is in state q_0, and so far no input has been read; this is an initial configuration. (b) The finite control is in state q_3, and the remaining input is 000; 00 has already been read.

*The **initial configuration** of M on input x is the configuration $(q_0, [1, x])$, or equivalently $(q_0, \tau^{Initial}(x))$. We use C_0 to denote the initial configuration when M and x are understood. For machine M, the set of all possible configurations for all possible inputs x is denoted by $\mathcal{C}(M)$.*

Figure 4.5 shows a pictorial representation of a couple of DFA configurations. The configurations corresponding to the snapshots of Figure 4.5 (a) and (b) are $(q_0, [1, 011])$ and $(q_3, [3, 00000])$, respectively. They have remaining inputs 011 and 000, respectively. Figure 4.5 (a) indicates an initial configuration; the initial configuration for the DFA shown in Figure 4.5 (b) is $(q_0, [1, 00000])$ (assuming q_0 is the machine's initial state).

How can we use the notion of configuration to discuss the computation of a DFA? It helps us define the *next move* relation, denoted $\vdash_M$, as shown in the following.

Definition 4.3.4   *Let $M = (Q, \Sigma, \delta, q_0, F)$ be a DFA. Let $\mathcal{C}(M)$ be the set of all configurations of M. Let $C_1 = (q_1, [p_1, x])$ and $C_2 = (q_2, [p_2, x])$ be two elements of $\mathcal{C}(M)$. $C_1 \vdash_M C_2$ if and only if $p_2 = p_1 + 1$ and there is a transition*

$$\delta(q_1, \sigma[p_1, x]) = q_2$$

$\vdash_M$ *is called the **next move**, **step**, or **yields** relation.*

Several remarks are in order regarding this definition. First, $\vdash_M$ is a relation defined on configurations. This means $\vdash_M \subseteq \mathcal{C}(M) \times \mathcal{C}(M)$. Since δ is a function, $\vdash_M$ is also a function. Definition 4.3.4 is saying that configuration C_1 yields configuration C_2 if there is a transition from C_1 that when executed brings M to the new configuration C_2. Depending on the context, we sometimes omit the subscript on $\vdash$.

As an example consider the DFA, call it M, whose transition function was depicted in Table 4.1. The initial configuration of M on input $x = 0011$ is $(q_0, [1, 0011])$. Applying transition 1 from Table 4.1, we see

$$(q_0, [1, 0011]) \vdash_M (q_1, [2, 0011])$$

The machine read a 0 and moved to state q_1. Continuing this *trace* (see Definition 4.3.5), we obtain the following series of configurations:

$$(q_1, [2, 0011]) \vdash_M (q_0, [3, 0011]) \qquad \text{(by transition 3)}$$
$$\vdash_M (q_2, [4, 0011]) \qquad \text{(by transition 2)}$$
$$\vdash_M (q_2, [5, 0011]) \qquad \text{(by transition 6)}$$

We say the DFA *halts* when there is no next state. This can occur whenever the state transition function is undefined. A *halting configuration* of a DFA is a configuration $C_h = (q, [p, x]) \in \mathcal{C}(M)$ with the property that $\delta(q, \sigma[p, x])$ is undefined.

If the DFA halts when there is no more input left to process—that is, it is in a configuration $C = (q, \tau^{Final}(x))$—then we say that the DFA is in a *final configuration*. That is, the DFA is in a configuration $C_h = (q, [p, x]) \in \mathcal{C}(M)$ with the property that $p = |x| + 1$.

The relation $\vdash_M$ was defined to aid in assisting with the descriptions of computations. But $\vdash_M$ stands for only one step. We would like to discuss computations of varying lengths, length zero included.

Definition 4.3.5   *Let M be a DFA with next move relation $\vdash_M$. Let $C_i \in \mathcal{C}(M)$, for $0 \leq i \leq n$, be a sequence of $n + 1$ configurations. Define $\vdash_M^*$ to be the reflexive, transitive closure of the relation $\vdash_M$.*

C_0 yields or leads to C_n if $C_0 \vdash_M^* C_n$.

A computation or trace of M is a sequence of configurations related by $\vdash_M$ as follows:

$$C_0 \vdash_M C_1 \vdash_M \cdots \vdash_M C_n$$

This computation has length n, or we say it has n steps. Sometimes, we write

$$C_0 \vdash_M^n C_n$$

to indicate a computation from C_0 to C_n of length n.

Notice that the term "yields" is used in Definition 4.3.4 in conjunction with the notation $\vdash_M$ to mean one step, and above in conjunction with the notation $\vdash_M^*$ to mean zero or more steps. Also observe that on an input x of length n, a DFA will run for at most n steps. If the state transition function is defined on

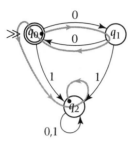

Figure 4.6

Thread of execution of the DFA of Table 4.1 on input 0011.

every state and data symbol, then the DFA will process its entire input and so will run for exactly n steps.

Thus, for the four–step computation traced above, we can write

$$(q_0, [1, 0011]) \vdash^*_M (q_2, [5, 0011])$$

or

$$(q_0, [1, 0011]) \vdash^4_M (q_2, [5, 0011])$$

with $(q_2, [5, 0011])$ the final configuration.

Another way of visualizing a DFA computation as it processes its input is through its *thread of execution*. The thread of execution can be visualized as follows. Begin with the state transition diagram drawn on a large table. Take a spool of string and anchor the free end at the start state. Now imagine tracing the execution of a DFA by moving the spool from the current state to the next state, unrolling string as required. Eventually the machine will run out of input and the trace will stop. The path that the string leaves through the state transition diagram represents the thread of execution, with distance along the string from the start state corresponding to time. This is illustrated in Figure 4.6, where the DFA described in Table 4.1 processes the input 0011.

As alluded to earlier, we would like to describe the computational capabilities of DFAs in terms of the languages they accept. First, we need to define what it means for a DFA to *accept* its input. The idea is simply that the machine reads all of its input and ends up in an accepting state.

Definition 4.3.6 *Let $M = (Q, \Sigma, \delta, q_0, F)$ be a DFA and $q \in Q$. M **accepts** input $x \in \Sigma^*$ if*

$$(q_0, \tau^{Initial}(x)) \vdash^*_M (f, \tau^{Final}(x))$$

where $f \in F$. This computation is called an **accepting computation**. A halting configuration $(q, \tau^{Final}(x))$ is called an **accepting configuration** of M if $q \in F$. If M does not accept its input x, then M is said to **reject** x. The computation of M on input x in this case is called a **rejecting computation**, and M was left in a **rejecting configuration**.

M begins computing in its initial state, with the input tape head scanning the first symbol of x. If M reads all of x and ends in an accepting state, it accepts. It is important to note that M reads its input only once and in an *online* fashion. This means M reads the input once from left to right and then must decide what to do with it. M cannot go back and look at the input again. In addition, even though M can sense the end of the input by detecting the $\rangle$ marker, this is only useful if M can reverse directions on the input tape. Thus M must be prepared to make a decision about accepting or rejecting assuming that the input might be exhausted after the symbol just read.

For example, the DFA with the transition function as shown in Figure 4.1 accepts the input $x = 0011$, since $q_0 \in F$ and

$$(q_0, [1, 0011]) \vdash^* (q_0, [5, 0011])$$

We can now define the *language accepted* by a DFA M as simply the set of all strings accepted by M.

Definition 4.3.7   *Let $M = (Q, \Sigma, \delta, q_0, F)$ be a DFA. The* **language accepted** *by M, denoted $L(M)$, is*

$$\{x \mid M \text{ accepts } x\}$$

The set of all languages accepted by DFAs is denoted $\mathcal{L}_{\mathbf{DFA}}$. That is,

$$\mathcal{L}_{\mathbf{DFA}} = \{L \mid \text{ there is a DFA } M \text{ with } L = L(M)\}$$

The DFA shown in Figure 4.1 accepts the language $(00)^*$. It follows that $(00)^* \in \mathcal{L}_{\mathbf{DFA}}$.

Table 4.2 summarizes all of the concepts presented regarding DFAs. Review these concepts carefully before moving on to study the other models defined in this chapter.

The description of DFAs is now complete: the model has been fully defined, and a terminology has been developed so that we can talk about DFA computations and language acceptance. But we have not described how to design such a machine to solve a given problem. Let's look at a couple of applications, and then we will make a few remarks about programming DFAs. A number of exercises involving DFAs are provided at the end of the chapter.

Concept	Reference
input tape	Section 4.2.1
finite control	Section 4.2.2
states	Definition 4.3.1
data alphabet	Definition 4.3.1
tape alphabet	Definition 4.3.1
transition function	Definition 4.3.1
initial state	Definition 4.3.1
accepting states	Definition 4.3.1
transition table	Page 93
configuration	Definition 4.3.3
initial configuration	Definition 4.3.3
next move, step, or yields	Definition 4.3.4
halting configuration	Page 95
final configuration	Page 95
computation	Definition 4.3.5
thread of execution	Definition 4.3.5
length or number of steps in computation	Page 96
accept a string	Definition 4.3.6
accepting configuration	Definition 4.3.6
rejecting configuration	Definition 4.3.6
accept a language	Definition 4.3.7
$\mathcal{L}_{\textbf{DFA}}$	Definition 4.3.7

Table 4.2

Summary of the terminology developed to define deterministic finite automata.

Example 4.3.8 Application of DFAs involving searching a text for a specified pattern

(You will no doubt recall a similar problem from Chapter 1 involving a C-- program to recognize strings containing the pattern "onto.")

We have alluded to the fact that DFAs are useful for pattern matching. In this application, we consider the problem of searching for a given pattern x in a file of text. We will assume our alphabet is $\{a, b, c\}$. The example can easily be generalized to larger alphabets. To further simplify the discussion, let's take x as the string *abac*. The techniques used here can be applied to any other string x. So we want to build a DFA that accepts the language

$$\{w \mid w \in \{a, b, c\}^* \text{ and } w \text{ contains the pattern } abac\}$$

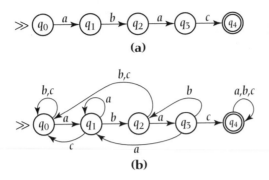

Figure 4.7

Steps in constructing a DFA to recognize a pattern x in a file of text. In this case corresponding to Example 4.3.8, $x = abac$. (a) Begin by "hard coding" the pattern into the machine's states. (b) Fill in all other transitions over the alphabet $\{a, b, c\}$, as appropriate.

The idea is to begin by "hard coding" the pattern x into the states of the machine. This is illustrated in Figure 4.7 (a). Since the pattern _abac_ has length four, four states are needed in addition to the initial state, q_0, to "remember" the pattern. You can think of each state as signifying that a certain amount of progress has been made so far in locating the pattern. So, for example, on reaching state q_2 the machine remembers that ab has been read.

We can only reach state q_4 if we have read the pattern $abac$, so q_4 is the only accepting state required. The next step is to fill in the remaining transitions on other characters in the alphabet. The complete DFA is shown in Figure 4.7 (b). Notice how in the figure there are some edges with more than one label. This simply means that arrow represents many transitions, one for each labeling symbol.

Let's explain how the extra transitions were added by examining state q_3. The following methodology can be applied in a similar fashion for the other states. From state q_3 on reading a "c," we enter the accepting state specifying that the pattern was indeed found; this is why state q_4 is an accepting state. From state q_3 on reading an "a," we return back to state q_1 because the "a" could be the start of the pattern $abac$. That is, we can make use of this "a." If we read a "b" from the state q_3, then we need to go all the way back to state q_0. The "b" nullifies all of the progress we had made, and we must now start over from the beginning.

The complete description of the DFA for recognizing strings containing the pattern $abac$ over the alphabet $\{a, b, c\}$ is

$$(\{q_0, q_1, q_2, q_3, q_4\}, \{a, b, c\}, \delta, q_0, \{q_4\})$$

State	Input Symbol	New State
q_0	a	q_1
q_0	b	q_0
q_0	c	q_0
q_1	a	q_1
q_1	b	q_2
q_1	c	q_0
q_2	a	q_3
q_2	b	q_0
q_2	c	q_0
q_3	a	q_1
q_3	b	q_0
q_3	c	q_4
q_4	a	q_4
q_4	b	q_4
q_4	c	q_4

Table 4.3

The transition table for the DFA described in Example 4.3.8 and shown in Figure 4.7.

where δ is as shown in Table 4.3. Test this DFA on some sample inputs until you are convinced that it is correct. One point worth noting is that once a pattern is found (that is, the first time an accepting state is entered), the text editor can notify the user of the pattern's location rather than continuing to process the remainder of the file. This is usually what text editors do.   ■

4.3.1   DFA Design

We return now to the discussion of DFA design. Like any type of design, a thorough understanding of what is legal and what is illegal is critical. But like all design, we can only provide you with an outline of a design strategy. Design is not taught; it is more like an apprenticeship. You learn design by doing it.

Basic Strategy for DFA Design

1. Try to focus on the key structural properties of the language you are designing for, and using this information, determine the state set required.
2. Decide what the initial state should be.

3. Imagine each input character coming out of a pipe. You do not see the character before it suddenly appears, and each time a character appears you must decide if the string pumped out so far would be accepted if the input ended at this point. This consideration has to be incorporated into the accepting state design because DFAs have no look-ahead feature.

4. For each state, decide on the transition to be made for each character of the alphabet. Make sure that leaving each state, if necessary, there is a transition for each symbol in the machine's alphabet.

5. Always test your prototype DFAs and final version on a number of "random" examples. In addition, test them on short strings, since these often need to be handled as special cases.

6. Do a final check. Make sure you have an initial state specified, all required transitions have been included, and the accepting states are correctly labeled.

Let's go through one more example, following the procedure for DFA design outlined above.

Example 4.3.9   Sample design of a DFA using our basic strategy

Let

$$L = \{x \mid x \in \{0, 1\}^* \text{ and } x \text{ has an odd number of 0's and an even number of 1's}\}$$

We begin by mulling over the language before beginning design. Let's consider the structure of this language as suggested in point 1 of the basic strategy. Given any string of 0's and 1's, after reading a character, we can either have seen

- an even number of 0's and an even number of 1's,
- an odd number of 0's and an odd number of 1's,
- an odd number of 0's and an even number of 1's, or
- an even number of 0's and an odd number of 1's.

Figure 4.8 (a) shows the four possible states. Specifying the start state is the second step of the design strategy. In our case we begin having seen no input, so the initial state is q_0, corresponding to the empty string—an even number of 0's and an even number of 1's. The next step in the basic design strategy is to determine the accepting states. We want to accept a given string if it has an odd number of 0's and an even number of 1's, so we see that state q_2 should be an accepting state. Carrying out step 4 yields the DFA shown in Figure 4.8 (b).

Let's test the machine M shown in Figure 4.8 (b) on a few inputs as suggested in step 5 of the basic strategy. On input Λ, we get

$$(q_0, [1, \Lambda]) \vdash_M^* (q_0, [1, \Lambda])$$

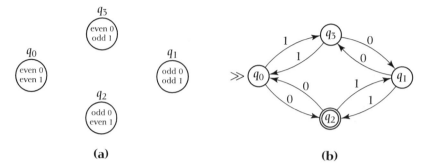

Figure 4.8

An illustration of the basic strategy for designing DFAs corresponding to Example 4.3.9. (a) The different possible states that could arise when considering the odd and even properties of a string of 0's and 1's. There are only four possible states. (b) The complete DFA for accepting strings that contain an odd number of 0's and an even number of 1's.

and since q_0 is not an accepting state, $\Lambda \notin L(M)$. This is good since $\Lambda \notin L$. On input 0, we get

$$(q_0, [1, 0]) \vdash_M^* (q_2, [2, 0])$$

and since q_2 is an accepting state, $0 \in L(M)$. This checks because $0 \in L$. Finally, let's test on input 01001; we get

$$(q_0, [1, 01001]) \vdash_M (q_2, [2, 01001])$$
$$\vdash_M (q_1, [3, 01001])$$
$$\vdash_M (q_3, [4, 01001])$$
$$\vdash_M (q_1, [5, 01001])$$
$$\vdash_M (q_2, [6, 01001])$$

so we have

$$(q_0, [1, 01001]) \vdash_M^* (q_2, [6, 01001])$$

Since q_2 is an accepting state of M, $01001 \in L(M)$. This checks because 01001 has three 0's and two 1's, and is therefore in L.

The last part of the basic DFA design strategy is to give the machine the "once-over." A careful check of Figure 4.8 reveals initial and accepting states have been marked, and there are two transitions (one on 0 and one on 1) for each state. This completes the design and analysis of the DFA for L. ∎

Clearly, the basic strategy may not work as well as it did on Example 4.3.9 in all cases. What is important though is that you follow a systematic procedure in designing DFAs so that you can reduce the chances of making an error. Some of the results presented in Chapter 5 will also help in DFA construction; they offer us certain possibilities for breaking a language into parts, designing a DFA for each part, and then combining. Such a divide–and–conquer strategy can often be very useful. One last point is that the DFAs we have presented in this section all have had only one accepting state. There are cases you will encounter in the exercises and in the next section where DFAs have more than one accepting state.

4.4 *Nondeterministic Finite Automata*

In this section we define the nondeterministic finite automata (NFAs). A DFA has only one possible thread of execution on any given input string because the state transition function has at most one possible next state given the current state and current input symbol. An NFA is an enhanced version of a DFA in which the state transition function is modified so that there may be many possible next states for the current state and input symbol. Thus an NFA, for a given input, has many possible threads of execution, and so its behavior is not predictable. So how does an NFA compute?

An NFA computation can be visualized as many superimposed potential threads. But an NFA is not a *parallel computer*; it does not have any ability to run simultaneous computations. Instead, you can imagine the NFA as behaving as follows: if the problem the NFA is solving has a solution, then the simultaneous threads will collapse into a single unique thread of computation that expresses a solution. If the NFA cannot solve the problem, the threads collapse into failure.

It is rather obvious that an NFA is not a machine that we can build directly. So why is it worth considering? Here are three reasons. The first is simply that this model has more expressive power than the DFA in the sense that it is easier to design NFAs than DFAs for some languages, and such NFAs usually have fewer states than the corresponding DFA.

A second reason is that the abstract concept of nondeterminism has proved very important in theoretical computer science and will be used later in other models described in this book. Thus it makes sense to introduce the concept early on in a simple model before moving to a more advanced model.

Third, although NFAs are more expressive when it comes to programming them, it turns out that any language that can be accepted by an NFA can also be accepted by a DFA. We prove this result via simulation in Section 4.5. This simulation, our first, will serve as a prototype for other simulations to come.

Nearly all of the basic definitions about DFAs carry over to NFAs. Let's mention the enhancements to a DFA that yield the NFA model and then look at some examples. The new features, in order of descending importance, are

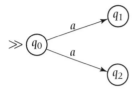

Figure 4.9

A partial NFA. From state q_0 there is a choice of either state q_1 or state q_2 on input a.

1. the use of *nondeterminism*,
2. the use of Λ-*transitions*, and
3. the use of transitions on arbitrary strings.

Nondeterminism means that the machine could potentially have two or more different computations on the same input. For example, in Figure 4.9 we show a portion of an NFA. In this NFA, from state q_0 on reading an a, the machine could go to either state q_1 or state q_2. This behavior is nondeterministic and was not allowed in the DFA. In our examples we will see that this feature is very useful for designing NFAs.

A Λ-*transition* allows the machine to change state without reading from the input tape or advancing the input head. It is useful to think of such a transition as a jump or goto. Why would such a jump be useful? As an example, suppose we want to recognize the language $a^* \cup b^*$ over the alphabet $\{a, b\}$. The NFA shown in Figure 4.10 accepts this language. Since NFAs, like DFAs, only get to read their input once, the two Λ-transitions start two threads of computation. One thread looks for an input that is all a's; the other looks for an input that is all b's. If either thread accepts its input, then the NFA stops and accepts. Thus we can accept (formally defined in this section) $a^* \cup b^*$ very easily; the design is also conceptually appealing. Notice that without using Λ-transitions the machine needs three accepting states.

A DFA for accepting the language $a^* \cup b^*$ is shown in Figure 4.10 (b). This machine is a bit more complex: it has one more state, a few more transitions, and three accepting states. It can be simplified a bit by taking advantage of the fact that if there is no transition from the current state for the current input symbol, the machine halts and rejects the input. Thus state q_3 could be removed.

Now let's focus on the third enhancement to DFAs. By "use of transitions on arbitrary strings," we mean that a transition can be labeled with any string in Σ^*. Essentially, this means an NFA is allowed to read more than one input symbol at a time (or none). How might this feature prove useful? Coupled with nondeterminism, this enhancement allows us to design simpler machines. As an example, recall the DFA presented in Figure 4.7 that accepted the language

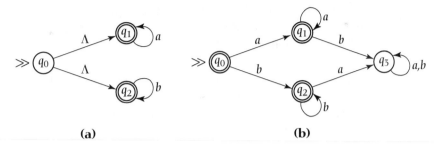

(a)   **(b)**

Figure 4.10

(a) An NFA for accepting the language $a^* \cup b^*$. (b) The smallest DFA for accepting the same language.

Figure 4.11

An NFA for accepting the language $\{x \mid x \in \{a, b, c\}^*$ and x contains the pattern $abac\}$. Compare this finite–state machine with the DFA shown in Figure 4.7 for accepting the same language.

$\{x \mid x \in \{a, b, c\}^*$ and x contains the pattern $abac\}$

An NFA for accepting this same language is shown in Figure 4.11. Until we formally define computations and acceptance for NFAs, think of this machine as gobbling up symbols unless it encounters the pattern $abac$, in which case it jumps to an accepting state and then continues to gobble up symbols. We have reduced the five–state DFA from Figure 4.7 to a two–state NFA using this new feature.

We are now ready to present the formal definition of an NFA. Rather than go through all of the definitions presented for DFAs again for NFAs, we highlight the changes.

Definition 4.4.1   *A **nondeterministic finite automaton (NFA)** is a five-tuple*

$$M = (Q, \Sigma, \Delta, q_0, F)$$

*that is defined similarly to a DFA except for the specification of the transitions. The **transition relation** Δ is a finite subset of*

$$Q \times \Sigma^* \times Q$$

Notice $Q \times \Sigma_T^* \times Q$ is an infinite set of triples, but we require Δ to be finite. NFAs, like DFAs, are restricted to a finite set of instructions.

The new specification of transitions handles all of the enhancements that were discussed above. Since we now have a relation instead of a function, the machine can be nondeterministic. That is, for a given state and string pair, it is possible for the machine to have a choice of next move. In Figure 4.9, for example, the two transitions (q_0, a, q_1) and (q_0, a, q_2) are shown. Of course, in a DFA this pair of transitions would not be allowed.

Since

$$\Delta \subseteq Q \times \Sigma_T^* \times Q$$

this model incorporates Λ–transitions and arbitrary string transitions. For example, in the NFA shown in Figure 4.10 (a), the two Λ–transitions (q_0, Λ, q_1) and (q_0, Λ, q_2) are shown. And in Figure 4.11 the transition from state q_0 to q_1 is $(q_0, abac, q_1)$.

Finally, since Δ is a relation that is not total, there can be state–string pairs for which Δ is not defined. In Figure 4.10 (a) the machine does not have a transition out of state q_0 on either a or b. So, in the full representation of Δ, there simply are no transitions (q_0, a, q) or (q_0, b, q) for any $q \in Q$. If a thread ever reaches such a dead end, it terminates with reject.

Nearly all of the other definitions for DFAs carry over with very little modification. For example, $\vdash$ still relates configurations, but now we might have $C_1 \vdash C_2$ and $C_1 \vdash C_3$, where $C_2 \neq C_3$, a situation that was not possible in a DFA. However, we need to change our notion of acceptance. Since NFAs are nondeterministic, there may be several possible computation threads on the same input. An NFA accepts its input as long as one thread accepts.

Definition 4.4.2   *Let $M = (Q, \Sigma, \Delta, q_0, F)$ be an NFA. M **accepts** input $x \in \Sigma^*$ if*

$$(q_0, \tau^{Initial}(x)) \vdash_M^* (f, \tau^{Final}(x))$$

*for some accepting state $f \in F$. Such a computation is called an **accepting computation**. Computations that are not accepting are called **rejecting computations**. The **language accepted** by M, denoted $L(M)$, is*

$$\{x \mid M \text{ accepts } x\}$$

The set of all languages accepted by NFAs is denoted $\mathcal{L}_{\mathbf{NFA}}$. That is,

$$\mathcal{L}_{\mathbf{NFA}} = \{L \mid \text{ there is an NFA } M \text{ with } L = L(M)\}$$

On a given input, an NFA may have both accepting and rejecting computations. If it has at least one accepting computation, then the input is accepted;

that is, the input is accepted if at least one thread leads to an accepting state. The language accepted by an NFA consists of all strings that the NFA accepts. Let's consider an example of two possible computations of the NFA shown in Figure 4.11, call it M, on input *abaca*.

The first is

$$(q_0, [1, abaca]) \vdash_M (q_0, [2, abaca])$$
$$\vdash_M (q_0, [3, abaca])$$
$$\vdash_M (q_0, [4, abaca])$$
$$\vdash_M (q_0, [5, abaca])$$
$$\vdash_M (q_0, [6, abaca])$$

and the second is

$$(q_0, [1, abaca]) \vdash_M (q_1, [5, abaca])$$
$$\vdash_M (q_1, [6, abaca])$$

Clearly, the two computations are very different. In the first one, we use up all of the input in five steps but do not end in an accepting state. Thus this is an example of a rejecting computation. In the second case, we use up all of the input in two steps and do end in an accepting state. Thus the latter computation is accepting. Since there is an accepting computation, the input *abaca* is accepted by M and $abaca \in L(M)$. To prove that an input is accepted by an NFA, we only need to demonstrate that a *single* accepting computation exists. However, to argue that an NFA does not accept a given string, we must show that *all* possible computations are rejecting. This is usually more difficult. The asymmetry just pointed out between accepting and rejecting in nondeterministic machines is an important one in complexity theory.

The basic strategy for designing DFAs outlined on page 100 can also be applied to NFAs.

4.5   *Equivalence of DFAs and NFAs*

NFAs possess many features that DFAs do not. These enhancements simplify the design of NFAs for certain languages. Do these new features actually make the NFA a more powerful model in the sense that it can accept languages that *no* DFA can? That is, is there some language L that an NFA can accept that no DFA can? Surprisingly, DFAs and NFAs accept exactly the same class of languages. We prove this theorem below via a technique known as *subset construction*. If you have difficulty understanding the proof, you may want to skip ahead and read Example 4.5.2 before going through all of the proof details.

Theorem 4.5.1   (Subset Construction)   *The language classes $\mathcal{L}_{\mathbf{DFA}}$ and $\mathcal{L}_{\mathbf{NFA}}$ are equal.*

Proof: We must show that $\mathcal{L}_{\mathbf{DFA}} = \mathcal{L}_{\mathbf{NFA}}$. Since this is really just demonstrating set equality, it is enough to prove that $\mathcal{L}_{\mathbf{DFA}} \subseteq \mathcal{L}_{\mathbf{NFA}}$ and $\mathcal{L}_{\mathbf{NFA}} \subseteq \mathcal{L}_{\mathbf{DFA}}$. As is customary, we perform the easy part of the proof first.

($\mathcal{L}_{\mathbf{DFA}} \subseteq \mathcal{L}_{\mathbf{NFA}}$) Suppose $L \in \mathcal{L}_{\mathbf{DFA}}$. We need to show that $L \in \mathcal{L}_{\mathbf{NFA}}$ to conclude that $\mathcal{L}_{\mathbf{DFA}} \subseteq \mathcal{L}_{\mathbf{NFA}}$. If $L \in \mathcal{L}_{\mathbf{DFA}}$, then there exists a DFA $M = (Q, \Sigma, \delta, q_0, F)$ such that $L(M) = L$. The idea is simply to view M as an NFA.

Define an NFA $N = (Q, \Sigma, \Delta, q_0, F)$, where $\delta(q, a) = q'$ if and only if $(q, a, q') \in \Delta$. We claim that $L(M) = L(N)$. It is easy to see that

$$(q_0, \tau^{Initial}(x)) \vdash_M^* (f, \tau^{Final}(x))$$

where $f \in F$ if and only if

$$(q_0, \tau^{Initial}(x)) \vdash_N^* (f, \tau^{Final}(x))$$

This simply says the machines have the same transitions, which is of course how M' was defined. Since $L(N) = L$, this shows $L \in \mathcal{L}_{\mathbf{NFA}}$ and we can conclude that $\mathcal{L}_{\mathbf{DFA}} \subseteq \mathcal{L}_{\mathbf{NFA}}$.

($\mathcal{L}_{\mathbf{NFA}} \subseteq \mathcal{L}_{\mathbf{DFA}}$) Suppose $L \in \mathcal{L}_{\mathbf{NFA}}$. We need to show that $L \in \mathcal{L}_{\mathbf{DFA}}$ to conclude that $\mathcal{L}_{\mathbf{NFA}} \subseteq \mathcal{L}_{\mathbf{DFA}}$. If $L \in \mathcal{L}_{\mathbf{NFA}}$, then there exists an NFA $M = (Q, \Sigma, \Delta, q_0, F)$ such that $L(M) = L$. We will construct a DFA M_3 such that $L(M_3) = L$.

The simulation of M will take place in three stages. In each stage, a new machine will be constructed that is equivalent to M but is more like a DFA than in the previous phase. In the third stage, the result is in fact a DFA. The first stage involves eliminating transitions of the form (q, γ, q'), where $|\gamma| > 1$. Stage two involves eliminating Λ–transitions. In the third stage, nondeterminism is removed. From M we construct M_1, from M_1 we define M_2, and from M_2 we build the desired DFA M_3. Since we will show $L(M_3) = L(M)$, this is enough to complete the proof of the theorem.

Constructing M_1: The idea in building M_1 is to add new states to M so that strings γ labeling transitions, with $|\gamma| > 1$, can be split up into single–symbol transitions as required in a DFA. You can think of splicing in new states in the transition diagram for any edge labeled by a string of length more than one. The five–tuple for M_1 is given by

$$M_1 = (Q_1, \Sigma, \Delta_1, q_0, F)$$

The new state set Q_1 consists of the states from Q and the additional states that we need to splice in. Δ_1 is defined in terms of Δ, except that transitions on strings of length more than one need to be replaced by a new set of equivalent transitions. The algorithm shown in Figure 4.12 describes exactly how Q_1 and Δ_1 are constructed.

begin
    comment: initialize
    $Q_1 \leftarrow Q$;
    $\Delta_1 \leftarrow \Delta$;
    comment: replace transitions of strings of length two or more
    for each transition $(q, \gamma, q') \in \Delta$ with $|\gamma| > 1$ **do**
        $\Delta_1 \leftarrow \Delta_1 - \{(q, \gamma, q')\}$;
        comment: suppose $|\gamma| = k$ for some $k > 1$
        comment: let $q_1, \ldots, q_{k-1}$ be new states not in Q_1
        $Q_1 \leftarrow Q_1 \cup \{q_1, \ldots, q_{k-1}\}$;
        $\Delta_1 \leftarrow \Delta_1 \cup \{(q, \gamma(1), q_1), (q_1, \gamma(2), q_2), \ldots, (q_{k-1}, \gamma(k), q')\}$;
end

Figure 4.12

The first stage of subset construction. This stage involves eliminating transitions of the form (q, γ, q'), where $|\gamma| > 1$.

The following three facts imply that $L(M) = L(M_1)$:

1. The set of accepting states in M_1 is the same as in M.

2. All transitions in Δ are in Δ_1, except for those on strings of length greater than one.

3. Transitions on strings of length greater than one in Δ were replaced by transitions in Δ_1 that achieved the same effect.

Constructing M_2: The second stage in the construction requires that we eliminate Λ-transitions from M_1. In the process we will define a new NFA

$$M_2 = (Q_2, \Sigma, \Delta_2, q_0, F_2)$$

We will not be adding any new states, so $Q_2 \subseteq Q_1$.

    The goal is to eliminate all Λ-transitions from M_1. In M_1, it is possible to move from a state q to state q' by a sequence of Λ-transitions, and then to read a symbol s and make a transition from q' to some other state q''. This is effectively the same as making the transition directly from q by reading symbol s and then moving to q''. So whenever it is possible to reach a state q'' from q by reading the symbol s, we want to add the transition (q, s, q'') to Δ_2.

    The algorithm shown in Figure 4.13 shows precisely how Δ_2 is constructed using this idea.

    Notice if there was some state $q \in Q_1$ that involved only Λ-transitions in M_1, it is possible that after applying the above construction of Δ_2 that state q becomes *unreachable*; that is, there is no way to make a transition *to* state q from the initial state. An unreachable state no longer plays any role in the strings accepted by

begin

 comment: initialize Δ_2

 $\Delta_2 \leftarrow \emptyset$;

 comment: eliminate Λ–transitions

 for each state $q \in Q_1$ **do**

  for each symbol $a \in \Sigma$ **do**

   $\Delta_2 \leftarrow \Delta_2 \cup \{(q, a, q') \mid (q, [1, a]) \vdash^*_{M_1} (q', [2, a])\}$;

end

Figure 4.13

The second stage of subset construction. This stage involves the elimination of Λ–transitions.

the machine, since it can no longer be entered by a computation starting from the initial state. So Q_2 is defined to be all the states of Q_1 reachable from the initial state under transition function Δ_2.

It is also possible for M_1 to move from a state q to state q' by a sequence of Λ–transitions and then halt. This means that if q' is an accepting state, then effectively so is q because when the machine runs out of input, it can still reach q' and accept.

So the final step in this construction is to identify all these kinds of new accepting states. They are simply

$$F_2 = Q_2 \cap \{q' \in Q_1 \mid (q', [1, \Lambda]) \vdash^*_{M_1} (f, [1, \Lambda]) \text{ for some } f \in F\}$$

This says that any state in M_1 from which we can reach an accepting state without using input (i.e., by processing the empty tape configuration $[1, \Lambda]$) becomes an accepting state in M_2. Note that this set also includes the original states in F that remain reachable in M_2.

We now argue that $L(M_1) = L(M_2)$. Suppose $x \in L(M_1)$. Then $(q_0, \tau^{Initial}(x)) \vdash^*_{M_1}$ $(f, \tau^{Final}(x))$ for some $f \in F$. This computation may involve Λ–transitions. Any series of Λ–transitions that are followed by a transition in which an individual symbol is read can be replaced by a single transition of M_2, resulting in M_2 having the same configuration as M_1. Any combination of Λ–transitions that occur after x has been completely read lead from some state $\widetilde{q}$ to f. Because of the way in which F_2 was defined, we see $\widetilde{q} \in F_2$, and so $x \in L(M_2)$. This shows $L(M_1) \subseteq L(M_2)$.

A related argument can be used to show that $L(M_2) \subseteq L(M_1)$ essentially by reversing the steps in the argument just presented. All this says is that we did not make M_2 accept more strings than M_1.

Constructing M_3: The third stage in the construction is to eliminate nondeterminism from M_2 in forming M_3. The idea is to consider all the possible threads of computation that M_2 could have active simultaneously. At any point in time, each of the threads is in a single well–defined state, that state being a consequence

begin
    comment: states of M_3 are sets of states of M_2
    $Q_3 \leftarrow \{ \{q_0\} \}$;
    $\delta_3 \leftarrow \emptyset$;
    comment: Q_u has unprocessed successor states from Q_3
    $Q_u \leftarrow Q_3$;
    while $Q_u \neq \emptyset$ **do**
        comment: get an unprocessed state from Q_u
        pick any $Q' \in Q_u$;
        $Q_u \leftarrow Q_u - \{Q'\}$;
        comment: compute successors of Q' for each input symbol a
        for each symbol $a \in \Sigma$ **do**
            comment: $R \in 2^{Q_2}$
            $R \leftarrow \emptyset$;
            for each state $q' \in Q'$ **do**
                for each state $q_2 \in Q_2$ **do**
                    if $(q', a, q_2) \in \Delta_2$ **then** $R \leftarrow R \cup \{q_2\}$;
            comment: add R to unprocessed set if a new state
            if $R \notin Q_3$ **then** $Q_u \leftarrow Q_u \cup \{R\}$;
            $Q_3 \leftarrow Q_3 \cup \{R\}$;
            $\delta_3 \leftarrow \delta_3 \cup \{(Q', a, R)\}$;
end

Figure 4.14

The third stage of subset construction. This stage involves the removal of nondeterminism.

of the nondeterminism and the transitions that were chosen in the past by the thread. So the current state of all the threads is a set of states. For every possible combination of thread states in M_2, there will be a single state in M_3; that is, the "current" states over all possible threads will be compressed into a single state in M_3. This means that the states in M_3 will be subsets of Q_2; that is, a state in M_3 is a set of M_2 states.

We define the new machine as the following DFA:

$$M_3 = (Q_3, \Sigma, \delta_3, \{q_0\}, F_3)$$

where

$$Q_3 \subseteq 2^{Q_2}$$

The new transition function δ_3 is formed as described in the algorithm depicted in Figure 4.14.

It is important to observe that the states of M_3 are sets of states of M_2. So the initial state of M_3 is now $\{q_0\}$ and not simply q_0, since it must be a set.

Finally we identify the accepting states of M_3 by observing that if any one of the threads reflected in a state of M_3 is accepting, then M_3 should accept.

$$F_3 = \{Q' \mid Q' \in Q_3 \text{ and } Q' \cap F_2 \neq \emptyset\}$$

Remember at this point that we are trying to eliminate nondeterminism from M_2. The idea behind the algorithm shown in Figure 4.14 is best explained via a simple example. Suppose that from state q, M_2 on reading an a could go to either state q_1 or state q_2. That is, M_2 from configuration $(q, [1, as])$ for any string s can make a nondeterministic move—either change to configuration $(q_1, [2, as])$ or to configuration $(q_2, [2, as])$. In M_3 then, we want to end up in configuration $(\{q_1, q_2\}, [2, as])$, since M_2 could be in either one of these states after reading the a. Of course, this is why we need sets to represent the states of M_3.

It is easy to see that M_3 is a DFA. The last statement in the code shown in Figure 4.14 dictates that exactly one transition is added to the relation δ_3 for each symbol and each state. Thus δ_3 is a function.

We must argue that $L(M_3) = L(M_2)$. Using the transitivity of equality, this will imply that $L(M_3) = L(M)$. So, this will complete the entire proof of the theorem.

First, we prove that $L(M_2) \subseteq L(M_3)$. Suppose $x \in L(M_2)$, with $n = |x|$. Then there exists a computation $(q_0, [1, x]) \vdash^*_{M_2} (f, [n + 1, x])$ for some $f \in F_2$. Since M_2 has no Λ–transitions and no transitions on strings of length more than one, this computation passes through exactly $n - 1$ states. The **if** statement of the algorithm shown in Figure 4.14 adds the appropriate state to the set R, and then in the last step of the algorithm the appropriate transition is added to δ_3, keeping track of all the possible states that M_2 could be in. Thus, for each step of the computation in M_2 involving a transition (q', a, q_2), there are corresponding sets of states Q' with $q' \in Q'$ and Q_2 with $q_2 \in Q_2$ in M_3, and a transition (Q', a, Q_2) in Δ_3. Therefore,

$$(\{q_0\}, [1, x]) \vdash^n_{M_3} (F', [n + 1, x])$$

where $f \in F'$. This shows that $x \in L(M_3)$, so $L(M_2) \subseteq L(M_3)$. By a related argument that essentially reverses the steps in this one, we can prove that $L(M_3) \subseteq L(M_2)$. The proof is now finished. ∎

The proof that any language accepted by an NFA is accepted by a DFA simply required the removal of each enhancement of the NFA. The fact that we could do this and still end up with a DFA, however, was not obvious. In practice, when forming M_3 using the algorithm of Figure 4.14, many of the states produced are unreachable. An example is presented below, where we trace the steps necessary for subset construction. Generally, we are able to shortcut stage three, keeping track of just the reachable states; the technique for doing this is also explained in the example.

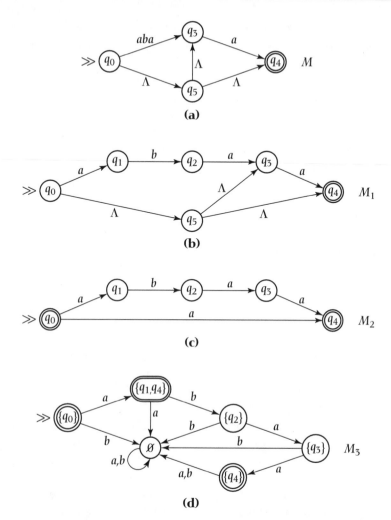

Figure 4.15

(a) A sample NFA to which subset construction is applied. (b) The resulting NFA after stage one of Theorem 4.5.1 has been applied. (c) The resulting NFA after stage two (d) The resulting DFA after stage three.

Example 4.5.2   Subset construction application to DFA

Consider the NFA shown in Figure 4.15 (a). subset construction to construct a DFA that accep NFA by carrying out the three stages of subset c Theorem 4.5.1. The results of each phase are shown in respectively. The example we have chosen is fairly simple, but it does illustrate all of the basic points. Additional subset constructions are asked for in the exercises.

A look at the machine in Figure 4.15 (a) reveals that it is not a DFA. There is a transition from state q_0 to state q_3, labeled with the string aba; three Λ–transitions; and some nondeterminism involving state q_5.

Let's begin converting M to a DFA by forming M_1, as done in Theorem 4.5.1. This involves splicing in new states q_1 and q_2. When you do your own subset constructions, you can create whatever new state names you like. The result of removing transition (q_0, aba, q_3) from M and adding transitions (q_0, a, q_1), (q_1, b, q_2), and (q_2, a, q_3) to M_1 is shown in Figure 4.15 (b). You can easily verify that $L(M) = L(M_1) = \{\Lambda, a, abab\}$.

Stage two of the subset construction procedure involves the elimination of Λ–transitions. In going from M_1 to M_2, shown in Figure 4.15 (c), all Λ–transitions were deleted from M_1, and the transition (q_0, a, q_4) was added to M_2. This transition was added because $(q_0, [1, a]) \vdash^*_{M_1} (q_4, [2, a])$. Notice state q_5 was deleted because it was no longer reachable. Additionally, state q_0 was made an accepting state because $(q_0, [1, \Lambda]) \vdash^*_{M_1} (q_4, [1, \Lambda])$ and $q_4 \in F$. Note that a DFA can accept Λ if and only if its initial state is an accepting state.

The last stage of the construction is to eliminate nondeterminism. Notice how in M_2 we can go to either state q_1 or state q_4 on reading an a. This stage is where the procedure derives its name from. In forming M_3's states, we use the power set of the states of M_2. $|Q_2| = 5$, so $|2^{Q_2}| = 32$; that is, the power set of Q_2 has 32 elements. Many of these will not be reachable from the initial state $\{q_0\}$ of M_3. This prompts us to begin from state $\{q_0\}$ of M_3 and then to trace each symbol $\sigma \in \Sigma$ to determine the set of states that M_2 could possibly be in at each given step. It is best if we order the symbols in Σ so that we have a fixed way of processing them when we move on to new states. A natural order is a first and b second.

From state q_0 of M_2 on an a, we could go to either state q_1 or q_4. Thus, in M_3, the state $\{q_1, q_4\}$ is reachable, and we draw it in the transition diagram for M_3. For emphasis, let us repeat that M_3 being in state $\{q_1, q_4\}$ means that a thread of M_2 could be occupying either one of these two states. Next we trace in M_2 from state q_0 on the symbol b. Notice from b we cannot reach any other state in M_2. This corresponds to R in Figure 4.14 being empty. Therefore, we add the state $\emptyset$ to M_3 and the transition $(\{q_0\}, b, \emptyset)$ to Δ_3.

Now we can continue processing the unfinished states in M_3. These are $\{q_1, q_4\}$ and $\emptyset$. Let's carry on from state $\{q_1, q_4\}$. Since there are no transitions out of q_1 or q_4 on an a, in M_3 we add the transition $(\{q_1, q_4\}, a, \emptyset)$. On a b from q_1 in M_2, we can go to state q_2, so we add the transition $(\{q_1, q_4\}, b, \{q_2\})$ to Δ_3.

If we continue processing in this manner, the result is the DFA shown in Figure 4.15 (d). Notice this machine has 6 states and 12 transitions, as you would expect since there are two symbols in the alphabet. Also observe that any state that contained an accepting state of M_2 as an element is marked as an accepting state. These states are $\{q_0\}$, $\{q_1, q_4\}$, and $\{q_4\}$. Lastly, notice that the language accepted by M_3 is $\{\Lambda, a, abaa\}$, so $L(M) = L(M_1) = L(M_2) = L(M_3)$.

The resulting DFA only has 6 states. What about the other 26 possible states? As we alluded to earlier, none of these are reachable; thus, they do not factor into the language that the machine accepts. We need not specify all of the transitions out of these states since the transition function for a DFA does not have to be defined everywhere. In general, you eliminate the unreachable states by not adding them to Q_3 in the first place. The final DFA produced in our example has states $\emptyset$, $\{q_0\}$, $\{q_2\}$, $\{q_3\}$, $\{q_4\}$, and $\{q_1, q_4\}$. ∎

The following checks are worth performing to give some level of confidence that the result of a subset construction is correct:

- Make sure that the initial state is properly labeled.
- Verify that the accepting states are properly labeled.
- Check that there are $|\Sigma|$ transitions leaving each reachable state in the final DFA.
- Make sure that all states in the completed DFA are sets.
- Trace several sample inputs as a check that the DFA constructed actually accepts the same language as the original NFA.

When two types of computational models accept exactly the same class of languages, we say they are *equivalent*. Thus DFAs and NFAs are equivalent. If two machines M_1 and M_2, possibly different types, are such that $L(M_1) = L(M_2)$, then we say M_1 and M_2 are *equivalent*.

4.6 *Equivalence of DFAs and C-- Programs*

Let's return to the C-- programs of Problems 1 to 3 in Chapter 1. For any given program, there are a fixed number of statements that assign to the state variable s, and thus s can take on only a finite range of values. The actual changes in s are driven by the characters read from the input. So C-- programs look very much like finite-state machines. In fact, the two models are equivalent, in that any DFA can be converted (compiled) into a C-- program, and any C-- program can be converted into a DFA.

Converting a DFA M to a C-- program is straightforward: values of s correspond to states in M, and there is a case for every possible state. Within each state case, there is a case for every possible symbol being read. This is exactly how the program Parity of Problem 2 is constructed.

Converting a C-- program to a DFA is a bit trickier, since not every C-- program has the nice structure of the Parity program. Instead you need to employ an argument similar to the discussion in Problem 3 to characterize what the C-- program does during the time between passes of the inspection point. The result is that you can view the C-- program as making a single state transition between any two passes of the inspection point, but this transition is labeled by a string, not just an individual symbol.

4.7   *Exercises*

Section 4.2   *Basic Machine Notions*

1. Draw pictures of tapes and tape heads corresponding to the following tape configurations:
   - (a) [5, 10101]
   - (b) [0, 111]
   - (c) [4, *aaa*]
   - (d) [6, *abaaaba*]
   - (e) [0, Λ]

2. What are $\sigma[p, x]$ and $\rho([p, x])$ in the following cases?
   - (a) [5, 1010]
   - (b) [2, 111]
   - (c) [0, 1110]
   - (d) [0, Λ]
   - (e) [1, Λ]

Section 4.3   *Deterministic Finite Automata*

3. Write a C-- program to accept the language (00)* over the alphabet {0, 1}. Test your program on the inputs Λ, 0, 0000, 0^{11}, 1, 00001, and 11111.

4. Present the formal definition of a DFA (without looking back).

5. Write out the five–tuple for the DFA shown in Figure 4.8 (b).

6. Write out the initial configurations for the DFA shown in Figure 4.10 (b) on inputs Λ, *aaaa*, and *ababa*.

7. In an *m*–state DFA *M*, what is the maximum number of possible configurations *M* could have on an input of length *n*?

8. Trace the DFA shown in Figure 4.1 using the ⊢ relation on the following inputs: 010101, 0000, Λ, and 111. Which of these inputs are accepted? Which are rejected?

9. Show that the following languages are in $\mathcal{L}_{\mathbf{DFA}}$ by constructing DFAs to accept them. In each problem, draw the transition diagram and write out the five–tuple for the machine. In each case, if they exist, write out

computations of length five for an input that is accepted and for one that is rejected. Use the ⊢ relation to write out the computations.

(a) Ø over the alphabet {0, 1}

(b) {0, 1}* over the alphabet {0, 1}

(c) {axa | a ∈ {0, 1}, x ∈ {0, 1}*} ∪ {0}

(d) (0 ∪ 1)*0110* over the alphabet {0, 1, 2}

(e) {x | x ∈ {0, 1}* and x contains an odd number of 1's}

(f) {x | x ∈ {1, 2, . . . , 9}{0, 1, . . . , 9}* and x is divisible by 3 when x is interpreted as a decimal number}

10. Let

$$M = (\{1, 2, 5\}, \{a, b\}, \{(1, b, 2), (2, a, 2), (5, a, 5), (5, b, 1), (1, a, 1), (2, b, 5)\}, 1, \{1\})$$

be a DFA. Here the transition function is spelled out with triples, that is, from state 1 on input b go to state 2, and so on. What language does M accept? Present your answer in words, and then give a regular expression for your answer.

11. Suppose M is a five-state DFA. On input $x \in \Sigma^*$, what is the maximum number of moves M can make if

(a) $\Sigma = Ø$?

(b) $\Sigma = \{a, b\}$?

(c) $\Sigma = \{0, 1, 2, 3\}$?

In all cases explain your answer.

12. Can a DFA have an infinite computation?

13. In this exercise you are to model traffic lights using a DFA. Consider a roadway intersection that forms a T. There are three different sets of lights, and each has the possibility of displaying green or red (there is no yellow in this case). Describe how you could use finite-state machines to model the intersection in terms of the arrival and control of cars and the changing of lights.

14. In this exercise you are to model a soda machine using a DFA. Suppose, like in the old days, a soda costs only 20 cents. Use as an input alphabet nickels, dimes, and quarters. Indicate how finite-state machines can be used to model the behavior of the soda machine.

15. In this exercise you are to model an elevator using a DFA. Suppose there is an elevator in a seven-story building. Model user requests and the state space for the elevator using finite-state machines. Consider how to add priorities of service to floors.

16. Let $L \subseteq \{a, b\}^*$ be a language.

    Define $\text{Prefix}(L) = \{w \in \{a, b\}^* \mid x = wy \text{ for some } x \in L, y \in \{a, b\}^*\}$.

    Show that if L is accepted by a DFA M, then there is another DFA M' that accepts $\text{Prefix}(L)$. Argue why your construction is correct.

17. Is every DFA equivalent to another DFA that has only one accepting state?

Section 4.4   Nondeterministic Finite Automata

18. Present the formal definition of an NFA (without looking back).

19. Examine each definition summarized in Table 4.2 for DFAs and note any changes that must occur when these definitions are adapted to NFAs.

20. Write out the five–tuples for the NFAs shown in Figures 4.10 (a) and 4.11.

21. Let $M = (\{s\}, \emptyset, \emptyset, s, \{s\})$. Is M an NFA? Justify your answer.

22. Write out the initial configurations for the NFA shown in Figure 4.10 (a) on inputs Λ, *aaaa*, and *ababa*.

23. Trace the NFA shown in Figure 4.10 using the $\vdash$ relation on the following inputs: *ababa*, *aaa*, Λ, and *bbba*. In each case trace *all* possible computations. Which of these inputs are accepted? Which are rejected?

24. True or false? Explain your answer.

    (a) $(\{1\}, \{a, b\}, \{((1, a), 1), ((1, b), 1)\}, s, \{1\})$ is a DFA.
    (b) Every NFA is a DFA.
    (c) If M is a DFA accepting the same language as NFA M', then M must have more states than M'.
    (d) An accepting computation in a DFA is always longer than an accepting computation of an equivalent NFA.
    (e) If the transition relation of an NFA is actually a function, then it must be one-to-one.
    (f) $(\{s\}, \{a\}, \emptyset, s, \{a\})$ is an NFA.

25. Show that the following languages are in $\mathcal{L}_{\mathbf{NFA}}$ by constructing NFAs to accept them. In each problem, draw the transition diagram and write out the five–tuple for the machine. In each case, if they exist, write out an accepting computation for an input of length five and a rejecting computation for an input of length five. Use the $\vdash$ relation to describe the computation.

    (a) $\emptyset$ over the alphabet $\{0, 1\}$
    (b) $\{0, 1\}^*$ over the alphabet $\{0, 1\}$
    (c) $(0 \cup 1)^*0110^*$ over the alphabet $\{0, 1, 2\}$
    (d) $\{x \mid x \in \{0, 1\}^* \text{ and } x \text{ does not contain the pattern } 1010\}$

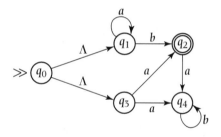

Figure 4.16

An NFA that needs to be converted into a DFA via subset construction.

    (e) $\{x \mid x \in \{0, 1\}^*$ and x when interpreted as a binary number is divisible by 2 or 3}

26. Can an NFA have an infinite thread of execution? Can it have an infinite computation in the sense that all threads are infinite?

Section 4.5 *Equivalence of DFAs and NFAs*

27. Let $M = (\{q_0, q_1\}, \{0, 1\}, \Delta, q_0, \{q_1\})$ be an NFA with

$$\Delta = \{(q_0, 0, q_0), (q_0, 0, q_1), (q_0, 1, q_1), (q_1, 1, q_0), (q_1, 1, q_1)\}$$

Draw the state transition diagram for M. Convert M to a DFA using subset construction.

28. Let $M = (\{q_0, q_1, q_2\}, \{0, 1\}, \Delta, q_0, \{q_2\})$ be an NFA with

$$\Delta = \{(q_0, 1, q_1), (q_1, 0, q_2), (q_2, 0, q_0), (q_2, 1, q_0)\}$$

Draw the state transition diagram for M. Convert M to a DFA using subset construction.

29. Apply the subset construction method to the NFA shown in Figure 4.10. Trace the resulting DFA on inputs Λ, *aaa*, *bb*, and *ab*.

30. Apply the subset construction method to the NFA shown in Figure 4.11. Trace the resulting DFA on inputs Λ and *abac*.

31. Apply the subset construction method to the NFA shown in Figure 4.16. Trace the resulting DFA on inputs Λ, *aaaaa*, and *aab*.

32. Write regular expressions for the languages accepted by the machines shown in Figure 4.17.

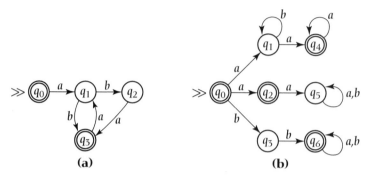

Figure 4.17

(a) A DFA. (b) An NFA.

33. Prove for every NFA there is an equivalent NFA that has only one final state.

34. Define a variant of an NFA that can have more than one initial state. Prove there is an equivalent NFA for each multiple initial state NFA.

35. How might you go about defining DFAs and NFAs that produce output?

CHAPTER 5

Properties of Finite–State Languages

I said, "Do you speak my language?" She just smiled and gave me a Vegemite sandwich.

—*Men at Work*

5.1 Introduction

This chapter focuses on the class of languages accepted by DFAs, the so–called finite–state languages. The goals of this chapter are

- to examine some important simulation results and methodologies,
- to show the class of languages represented by regular expressions ($\mathcal{L}_{\mathbf{RE}}$) is equal to those accepted by finite automata ($\mathcal{L}_{\mathbf{DFA}}$),
- to provide more examples of interesting languages,
- to illustrate a method to prove a language is *not* in a given class, and
- to describe closure properties of finite–state languages.

This course of presentation will give you more experience with finite–state machines and the techniques employed for studying them.

In Section 5.2 a number of simulation techniques are illustrated. These results are useful in determining whether a given language is in a particular language class. For example, suppose we know a language $L \subseteq \Sigma^*$ is in the language class C. Does this imply that $\overline{L}$ is also in C? What about L^*? Or suppose we know languages L_1 and L_2 are in the class C. Does this mean that $L_1 \cup L_2$, $L_1 \cap L_2$, and $L_1 \circ L_2$ are also in C? The simulation results in this section will answer these questions for the class of languages accepted by finite automata. More general versions of the questions will be addressed in Chapter 7. The results contained in this section are not difficult to prove if we choose the right machine model for the proofs.

The next major result in this chapter is that $\mathcal{L}_{\mathbf{RE}}$ equals $\mathcal{L}_{\mathbf{DFA}}$; that is, the class of languages that can be represented by regular expressions is exactly the same class of languages as can be accepted by deterministic finite automata. Since we know $\mathcal{L}_{\textbf{DFA}}$ equals $\mathcal{L}_{\textbf{NFA}}$, this implies $\mathcal{L}_{\textbf{RE}}$ equals $\mathcal{L}_{\textbf{NFA}}$ as well. This theorem shows how two very different formalisms can be unexpectedly related.

In this text, there are a wide variety of language classes: $\mathcal{L}_{\textbf{RE}}$, $\mathcal{L}_{\textbf{DFA}}$, $\mathcal{L}_{\textbf{NFA}}$, $\mathcal{L}_{\textbf{DPDA}}$, $\mathcal{L}_{\textbf{PDA}}$, $\mathcal{L}_{\textbf{DTM}}$, and $\mathcal{L}_{\textbf{NTM}}$. The general strategy for showing that a given language is in a particular class is to provide a machine to accept the language. How do we show that a specific language L is *not* in some language class?

For classes that are characterized by machines, it is sufficient to show that it is impossible to construct a machine for L. So for a class like $\mathcal{L}_{\textbf{DFA}}$, it is sufficient to show that no DFA can accept L. The adversary technique that was used in Problem 3 for the C-- program in Chapter 1 applies here also. One of its generalizations is captured in the so-called *Pumping Lemma*.

Since the Pumping Lemma is important, we devote another section to illustrating how it can be used effectively. We provide both positive and negative applications to languages that either satisfy the lemma or do not. The Pumping Lemma has many variants within the framework of regular languages, and it can also be generalized to other language classes. In this chapter, we focus only on one particular form of the lemma and only for regular languages.

Many of the methods employed in this chapter are fundamental to the study of computability theory and can be generalized. The exercises and references present pointers to this rich area of computability theory.

5.2   *Machines for Five Language Operations*

This section presents five different simulations involving finite automata. The results show, when given two finite automata M_1 and M_2, how to construct machines for accepting the following languages:

1. the complement of $L(M_1)$, $\overline{L(M_1)}$,

2. the union of $L(M_1)$ and $L(M_2)$, $L(M_1) \cup L(M_2)$,

3. the intersection of $L(M_1)$ and $L(M_2)$, $L(M_1) \cap L(M_2)$,

4. the Kleene star of $L(M_1)$, $L(M_1)^*$, and

5. the concatenation of $L(M_1)$ and $L(M_2)$, $L(M_1) \circ L(M_2)$.

The proof techniques used to derive these theorems are important and are the first step towards understanding a number of other simulation results in computability theory.

As a corollary to the five theorems, we obtain that the finite–state languages (i.e., $\mathcal{L}_{\textbf{DFA}} = \mathcal{L}_{\textbf{NFA}}$) are *closed* under complementation, union, intersection, Kleene star, and concatenation. By "closed," we mean that you can take any languages in the class, apply these operations to them, and the resulting language will still be in the class. The proofs given in this section show how to build the corresponding finite automata directly.

Later, in Theorem 5.3.1, we will establish that $\mathcal{L}_{\mathbf{DFA}}$ is the same class of languages as $\mathcal{L}_{\mathbf{RE}}$, and from Observation 3.3.4 we know this is just the set of regular languages. From the definition of the regular languages, Definition 3.2.1, we already know they are closed under union, concatenation, and Kleene star. Their relationship with finite automata allows us to conclude that the regular languages are also closed under intersection and complementation. This illustrates how a change to an equivalent model can often simplify proofs.

The basic strategy of the following proofs is to manipulate languages by manipulating the machines that accept them. For example, we take a machine M that accepts some language L, and transform it into another machine M' that accepts $\overline{L}$. Since $\mathcal{L}_{\mathbf{DFA}}$ equals $\mathcal{L}_{\mathbf{NFA}}$, the proofs can be based on either deterministic or nondeterministic finite automata. We use the model that simplifies the particular proof.

Another way of viewing the results in this section is that we are checking a class of languages to see if it has certain desirable closure properties. As we will see in Chapter 7, not all classes of languages possess the closure properties we investigate in this section.

5.2.1   Closure under Complement

After membership *in* a language, one of the most natural questions to ask is about *non*-membership. That is, given a machine for accepting L, is there a machine that picks out the strings that are not in L, and so accepts $\overline{L}$? This can be surprisingly simple to answer, as in the case of DFA languages, or it can be remarkably difficult, with many such questions still unsolved (see the references).

Theorem 5.2.1   *Let $M = (Q, \Sigma, \delta, q_0, F)$ be a DFA. The language $\overline{L(M)}$ is accepted by a DFA. That is, the languages accepted by DFAs are closed under complementation.*

Proof: Intuitively, we simply want to accept all the strings that M rejected and reject all the strings that M accepted. What happens if we just swap all accepting and rejecting states of M?

Without loss of generality, we can assume that δ is defined on all $Q \times \Sigma$ pairs. If it is not, we can simply add a new state q_a to M that is not accepting, and make all previously undefined transitions now send the machine to state q_a. The state q_a is made to be absorbing, so that all of its transitions are directed back to it (i.e., $\delta(q_a, s) = q_a$ for all $s \in \Sigma$).

We define a new machine $\overline{M}$ such that $L(\overline{M}) = \overline{L(M)}$. Define $\overline{M} = (Q, \Sigma, \delta, q_0, Q - F)$; that is, $\overline{M}$ is the same as M except the rejecting states of M are accepting states of $\overline{M}$ and vice versa. It is clear that $\overline{M}$ is in fact a DFA. Figure 5.1 illustrates the transformation of M to $\overline{M}$ for a hypothetical machine M.

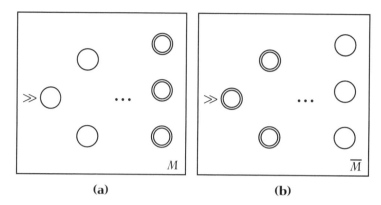

(a)   **(b)**

Figure 5.1

An illustration of the construction used in Theorem 5.2.1 to show that the complement of a language accepted by a DFA is itself accepted by a DFA. Accepting and rejecting states have been switched. (a) The original DFA. (b) The result of the transformation.

We claim that $L(\overline{M}) = \overline{L(M)}$. Since both machines are deterministic and have the same transition function, they will halt in the same state after reading all of their input; that is, their computations can be described as

$$(q_0, [1, x]) \vdash^*_M (q', [|x| + 1, x]) \text{ and } (q_0, [1, x]) \vdash^*_{\overline{M}} (q', [|x| + 1, x])$$

where both machines halt in state q'. State q' is an accepting state of M if and only if it is a rejecting state of $\overline{M}$. That is, $x \in L(\overline{M})$ if and only if $q' \notin F$ if and only if $x \notin L(M)$ if and only if $x \in \overline{L(M)}$.

Thus $\overline{L(M)} = L(\overline{M})$. This completes the proof.   ∎

Although the proof of Theorem 5.2.1 is simple, it depends crucially on the fact that the machine we started with is deterministic. This means that there is exactly one sequence of transitions followed by the machine on input x. In other words, on input x, exactly one thread is followed by M, and it is either accepting or rejecting. Whether the states on the thread are accepting or rejecting is incidental to the path followed. Input x defines the same thread through the state transition diagrams of M and $\overline{M}$. Flipping the meaning of accept and reject states does not destroy deterministic behavior, and so $\overline{M}$ must reject exactly when M accepts, and vice versa. (Note that the proof still works even if we did not require DFAs to read all of their input before halting.)

But this technique will not work in general with NFAs. Consider a string x in the language accepted by an NFA M. M can have many rejecting threads for x along with at least one accepting thread for x. If there is even one rejecting thread for x, then the NFA with flipped accept and reject states will also accept x. So x will be in both $L(M)$ and $L(\overline{M})$. In fact, if we are given an NFA M and asked to build a machine for $\overline{L(M)}$, we will usually have to construct the equivalent DFA first and then complement it.

Figure 5.1 schematically represents the transformation applied in Theorem 5.2.1. The proof works for *any* DFA, but in our figure we had to represent a DFA with some fixed number of accepting states—in this case we used three. We will represent the other proofs in this section pictorially as well. Keep in mind that with these figures we are not able to represent all cases, so they are not completely general. For example, in Figure 5.1 the initial state could also be an accepting state in some cases.

5.2.2   Closure under Union

We continue by showing that the languages accepted by finite automata are closed under union. In this case it is most convenient to begin with NFAs, but of course the result holds for DFAs as well.

Theorem 5.2.2   *Let $M_1 = (Q_1, \Sigma_1, \Delta_1, q_1, F_1)$ and $M_2 = (Q_2, \Sigma_2, \Delta_2, q_2, F_2)$ be NFAs. The language $L(M_1) \cup L(M_2)$ is accepted by an NFA. That is, the languages accepted by NFAs are closed under union.*

Proof: The intuitive idea behind this proof is to guess whether the input string is part of the language of M_1 or part of the language of M_2. In what follows, we show how to construct an NFA that does this.

Without loss of generality, we may assume that $Q_1 \cap Q_2 = \emptyset$. This can be achieved by a renaming of states in Q_2 and then updating Δ_2 and F_2 appropriately. We define a new machine M and then prove that $L(M) = L(M_1) \cup L(M_2)$. Define $M = (Q, \Sigma, \Delta, q_0, F)$, where $q_0 \notin Q_1 \cup Q_2$ and

$Q = Q_1 \cup Q_2 \cup \{q_0\}$

$\Sigma = \Sigma_1 \cup \Sigma_2$

$\Delta = \Delta_1 \cup \Delta_2 \cup \{(q_0, \Lambda, q_1), (q_0, \Lambda, q_2)\}$

$F = F_1 \cup F_2$

That is, M combines M_1 and M_2 via a new state q_0 with Λ-transitions to the initial states of M_1 and M_2. M has two new transitions and the accepting states of M are simply the union of the accepting states of M_1 and M_2. It is clear that M is an NFA. Figure 5.2 illustrates the transformation of M_1 and M_2 to M. Notice how M_1 and M_2 have been drawn with disjoint state sets.

We claim that $L(M) = L(M_1) \cup L(M_2)$. To show this, we need to prove that $L(M) \subseteq L(M_1) \cup L(M_2)$ and that $L(M_1) \cup L(M_2) \subseteq L(M)$.

First, let's prove that $L(M) \subseteq L(M_1) \cup L(M_2)$. Suppose $x \in L(M)$. This means $(q_0, [1, x]) \vdash_M^* (f, [|x| + 1, x])$ for some $f \in F$. There are only two possible transitions out of q_0. Notice that one of these must be taken, since $q_0 \notin F = F_1 \cup F_2$. That is, f is

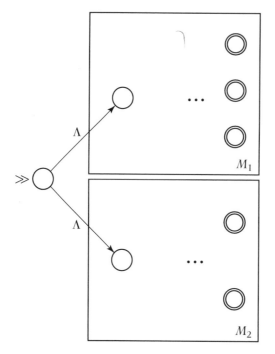

Figure 5.2

An illustration of the construction used in Theorem 5.2.2 to show that the union of two languages accepted by NFAs M_1 and M_2 is itself accepted by an NFA.

not q_0. Without loss of generality, suppose the first transition in this computation on x goes to q_1. A similar argument could be used if the computation went to q_2 instead. Then we have

$$(q_0, [1, x]) \vdash_M (q_1, [1, x]) \vdash_M^* (f, [|x| + 1, x]) \tag{5.1}$$

where $f \in F_1$. We are able to conclude that $f \in F_1$, since $Q_1 \cap Q_2 = \emptyset$. Observing that from state q_1 only transitions from Δ_1 are applicable and that

$$\Delta = \Delta_1 \cup \Delta_2 \cup \{(q_0, \Lambda, q_1), (q_0, \Lambda, q_2)\}$$

we can rewrite the second part of Equation 5.1 in terms of transitions only from M_1, as

$$(q_0, [1, x]) \vdash_M (q_1, [1, x]) \vdash_{M_1}^* (f, [|x| + 1, x]) \tag{5.2}$$

Rewriting the second part of this, we get $(q_1, [1, x]) \vdash_{M_1}^* (f, [|x| + 1, x])$, where $f \in F_1$. This means $x \in L(M_1)$. Therefore, $L(M) \subseteq L(M_1) \cup L(M_2)$.

To complete the proof, we need to show that $L(M_1) \cup L(M_2) \subseteq L(M)$. Suppose $x \in L(M_1) \cup L(M_2)$. Then $x \in L(M_1)$ or $x \in L(M_2)$. Without loss of generality, suppose $x \in L(M_1)$. A similar argument holds if $x \in L(M_2)$. Since $x \in L(M_1)$, we have $(q_1, [1, x]) \vdash^*_{M_1} (f_1, [|x| + 1, x])$ for some $f_1 \in F_1$. Since $\Delta_1 \subset \Delta$, $F_1 \subseteq F$, and $(q_0, \Lambda, q_1) \in \Delta$, we see that $(q_0, [1, x]) \vdash_M (q_1, [1, x]) \vdash^*_M (f_1, [|x| + 1, x])$ with $f_1 \in F$. Therefore, $x \in L(M)$. This shows that $L(M_1) \cup L(M_2) \subseteq L(M)$ and completes the proof. ∎

Figure 5.2 illustrates the simulation used in Theorem 5.2.2. Notice the proof would have worked equally well had M_1 and M_2 been deterministic. The end result would still have been nondeterministic though. In the proof we allowed the machines to have different alphabets Σ_1 and Σ_2. We leave it as an exercise to show that we could have assumed the machines had the same alphabets. This exercise shows that we could have also made the same assumption in the other results to follow.

5.2.3 Closure under Intersection

In our proof that the languages accepted by finite automata are closed under intersection, we begin with two DFAs.

Theorem 5.2.3 *Let $M_1 = (Q_1, \Sigma_1, \delta_1, q_1, F_1)$ and $M_2 = (Q_2, \Sigma_2, \delta_2, q_2, F_2)$ be DFAs. The language $L(M_1) \cap L(M_2)$ is accepted by a DFA. That is, the languages accepted by DFAs are closed under intersection.*

Proof: The intuitive idea behind the proof is to simulate running the two machines in parallel; that is, each machine is run independently but simultaneously on the input. If both machines accept, then the input is accepted; otherwise it is rejected. The argument given below shows how to formalize this.

Without loss of generality, we may assume that $Q_1 \cap Q_2 = \emptyset$. We define a new machine M, which simulates the parallel execution of M_1 and M_2, and then prove that $L(M) = L(M_1) \cap L(M_2)$. Define $M = (Q, \Sigma, \delta, q_0, F)$, where

$Q = Q_1 \times Q_2$

$\Sigma = \Sigma_1 \cap \Sigma_2$

$\delta = \{((p_1, p_2), a, (q_1, q_2)) \mid (p_1, a, q_1) \in \delta_1 \text{ and } (p_2, a, q_2) \in \delta_2\}$

$q_0 = (q_1, q_2)$

$F = F_1 \times F_2$

Note that the new alphabet Σ is the intersection of the two machine alphabets, since any string composed of symbols not in both alphabets cannot be in the intersection of the two languages.

In order for M to run M_1 and M_2 in parallel, it must keep track of the current state q_1 of M_1 and the current state q_2 of M_2. In general, M_1 can be in any state of

Q_1, and M_2 in any state of Q_2, so M can be in any pair of states (q_1, q_2) of $Q_1 \times Q_2$. An exercise asks you to carefully verify that M is, in fact, a DFA.

We need to prove that the simulation works. We claim that $L(M) = L(M_1) \cap L(M_2)$. Because M is deterministic, we can show this directly (rather than having to show $L(M) \subseteq L(M_1) \cap L(M_2)$ and that $L(M_1) \cap L(M_2) \subseteq L(M)$).

Suppose $x \in L(M)$. This is true if and only if

$$(q_0, [1, x]) \vdash_M^* (f, [|x| + 1, x])$$

for some $f \in F$, with $q_0 = (q_1, q_2) \in Q_1 \times Q_2$ and $f = (f_1, f_2) \in F_1 \times F_2$. But, from the definition of δ, this is true if and only if

$$(q_1, [1, x]) \vdash_{M_1}^* (f_1, [|x| + 1, x])$$

and

$$(q_2, [1, x]) \vdash_{M_2}^* (f_2, [|x| + 1, x])$$

This is true if and only if $x \in L(M_1)$ and $x \in L(M_2)$, respectively.

Therefore, $L(M) = L(M_1) \cap L(M_2)$.   ∎

5.2.4 Closure under Concatenation

Our next simulation in this section involves concatenation. In this case we begin with NFAs.

Theorem 5.2.4   *Let $M_1 = (Q_1, \Sigma_1, \Delta_1, q_1, F_1)$ and $M_2 = (Q_2, \Sigma_2, \Delta_2, q_2, F_2)$ be NFAs. The language $L(M_1) \circ L(M_2)$ is accepted by an NFA. That is, the languages accepted by NFAs are closed under concatenation.*

Proof: The idea behind this result is to run the machines serially. We build a new NFA that runs M_1 until an accepting state is reached, jumps to the initial state of M_2, and runs M_2 on the remainder of the input. The key is when to decide that it is time to switch to M_2. The proof given below shows how to implement this strategy.

Without loss of generality, we may assume that $Q_1 \cap Q_2 = \emptyset$. We define a new machine M and then prove that $L(M) = L(M_1) \circ L(M_2)$. Define $M = (Q, \Sigma, \Delta, q_1, F_2)$, where

$Q = Q_1 \cup Q_2$

$\Sigma = \Sigma_1 \cup \Sigma_2$

$\Delta = \Delta_1 \cup \Delta_2 \cup \{(f, \Lambda, q_2) \mid f \in F_1\}$

M has Λ–transitions from all of its accepting states to the initial state of M_2; this allows us to run the machines in serial. It should be clear that M is indeed

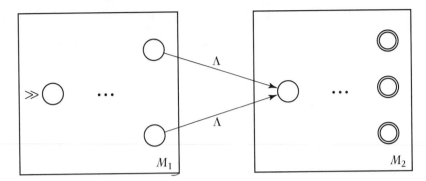

Figure 5.3

An illustration of the construction used in Theorem 5.2.4 to show that the concatenation of two languages accepted by NFAs is itself accepted by an NFA. Accepting states of M_1 are no longer accepting in M, but the accepting states of M_2 are retained.

an NFA. Figure 5.3 illustrates the transformation of M_1 and M_2 to M. Notice how M_1 and M_2 have been drawn with disjoint state sets.

We claim that $L(M) = L(M_1) \circ L(M_2)$. To show this we need to prove that $L(M) \subseteq L(M_1) \circ L(M_2)$ and that $L(M_1) \circ L(M_2) \subseteq L(M)$.

First, let's prove that $L(M) \subseteq L(M_1) \circ L(M_2)$. Suppose $x \in L(M)$, with $n = |x|$. This means $(q_1, [1, x]) \vdash_M^* (f_2, [n+1, x])$ for some $f_2 \in F$. Since $f_2 \in F_2$ and $Q_1 \cap Q_2 = \emptyset$, M must have crossed into M_2 by entering the state q_2 at some point in its computation. Let f_1 be the last state used in M_1 before entering q_2. It is clear from the definition of Δ that $f_1 \in F_1$. Let $x = x_1 x_2$, where x_2 is the remainder of the string x when M entered state q_2. We can therefore express an accepting computation of M on input x as follows:

$$
\begin{aligned}
(q_1, [1, x_1 x_2]) &\vdash_M^* & (f_1, [|x_1| + 1, x_1 x_2]) \\
&\vdash_M & (q_2, [|x_1| + 1, x_1 x_2]) \\
&\vdash_M^* & (f_2, [|x_1 x_2| + 1, x_1 x_2])
\end{aligned}
\tag{5.3}
$$

But because the input tape is one–way, and by the definition of the transition function of M from M_1 and M_2, this implies

$$(q_1, [1, x_1]) \vdash_{M_1}^* (f_1, [|x_1| + 1, x_1]) \text{ and } (q_2, [1, x_2]) \vdash_{M_2}^* (f, [|x_2| + 1, x_2])$$

This implies $x_1 \in L(M_1)$ and $x_2 \in L(M_2)$. Therefore, $x = x_1 x_2 \in L(M_1) \circ L(M_2)$, and we have shown that $L(M) \subseteq L(M_1) \circ L(M_2)$.

To complete the proof, we need to show that $L(M_1) \circ L(M_2) \subseteq L(M)$. Suppose $x \in L(M_1) \circ L(M_2)$. By the definition of concatenation, there exist x_1 and x_2 such that $x = x_1 x_2$, where $x_1 \in L(M_1)$ and $x_2 \in L(M_2)$. So, we can write

$$(q_1, [1, x_1]) \vdash^*_{M_1} (f_1, [|x_1| + 1, x_1]) \text{ and } (q_2, [1, x_2]) \vdash^*_{M_2} (f, [|x_2| + 1, x_2])$$

Since $(f_1, \Lambda, q_2) \in \Delta$, $\Delta_1 \subseteq \Delta$, and $\Delta_2 \subseteq \Delta$, it follows that

$$(q_1, [1, x]) = (q_1, [1, x_1 x_2]) \vdash^*_M (f_1, [|x_1| + 1, x_1 x_2])$$

$$\vdash_M (q_2, [|x_1| + 1, x_1 x_2])$$

$$\vdash^*_M (f_2, [|x_1 x_2| + 1, x_1 x_2]) = (f_2, [|x| + 1, x])$$

Since $f_2 \in F_2 = F$, it follows that $x \in L(M)$. This shows that $L(M_1) \circ L(M_2) \subseteq L(M)$ and completes the proof. ∎

5.2.5   Closure under Kleene Star

The final simulation presented in this section is a little trickier than the ones presented thus far.

Theorem 5.2.5   *Let $M = (Q, \Sigma, \Delta, q_0, F)$ be an NFA. The language $L(M)^*$ is accepted by an NFA. That is, the languages accepted by NFAs are closed under Kleene star.*

Proof: We begin with an NFA. Intuitively, what we need is an NFA that is allowed to concatenate copies of any accepted strings together, and then accept. We need to allow jumps from accepting states back to the initial state and also make sure we accept the empty string. Some care must be taken to make sure we do not accept any "extra" strings.

We define a new machine M^* and then prove that $L(M^*) = L(M)^*$. Let q_0' be a new state not in Q. Define $M^* = (Q', \Sigma, \Delta', q_0', F')$, where

$$Q' = Q \cup \{q_0'\}$$

$$\Delta' = \Delta \cup \{(q_0', \Lambda, q_0)\} \cup \{(f, \Lambda, q_0) \mid f \in F\}$$

$$F = F \cup \{q_0'\}$$

M^* is constructed from M by adding a new initial state that is also an accepting state, and then adding Λ-transitions from all accepting states to the old initial state, q_0. These transitions are the jumps alluded to earlier. It is clear that M^* is in fact an NFA. Figure 5.4 illustrates the transformation of M to M^* for a hypothetical machine M.

We need to prove that the simulation works. We claim that $L(M^*) = L(M)^*$. To show this, we need to prove that $L(M^*) \subseteq L(M)^*$ and that $L(M)^* \subseteq L(M^*)$.

First, we show that $L(M^*) \subseteq L(M)^*$. Suppose $x \in L(M^*)$. Then $(q_0', [1, x]) \vdash^*_{M^*} (f, [|x| + 1, x])$ for some $f \in F'$. If f equals q_0', then we must have $x = \Lambda$, and since $\Lambda \in L(M)^*$, we are done. Suppose f does not equal q_0'. Then consider any accepting computation thread on input x. Let $f_1, \ldots, f_{k-1}$ denote the states in F (in order) that M^* leaves via transitions of the form (f_i, Λ, q_0) as it processes x. Note that if $x \in L(M)$, there will be no such transitions.

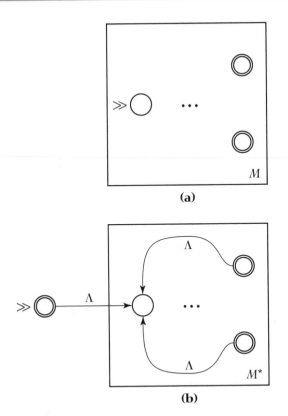

Figure 5.4

An illustration of the construction used in Theorem 5.2.5 to show that the Kleene star of a language accepted by an NFA is itself accepted by an NFA. (a) The original NFA. (b) The NFA produced by the simulation.

Let $x_1, \ldots, x_{k-1}$ denote the substrings of the input used in each case between such transitions, and let x_k denote the remainder of the input after the last such transition is executed. Note that $x = x_1 \cdots x_k$. We can rewrite the computation of M^* on input x as follows:

$$(q_0', [1, x]) \vdash_{M^*}^* (q_0, [1, x_1 x_2 \cdots x_k]) \tag{5.4}$$

$$\vdash_{M^*}^* (f_1, [|x_1| + 1, x_1 x_2 \cdots x_k])$$

$$\vdash_{M^*}^* (q_0, [|x_1| + 1, x_1 x_2 \cdots x_k])$$

$$\vdash_{M^*}^* (f_{k-1}, [|x_1 \cdots x_{k-1}| + 1, x_1 x_2 \cdots x_k])$$

$$\vdash_{M^*}^* (q_0, [|x_1 \cdots x_{k-1}| + 1, x_1 x_2 \cdots x_k])$$

$$\vdash_{M^*}^* (f_k, [|x_1 \cdots x_k| + 1, x_1 x_2 \cdots x_k])$$

From Equation 5.4, the definition of Δ', and the definition of NFAs, it follows that $(q_0, [1, x_i]) \vdash_M^* (f_i, [|x_i| + 1, x_i])$ for $1 \le i \le k$. This means $x_i \in L(M)$ for $1 \le i \le k$. Therefore, $x_1 \cdots x_k = x \in L(M)^*$. This shows that $L(M^*) \subseteq L(M)^*$.

To complete the proof, we must show that $L(M)^* \subseteq L(M^*)$. Suppose $x \in L(M)^*$. If x equals Λ, clearly $x \in L(M^*)$, since q_0' is an accepting state. If x does not equal Λ, by the definition of Kleene star (see page 34), $x = x_1 \cdots x_k$ for some k greater than 0, and $x_i \in L(M)$ for $1 \le i \le k$. That is, there exist $f_1, \ldots, f_k \in F$ such that $(q_0, [1, x_i]) \vdash_M^* (f_i, [|x_i| + 1, x_i])$ for $1 \le i \le k$. Using the definition of Δ' and that of NFAs, we can write the same computation as given in Equation 5.4 for M^*. This implies $x \in L(M^*)$, since f_k is also an accepting state of M^*. Therefore, $L(M)^* \subseteq L(M^*)$, and the proof is complete: ∎

We summarize the results proved in this section and in Exercise 24 with the following corollary.

Corollary 5.2.6   *The language classes $\mathcal{L}_{\mathbf{DFA}}$ and $\mathcal{L}_{\mathbf{NFA}}$ are closed under the operations of union, concatenation, Kleene star, intersection, complementation, and reversal.*

Proof: Combining Theorems 5.2.1–5.2.5 and Exercise 24 with the result that $\mathcal{L}_{\mathbf{DFA}}$ equals $\mathcal{L}_{\mathbf{NFA}}$, the result follows. ∎

We have provided a number of exercises concerning Theorems 5.2.1–5.2.5, but you should practice combining various finite automata until the techniques of this section have been fully mastered. After carrying out one of the constructions given in this section in a specific case, test the result on some sample input strings to make sure the resulting machine behaves as desired. This is one way to be confident that the construction was carried out correctly.

Theorems 5.2.1–5.2.5 are useful for designing finite automata using a divide-and-conquer strategy. That is, it is often helpful to split a language up into several component languages, build machines for each component, and then combine them using Theorems 5.2.1–5.2.5. This technique of splitting a problem up into subproblems that are easier to solve is a theme that runs throughout computer science.

5.3   *Equivalence of Regular Expressions and Finite Automata*

The main result of this section is that the language class $\mathcal{L}_{\mathbf{RE}}$ is equal to the language class $\mathcal{L}_{\mathbf{DFA}}$, which we know equals $\mathcal{L}_{\mathbf{NFA}}$. The result is expressed in the following theorem.

Theorem 5.3.1   *The class of languages represented by regular expressions is equal to the class of languages accepted by finite automata. That is,*

$$\mathcal{L}_{\mathbf{RE}} = \mathcal{L}_{\mathbf{DFA}} = \mathcal{L}_{\mathbf{NFA}}$$

Proof: Each half of this theorem requires some work in order to prove. Theorem 5.3.2 shows that $\mathcal{L}_{\mathbf{RE}} \subseteq \mathcal{L}_{\mathbf{NFA}}$ by inductively constructing an NFA to accept the language represented by a given regular expression. Theorem 5.3.4 proves that $\mathcal{L}_{\mathbf{DFA}} \subseteq \mathcal{L}_{\mathbf{RE}}$. In the proof, a new variant of the finite automaton is introduced, where we allow regular expressions to label transitions. We provide an algorithm that takes as input one of these new finite automata and builds a regular expression to represent it.   ∎

Let's begin by proving that every language represented by a regular expression can be accepted by a finite automaton.

Theorem 5.3.2   *If L is a language that is represented by a regular expression R, then $L \in \mathcal{L}_{\mathbf{NFA}}$.*

Proof: Let R be an arbitrary standard regular expression (as per Definition 3.3.1) over an alphabet Σ. The key idea is to use the methods developed in the last section concerning $\cup$, $*$, and $\circ$ to build an NFA M that accepts the same language as R represents. The construction of M will mirror the structure of R. The proof is constructive, and we split it into several cases according to the form of R. In each case we inductively build an NFA M such that $L(M) = L(R)$.

Suppose, for induction, that for all regular expressions R' that are shorter than R, there exists an NFA M' such that $L(M') = L(R')$. We now consider the structure of R, and construct an M such that $L(M) = L(R)$.

1. Case $R = (\ )$.
   Let $M = (\{q_0\}, \Sigma, \emptyset, q_0, \emptyset)$. It is clear that M is an NFA and that $L(M) = \emptyset$. Therefore, $L(R) = \emptyset = L(M)$.

2. Case $R = \sigma$ for some $\sigma \in \Sigma$.
   Let $M = (\{q_0, q_1\}, \Sigma, \{(q_0, \sigma, q_1)\}, q_0, \{q_1\})$. It is clear that M is an NFA and that $L(M) = \{\sigma\}$. Therefore, $L(R) = \{\sigma\} = L(M)$.

3. Case $R = (R_1 | R_2)$. Then (by Definition 3.3.2) $L(R) = L(R_1) \cup L(R_2)$.
   Since R_1 and R_2 are shorter than R, by the induction hypothesis, there are NFAs M_1 and M_2 such that $L(M_1) = L(R_1)$ and $L(M_2) = L(R_2)$. Using Theorem 5.2.2, form M such that $L(M) = L(M_1) \cup L(M_2) = L(R)$.

4. Case $R = (R_1 R_2)$. Then $L(R) = L(R_1) \circ L(R_2)$.
   Since R_1 and R_2 are shorter than R, by the induction hypothesis, there are NFAs M_1 and M_2 such that $L(M_1) = L(R_1)$ and $L(M_2) = L(R_2)$. Using Theorem 5.2.4, form M such that $L(M) = L(M_1) \circ L(M_2) = L(R)$.

5. Case $R = R_1*$. Then $L(R) = L(R_1)^*$.
   Since R_1 is shorter than R, by the induction hypothesis, there is an NFA M_1 such that $L(M_1) = L(R_1)$. Using Theorem 5.2.5, form M such that $L(M) = L(M_1)^* = L(R)$.

Thus the NFA M constructed by the procedure described above satisfies $L(M) = L(R)$. ■

Note that, since regular expressions and regular constructions are equivalent (by Observation 3.3.4), we could have done a similar proof but using regular constructions instead. The reason for working with regular expressions is that the process of transforming a regular expression into an NFA illustrates the process of compiling a language into a machine.

To convert a regular expression R into an NFA, you start with the smallest components of R and build up the NFA as in the proof. We present an example below.

Example 5.3.3   How to construct an NFA accepting the language represented by a regular expression

Consider the following regular expression:

$R = (0*(0 \mid (11)))$

which is, of course, equivalent to the regular construction $0^*(0 \cup 11)$. There are four operations in this regular expression as well as two symbols. Figure 5.5 illustrates how Theorem 5.3.2 can be applied to construct an NFA for accepting $L(R)$.

In Figure 5.5 (b), two simple machines are formed via the method explained in the base case of Theorem 5.3.2. For example, the machine to accept the language $\{0\}$ is simply $(\{q_0, q_1\}, \{0, 1\}, \{(q_0, 0, q_1)\}, q_0, \{q_1\})$. The machine to accept the language $\{1\}$ is similar.

In Figure 5.5 (c), the construction of Theorem 5.2.4 is applied to two separate copies of the machine for accepting the language $\{1\}$. The construction keeps the initial state of the first machine and adds Λ–transitions from any accepting states in the first machine to the initial state of the second machine. The accepting states of the new machine are exactly those from the second machine. It is easy to see that the resulting machine accepts the language $\{11\}$, that is, the concatenation of the language $\{1\}$ with itself.

In Figure 5.5 (d), the construction of Theorem 5.2.5 is applied to the machine accepting the language $\{0\}$ to obtain a machine that accepts $\{0\}^*$. A new initial state is added that is also an accepting state, and from all old accepting states (of which there is one), Λ–transitions are added to the old initial state. It should be clear that the resulting machine accepts the regular language 0^*.

In Figure 5.5 (e), the construction of Theorem 5.2.2 is applied to the machines accepting the languages $\{0\}$ and $\{11\}$. A new initial state is added, as are Λ–transitions from this state to each of the initial states of the two machines being combined. The accepting states of the submachines are left as accepting states in the new machine. The new machine accepts the language $\{0, 11\}$.

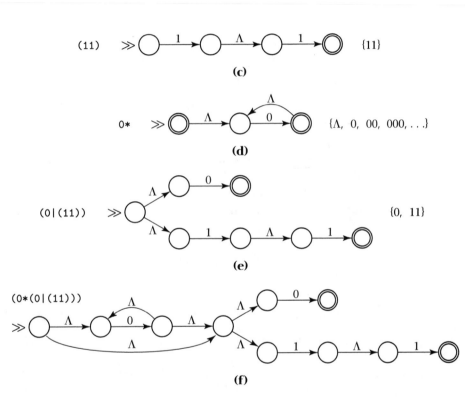

Figure 5.5

An illustration of how to convert a regular expression into an NFA that accepts the same language as the regular expression represents. (a) The original regular expression, R. (b) The base case of Theorem 5.3.2 is applied to R. (c) A concatenation construction. (d) A Kleene star construction. (e) A union construction. (f) The final NFA, a concatenation of the submachines given in (d) and (e). The procedure for building the machines is discussed further in Example 5.3.3.

In Figure 5.5 (f), the two submachines shown in (d) and (e) are combined, using another application of Theorem 5.2.4. The resulting machine accepts the language represented by R.

The construction is easy to apply and completely general purpose. The trade-off is that it does not yield a minimal NFA for $L(R)$. An inspection of Figure 5.5 (f) reveals a number of states that could easily be eliminated.   ∎

In the exercises we ask you to construct NFAs for several regular expressions by applying the method of Theorem 5.3.2. Although in some cases ad hoc techniques may be used successfully to design an NFA from scratch for a given regular expression, we prefer that you learn and practice the general method.

To complete the second part of Theorem 5.3.1, we need to prove the following result. Our proof is based on that given by Derick Wood [46].

Theorem 5.3.4   *If L is a language that is accepted by a DFA M, then $L \in \mathcal{L}_{\mathbf{RE}}$.*

Proof: There are two key steps in the proof. The first is to show that every language accepted by a DFA can be accepted by a new variant of the finite automaton, called an *extended finite automaton* (EFA). In an EFA, regular expressions are allowed to label transitions. The second step is to design an algorithmic procedure for eliminating states from EFAs until we are left with just two states: an initial state and an accepting state. The regular expression labeling the transition between these two states is the desired regular expression representing the original language. The proof given below formalizes these steps.

Let's begin by defining the EFA model of computation as proposed by Wood.

Definition 5.3.5   *An **extended finite automaton (EFA)** is a five-tuple*

$$M = (Q, \Sigma, \delta, q_0, \{f\})$$

that is defined similarly to a DFA except for the specification of the transitions, the fact that there is only a single accepting state f, and the requirement that the accepting state is not the same as the initial state. Let R_Σ represent the set of all regular expressions over the alphabet Σ. The transition function δ is a total function mapping from $Q \times Q$ to R_Σ.

The main difference between an EFA and a DFA is that the transitions in the EFA can be labeled by arbitrary regular expressions over Σ instead of just single characters. If $\delta(q, q') = R'$ is a transition in an EFA, then R' is a regular expression representing *all* labels that permit the machine to make a transition from state q to state q'. For example, if $\delta(q, q') = 0*$, then on Λ or any string of 0's the machine can move from state q to q'. Such transitions allow the EFA to exhibit nondeterministic behavior even though the transitions are defined by a function.

The restriction of EFAs to a single accepting state is not a serious restriction since for every NFA N possessing more than one accepting state there is an equivalent single accepting state NFA N' such that $L(N) = L(N')$.

```
begin
    let M = (Q, Σ, δ, q_0, {f}) be an EFA;
    while |Q| > 2 do
        pick a state q ∈ Q − {q_0, f};
        R_2 ← δ(q, q);
        for each pair of states p and r do
            R_1 ← δ(p, q);
            R_3 ← δ(q, r);
            comment: add transition δ(p, r) = (R_1(R_2*R_3)) to δ
            δ ← δ ∪ {(p, r, (R_1(R_2*R_3)))};
        Q ← Q − {q};
        comment: remove all transitions from δ involving q
        δ ← δ restricted to Q;
    output the value of δ(q_0, f);
end
```

Figure 5.6

High–level code for converting an EFA into a two–state EFA whose only transition is labeled by a regular expression R representing the language of the original EFA M. The code is discussed in Theorem 5.3.4 and Example 5.3.6.

Other concepts defined for DFAs in Chapter 4 can be extended in natural ways to EFAs.

It is a simple exercise to show that, given any DFA, there is an equivalent EFA. This really amounts to converting the DFA into an NFA having only a single accepting state f and then viewing the labels on the transitions in this NFA as being regular expressions. For example, a Λ–transition would be labeled by the regular expression ( )* in the EFA. Furthermore, without loss of generality, we may assume that there are no transitions into state q_0 and no transitions out of state f.

Let $M' = (Q', \Sigma, \delta', q_0, F')$ be a DFA. The first step in the construction is to build an equivalent EFA $M = (Q, \Sigma, \delta, q_0, \{f\})$, where q_0 is different than f. This can be accomplished as discussed above.

The second step in the process of constructing an equivalent regular expression is to eliminate states from Q one at a time until there are only two states left, namely q_0 and f. The desired regular expression is the one labeling the transition from q_0 to f. When a state is removed during this elimination process, the transitions need to be changed accordingly to reflect this. Each time a state is removed, the machine is updated so that the new machine accepts the same language as the old one.

Figure 5.6 depicts the high–level code for implementing the procedure just described. We are interested in removing states from Q until only q_0 and f are left. The **while** loop runs until we reach this situation. When a state q is eliminated

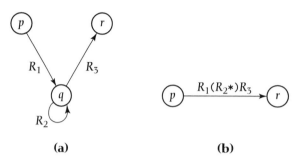

(a)   (b)

Figure 5.7

An illustration of how eliminated states are shortcut in the proof of Theorem 5.3.4. (a) The original situation, with transitions passing through state q. (b) Replacing these transitions by an equivalent, direct transition from state p to state r.

from Q, the code specifies that any transitions involving q are "shortcut." That is, if we could go from state p to state q on a string in R_1, "spin" in state q on strings in R_2, and then go from state q to state r on a string in R_3, we can concatenate these transition labels and go directly from p to r. In this case the algorithm adds the transition $\delta(p,r) = (R_1(R_2*R_3))$ to δ. When this process has been carried out for all possible pairs of states p and r, then all transitions involving q are removed by restricting δ to $Q - \{q\}$; that is, q is deleted from Q. Figure 5.7 illustrates this elimination procedure.

It is clear that when the algorithm terminates, only states q_0 and f are left in Q. Additionally, by our assumption that there were no transitions into state q_0 and no transitions out of f, at the termination point there is only one transition left, namely the one from state q_0 to f. Let M_i, for $1 \leq i \leq |Q| - 2$, represent the EFA formed during completion of the ith iteration of the **while** loop. An easy induction proof can be used to show that

$$L(M) = L(M_1) = \cdots = L(M_{|Q|-2}) \tag{5.5}$$

Since there is only one transition in $M_{|Q|-2}$ and it is labeled by $\delta(q_0, f)$, it is clear that $L(M_{|Q|-2}) = L(\delta(q_0, f))$. That is, the language of $M_{|Q|-2}$ consists of all strings represented by the regular expression labeling its transition from the initial state to the accepting state. By Equation 5.5, this language is the same as $L(M)$. Therefore, the regular expression $\delta(q_0, f)$ represents $L(M)$. Since $L(M') = L(M)$, this means we have successfully constructed a regular expression to represent the language of the original DFA M'. ∎

Let's look at an example of how Theorem 5.3.4 is applied.

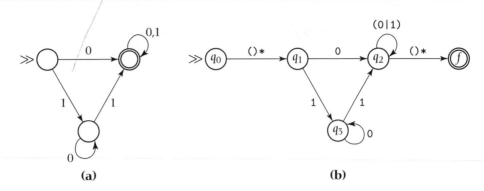

(a)   **(b)**

Figure 5.8

(a) The sample DFA used in Example 5.3.6. (b) The conversion of the DFA into an EFA; the algorithm shown in Figure 5.6 can be applied directly to this EFA.

Example 5.3.6   How to construct a regular expression representing the language accepted by a DFA

Figure 5.8 (a) shows a picture of a DFA whose language we would like to determine a regular expression for. Figure 5.8 (b) shows how we can convert this machine to an equivalent EFA in which there are no transitions into the initial state, no transitions out of the accepting state, and a single accepting state. Notice that transitions on ( ) are not shown. For example, $\delta(q_0, q_3) = (\ )$, which merely indicates that we cannot make a transition from state q_0 to state q_3.

The algorithm given in Figure 5.6 does not specify an order in which states must be eliminated from the EFA. Oftentimes it is easier to carry out the construction if the states having the fewest number of incoming and outgoing edges are selected for removal first. For illustration purposes in this case, we will remove states in the order q_2, q_3, and q_1. If another order is selected, usually a different regular expression will be produced. However, the regular expressions produced by various elimination orders are equivalent.

Figure 5.9 illustrates what happens when we remove state q_2. When we consider all possible pairs of states that have a path going through state q_2, only the paths involving states q_1, q_2, and f, and states q_3, q_2, and f, play an important role. Other paths, such as q_0, q_2, and f, involve at least one transition that is labeled by ( ). When this label gets concatenated with other labels, the resulting transition is also labeled with ( ). Thus we only need to consider pairs of states in which both labels are different than ( ).

Let's consider the path involving states q_1, q_2, and f. We can go from state q_1 to q_2 on reading a 0. Because $\delta(q_2, q_2) = (0|1)$, we can remain in state q_2 while reading any combination of 0's and 1's. From q_2 we can then go to state f using a Λ-transition. The result of this path means, in going from state q_1 to state f, we

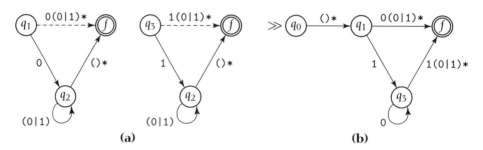

(a) **(b)**

Figure 5.9

(a) The two paths through state q_2 that need to be shortcut. (b) The new EFA after state q_2 has been eliminated.

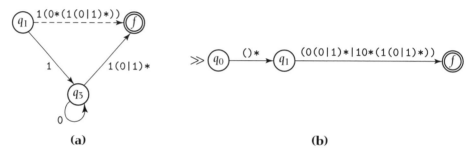

(a) **(b)**

Figure 5.10

(a) The path through state q_3 that needs to be shortcut. (b) The new EFA after state q_3 has been eliminated.

could read a 0 followed by any combination of 0's and 1's. A regular expression representing such patterns is $(0(0|1)*)$. In Figure 5.9 (a), we illustrate this bypass of state q_2 with a dotted line. A similar process is used to go directly from state q_3 to f without going through state q_2. In this case the resulting transition is $\delta(q_3, f) = (1(0|1)*)$. Figure 5.9 (b) shows the result of removing state q_2 and its associated transitions, and then adding in the two bypass transitions.

Figure 5.10 illustrates what happens when we remove state q_3. In this case there is only one path to consider; it goes from state q_1 to q_3 to f. Figure 5.10 (b) shows the new equivalent EFA once state q_3 has been eliminated. Notice how the 0–transition on state q_3 is incorporated within the regular expression as $0*$.

Now the modified EFA just has three states, so only state q_1 still needs to be removed. Figure 5.11 illustrates what happens when it is eliminated. The final regular expression that represents the same language as the original DFA shown

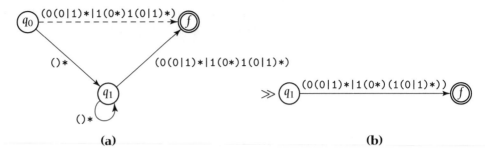

(a)   **(b)**

Figure 5.11

(a) The path through state q_1 that needs to be shortcut. (b) A two–state EFA whose only transition is labeled by a regular expression that represents the same language as the original DFA in Figure 5.8 accepts.

in Figure 5.8 (a) accepts is the label on the transition from state q_0 to state f. In this case it is

$$((0(0|1)*)|(1(0*(1(0|1)*))))$$

This expression does indeed capture the language accepted by the DFA of Figure 5.8. ∎

In the exercises we ask you to find regular expressions for various DFAs using the method of Theorem 5.3.4. Although in some cases ad hoc techniques may be used successfully to find a regular expression from scratch for a given DFA, we prefer that you learn and practice the general method for doing this. Because the method does no optimization, many of the regular expressions formed by using this technique are not as short as possible.

As an immediate corollary of Theorem 5.3.1, we obtain the following result.

Corollary 5.3.7 $\mathcal{L}_{\textbf{DFA}} = \mathcal{L}_{\textbf{NFA}} = \mathcal{L}_{\textbf{RE}} = \mathcal{L}_{\textbf{EFA}}$

Proof: Theorem 5.3.4 shows that $\mathcal{L}_{\textbf{EFA}} \subseteq \mathcal{L}_{\textbf{RE}}$, and Theorem 5.3.2 shows that $\mathcal{L}_{\textbf{RE}} \subseteq \mathcal{L}_{\textbf{NFA}} = \mathcal{L}_{\textbf{DFA}}$. One of the exercises requires the straightforward proof that $\mathcal{L}_{\textbf{DFA}} \subseteq \mathcal{L}_{\textbf{EFA}}$. The resulting circle of inclusions implies that all four classes are equal. ∎

As a second corollary we obtain the following result involving closure properties of EFAs and regular languages. Remember that a language is a regular language if and only if it can be represented by a regular expression (see Observation 3.3.4).

Corollary 5.3.8 $\mathcal{L}_{DFA} = \mathcal{L}_{NFA} = \mathcal{L}_{RE} = \mathcal{L}_{EFA}$ *are closed under the operations of union, concatenation, Kleene star, intersection, and complementation.*

Proof: The result follows from Corollaries 5.2.6 and 5.3.7.   ∎

Now we have four formalisms for describing the regular languages: DFAs, NFAs, EFAs, and regular expressions. A fifth representation, *regular grammars*, is described in Chapter 7. All of these computational models can be used for proving that a language is regular. The techniques described thus far are valuable because they suggest a natural divide–and–conquer strategy for showing a language is regular. However, we do not have any method for demonstrating that a language is *not* regular. In the next section we remedy this situation by proving the Pumping Lemma.

5.4   *Pumping Lemma for Regular Languages*

In this section we cover one of the fundamental tools for proving that a language is *not* regular. The method is contained in a lemma known as the *Pumping Lemma*. There are many versions of this lemma, and we present two: a simple straightforward form, and a more useful general form. Another variant, sometimes referred to as the *Strong Pumping Lemma*, appears in the exercises. Let's begin with some observations about regular languages.

Recall that any regular language can be represented by each of the following formalisms: a DFA, an NFA, an EFA, or a regular expression. If L is any finite language, then L is regular. Why? Because, for example, we could produce an NFA having $|L|$ transitions, with each labeled by a different string in L.

But when L is an infinite language, it must contain arbitrarily long strings. Our intuition would tell us that, in general, the longer a string x is, the more memory it will take to determine if $x \in L$. Since DFAs have only a constant amount of memory, they would not be able to process long strings unless the strings had some kind of repeated patterns that a DFA could detect independent of the length of the string. So any DFA that accepts L must have cycles that detect repeated patterns in the strings of L. Similarly, any regular expression that generates L must have a pattern enclosed in an $*$.

The leads us to suspect that any infinite regular language must contain long strings that have some type of simple repetitive patterns in them. This fact is captured by the Pumping Lemma.

The interesting thing about the Pumping Lemma is that, although it is a statement about the patterns that any infinite regular language must have, its main application is to show that an infinite language cannot be regular. Since every regular language must satisfy the Pumping Lemma, to show that a language L is not regular we need only demonstrate some feature of L that contradicts the lemma. We begin by proving a simple version of the Pumping Lemma that is, in practice, a bit inconvenient to use.

Lemma 5.4.1   (Basic Pumping Lemma)   *Suppose L is an infinite regular language. Then there exist strings x, y, and z satisfying the following properties:*

1. *$y \neq \Lambda$ and*
2. *$xy^n z \in L$ for all $n \in \mathbb{N}$.*

Proof: The intuitive idea behind the proof is that a DFA, which has a fixed number of states, in processing a very long input must repeat some state during its computation. The string represented by the concatenation of the labels on the transitions that are applied during this loop is the string y that can be repeated any number of times. We now formalize this intuition.

Since L is a regular language, by Theorem 5.3.1 there exists a DFA $M = (Q, \Sigma, \delta, q_0, F)$ such that $L(M) = L$. Any sufficiently long string w will do. We will consider the computation of M on a "long" string and show that M's transition diagram must contain a cycle whose edge labels concatenated together form the desired string y.

Suppose $|Q| = k$. Since L is an infinite language, there exists a string $w = w(1) \cdots w(m)$ such that $|w| = m \geq k$, $w \in L(M)$. Consider the computation of M on input w. Instead of writing it as a sequence of configurations, we will write it as a sequence of transitions, with each transition labeled with the input symbol that triggered the transition.

$$q_0 \xrightarrow{w(1)} q_1 \xrightarrow{w(2)} q_2 \xrightarrow{w(3)} \cdots \xrightarrow{w(m-1)} q_{m-1} \xrightarrow{w(m)} q_m$$

where $q_1, \ldots, q_{m-1} \in Q$ and $q_m \in F$.

Since $|w| = m \geq k = |Q|$, the Pigeonhole Principle implies there exist natural numbers i and j such that $0 \leq i < j \leq m$ and q_i equals q_j. For these i and j we have

$$q_i \xrightarrow{w(i+1)} \cdots \xrightarrow{w(j-1)} q_{j-1} \xrightarrow{w(j)} q_j = q_i$$

Since $i + 1 \leq j$, the length of $w(i + 1) \cdots w(j)$ is greater than or equal to 1. Let $y = w(i + 1) \cdots w(j)$. Notice that y could be deleted from w or additional copies of y could be inserted, and M would still accept the new string. That is,

$$w(1) \cdots w(i) \circ y^n \circ w(j + 1) \cdots w(m) \in L(M)$$

for each $n \in \mathbb{N}$. Taking $x = w(1) \cdots w(i)$ and $z = w(j + 1) \cdots w(m)$, we have $xy^n z \in L(M) = L$ for all $n \in \mathbb{N}$. Since $y = w(j + 1) \cdots w(m) \neq \Lambda$, the proof is complete.   ∎

You may have noticed some similarities between this proof and the one in Section 1.1.4 where we argued that no C-- program could be devised to accept the language consisting of strings having an equal number of a's and b's. The two

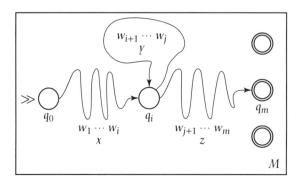

Figure 5.12

An illustration of the strings x, y, and z in the Pumping Lemma. The loop on state q_i labeled y may be repeated any number of times given the appropriate input. For example, on xy^0z it is used zero times, on xy^1z once, on xy^2z twice, and so on.

arguments are essentially the same, except for the difference in computational models.

Inspecting the proof of the Basic Pumping Lemma reveals that we can actually say more. The pigeonhole argument will work for any sufficiently long *substring* of the string in L. This lets us have finer control on what part of the string actually gets pumped, where "pumping" refers to replacing y with y^n for some $n \in \mathbb{N}$. This gives us the General Pumping Lemma:

Lemma 5.4.2 (General Pumping Lemma) *Suppose that L is an infinite regular language. Then there exists a constant $k > 0$ such that the following holds: Take any string $w \in L$ with $|w| > k$. Pick any two positions i, j in w such that $0 < i$ and $i + k < j \leq |w|$. Then there exist strings x, y, z such that*

1. $w = xyz$,

2. $i \leq |x|$, *that is, position i is in string x,*

3. $0 < |y| \leq k$,

4. $|xy| < j$, *that is, position j is in string z,*

5. $xy^nz \in L$ *for all $n \in \mathbb{N}$.*

Figure 5.12 provides an illustration of the Pumping Lemma. The picture shows that the loop, whose edge labels concatenated together yield y, can be skipped entirely or repeated any number of times and the corresponding input will be accepted.

In the next section we show how the Pumping Lemma is applied to prove a language is not regular. This gives us our first technique for showing that a language is not in a specific language class.

<table>
</table>

5.5	*Applications of the Pumping Lemma*

In this section our goal is to help you develop an intuition for recognizing nonregular languages and then to illustrate how to apply the Pumping Lemma to formally prove this intuition is correct. This is best done via examples. First, we consider some positive examples of some familiar infinite regular languages and see that appropriate x, y, and z exist as specified in the Pumping Lemma.

Example 5.5.1   Positive applications of the Pumping Lemma

1. Consider the language $L = \{\Lambda, 0, 00, \ldots\}$ over the alphabet $\{0, 1\}$. L is represented by the regular construction 0^* and so is regular. Furthermore, L is infinite. Therefore, the Pumping Lemma applies. The Pumping Lemma states that there exist three strings x, y, and z such that $xy^nz \in L$ for all $n \in \mathbb{N}$. Where do these strings come from? We must do two things. First we need a DFA M with $L(M) = L$. The one shown in Figure 5.13 will do. Then we need a string from L at least as long as $|Q|$. Take 000, for example. Next we have to trace the execution of M as it accepts 000. In general, we will have many possible points where a state is repeated. In this case, picking one, we obtain $x = 0$, $y = 0$, and $z = \Lambda$. We see that $y \neq \Lambda$ and that $xy^nz = 00^n \in L$ for all $n \in \mathbb{N}$.

2. Consider the infinite regular language $L = (01)^*$ accepted by the DFA shown in Figure 5.14. Choosing $w = 010101$, we can have the splitting $x = 0$, $y = 1010$, and $z = 1$, among others. Note that, although choosing $y = 01$ would also satisfy the conditions of the Pumping Lemma, such a y could not be obtained from the DFA we used. ■

In general, positive aspects of the Pumping Lemma are not all that useful. Just because we have a language L and strings x, y, and z satisfying the conditions of the Pumping Lemma, we *cannot* conclude that L is a regular language. That is, the

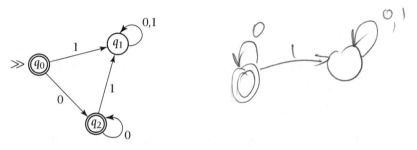

Figure 5.13

A DFA for accepting the regular language 0^*.

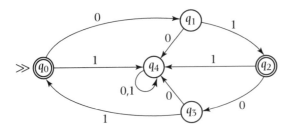

Figure 5.14

A DFA for accepting the regular language $(01)^*$.

converse of the Pumping Lemma is not true. The lemma specifies a property of all infinite regular languages, but other infinite languages, which are not regular, may also have this property.

The real purpose of the Pumping Lemma is for proving that languages are *not* regular.

Example 5.5.2 Applications of the Pumping Lemma to prove a language is not regular

1. $L = \{0^i 1^i \mid i \geq 0\}$ is nonregular.

   Proof: It is clear that L is infinite. We proceed via a proof by contradiction.

   Suppose L is regular. Since L is infinite and by assumption regular, the General Pumping Lemma applies. First, let k be given to us by the lemma. Now choose string $w = 0^{3k} 1^{3k}$. We have $w \in L$, and also long enough that we can pick position $i = 3k + 1$ and $j = 3k + k + 2$, so that $i + k < j$ as required by the lemma.

   Then there exist strings x, y, z so that $w = xyz$, $0 < |y|$, position i is in x, and position j is in z. Our choice of i and j means that y consists only of 1's.

   Choose $n = 0$ in the last condition of the Pumping Lemma, so that $xz \in L$. So xz has $3k - |y|$ 1's in it. But xz still has $3k$ 0's. So xz cannot be in L.

   This contradiction means that our only assumption, that L is regular, must be false.   ■

2. $L = \{0^i \mid$ where i is a prime number$\}$.

   Proof: Since the number of primes is infinite, so is L. We suppose that L is regular and proceed via a proof by contradiction.

   Since L is infinite and regular, the General Pumping Lemma applies. First, let k be given to us by the lemma. Now pick any prime $p > k + 1$ and

}

1. Suppose the infinite language under consideration is regular.

2. Introduce the fixed, but unknown, k from the lemma.

3. Select a string w from L that has a substring that when pumped will violate the conditions for membership in L. Make sure that w is long enough to allow the selecting of the positions i and j such that $i + k < j$.

4. Consider *all possible* forms of strings x, y, and z that satisfy the conditions of the Pumping Lemma.

5. Examine the different possible forms for y^n. Do not forget the possibility of choosing $n = 0$ and deflating w.

6. Derive a contradiction.

7. Conclude that the given infinite language is not regular.

Figure 5.15

A high–level summary of the steps involved in a proof using the General Pumping Lemma.

choose string $w = 0^p$. We have $w \in L$. Pick positions $i = 1, j = |w|$, so we have $i + k < j$. We do not need these positions in our argument below.

Then there exist strings x, y, z so that $w = xyz$. Note that $x = 0^q$, $y = 0^r$, $z = 0^s$ for some $q, r, s \in \mathbb{N}$, and $0 < r$. Choose $n = p + 1$ in the last condition of the Pumping Lemma, so that $xy^{p+1}z \in L$. That is, $0^q 0^{(p+1)r} 0^s \in L$.

But $q + (p + 1)r + s = p(r + 1)$ is not a prime number, so $xy^{p+1}z \notin L$. This contradiction means that our only assumption, that L is regular, must be false. ∎

One of the beauties of the Pumping Lemma is that its applications have basically the same structure. Pick a target string in L and isolate a section of it that when pumped will violate the definition of L. We summarize the steps required for such a proof in Figure 5.15.

We should caution that the Pumping Lemmas are not always applicable to every nonregular language. The next section presents some alternative methods for showing nonregularity.

5.6   *Using Closure Properties to Deduce That a Language Is Nonregular*

In this section we use closure properties as an alternative strategy to show that certain languages are nonregular. This contrasts with the way we used closure properties earlier in the chapter; there we explained how they could be employed using a divide–and–conquer strategy for proving that certain languages *are* regular. How can we use them to show that languages are not regular? Suppose $L = L_1 \cup L_2$. If L is a language that we know is *not* regular and L_2 is a language that we know *is* regular, then it follows that L_1 is *not* regular. Why? Since regular languages are closed under union, if both L_1 and L_2 were regular, then it would follow that L is also regular. This methodology can be applied quite generally, and below we look at several examples. Most frequently, closure under intersection is used in such proofs.

Example 5.6.1   Applications of closure properties to prove some languages are not regular

1. The language $L = \{w \mid \#_0(w) = \#_1(w)\}$ is not regular. Suppose L is regular for contradiction. Then $L \cap 0^*1^*$ is a regular language, since 0^*1^* is regular and by Corollary 5.3.8 the regular languages are closed under intersection. But $L \cap 0^*1^* = \{0^i1^i \mid i \geq 0\}$, which was earlier proved to be nonregular. This gives the desired contradiction and shows L is not regular.

   You might wonder (as former student Chad Boucher did) where the 0^*1^* came from. That is, why did we pick this and not some other regular language? In general, when using the intersection operation to obtain a contradiction in this style, we need to work towards a language that is already known to be nonregular or can easily be shown to be nonregular (see case 3 below).

2. The language $L = \{0, 1\}^* - \{0^i1^i \mid i \geq 0\}$ is not regular. Suppose L is regular for contradiction. Then the complement of L, $\bar{L}$, is regular by Corollary 5.3.8. But $\bar{L} = \{0^i1^i \mid i \geq 0\}$, which is not regular. This contradicts the assumption that L was regular.

3. The language $L = \{xx \mid x \in \{0, 1\}^*\}$ is not regular. Suppose L is regular for contradiction. Then $L \cap 0^*10^*1$ is regular, since 0^*10^*1 is regular and by Corollary 5.3.8 the regular languages are closed under intersection. Let

$$L' = L \cap 0^*10^*1 = \{0^i10^i1 \mid i \geq 0\}$$

It is not hard to prove that L' is nonregular using the Strong Pumping Lemma (see Exercise 30). This contradicts the assumption that L was regular.

5.7   *Exercises*

Section 5.2   *Machines for Five Language Operations*

1. Construct a DFA M to accept the language L represented by 0^* over the alphabet $\Sigma = \{0, 1\}$. Apply the construction of Theorem 5.2.1 to produce a new machine $\bar{M}$. What language does $\bar{M}$ accept? Trace your machine on an input that is accepted and also on one that is rejected.

2. Construct a DFA to accept the language

   $$L = \{x \mid x \text{ does not contain the pattern } 01001 \text{ and } L \subseteq \{0, 1\}^*\}$$

Trace your machine on an input that is accepted and also on one that is rejected.

3. Fully specify an NFA M and show explicitly that the construction used to prove Theorem 5.2.1 does not apply. That is, apply the construction but show $L(\overline{M})$ does not equal $\overline{L(M)}$. Does this mean the languages accepted by NFAs are not closed under complement?

4. Construct an NFA that is not a DFA and show that the construction given in Theorem 5.2.1 works for your NFA.

5. Design a constructive method to prove that the complement of the language accepted by an NFA is accepted by a DFA.

6. Given two NFAs M_1 and M_2 with state sets Q_1 and Q_2, respectively, show that if Q_1 and Q_2 have states in common, then Theorem 5.2.2 does not necessarily work. This illustrates why we need the first sentence in the proof of Theorem 5.2.2.

7. Given two NFAs M_1 and M_2, how is it possible to view them over the same alphabet? For example, in Theorem 5.2.2, say we would like to use one alphabet. What should the alphabet be? How does this affect the other components of the machines? What about for DFAs?

8. Show that the language $0^* \cup 1^*$ is accepted by an NFA. Use the construction from Theorem 5.2.2. Trace your machine on an input that is accepted and also on one that is rejected.

9. Show that the language $(01)^* \cup \{x \mid x$ does not contain the pattern $010\}$ is accepted by an NFA. Trace your machine on an input that is accepted and also on one that is rejected.

10. Design a DFA to accept the language

$$L = \{x \mid x \text{ does not contain the pattern } 011 \text{ or } |x| < 3\}$$

where $L \subseteq \{0, 1\}^*$. Trace your machine on an input that is accepted and also on one that is rejected.

11. If M_1 and M_2 in Theorem 5.2.2 are deterministic and the construction given in the theorem is applied, followed by subset construction to obtain a DFA, how much larger can the resulting DFA be?

12. Prove that the machine M defined in Theorem 5.2.3 is in fact a DFA.

13. In the proof of Theorem 5.2.3, could NFAs M_1 and M_2 have been used? Explain your answer. How about a DFA and an NFA?

14. Design a DFA to accept the language

$$L = \{x \mid x \text{ contains the pattern } 011 \text{ and } |x| > 5\}$$

where $L \subseteq \{0, 1\}^*$. Trace your machine on an input that is accepted and also on one that is rejected.

15. Let $\Sigma = \{0, 1\}^*$. Design a DFA to accept the language

$$L = \{x \mid \#_0(x) \text{ is even, and } x \text{ represents a binary number divisible by 3}\}$$

Trace your machine on an input that is accepted and also on one that is rejected.

16. Why was it necessary to introduce a new initial state in the construction given in Theorem 5.2.5? Are there situations in which it is not needed? Does the new initial state always have to be an accepting state?

17. Apply the construction given in Theorem 5.2.5 to obtain machines for the following languages:

(a) $\emptyset^*$
(b) 1^*
(c) $\{0, 1\}^*$
(d) $\{x \mid x \in \{0, 1\}^* \text{ and } x \text{ does not contain the pattern } 00011\}$

18. Let L_1 be the language represented by $0^* \cup 1^*$. Let L_2 be the language $\{x \mid x \in \{0, 1\}^* \text{ and } x \text{ has an even number of 0's}\}$. Let $L_3 = \emptyset$. Apply the construction given in Theorem 5.2.4 to obtain NFAs for the following languages:

(a) $L_1 \circ L_2$
(b) $L_2 \circ L_1$
(c) $L_1 \circ L_3$
(d) $L_3 \circ L_2$
(e) $L_1 \circ (L_2 \circ L_3)$
(f) $(L_1 \circ L_2) \circ L_3$

19. Let M_1 and M_2 be finite automata with input alphabet Σ. Design algorithms to answer the following questions about finite automata:

(a) Let $x \in \Sigma^*$. Is $x \in L(M_1)$?
(b) Is $L(M_1) = \emptyset$?
(c) Is $L(M_1) = \Sigma^*$?
(d) Is $L(M_1) \subseteq L(M_2)$?
(e) Is $L(M_1) = L(M_2)$?
(f) Is $L(M_1) \cup L(M_2) = \Sigma^*$?

20. Prove that Equation 2.4 can be used to show that finite automata are closed under intersection.

21. Construct a finite automaton whose language is the intersection of the two languages L_1 and L_2 that are accepted by machines M_1 and M_2 as specified in Figure 5.16. Perform a direct construction. Write out the corresponding five–tuple for your answer.

22. Build a table analyzing, for each of the five theorems in this section, how the new machine constructed compares in size to the original machine(s).

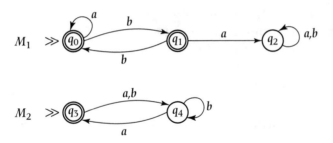

Figure 5.16

Two DFAs whose intersection is needed in Exercise 21.

Express the entries in the table for Q, Σ, δ or Δ, and F in terms of the size(s) of the original machine(s).

23. Prove that the language L consisting of strings over the alphabet $\{0, 1, 2, \ldots, 9\}$ that represent decimal numbers with no leading zeros and that are evenly divisible by two and three, or by five can be accepted by a DFA. For example, $012 \notin L$, $12 \in L$, $8 \notin L$, and $92350 \in L$.

24. Let M be a DFA. Show how to construct an NFA M' such that $L(M') = L(M)^R$.

Section 5.3   Equivalence of Regular Expressions and Finite Automata

25. Let M be an arbitrary DFA. Prove that there is an equivalent EFA. That is, there is an EFA M' such that $L(M') = L(M)$.

26. Use the techniques of Theorem 5.3.2 to design NFAs that accept the following regular languages:

    (a) $\varnothing^*$
    (b) $(0 \cup 1)^*$
    (c) 0^*1^*
    (d) $0^*(00 \cup 11)$
    (e) $((0 \cup 11)^* \circ (111 \cup 01)^*)$

27. Find a regular expression or construction for the language of the DFA in Example 4.3.9. That language contains those strings with an odd number of 0's and an even number of 1's.

28. Find regular expressions or constructions to represent the same languages as accepted by the following finite automata. Use the algorithm given in Theorem 5.3.4. In some cases you may need to make small modifications to the machines before the algorithm can be directly applied.

    (a) The DFA shown in Figure 4.1
    (b) The DFA M_2 shown in Figure 5.16

(c) The DFA M_1 shown in Figure 5.16

(d) The DFA shown in Figure 4.7

(e) The DFA shown in Figure 4.8

(f) The NFA shown in Figure 4.10

(g) The NFA shown in Figure 4.17 (b)

Section 5.4   Pumping Lemma for Regular Languages

29. Construct DFAs for the following languages, and then use the DFAs to obtain strings x, y, and z for the Pumping Lemma. (You may want to read Section 5.6 before proceeding.)

(a) $a^* \cup b^*$

(b) $(0 \cup 1)^* 0 (0 \cup 1)^*$

(c) $000 (0 \cup 1)^*$

(d) $\{x \mid x \in \{0, 1\}^* \text{ and } \#_1(x) \leq 3\}$

30. In this exercise we present a variant of the Pumping Lemma that is sometimes referred to as the *Strong Pumping Lemma*. This lemma is more general than the Pumping Lemma and can occasionally be used to show a language is nonregular when the Pumping Lemma cannot be applied.

> **Lemma 5.7.1   (Strong Pumping Lemma)**   *Suppose L is an infinite regular language and is accepted by the DFA $M = (Q, \Sigma, \delta, q_0, F)$. Let w be any string in L with $|w| \geq |Q|$. Then there are strings x, y, and z satisfying the following properties:*
>
> *(a) $w = xyz$,*
>
> *(b) $|xy| \leq |Q|$,*
>
> *(c) $y \neq \Lambda$, and*
>
> *(d) $xy^n z \in L$ for all $n \in \mathbb{N}$.*

     What are the differences between the Strong Pumping Lemma and the General Pumping Lemma?

     Prove the Strong Pumping Lemma.

31. For each language described in Exercise 29, provide strings w, x, y, and z such that the Strong Pumping Lemma holds. Of course, you will need to provide DFAs for the languages first.

Section 5.5   Applications of the Pumping Lemma

32. Prove the following languages are not regular using the Pumping Lemma:

(a) $\{x \mid x \in \{a, b\}^* \text{ and } \#_a(x) = \#_b(x)\}$

(b) $\{0^{i^2} \mid i \geq 0\}$

(c) $\{0^i 1^i 0^i \mid i \geq 0\}$

(d) $\{0^{2^i} \mid i \geq 0\}$

(e) $\{0^i1^i0^j \mid i,j \geq 0\}$

(f) $\{0^i10^i1 \mid i \geq 0\}$

(g) $\{x \mid x \in \{0, 1\}^* \text{ and } x = x^R\}$

(h) $\{xx^R \mid x \in \{0, 1\}^*\}$

(i) $\{x \Diamond x^R \mid x \in \{0, 1\}^*\}$

33. Define your own nonregular language, a language that is not a simple twist on one of the nonregular languages already defined. Prove that it is nonregular using one of the pumping lemmas.

34. Let $\Gamma = \{0, 1, \ldots, 9\}$. Which of the following languages are regular? Justify your answers.

(a) $\{0^i1^j0^i \mid i,j \geq 0\}$

(b) $\{0^i1^j2^k \mid i > j > k \geq 0\}$

(c) $\{x \mid x \in (\Gamma - \{0\})\Gamma^* \text{ and } x \bmod 7 \equiv 0\}$

(d) $\{x \Diamond y \Diamond z \mid x + y = z \text{ and } x, y, z \in \{0, 1\}^*\}$

(e) $\{0^i1^j \mid j \leq i \leq 2j\}$

Section 5.6 Using Closure Properties to Deduce That a Language Is Nonregular

35. Prove that the following languages are not regular by using closure properties:

(a) $\{xy \mid x, y \in \{0, 1\}^* \text{ and } y \neq x^R\}$

(b) $\{0^i1^j0^{i+j} \mid i,j \geq 0\}$

(c) $\{0^i1^j2^k3^l \mid i,j,k,l \geq 1\}$

36. Is $\{0^i10^j \mid i \neq j \text{ and } i,j \geq 0\}$ regular?

37. Which of the following statements are true?

(a) If L_1 and L_2 are not regular, then neither is $L_1 \cup L_2$.

(b) If L_1 and L_2 are not regular, then neither is $L_1 \cap L_2$.

(c) If L_1 and L_2 are not regular, then neither is $L_1 \circ L_2$.

38. Specify a language $L \subseteq \{0, 1\}^*$ such that L^* is not regular.

39. Specify a language $L \subseteq \{0, 1\}^*$, which is not regular, such that L^* is regular.

40. Are the regular languages closed under infinite union?

41. Prove that the regular languages are closed under general language homomorphism.

CHAPTER 6

Fundamental Machines Part II: Stack and Tape Machines

There are many models that have been defined in the theory of computation. The pushdown automaton and Turing machine are among the most important.
—*Raymond Greenlaw*

6.1 Pushdown Automata

Regular languages have broad application in computer science, but many useful languages are not regular and so cannot be accepted by DFAs and NFAs. For example, no DFA can accept the language consisting of nested, balanced parentheses:

$$L_0 = \{\Lambda, (), ()(), (()), ((())), (()), ()(), \ldots\}$$

Languages like this are important from the perspective of programming languages as they correspond to the nesting of expressions and program blocks. Intuitively, a DFA cannot accept a language like L_0 because the only way the machine can store information is in its current state, so on sufficiently long inputs the machine loses track of the pattern of parentheses.

Another example of a language beyond the capability of a DFA is the one from Chapter 1 consisting of strings having an equal number of a's and b's. There we argued that this language could not be recognized by any C-- program, and thus not by any DFA, since C-- programs have the same computational power as DFAs.

Whenever we encounter limitations to a computational model, the natural question to ask is, What features can we add to the model to make it more powerful? Since memory is a limitation for DFAs, it seems reasonable to add memory other than that provided by just the states. How sophisticated should this memory be? Supposing that we want to minimize the changes we make in our hardware, one of the simplest forms of additional memory is a stack. It has a very simple interface (push and pop), yet arbitrary numbers of symbols can be put onto the stack. The only limitation is that access to the stack contents is restricted to just the top symbol.

The resulting *pushdown automata* allow us to accept a richer class of languages than the finite automata, and their main contribution has been in the area of parsing and compiler construction. We will expand on their relation to programming languages in Chapter 7, when these machines are related to grammars.

Since deterministic and nondeterministic finite automata have the same computational power, it seems reasonable that we keep things simple and initially add the stack to just the DFA model. This results in the *deterministic pushdown automaton* (DPDA) model. It turns out that adding a stack actually makes nondeterministic behavior more powerful than deterministic behavior, and so we will also add a stack to the NFA model, resulting in the *nondeterministic pushdown automaton* (PDA) model.[1]

The stack is implemented by adding an extra tape to our finite automaton model. This extra stack tape will be writable, unlike the input tape. However, there will be restrictions on how this tape can be manipulated. Its initial stack configuration is $[1, \Lambda]$, the *empty stack*. The right end tape mark is the bottom-of-stack marker, and the stack tape head will always be positioned over the top symbol of the stack. There are two primitives that are used to write to the stack: a basic push and a basic pop.

1. *Basic push:* The head moves left one square onto the $\langle$ mark and then writes a symbol from the data alphabet Σ. This symbol is thus pushed onto the stack and becomes the new top of stack.

2. *Basic pop:* If the stack is not empty—that is, the head is not over the $\rangle$ mark—then a $\langle$ mark is written to the stack to erase the top, and the head advanced one square to the right. This results in the top symbol being popped off the stack. If the stack is empty, then a basic pop does not change the state of the stack.

6.1.1 Deterministic Pushdown Automata

The finite control can read symbols from the stack as well as inspect the current state and input tape symbol before making a transition. In a DFA, whenever the input tape is inspected, the input head advances one square to the right if possible. When we also have a stack, we do not necessarily want to move the input head at every step, nor do we necessarily want to manipulate the stack at every step. This makes the description of the PDA instructions a bit more complicated.

---

1. For historical reasons we use the acronyms DPDA and PDA rather than DPA and NPA, as you might expect.

The transition function δ will take a triple of (current state, input symbol, top-of-stack symbol) and produce an instruction triple of (next state, input head move, stack operation). The result of executing this instruction is the next configuration of the machine.

Definition 6.1.1   *A **deterministic pushdown automaton (DPDA)** is a five-tuple*

$$M = (Q, \Sigma, \delta, q_0, F)$$

with components

1. *Q—A finite, nonempty set of **states***
2. *Σ—The **data alphabet** (which induces **tape alphabet** $\Sigma_T = \Sigma \cup \{\langle, \rangle\}$)*
3. *δ—The **transition function** or **finite control** that maps a triple (q, t, s), where $q \in Q$ and $t, s \in \Sigma_T$, to a triple (q', i, d), where*

    $q' \in Q$

    $i \in \{\circ, +\}$

    $d \in \{\circ, \text{pop}\} \cup \{\text{push } a \mid a \in \Sigma\}$

4. *q_0—The **initial state** or **start state**, $q_0 \in Q$*
5. *F—The set of **accepting states**, $F \subseteq Q$*

For a pushdown automaton, the configuration also needs to capture the state of the stack:

Definition 6.1.2   *A **configuration** of a DPDA $M = (Q, \Sigma, \delta, q_0, F)$, on input $x \in \Sigma^*$, is a triple $(q, [p, x], [1, \gamma])$, where*

1. *$q \in Q$.*
2. *$[p, x]$ is a configuration of the input tape.*
3. *$[1, \gamma]$ is a configuration of the stack tape, which always has its head over the top of the stack.*

*The **initial configuration** of M on input x is the configuration $(q_0, [1, x], [1, \Lambda])$. We use C_0 to denote the initial configuration when M and x are understood. For machine M, the set of all possible configurations for all possible inputs x is denoted by $\mathcal{C}(M)$.*

Definition 6.1.3   *Let $M = (Q, \Sigma, \delta, q_0, F)$ be a DPDA. Let $\mathcal{C}(M)$ be the set of all configurations of M. Let $C_1 = (q_1, [p_1, x], [1, \gamma])$ and $C_2 = (q_2, [p_2, x], [1, \gamma'])$ be two elements of $\mathcal{C}(M)$. Configuration C_1 specifies a current state and symbols under the input and stack tape head, which is the triple $(q, \sigma[p_1, x], \sigma[1, \gamma])$. Let (q', i, d) be the result of applying δ to this triple. Then $C_1 \vdash_M C_2$ if and only if the following two conditions hold:*

Input tape motion condition:

$i = \circ$ and $p_2 = p_1$

or

$i = +$ and $p_2 = 1 + p_1$

and

Stack tape operation condition:

$i = \circ$ and $\gamma = \gamma'$

or

$i = \mathrm{pop}$ and $\gamma = a\gamma'$ for some $a \in \Sigma$

or

$i = \mathrm{pop}$ and $\gamma = \gamma' = \Lambda$

or

$i = \mathrm{push}\, a$ and $a\gamma = \gamma'$ for some $a \in \Sigma$

$\vdash_M$ *is called the* **next move**, **step**, *or* **yields** *relation.*

Like the DFA, δ does not have to be defined on every possible triple, and so not every configuration has a successor configuration. Configurations with no successors are called halting configurations.

The last notion we need is of acceptance of an input. It is similar to that of a DFA in that all of the input must be read. In addition the stack must be empty.

Definition 6.1.4   *Let $M = (Q, \Sigma, \delta, q_0, F)$ be a DPDA and $q \in Q$. M* **accepts** *input $x \in \Sigma^*$ if*

$$(q_0, \tau^{Initial}(x), [1, \Lambda]) \vdash_M^* (f, \tau^{Final}(x), [1, \Lambda])$$

where $f \in F$. This computation is called an **accepting computation**. *A configuration $(q, \tau^{Final}(x), [1, \Lambda])$ with no successors is called an* **accepting configuration** *of M if $q \in F$. If M does not accept its input x, then M is said to* **reject** *x. The computation of M on input x in this case is called a* **rejecting computation**, *and M was left in a* **rejecting configuration**.

How could a DFA augmented with a stack be used to recognize the balanced parentheses language $L_{()}$ from above? Intuitively, we could use the stack to store the unmatched left parentheses. For each right parenthesis we encounter, a left

Transition Number	Current State	Input Symbol	Stack Top	New State	Input Op	Stack Op
1	q_0	(	)	q_0	+	push (
2	q_0	(	(	q_0	+	push (
3	q_0	)	(	q_0	+	pop
4	q_0	)	)	q_1	○	○
5	q_0	)	(	q_2	○	○
6	q_0	)	)	q_2	○	○

Table 6.1

The transition table for the DPDA described in Example 6.1.5.

parenthesis could be popped off the stack. If we run out of right parentheses exactly when the stack is empty, then we know that the parentheses are balanced.

Example 6.1.5   A DPDA to accept L_0, the language of nested, balanced parentheses

As mentioned earlier, the key idea is to store all left parentheses on the stack and then pop them off as each one matches a right parenthesis. Define

$$M = (\{q_0, q_1\}, \{(,)\}, \delta, q_0, \{q_1\})$$

where δ is as given in Table 6.1.

Transitions (1) and (2) are used to push opening parentheses on the stack; transition (3) is used to match a closing parenthesis with an open one on the stack; (4) accepts the input, and (5) and (6) send the machine into a rejecting state, which halts the machine.

Consider M on input (()()):

$$(q_0, [1, (()())], [1, \Lambda]) \vdash_M (q_0, [2, (()())], [1, (])$$
$$\vdash_M (q_0, [3, (()())], [1, ((])$$
$$\vdash_M (q_0, [4, (()())], [1, (])$$
$$\vdash_M (q_0, [5, (()())], [1, ((])$$
$$\vdash_M (q_0, [6, (()())], [1, (])$$
$$\vdash_M (q_0, [7, (()())], [1, \Lambda])$$
$$\vdash_M (q_1, [7, (()())], [1, \Lambda])$$

Therefore,

$$(q_0, [1, (()())], [1, \Lambda]) \vdash_M^* (q_1, [7, (()())], [1, \Lambda])$$

and since q_1 is an accepting state, all input has been read, and the stack is empty, we have $(()()) \in L(M)$.

Now consider M on the input string $())$. We get the following computation:

$$(q_0, [1, ())], [1, \Lambda]) \vdash_M (q_0, [2, ())], [1, (])$$

$$\vdash_M (q_0, [3, ())], [1, \Lambda])$$

$$\vdash_M (q_2, [3, ())], [1, \Lambda])$$

Notice that no further transitions of M can be applied, q_2 is not an accepting state, and so $()) \notin L_0$. ∎

6.1.2   Nondeterministic Pushdown Automata

Let's begin by presenting the definition of a nondeterministic pushdown automaton.

Definition 6.1.6   *A **nondeterministic pushdown automaton (PDA)** is a five-tuple*

$$M = (Q, \Sigma, \Delta, q_0, F)$$

that is defined similarly to the DPDA except for the specification of the transitions.

*The **transition relation** Δ is a set of six-tuples of the form*

$$(q, t, s, q', i, d)$$

where

$q, q' \in Q$

$t, s \in \Sigma_T$

$i \in \{\circ, +\}$

$d \in \{\circ, \text{pop}\} \cup \{\text{push } a \mid a \in \Sigma\}$

The main change from the DPDA to the PDA is, of course, the addition of nondeterminism. Thus, from some configurations in a PDA, it is possible that the machine could follow one of several different threads. Language acceptance is defined for PDAs exactly as for NFAs. A string x is in $L(M)$ if and only if there is at least one computation on x that reads all of the input and halts in an accepting state with the stack empty.

We can define corresponding language classes for pushdown automata in the same way that we did for finite automata.

Definition 6.1.7 $\mathcal{L}_{\textbf{DPDA}}$ *(or $\mathcal{L}_{\textbf{PDA}}$) represents the class of languages accepted by DPDAs (or, respectively, PDAs). That is,*

$$\mathcal{L}_{\textbf{DPDA}} = \{L \mid \text{there exists a DPDA } M \text{ with } L = L(M)\}$$

and

$$\mathcal{L}_{\textbf{PDA}} = \{L \mid \text{there exists a PDA } M \text{ with } L = L(M)\}$$

6.1.3 Inequivalence of DPDAs and PDAs

Are the language classes $\mathcal{L}_{\textbf{DPDA}}$ and $\mathcal{L}_{\textbf{PDA}}$ the same? In the case of finite automata, the corresponding classes, $\mathcal{L}_{\textbf{DFA}}$ and $\mathcal{L}_{\textbf{NFA}}$, are equal. In the present case the language classes are not equal. That is, $\mathcal{L}_{\textbf{DPDA}} \subseteq \mathcal{L}_{\textbf{PDA}}$, but the reverse is not true. Let's look at an example of a language accepted by a PDA but not by any DPDA. We will only give an informal argument as to why the language is not accepted by any DPDA. However, the example should make it clear why some languages accepted by PDAs cannot be accepted by DPDAs. In addition, the example will illustrate how to program a PDA. The general strategy outlined for designing finite automata can be extended to pushdown automata; when asked to design pushdown automata in the exercises, you may want to start by following that procedure.

Example 6.1.8   A language accepted by a PDA but not by any DPDA

Consider the language

$$L = \{0^i 1^i \mid i \geq 0\} \cup \{0^j 1^{2j} \mid j \geq 0\}$$

We will construct a PDA M to accept L. Define

$$M = (\{q_0, q_1, q_2, q_3, q_4\}, \{0, 1\}, \Delta, q_0, \{q_1\})$$

where Δ is as given in Table 6.2.

The purpose of transitions (1), (2), (3) is to stack all the leading 0's. Transitions (4) and (5) make a nondeterministic choice to match single or double 1's; that is, the execution thread forks into two possible execution threads. Transitions (6) and (7) match each stacked 0 with an input 1, while transitions (8), (9), (10) match two 1's for each 0.

Let's consider some computations of M. Consider M on the input 0011. The following computation is an accepting computation:

$$(q_0, [1, 0011], [1, \Lambda]) \vdash_M (q_0, [2, 0011], [1, 0])$$
$$\vdash_M (q_0, [3, 0011], [1, 00])$$
$$\vdash_M (q_2, [3, 0011], [1, 00])$$
$$\vdash_M (q_2, [4, 0011], [1, 0])$$
$$\vdash_M (q_2, [5, 0011], [1, \Lambda])$$
$$\vdash_M (q_1, [5, 0011], [1, \Lambda])$$

Transition Number	Current State	Input Symbol	Stack Top	New State	Input Op	Stack Op
1	q_0	⟩	⟩	q_1	○	○
2	q_0	0	⟩	q_0	+	push 0
3	q_0	0	0	q_0	+	push 0
4	q_0	1	0	q_2	○	○
5	q_0	1	0	q_3	○	○
6	q_2	⟩	⟩	q_1	○	○
7	q_2	1	0	q_2	+	pop
8	q_3	⟩	⟩	q_1	○	○
9	q_3	1	0	q_4	+	○
10	q_4	1	0	q_3	+	pop

Table 6.2

The transition table for the PDA described in Example 6.1.8.

This computation is accepting, since all the input was read, q_1 is an accepting state, and the stack is empty.

M also has rejecting computations on input 0011. For example, the thread

$$(q_0, [1, 0011], [1, \Lambda]) \vdash_M (q_0, [2, 0011], [1, 0])$$

$$\vdash_M (q_0, [3, 0011], [1, 00])$$

$$\vdash_M (q_3, [3, 0011], [1, 00])$$

$$\vdash_M (q_4, [4, 0011], [1, 00])$$

$$\vdash_M (q_3, [5, 0011], [1, 0])$$

The last state q_3 has no successor, so the thread halts, and since q_3 is not an accepting state, the input is rejected. As usual with nondeterministic models, if there is at least one accepting computation, then the string is accepted. Thus $0011 \in L(M)$.
∎

For finite automata, Theorem 4.5.1 showed that $\mathcal{L}_{\textbf{DFA}} = \mathcal{L}_{\textbf{NFA}}$, and as we will see in the next section for Turing machines, Theorem 6.2.19 shows that $\mathcal{L}_{\textbf{DTM}} = \mathcal{L}_{\textbf{NTM}}$. This is *not* the case for pushdown automata, as the following theorem shows. (The proof of this theorem can be found in [26].)

Theorem 6.1.9 *The language classes $\mathcal{L}_{\textbf{DPDA}}$ and $\mathcal{L}_{\textbf{PDA}}$ are not equal.*

Are the pushdown automata completely general models of computation? Intuitively, it seems very unlikely, since they can only read their input once, and furthermore the only mechanism for storing the input they possess is a stack. In Chapter 7 we will show that the language:

$$\{a^i b^i c^i \mid i \geq 0\}$$

is not context–free. Chapter 7 we will also revisit the pushdown automata to examine their link with context–free grammars and parsing.

In the next section we turn to our last finite–state control machine, the Turing machine. A Turing machine to accept the language $\{a^i b^i c^i \mid i \geq 0\}$ is provided in the next section. As opposed to the finite automata and pushdown automata, Turing machines are a completely general model of computing (subject to the Church–Turing Thesis, of course).

6.2   *Turing Machines*

We have seen that our first two classes of computational models, the finite automata and pushdown automata, are not completely general: there were some simple languages that the models could not accept. What is the minimum extension we can make to these models so that they become so powerful that any further extensions can only add convenience, not intrinsic capability? That is, if it is possible, how can we extend the automata to be general computational models? Interestingly, simply adding a read/write *work tape* to the DFA is sufficient to produce a machine, called the *Turing machine*, which is as powerful as any other computing device.

Before defining the Turing machine, we present an informal description of the new components of the model and consider an analogy with everyday programming.

The writer of a C program defines data structures and develops instructions for manipulating this data. Many programs require input, and the appropriate code must be placed in the program to accept and store the input data. Once a program is compiled, the executable file can be run on the underlying hardware, for example, a personal computer (PC). Similarly, you can write a Turing machine program. Like C, only certain types of Turing machine constructs are syntactically correct. Since Turing machines are rather inefficient, and consequently are not in great demand, their hardware is not as readily available as that of a PC. The execution of a Turing machine program is usually carried out by hand via the formal definition of the Turing machine.

Figure 6.1 depicts the steps involved in running a C program, shows schematically how the data is typically input to the program, and how output is produced. Once the program is coded, it can be saved as an ASCII file and compiled. If the program is syntactically correct, an executable file a.out is produced that can then be run. Contrast this process with the one illustrated in Figure 6.2.

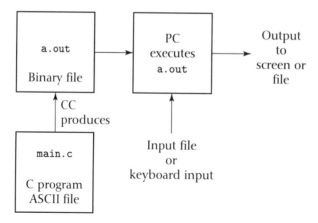

Figure 6.1

The compile and execute cycle for a C program.

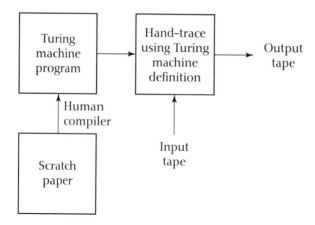

Figure 6.2

The compile and execute cycle of a Turing machine program.

Figure 6.2 demonstrates the experience that most Turing machine program-mers have. They develop a program on scratch paper, "compile" the program by hand, and then hand–trace the execution of the program, carrying out the steps defined by it according to the definition of the Turing machine.

It is relatively easy to write a Turing machine simulator program in C, since the "operations" that a Turing machine can perform are quite limited in nature. Thus the process shown in Figure 6.2 can be automated. A Turing machine program can then be input from a file to a C program; the Turing machine program can be executed on a personal computer. The process of building this simulator can greatly enhance your understanding of Turing machines. It can even be used to test and debug your Turing machine programs.

What is a Turing machine, and why is it important? A deterministic (or nondeterministic) Turing machine is simply a DFA (or, respectively, NFA) that has two-way read-only access to its input tape and a read/write work tape for storing data.

The Turing machine is important because it is the simplest model that *any* algorithm can be programmed on (subject to the Church–Turing Thesis). The work tape provides a very simple model of an infinitely extensible memory; you can imagine a device that fabricates additional tape so long as it is given sufficient raw materials. In terms of measuring resource usage, the Turing machine is mathematically easy to work with, as we will see in Chapter 8. Thus, it is well suited for studying the intrinsic computational nature of problems. The Turing machine helps us to capture the essential time and memory bounds required to solve problems, even though it is somewhat inadequate to capture the details important to everyday computations.

All of the concepts of automata carry over to Turing machines; in fact, we complicated the finite automata models more than normal so that they would look like crippled Turing machines. We can easily generalize them. Like the other computational models introduced so far, our primary focus is on viewing Turing machines as language acceptors, and so we do not need to generate any "output" other than accept/reject. On the other hand, if we want to compute functions, then we will have to produce output; such an output will typically be written on a designated *output tape*. But an output tape is not just a Turing machine option. It could be added to finite or pushdown automata as well.

6.2.1 Deterministic Turing Machines

Let's begin this section by presenting the definition of a deterministic Turing machine.

Definition 6.2.1 *A **deterministic Turing machine (DTM)** is a five-tuple*

$$M = (Q, \Sigma, \delta, q_0, F)$$

that is defined similarly to a DFA, except now we allow two-way read-only access to the input tape and incorporate a work tape. The **transition function** *or* **finite control** δ *is a function*

Tape alphabet

$$\delta : Q \times \Sigma_T \times \Sigma_T \mapsto Q \times \{-1, 0, +1\} \times \Sigma_T \times \{-1, 0, +1\}$$

The current state of the DTM, and the current configurations of its input and work tapes, are used by δ to compute the next state and to manipulate the tapes.

State	Input Symbol	Work Tape Symbol	New State	Move on Input Tape	Symbol Written on Work Tape	Move on Work Tape
q	a	b	q_1	d_1	c	d_2

Table 6.3

A convenient method for representing the transition function of a Turing machine. The transition $\delta(q, a, b) = (q', d_1, c, d_2)$ is shown.

δ takes a state, a symbol from the input tape alphabet, and a symbol from the work tape alphabet as arguments. It generates a four-tuple that indicates the next state of the finite control, a change in position of the input tape head, a symbol to be written to the work tape head, and a change in position of the work tape head. A change in head position is one of -1, 0, or $+1$. A -1 moves left one cell, a $+1$ moves right one cell, and a 0 means do not move.

Suppose $q \in Q$, $a, b \in \Sigma_T$, and $\delta(q, a, b) = (q', d_1, c, d_2)$, where $q' \in Q$, $c \in \Sigma_T$, and $d_1, d_2 \in \{-1, 0, +1\}$. The value of δ, (q', d_1, c, d_2), is called a *transition* and is interpreted as the new state that M is to enter, q'; a left, right, or stationary "move" of the input tape head depending on the value of d_1; a symbol c to be written on the work tape over symbol b; and a left, right, or stationary "move" of the work tape head according to the value of d_2. If M tries to move left of $\langle$ or to the right of $\rangle$, the machine *hangs*. That is, in these circumstances, by convention the machine "core dumps" and ceases running.

Since δ is a function, the DTM behaves deterministically. Another way of saying this is that the machine has only one "choice" for its next transition, just like for DFAs and DPDAs. Sometimes it is convenient to view the function δ as a relation, that is, to list δ as a set of ordered pairs. For example, if $\delta(q, a, b) = (q', d_1, c, d_2)$, then $((q, a, b), (q', d_1, c, d_2)) \in \delta$.

As with automata, the finite control is often more easily understood and presented via a table, as shown in Table 6.3. Each row in the table stands for a transition of a Turing machine. The transition $\delta(q, a, b) = (q', d_1, c, d_2)$ is shown, using the obvious isomorphism between functions and their relational representations.

Figure 6.3 depicts a DTM M with $Q = \{q_0, q_1, q_2, q_3\}$, $\Sigma = \{0, 1\}$, $F = \{q_2, q_3\}$, and q_0 the initial state. The arrow pointing to q_1 indicates the current state of M is q_1. To illustrate how δ works, suppose $\delta(q_1, 0, 0) = (q_2, +1, 1, -1)$. The result of executing this transition is shown in Figure 6.4. Notice the state changed to q_2; the input tape head moved one square to the right, corresponding to the $+1$; a 1 was written on the work tape; and the work tape head was moved one square to the left, corresponding to the -1.

Before proceeding further, let's consider a full example.

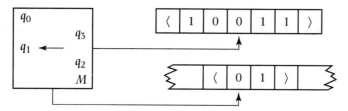

Figure 6.3

A DTM's finite control, input tape, and work tape. The machine is currently in state q_1.

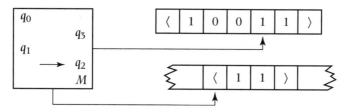

Figure 6.4

The same DTM as in Figure 6.3 after the execution of the transition $\delta(q_1, 0, 0) = (q_2, +1, 1, -1)$.

Example 6.2.2   A simple DTM

Let $M = (Q, \Sigma, \delta, q_0, F)$, with $Q = \{q_0, q_1, q_2, q_3, q_4\}$, $\Sigma = \{0, 1\}$, δ as shown in Table 6.4, start state q_0, and accepting states $\{q_3\}$. We will have more to say about this example below. ■

The descriptions in Figures 6.3 and 6.4 clearly explain one move of a DTM but are quite cumbersome. Imagine trying to discuss the full execution of a DTM in this form. As was done for automata, we use a shorthand notation in order to simplify the description of a computation. We define the standard notation in the following and then apply it to examples involving M, the DTM defined in Example 6.2.2.

In order to describe a computation of a DTM, we need to specify "snapshots" of the machine like those shown in Figures 6.3 and 6.4, as we have done for the other computational models described thus far.

Definition 6.2.3   *A* **configuration** *of a DTM* $M = (Q, \Sigma, \delta, q_0, F)$ *on input* $x \in \Sigma'$, $|x| = n$, *is a three-tuple* (q, c_I, c_W), *where*

  1. $q \in Q$,

State	Input Symbol	Work Tape Symbol	New State	Move on Input Tape	Symbol Written on Work Tape	Move on Work Tape
q_0	)	)	q_3	0	)	0
q_0	1	)	q_4	+1	)	0
q_0	0	)	q_1	+1	0	+1
q_1	0	)	q_1	+1	0	+1
q_1	1	)	q_2	0	)	-1
q_2	1	0	q_2	+1	)	-1
q_2	)	(	q_3	0	(	+1

Table 6.4

The transition table for δ of a DTM M that is used as an example throughout this section.

2. c_I is the input tape configuration, and

3. c_W is the work tape configuration.

The **initial configuration** of M is $(q_0, [1, x], [1, \Lambda])$.

As before, the initial configuration is denoted C_0, and the set of all possible configurations that the machine M could ever be in is denoted $\mathcal{C}(M)$.

Example 6.2.4   Sample Turing machine configurations

The configurations corresponding to the snapshots of Figures 6.3 and 6.4 are $(q_1, [3, 10011], [1, 01])$ and $(q_2, [4, 10011], [0, 11])$, respectively. The initial configuration of the machine depicted in Figure 6.3 is $(q_0, [1, 10011], [1, \Lambda])$. ■

How can we use the notion of configuration to discuss the computation of a Turing machine? Configurations are useful in defining the *next move* relation, denoted $\vdash_M$, as shown in the following. Although $\vdash_M$ is more complex for Turing machines than for automata, the ideas are the same.

Definition 6.2.5   *Let $M = (Q, \Sigma, \delta, q_0, F)$ be a DTM. Let $\mathcal{C}(M)$ be the set of all configurations of M. Let $C_1 = (q_1, [h_1, s_1], [k_1, t_1])$ and $C_2 = (q_2, [h_2, s_2], [k_2, t_2])$ be configurations in $\mathcal{C}(M)$. Since C_1 and C_2 are legitimate configurations, we can assume that their input and work tape head positions are within the correct bounds. Let $d_1, d_2 \in \{-1, 0, +1\}$ and $c \in \Sigma_T$. Let $a, b \in \Sigma_T$ be the contents of the cells under the input and work tape heads, respectively, of configuration C_1. That is, $a = s_1(h_1)$ and $b = t_1(k_1)$.*
   $C_1 \vdash_M C_2$ if and only if there is a transition

$$\delta(q_1, a, b) = (q_2, d_1, c, d_2)$$

where

1. $s_2 = s_1$, $0 \le h_2 \le |s_2| + 1$, *and* $h_2 = h_1 + d_1$
2. *if* $|t_1| = |t_2|$, *then* $k_2 = k_1 + d_2$ *and*

$$t_2 = t_1(1) \circ \cdots \circ t_1(k_1 - 1) \circ c \circ t_1(k_1 + 1) \circ \cdots \circ t_1(|t_1|)$$

3. *if* $|t_1| < |t_2|$, *then*
   (a) *if* $k_1 = 0$, *then* $k_2 = d_2 + 1$ *and* $t_2 = c \circ t_1$
   (b) *if* $k_1 = |t_1| + 1$, *then* $k_2 = |t_1| + 1 + d_2$ *and* $t_2 = t_1 \circ c$
4. *if* $|t_1| > |t_2|$, *then*
   (a) *if* c *is* $\langle$, *then* $k_2 = d_2$ *and* $t_2 = t_1(k_1 + 1) \circ \cdots \circ t_1(|t_1|)$
   (b) *if* c *is* $\rangle$, *then* $k_2 = k_1 + d_2$ *and* $t_2 = t_1(1) \circ \cdots \circ t_1(k_1 - 1)$

$\vdash_M$ *is called the* **next move**, **step**, *or* **yields** *relation.*

Several remarks are in order regarding this definition. First, $\vdash_M$ is a relation defined on configurations. This means $\vdash_M \subseteq \mathcal{C}(M) \times \mathcal{C}(M)$. Since δ is a function, $\vdash_M$ is also a function. Intuitively, it is clear what Definition 6.2.5 is saying: Configuration C_1 yields configuration C_2 if there is a transition from C_1 that when executed brings M to the new configuration C_2. The definition specifies this in detail. Let's break down what each step in the definition is saying.

Part 1 requires that the input tape is unchanged, that the tape head is in the input range after the transition is executed, and that h_2 is the resulting head position. That is, we cannot move left on $\langle$ or right on $\rangle$. h_2 is either one less than h_1, one more, or equal to it. These three cases correspond to a left move, a right move, or remaining stationary.

Part 2 applies when the write to the tape occurs in the tape contents between tape marks. It says that k_2 is the resulting head position after the move d_2 is added to the old work tape head position k_1. The new work tape is the same as the original work tape, except for the possible change of one character at position k_1. We define $t_1(-1) = \Lambda$ to handle the case where $k_1 = 0$.

Part 3 handles the case of writing a character from the data alphabet on top of a tape mark. This has the effect of extending the work tape by one cell.

Part 4 handles the case of writing a tape mark on the interior of the work tape. This has the effect of shortening the work tape, placing the work tape head at either end of the tape. In case (a), if $d_2 = -1$, the machine hangs. In case (b), if $d_2 = +1$, the machine hangs.

The relation $\vdash_M$ helps us to define what it means for a DTM to stop executing, that is, to *halt*.

Definition 6.2.6 *Let M be a DTM with next move relation $\vdash_M$. A* **halting configuration** *or* **final configuration** *of M is a configuration $C_h \in \mathcal{C}(M)$ with the property that* *for all $C \in \mathcal{C}(M)$, $C_h \vdash_M C$ does not hold. When a machine enters a halting configuration, it is said to **halt**.*

The definition specifies a configuration to be a halting configuration if there is no possible next move. The concepts of *halting* and *hanging* are sometimes confused: Hanging signifies the machine tried to do something illegal, such as moving off the input tape or work tape. Halting means that, from the current configuration, there is no possible transition to execute.

In analogy with the other models, we can extend $\vdash$ to its reflexive, transitive closure $\vdash^*$.

As an example, consider the DTM M, whose transition function is depicted in Table 6.4, on input $x = 0011$. The initial configuration of M on x is $(q_0, [1, 0011], [1, \Lambda])$. Applying the third transition in Table 6.4, we see

$$(q_0, [1, 0011], [1, \Lambda]) \vdash_M M(q_1, [2, 0011], [2, 0])$$

Continuing this a bit more:

$$(q_0, [1, 0011], [1, \Lambda]) \vdash_M (q_1, [2, 0011], [2, 0])$$
$$\vdash_M (q_1, [3, 0011], [3, 00])$$
$$\vdash_M (q_2, [3, 0011], [2, 00])$$
$$\vdash_M (q_2, [4, 0011], [1, 0])$$
$$\vdash_M (q_2, [5, 0011], [0, \Lambda])$$
$$\vdash_M (q_3, [5, 0011], [1, \Lambda])$$

From the last configuration shown above, there is no transition of δ that can be applied. Thus, $(q_3, [5, 0011], [1, \Lambda])$ is an example of a halting configuration. The computation shown has six steps or is of length six.

Now we can define what it means for a DTM to *accept* its input. The ideas are similar to what we developed for automata.

Definition 6.2.7   *Let $M = (Q, \Sigma, \delta, q_0, F)$ be a DTM. Suppose $x \in \Sigma^*$ and*

$$(q_0, [1, x], [1, \Lambda]) \vdash_M^* (f, [h, x], [k, s]) = C_f$$

*where C_f is a halting configuration. When $f \in F$, M **accepts** x, and C_f is called an **accepting configuration** of M. When $f \notin F$, then M is said to **reject** x, and C_f is a **rejecting configuration**.*

Note that the DTM must be in a halted state for the machine to accept or reject its input. Thus simply passing through a state in F during execution does not accept an input. It is also quite possible that the machine does not halt on a given input x. In this case the input is neither accepted nor rejected.

For example, M accepts the input $x = 0011$ since

$$(q_0, [1, 0011], [1, \Lambda]) \vdash_M^* (q_3, [5, 0011], [1, \Lambda])$$

as shown earlier.

We can now define the *language accepted* by a DTM.

Definition 6.2.8 *Let $M = (Q, \Sigma, \delta, q_0, F)$ be a DTM. The* **language accepted** *by M, denoted $L(M)$, is*

$$\{x \mid M \text{ accepts } x\}$$

The class of languages accepted by DTMs is denoted $\mathcal{L}_{\mathbf{DTM}}$. That is,

$$\mathcal{L}_{\mathbf{DTM}} = \{L \mid \text{ there exists a DTM } M \text{ with } L = L(M)\}$$

If $L \in \mathcal{L}_{\mathbf{DTM}}$, then L is **recursively enumerable**.

If M accepts a language L, then the definition specifies that M halts on all $x \in L$. However, there is an asymmetry in the definition, since for $x \notin L$, M is not required to halt; that is, M could hang or go into an infinite loop. A special case of acceptance is when M halts on every input, and either rejects or accepts x.

Definition 6.2.9 *Let $M = (Q, \Sigma, \delta, q_0, F)$ be a DTM. Suppose that on every input $x \in \Sigma^*$ that M halts. In this case we say that M* **decides** *$L(M)$.*

The class of languages decided by DTMs is denoted $\mathcal{L}_{\mathbf{REC}}$. That is,

$$\mathcal{L}_{\mathbf{REC}} = \{L \mid \text{ there exists a DTM } M \text{ that decides } L\}$$

If $L \in \mathcal{L}_{\mathbf{REC}}$, then L is said to be recursive or decidable. If $L \notin \mathcal{L}_{\mathbf{REC}}$, then L is **undecidable**.

A careful inspection of the machine M, whose transition function is provided in Table 6.4, shows that $L(M) = \{0^i 1^i \mid i \geq 0\}$, a language we visited earlier in Section 2.6. Note $\Lambda \in \{0^i 1^i \mid i \geq 0\}$. Let's verify that M accepts Λ. The initial configuration of M on input Λ is $C_0 = (q_0, [1, \Lambda], [1, \Lambda])$. Using the first transition in Table 6.4, we see $C_0 \vdash_M (q_3, [1, \Lambda], [1, \Lambda])$. The latter configuration is a halting configuration, since q_3 has no transitions leaving it. Since $q_3 \in F$, M accepts Λ; that is, $\Lambda \in L(M)$. Knowing that $L(M) = \{0^i 1^i \mid i \geq 0\}$ means $L(M) \in \mathcal{L}_{\mathbf{DTM}}$. Since this machine always halts on its inputs, it decides the language, and thus $L(M) \in \mathcal{L}_{\mathbf{REC}}$. No doubt you have noticed the similarities between this language and that of nested, balanced parentheses discussed in Section 6.1. Also observe that in this case we used the tape as a stack.

The next lemma illustrates the ideas involved in simulating one DTM by another; we prove that we may assume a DTM has only a single accepting state, that it reads the entire input before accepting, and that if it halts, it only does so in an accepting state.

Lemma 6.2.10   Let $M = (Q, \Sigma, \delta, q_0, F)$ be a DTM. Then there exists another DTM M' that accepts $L(M)$ but that

1. has only one accepting state,

2. is such that the accepting state is entered exactly once, at which point the machine halts,

3. on acceptance of input x, the input tape configuration is $[|x| + 1, x]$, and

4. if input $x \notin L(M)$, then the machine does not halt.

Proof: The idea of the proof is to form a new machine M' that has the same states as M and three additional states h, h_a, and l_r. The new, unique accepting state is h_a. The state h is responsible for moving the input head to the $\rangle$ marker if it is not already there. The state l_r is responsible for entering an infinite loop in the event that the original machine would reject the input. From all the accepting states of M, transitions are added to h. The precise definition of M' is given below.

Let h and h_a be new states not in Q. We define a new machine M' and then prove that M' is the desired machine.

Let $M' = (Q \cup \{h, h_a\}, \Sigma, \delta', q_0, \{h_a\})$, where

$$\delta' = \delta \cup \{((f, c, d), (h, 0, d, 0)) \mid \delta(f, c, d) \text{ is undefined, } f \in F, \ c, d \in \Sigma_T\}$$
$$\cup \{((q, c, d), (l_r, 0, d, 0)) \mid \delta(q, c, d) \text{ is undefined, } q \notin F, \ c, d \in \Sigma_T\}$$
$$\cup \{((h, c, d), (h, +1, d, 0)) \mid c \in \Sigma \cup \{\langle\}, \ d \in \Sigma_T\}$$
$$\cup \{((h, \rangle, d), (h_a, 0, d, 0)) \mid d \in \Sigma_T\}$$
$$\cup \{((l_r, c, d), (l_r, 0, d, 0)) \mid c, d \in \Sigma_T\}$$

It is clear that M' is indeed a DTM.

We claim that $L(M) = L(M')$. Consider the behaviors of M and M' on an input x. Both machines have the same initial configuration, and their transition functions δ and δ' are identical, except for the new transitions added to δ.

These new transitions are encountered in the execution of M' only when an accepting state $f \in F$ is encountered. So long as no states in F are encountered during execution, both M and M' behave exactly the same.

Now, when M encounters a state f in F, it may halt (because δ is undefined and so there is no transition out of f for the current configuration) or simply pass through by making another transition. If M simply passes through state f during execution, so does M' because δ' has the same transition.

The behavior of M and M' begin to differ only when M halts. Machine M halts in a state $f \in F$ and accepts x if and only if M' makes a transition to state h (from which it eventually accepts x by halting in state h_a).

Machine M halts in a state $f \notin F$ if and only if M' makes a transition to state l_r (and loops forever). So for $x \notin L(M)$, machine M' never halts.

begin
    copy input tape to work tape, during the copy verify that
        a's come first, then *b*'s, and then *c*'s;
    if input not in proper format **then** reject;
    while true **do**
        reset the work tape head to the left;
        make a pass over the work tape, replacing one occurrence
            each of *a*, *b*, and *c* by *X*;
        if there were no *a*'s, *b*'s, and *c*'s replaced **then** accept;
        if not all three were replaced **then** reject;
end

Figure 6.5

High–level code for accepting the language that consists of strings containing the
same number of *a*'s, *b*'s, and *c*'s with the symbols coming in this order. The details of
the machine are provided in Example 6.2.11.

Thus M accepts x if and only if M' accepts x, and so $L(M) = L(M')$.
This completes the proof.   ■

Many simulations in computability theory follow the same basic steps as contained in this lemma. It is useful in some proofs (in order to simplify them) to assume that DTMs have only one accepting state. This lemma provides justification for such an assumption.

Let's look at another example of a DTM. In the exercises we ask you to develop a few other DTM programs.

Example 6.2.11   A DTM to accept the language $\{a^i b^i c^i \mid i \geq 0\}$

Let's look at a high–level description of an algorithm for accepting this language before presenting the five–tuple of a DTM for it. In Figure 6.5 we show one approach for accepting this language. On an input x of length n, the idea is to make at most $n/3 + 1$ left–to–right passes over the input once it has been copied to the work tape. If possible during each pass, an a, b, and c are crossed off, in this order. If at any time one or two symbols become exhausted, the input is rejected, as it is if the symbols appear in an incorrect order. While copying the input to the work tape, we check that the symbols are in the correct order. In the situation when all symbols run out at the same time, the input is accepted.

Let $M = (\{q_0, q_1, q_2, q_3, q_4, q_5, q_6, q_7, q_8, q_9\}, \{a, b, c, X\}, \delta, q_0, \{q_9\})$, where δ is given as described in Table 6.5. The first transition in the table is so that we can accept Λ. Transitions involving states q_1, q_2, and q_3 are used to copy the input to the work tape and to make sure the symbols appear in the correct order. State q_4 is used to reset the work tape head to its left end. State q_5 is used to find the first unmarked a and then mark it. If in state q_5 a ⟩ is seen on the work tape, then we

State	Input Symbol	Work Tape Symbol	New State	Move on Input Tape	Symbol Written on Work Tape	Move on Work Tape
q_0	⟩	⟩	q_5	0	⟩	0
q_0	a	⟩	q_1	+1	a	+1
q_1	a	⟩	q_1	+1	a	+1
q_1	b	⟩	q_2	+1	b	+1
q_2	b	⟩	q_2	+1	b	+1
q_2	c	⟩	q_3	+1	c	+1
q_3	c	⟩	q_3	+1	c	+1
q_3	⟩	⟩	q_4	0	⟩	−1
q_4	⟩	a	q_4	0	a	−1
q_4	⟩	b	q_4	0	b	−1
q_4	⟩	c	q_4	0	c	−1
q_4	⟩	⟨	q_5	0	⟨	+1
q_4	⟩	X	q_4	0	X	−1
q_5	⟩	a	q_6	0	X	+1
q_5	⟩	b	q_8	0	b	+1
q_5	⟩	c	q_8	0	c	+1
q_5	⟩	X	q_5	0	X	+1
q_5	⟩	⟩	q_9	0	⟩	0
q_6	⟩	a	q_6	0	a	+1
q_6	⟩	b	q_7	0	X	+1
q_6	⟩	X	q_6	0	X	+1
q_7	⟩	b	q_7	0	b	+1
q_7	⟩	c	q_4	0	X	−1
q_7	⟩	X	q_7	0	X	+1

Table 6.5

The transition table for a DTM to accept the language $\{a^i b^i c^i \mid i \geq 0\}$. The remainder of the machine is formally specified in Example 6.2.11.

have successfully marked all of the work tape contents. In this case we transfer to state q_9 and the input is accepted. The transitions involving state q_6 are to locate and mark the next b, and similarly for state q_7 except the next c is marked. State q_8 is used to reject inputs that did not contain enough a's.

Let's consider a trace of M on input ab.

$$(q_0, [1, ab], [1, \Lambda]) \vdash_M (q_1, [2, ab], [2, a])$$

$$\vdash_M (q_2, [3, ab], [3, ab])$$

Since q_2 is not an accepting state and no transitions involving q_2 are applicable, we see $ab \notin L(M)$. We ask you to trace M on a few other inputs in the exercises. ∎

Concept	Reference
input tape	Section 4.2.1
states	Definition 6.1.1
data alphabet	Definition 6.1.1
tape alphabet	Definition 6.1.1
initial state	Definition 6.1.1
accepting states	Definition 6.1.1
work tape	Page 163
output tape	Page 165
finite control	Definition 6.2.1
transition function	Definition 6.2.1
transition table	Page 166
configuration	Definition 6.2.3
initial configuration	Definition 6.2.3
next move, steps, or yields	Definition 6.2.5
halting configuration	Definition 6.2.6
halt	Definition 6.2.6
hang	Page 170
accept a string	Definition 6.2.7
accepting configuration	Definition 6.2.7
rejecting configuration	Definition 6.2.7
accept a language	Definition 6.2.8
$\mathcal{L}_{\mathbf{DTM}}$	Definition 6.2.8
recursively enumerable language	Definition 6.2.8
decidable/recursive language	Definition 6.2.9
undecidable language	Definition 6.2.9

Table 6.6

This table summarizes the terminology developed to define DTMs and make use of them for studying computations.

We conclude this section by summarizing in Table 6.6 the basic concepts that are associated with DTMs. In the next section we explore the consequences of adding additional work tapes to a DTM.

6.2.2   Multiple–Work–Tape Turing Machines

One way of evaluating the quality of our computational models is to see how their capabilities change as we add or delete features. Our DTMs have one input tape and a single work tape. What happens if we add additional work tapes? This is certainly convenient from a programming standpoint. It is often much easier to design a k-work-tape DTM ($k > 1$) than a 1-work-tape DTM. We abbreviate "k–work–tape" to just "k–tape." All of the basic definitions in Table 6.6 can be extended in a natural way to k-tape DTMs. We ask you to present the formal definition of a k-tape DTM in the exercises.

Is the k-tape machine more powerful in the sense that it can accept new languages? The following theorem shows that the answer to this question is no; that is, any language accepted by a k-tape DTM can also be accepted by a 1-tape DTM.

Theorem 6.2.12 *Let $M = (Q, \Sigma, \delta, q_0, F)$ be a k-tape DTM. Then $L(M)$ is accepted by a 1-tape DTM.*

Proof: If k equals 1, the result is trivial. We sketch the result for the case k greater than 1 and ask you to complete the argument in the exercises. We will build a 1-tape DTM M' to simulate M.

Each step of M is simulated by a phase of M', where a phase of M' consists of a number of sweeps over its work tape. The key idea is to view M''s work tape as having multiple tracks. Figure 6.6 shows the correspondence between M and M''s work tapes in the case k equals 2. The odd–numbered tracks (in this case 1 and 3) are used to hold the work tape contents of M, and the even–numbered tracks are used to record the tape head positions on the work tapes. A 0 indicates M is not scanning the square, and a 1 indicates it is. So, on each even–numbered track there is exactly one 1. Using the 1's as tape head marker positions, M' can determine what symbols M is scanning at any given step.

First we present a high–level sketch of the simulation, and then look at it in more detail. Simulating one move of M can be done using a phase of six sweeps over M''s work tape as follows:

Sweep 1: Acquire the symbols that the tape heads of M are currently scanning and store them in the finite control.

Sweep 2: Rewrite the symbols that the tape heads of M are scanning according to the transition function of M.

Sweep 3: "Extend" the right end of the virtual work tapes if necessary.

Sweep 4: "Extend" the left end of the virtual work tapes if necessary.

Sweep 5: Move all tape heads that need to go to the right.

Sweep 6: Move all tape heads that need to go to the left.

What does the data alphabet, Γ, of M' look like? It certainly must contain Σ, since the input tape remains the same. It must also be able to encode the configurations of the k work tapes that are being compressed onto a single tape. Each virtual work tape has two tracks. Tape squares on the first track contain a symbol from $\Sigma \cup \{L, R\}$, and on the second track contain a symbol from $\{0, 1\}$. We

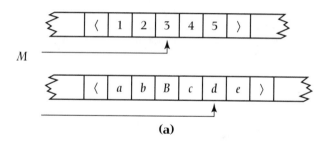

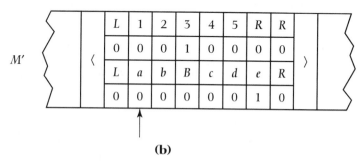

Figure 6.6

The correspondence between the work tapes of M and M' in the proof of Theorem 6.2.12 in the case where k equals 2. We view M''s single work tape as having $2k$ tracks. The 1's in the even–numbered tracks mark the work tape head positions of M.

need to introduce the two extra symbols, L and R, to act as end–of–tape markers for the new virtual work tapes. Thus

$$\Gamma = \Sigma \cup ((\Sigma \cup \{L, R\}) \times \{0, 1\})^k$$

Symbols from the Cartesian product portion of Γ are written as $2k$-tuples.

The behavior of M' is as much like M's as possible, except that M' supports the unpacking and packing of the work tape configurations.

Let's expand a bit further about how the simulation is performed.

1. M' is fed the same input as M. Since $M''s$ input tape has its own tape head, the input tape of M' essentially mimics the input tape of M. There will be times when the input head of M' remains stationary during sweeps over its work tapes.

2. As part of its initialization, M' has to set up an initial configuration for each of the virtual work tapes; that is, each of the work tapes should be empty with the head positioned over the right end marker. So M' writes

$$\underbrace{(L, 0, L, 0, \cdots, L, 0)}_{2k \text{ symbols}} \circ \underbrace{(R, 1, R, 1, \cdots, R, 1)}_{2k \text{ symbols}}$$

to its work tape. Note how $2k$ symbols are packed into 1 on the tape. M' is then initialized to state q_0.

3. M' sweeps from left to right, storing (in the finite control) the symbols $a_1, a_2, \ldots, a_k$ that appear above the symbol 1 in an even-numbered track of M''s work tape. These k symbols plus the current input symbol, x_i, are what M needs in order to determine its next transition. Note that a left-to-right sweep is completed when the $\rangle$ mark is encountered; a right-to-left when the $\langle$ mark is encountered.

4. Suppose q is the current state of M and

$$\delta(q, x_i, a_1, \ldots, a_k) = (\widetilde{q}, d_0, b_1, d_1, \ldots, b_k, d_k)$$

where $d_j \in \{-1, 0, +1\}$ for $0 \leq j \leq k$ and $b_j \in \Sigma$ for $1 \leq j \leq k$. Note that, if δ is undefined on $(q, x_i, a_1, \ldots, a_k)$, then so is δ'—the transition function of M'.

5. Move M''s input tape head in direction d_0. No more movement of the input head is performed until the next phase.

6. Sweep from right to left, replacing a_i by b_i for $1 \leq i \leq k$ above the 1's as in step 3. This writes the new symbols to the tape, but does not adjust for insertions and deletions. If M would have written a $\langle$ (or $\rangle$) onto the work tape, M' writes an L (or, respectively, R) instead.

7. Sweep from left to right, writing an R in all cells of a virtual work tape that occur to the right of the first R in the virtual work tape. If there is a virtual work tape that is missing an R at the end, write an R. If the write to the actual work tape would be onto the $\rangle$ mark, then write $(R, 0, R, 0, \ldots, R, 0)$ to extend the virtual work tapes.

8. Sweep from right to left, writing an L in all cells of a virtual work tape that occur to the left of the first L in the virtual work tape. If there is a virtual work tape that is missing an L at the end, write an L. If the write to the actual work tape would be onto the $\langle$ mark, then write $(L, 0, L, 0, \ldots, L, 0)$ to extend the virtual work tapes.

9. Sweep from left to right, moving the tape head marker one cell to the right for each even-numbered track where $d_i = +1$. If you reach a tape cell in which all virtual tape cells are R, then move right one cell and write $\rangle$ to truncate the work tape.

10. Sweep from right to left, moving the tape head marker one cell to the left for each even-numbered track where $d_i = -1$. If you reach a tape cell in which all virtual tape cells are L, then move left one cell and write $\langle$ to truncate the work tape.

11. Set the state of M' to $\tilde{q}$.

12. Go to step 3 and simulate the next step of M.

This completes the sketch of the proof. It should be clear that $L(M') = L(M)$, since M' simulates each move of M and the accepting states of M' are the same as those of M. ∎

A different approach to the proof of Theorem 6.2.12 is to string out all of M's work tapes sequentially on M''s work tape. So, the work tape for M' looks something like the following:

(work tape 1 contents)(work tape 2 contents) $\cdots$ (work tape k contents)

We ask you to expand on this approach in the exercises.

We have now seen that adding extra work tapes to a DTM does not add new computational power—no new languages can be accepted. In fact, all other "reasonable" enhancements to DTMs that have been thought of also provably do not add more power to DTMs. These observations provide more evidence for the Church–Turing Thesis. Several exercises consider extensions to DTMs, and you are asked to show the equivalence of the new models with the original DTM.

In view of the Church–Turing Thesis and the remarks provided above, we know that anything that is considered computable can be computed by a DTM. Thus, for example, we know that DTMs can be designed for simple tasks such as multiplication, division, counting the number of one type of symbol in the input, and so on. Additionally, any computation that a C program can carry out a DTM can also perform. In light of these observations, we find it more convenient to discuss "Turing machine" programs at a high level in an algorithmic language. Let us present an example of this. In principle, for any high–level code we design in this book, a DTM could be produced that carries out the same computation.

There is one important thing to remember when writing high–level algorithms. Each operation mentioned in the algorithm must itself be justified by being computable by a Turing Machine. For example, the high–level algorithm for the clique problem of Example 6.2.13 has an iteration over every possible subset of five vertices. It is clear that this enumeration is possible. On the other hand, we could not have an iteration over every possible subset of the integers.

Example 6.2.13 A high–level description of a DTM to accept the language

$\{G = (V, E) \mid G$ has a clique of size at least five$\}$

A *clique* is a set of vertices that are pairwise adjacent. That is, $V' \subseteq V$ is a clique if for all $u, v \in V'$, $\{u, v\} \in E$. The *size* of a clique is the number of vertices in it. The language under consideration in this example consists of all undirected graphs

begin
 if the input is not a valid encoding of an undirected graph **then** reject;
 if $|V| < 5$ **then** reject;
 for each possible subset of five vertices V' of V **do**
  if the vertices in V' form a clique **then** accept;
 reject;
end

Figure 6.7

High–level code for accepting the language consisting of strings that are encodings of undirected graphs that have a clique of size five or more. The code is discussed in Example 6.2.13.

that have a clique of size five. We have not specified an encoding for the graph G, but any of those studied in Section 2.9.1 suffices. For example, the graph may be coded using an adjacency matrix, an edge list, or adjacency lists.

Figure 6.7 depicts the code for accepting this language. The first step in the algorithm is simply to verify that the input encodes an undirected graph. Once an encoding scheme has been agreed on, it is easy for a DTM to check that a given input meets the requirements of the encoding scheme. If the graph does not have at least five vertices, then clearly it cannot have a clique of size five. The **for** loop tests each subset of five vertices of V to see if they form a clique. Note that if a graph has a clique of size five or more, then it must have a clique of size exactly five. If five vertices are found that form a clique, the input is accepted; otherwise, the input is rejected. ∎

In the exercises we ask you to specify high–level code for accepting some similar languages. Now let's turn to the nondeterministic variant of DTMs.

6.2.3   Nondeterministic Turing Machines

In this section we add nondeterminism to the Turing machine. As we have seen, nondeterminism is very useful for modeling and simplifying solutions to computations. We have already mentioned that DTMs are as powerful in terms of language acceptance as any computational model. Thus we know that the addition of nondeterminism to a DTM will not add more computing power in this sense. It is very instructive though to show how a nondeterministic Turing machine (NTM) can be simulated by a DTM. Recall that for automata we saw that DFAs could simulate NFAs, but DPDAs could not simulate PDAs.

In a deterministic computation, the next move of a Turing machine is determined uniquely by δ, since δ is a function. In an NTM we allow the possibility of more than just one next move. That is, the computation may branch at each

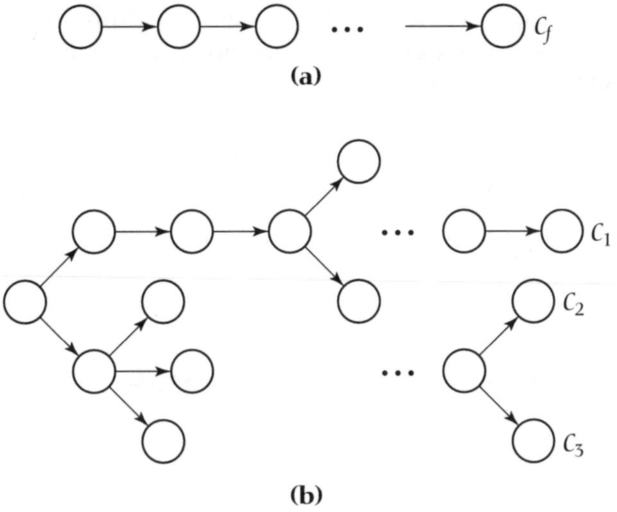

(a)

(b)

Figure 6.8

Configurations are represented by circles and transitions by arrows. (a) A deterministic computation: there is only one next possible configuration at each step in the computation. (b) A nondeterministic computation: at certain points the computation may branch, creating multiple threads.

configuration; there can be several different possible threads. Figure 6.8 illus-trates this schematically. The computation of a DTM can be viewed as a "tree" with only one branch, whereas the computation of an NTM can be viewed as a "tree" having many possible branches. Each computation of an NTM is allowed to follow one branch or thread. How are these threads incorporated into the syntax of an NTM? The following definition specifies how.

Definition 6.2.14   *A **nondeterministic Turing machine (NTM)** is a five-tuple*

$$M = (Q, \Sigma, \Delta, q_0, F)$$

*that is defined similarly to a DTM except for the specification of the transitions. The **transition relation** Δ is a finite subset of*

$$Q \times \Sigma_T \times \Sigma_T \times Q \times \{-1, 0, +1\} \times \Sigma_T \times \{-1, 0, +1\}$$

Nearly all of our definitions for DTMs (see Table 6.6) carry over in a natural way to NTMs. The main difference is in the transition relation versus the transition function. Δ is a finite relation that is no longer necessarily a function. In particular, this means $\vdash_M$ and $\vdash_M^*$ are no longer necessarily functions. It is nevertheless convenient to use function notation to express transitions, such as $\Delta(q, a, b) = (q', d_1, c, d_2)$, but keep in mind that Δ need not be a function.

If an NTM has several computations on a given input, how do we define acceptance? We use the same convention as we did for NFAs and PDAs; if *any* computation path leads to acceptance, then the input is accepted. That is, if at least one thread leads to acceptance, the input is accepted. More formally:

Definition 6.2.15   *Let $M = (Q, \Sigma, \Delta, q_0, F)$ be an NTM. Suppose $x \in \Sigma^*$ and*

$$(q_0, [1, x], [1, \Lambda]) \vdash_M^* (f, [h, x], [k, s]) = C_f$$

where C_f is a halting configuration. When $f \in F$, M **accepts** *x.*
    The **language accepted** *by M, denoted $L(M)$, is*

$$\{x \mid M \text{ accepts } x\}$$

The class of languages accepted by all NTMs is denoted $L_{\mathbf{NTM}}$. That is,

$$\mathcal{L}_{\mathbf{NTM}} = \{L \mid \text{there exists an NTM } M \text{ with } L = L(M)\}$$

Theorem 6.2.12 generalizes in a straightforward manner to yield the following analogous theorem for NTMs.

Theorem 6.2.16   *Let $M = (Q, \Sigma, \Delta, q_0, F)$ be a k-tape NTM. Then $L(M)$ is accepted by a 1-tape NTM.*

Proof: The proof is left as a potentially nasty exercise.   ∎

Let's look at a couple of examples of NTMs. We present descriptions at a high level and ask you to specify the full five–tuples for the machines in the exercises.

Example 6.2.17   An NTM to accept the language

$$\{x \diamondsuit y \mid x, y \in \{0, 1\}^* \text{ and } x \neq y\}$$

This language consists of two unequal bit strings that are separated by the delimiter $\diamondsuit$. Two strings x and y are *equal* if $|x| = |y|$ and $x(i) = y(i)$ for $1 \leq i \leq |x| = |y|$. The intuitive idea to accept such a language is to use nondeterminism to "guess" the position i, $1 \leq i \leq |x|$, verifying that $x(i) \neq y(i)$. Assuming the input has the correct form and such an i exists, then we should accept it. Of course, if the input has the correct form and $|x| \neq |y|$, then we should also accept it regardless of whether such an i can be found.

Figure 6.9 depicts the code for accepting this language. The first step in the algorithm is simply to verify that the input is properly encoded (i.e., consists of a bit string, followed by the only $\diamondsuit$ in the input, and then followed by a bit

begin
    if (the input is not a bit string x, followed by a single delimiter $\diamond$,
        followed by a bit string y) **then** reject;
    if $|x| \neq |y|$ **then** accept;
    guess a natural number i (represented in binary) such that $1 \leq i \leq |x|$;
    if $x(i) \neq y(i)$ **then** accept **else** reject;
end

Figure 6.9

High–level code for accepting the language consisting of strings $x \diamond y$ such that $x \neq y$ and $x, y \in \{0, 1\}^*$. The code is elaborated on in Example 6.2.17.

State	Input Symbol	Work Tape Symbol	New State	Move on Input Tape	Symbol Written on Work Tape	Move on Work Tape
q	a	$\rangle$	q	0	0	+1
q	a	$\rangle$	q	0	1	+1
q	a	$\rangle$	$\tilde{q}$	0	$\rangle$	0

Table 6.7

Transitions illustrating how an NTM can guess a bit string from a state q and then resume computation from state $\tilde{q}$ at any time. Such a guess is needed in Example 6.2.17.

string). The second step is to check if the strings have different lengths. If they do, the NTM accepts, since the strings themselves must be different in this case. The next step is to try and "guess" a position in the strings where they differ. This amounts to finding a proof that the strings are different. Abstractly, we can view the guessing as starting many threads, each thread testing a single position.

How can we implement such a guess in an NTM? The idea is to have a state q in the NTM from which either a 0 or a 1 can be written on the work tape, followed by moving the work tape head one square to the right, and then returning to state q. Out of state q a transition is required, which can be applied at any time via nondeterminism, to another state $\tilde{q}$, from which the writing of the guess stops and the next part of the computation resumes. Table 6.7 shows the transitions needed. To upper–bound the length of the guess, a shell consisting of a **for** loop can be added around state q's transitions. Remember that for an NTM to accept its input, only one thread needs to lead to acceptance. Thus, if there is some i such that $x(i) \neq y(i)$, the NTM will guess i on the computation when it writes i on the work tape and find that $x(i) \neq y(i)$. ■

begin
    if (the input is not an encoding of an undirected graph $G = (V, E)$,
        followed by the delimiter $\diamond$,
        concatenated with a vertex $s \in V$,
        followed by the delimiter $\diamond$,
        and concatenated with a vertex $t \in V$) **then** reject;
    if $s = t$ **then** accept;
    guess a sequence of vertices $s = v_1, \ldots, v_k = t$, where $2 \le k \le |V|$;
    for $l \leftarrow 1$ **to** $k - 1$ **do**
        if $\{v_l, v_{l+1}\} \notin E$ **then** reject;
    accept;
end

Figure 6.10

High–level code for accepting the language consisting of strings $G \diamond s \diamond t$, where $G = (V, E)$ is an undirected graph; $s, t \in V$; and there is a path in G from s to t. This NTM algorithm is discussed further in Example 6.2.18.

Example 6.2.18   An NTM to accept the language

$\{G \diamond s \diamond t \mid G$ is an encoding of an undirected graph $G = (V, E), s, t \in V$, and there is a path from s to t in $G\}$

This language consists of strings that encode an undirected graph delimited with $\diamond$ from a node s in the graph, delimited with $\diamond$ from a node t in the graph, and such that there is a *path* from s to t. A **path** in the graph is a sequence of vertices $s = v_1, \ldots, v_k = t$, where $k \ge 1$, $\{v_i, v_{i+1}\} \in E$ for $1 \le i \le k - 1$. The idea is to use nondeterminism to guess such a path if it exists and then to verify that the guessed path is in fact a path from s to t.

Figure 6.10 depicts the code for accepting this language. The first phase of the algorithm is simply to verify that the input is properly encoded. We have not specified a particular encoding for G but any of those described in Section 2.9.1 suffice. The second phase is to guess a sequence of vertices from V. The final phase is to check that the sequence of guessed vertices forms a path from s to t in G. The manner in which the vertices are guessed is similar to the method used in Example 6.2.17 for guessing a natural number. ∎

In the next section we relate DTMs and NTMs.

6.2.4   Equivalence of DTMs and NTMs

The following theorem shows that any language that can be accepted by an NTM can also be accepted by a DTM. The theorem is actually slightly stronger than this in that it proves $\mathcal{L}_{\textbf{DTM}} = \mathcal{L}_{\textbf{NTM}}$. We will see later in this text that NTMs seem to be more efficient than DTMs, and this apparent difference is one of the most fundamental open problems in computer science—the P versus NP question.

Theorem 6.2.19 *The language classes $\mathcal{L}_{\textbf{DTM}}$ and $\mathcal{L}_{\textbf{NTM}}$ are equal.*

Proof: To prove the result, we need to show $\mathcal{L}_{\textbf{DTM}} \subseteq \mathcal{L}_{\textbf{NTM}}$ and that $\mathcal{L}_{\textbf{NTM}} \subseteq \mathcal{L}_{\textbf{DTM}}$.

($\mathcal{L}_{\textbf{DTM}} \subseteq \mathcal{L}_{\textbf{NTM}}$) First we prove that determinism is a special case of nondeterminism. We show $\mathcal{L}_{\textbf{DTM}} \subseteq \mathcal{L}_{\textbf{NTM}}$. Let $L \in \mathcal{L}_{\textbf{DTM}}$. Then there exists a DTM $M = (Q, \Sigma, \delta, q_0, F)$ such that $L(M) = L$. Define an NTM $N = (Q, \Sigma, \Delta, q_0, F)$, where if

$$\delta(q, a, b) = (q', d_1, c, d_2)$$

then

$$((q, a, b), (q', d_1, c, d_2)) \in \Delta$$

It is easy to see that these machines have the same transitions, so they behave the same, and so $L(M) = L(N)$. Since $L(N) = L$, this shows $L \in \mathcal{L}_{\textbf{NTM}}$, and we can conclude that $\mathcal{L}_{\textbf{DTM}} \subseteq \mathcal{L}_{\textbf{NTM}}$.

($\mathcal{L}_{\textbf{NTM}} \subseteq \mathcal{L}_{\textbf{DTM}}$) Now let's show the more interesting case that nondeterminism can be simulated by determinism. That is, we show $\mathcal{L}_{\textbf{NTM}} \subseteq \mathcal{L}_{\textbf{DTM}}$. Let $L \in \mathcal{L}_{\textbf{NTM}}$. Then there exists an NTM $N = (Q, \Sigma, \Delta, q_0, F)$ such that $L(N) = L$. By Theorem 6.2.16 we can assume without loss of generality that N only has one work tape.

For each triple $(q, a, b) \in Q \times \Sigma_T \times \Sigma_T$, observe that there can be at most $|Q| \times |\{-1, 0, +1\}| \times |\Sigma_T| \times |\{-1, 0, +1\}| = 9|Q| \cdot |\Sigma_T|$ different elements related to it in Δ. Let $p = 9|Q| \cdot |\Sigma_T|$; that is, for a fixed triple, N has at most p possible next moves. Another way of saying this is that the maximum number of threads N that can begin from any configuration is p. We can view the moves of N out of a given triple as being labeled $1, \ldots, p$. Since there may be triples that do not have p moves out of them, some labels will correspond to "dummy" transitions.

A computation of N of length t can now be viewed as a sequence $c_1, c_2, \ldots, c_t$ of transitions, where $1 \leq c_i \leq p$ for $1 \leq i \leq t$ and each c_i represents the move chosen at the ith step in the computation. Figure 6.11 depicts the situation.

A DTM M will simulate N by exploring this computation tree of N in a breadth-first manner. (Note that a depth-first approach would not work, since we might end up following an infinite branch and never return.) M will have two work tapes in addition to its input tape. Then by applying Theorem 6.2.12, the result will follow.

On its first work tape, M generates, term by term, a sequence of digit strings of the following form:

$$1, 2, \ldots, p, 11, 12, \ldots, pp, 111, \ldots, 1pp, \ldots, p11, \ldots, ppp, 1111, \ldots$$

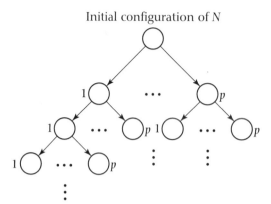

Initial configuration of N

Figure 6.11

The computation tree of an NTM corresponding to the proof of Theorem 6.2.19. Each circle represents a configuration of N. There are at most p next possible configurations at each step.

Each string of digits of length n is the label of a path from the root to a node of depth n in the computation tree of Figure 6.11. Ordering the paths by increasing length gives the breadth–first traversal of the computation tree. In other words, M will be generating all the paths in the computation tree in enumeration order.

After generating on work tape one a new term α in the sequence of paths, M resets its input head and simulates N on the sequence α, using its second work tape as N's work tape. The values of α dictate which transition of N is to be applied. If N accepts, then M accepts. If the path does not lead to acceptance, M generates the next path in order, cleans up its work tape, resets its input tape head, and continues. This process is depicted in a high–level algorithm in Figure 6.12.

We claim that $L(M) = L(N)$. Consider N on input x. Let C_0 denote the initial configuration of N on input x. If $x \in L(N)$, then $C_0 \vdash_N^* C_f$ for some accepting configuration C_f of N. Over all the paths in the computation tree of N that lead to acceptance of x, there will be a first one in enumeration order. Let α denote this path. Then for all paths $\alpha' <_{\text{enum}} \alpha$, M will not accept x. Therefore, α will be produced on work tape one. On sequence α, M will accept x.

If N does not accept x, then no accepting path in the computation tree exists, and so M will never halt, and so M does not accept x.   ∎

The relationship between DTMs and NTMs is considered further in Chapters 8, 10, and 11, where we investigate resource–bounded computations.

begin
    $\alpha \leftarrow 1$;
    while M has not accepted **do**
        increment α on work tape one of M;
        reset M's input tape head;
        clear work tape two of M and reset its tape head;
        simulate N on work tape two using work tape
            one to determine next moves;
    if N would accept **then** M accepts;
end

Figure 6.12

High–level code illustrating how the DTM M simulates the NTM N in Theorem 6.2.19.

6.3 *Undecidable Languages*

The set of Turing machines that halt on every possible input is rather obviously a subset of the set of Turing machines that do not necessarily halt on every input. Thus it is clear that

$$\mathcal{L}_{\textbf{REC}} \subseteq \mathcal{L}_{\textbf{DTM}}$$

We now show that this inclusion is proper. That is, there is a language L such that $L \in \mathcal{L}_{\textbf{DTM}}$ but $L \notin \mathcal{L}_{\textbf{REC}}$.

First, we appeal to our programming intuition and assume that we can build a DTM simulator. To do this, we first have to decide on an appropriate encoding scheme for DTM tuples. Any reasonable one will do. Then our simulator, call it M_{sim}, will take a DTM encoding P, and an input x separated by $\diamond$, and proceed to simulate the operations of the machine, beginning with the initial configuration and continuing one transition at a time. Now the simulator will be able to tell if P halts or hangs, but if P runs forever, so will the simulation. Suppose that the simulator halts and accepts whenever P on input x halts (it does not matter if P halts rejecting or accepting).

Thus, M_{sim} accepts the following language:

$$L_{\text{halt}} = \{P \diamond x \mid \text{DTM described by } P \text{ halts on } x\}$$

The existence of M_{sim} means that $L_{\text{halt}} \in \mathcal{L}_{\textbf{DTM}}$.

Is $L_{\text{halt}} \in \mathcal{L}_{\textbf{REC}}$? If so, we have exactly the situation we had in Problem 4 of Section 1.1.5. And we can use exactly the same diagonalization argument to show that $L_{\text{halt}} \notin \mathcal{L}_{\textbf{REC}}$.

Theorem 6.3.1 L_{halt} *is not decidable, and thus* $\mathcal{L}_{\textbf{REC}} \subset \mathcal{L}_{\textbf{DTM}}$.

Proof: Assume for contradiction that $L_{halt} \in \mathcal{L}_{\mathbf{REC}}$. Then there is a DTM, M_{halt}, that decides L_{halt}. We can do a simple modification of the description of M_{halt} to produce a new machine M_D that takes input x and does the following:

> **begin** M_D
> > **comment:** Input is a string x
> > run M_{halt} on input $x \Diamond x$;
> > **comment:** M_{halt} is guaranteed to halt
> > **if** M_{halt} accepts **then** loop forever **else** accept;
> **end**

Let P_D be the encoded description of M_D. Is $P_D \in L(M_D)$? No, because the following argument leads to a contradiction:

$P_D \in L(M_D)$ if and only if M_D accepts input P_D

if and only if M_{halt} rejects input $P_D \Diamond P_D$

if and only if M_D does not halt on input P_D

if and only if M_D rejects P_D

if and only if $P_D \notin L(M_D)$

Thus $L_{halt} \notin \mathcal{L}_{\mathbf{REC}}$.   ■

6.4   *Relations among Language Classes*

In this section we put together the relationships that have been proved so far in this chapter involving the various language classes. In Section 4.5 we proved that $\mathcal{L}_{\mathbf{DFA}} = \mathcal{L}_{\mathbf{NFA}}$. We were unable to prove a similar result for pushdown automata; however, we do know that $\mathcal{L}_{\mathbf{DPDA}} \subset \mathcal{L}_{\mathbf{PDA}}$. Since a DPDA is merely an extension of a DFA, we know that $\mathcal{L}_{\mathbf{DFA}} \subseteq \mathcal{L}_{\mathbf{DPDA}}$. This, combined with the fact that $\mathcal{L}_{\mathbf{DFA}} = \mathcal{L}_{\mathbf{NFA}}$, implies that $\mathcal{L}_{\mathbf{NFA}} \subseteq \mathcal{L}_{\mathbf{DPDA}}$. In fact, we know more. We mentioned that languages such as

$\{x \mid x \in \{a, b\}^* \text{ and } \#_a(x) = \#_b(x)\}$

are in $\mathcal{L}_{\mathbf{DPDA}}$ but not in $\mathcal{L}_{\mathbf{DFA}}$. Therefore, $\mathcal{L}_{\mathbf{DFA}} \subset \mathcal{L}_{\mathbf{DPDA}}$. Later we proved that $\mathcal{L}_{\mathbf{DTM}} = \mathcal{L}_{\mathbf{NTM}}$, and since we have seen how to implement a stack by a work tape, $\mathcal{L}_{\mathbf{DPDA}} \subset \mathcal{L}_{\mathbf{PDA}} \subseteq \mathcal{L}_{\mathbf{DTM}}$. In fact, languages such as

$\{a^i b^i c^i \mid i \geq 0\}$

are not accepted by any PDA (see Chapter 7) but are accepted by DTMs, as shown in Example 6.2.11. Putting everything together, we get the following series of equalities and inclusions.

$$\mathcal{L}_{\mathbf{DFA}} = \mathcal{L}_{\mathbf{NFA}} \subset \mathcal{L}_{\mathbf{DPDA}} \subset \mathcal{L}_{\mathbf{PDA}} \subset \mathcal{L}_{\mathbf{REC}} \subset \mathcal{L}_{\mathbf{DTM}} = \mathcal{L}_{\mathbf{NTM}} \qquad (6.1)$$

We will examine some of the subclasses of $\mathcal{L}_{\mathbf{DTM}}$ and $\mathcal{L}_{\mathbf{NTM}}$ in Chapters 8, 10, and 11. The results discussed there will reveal more to us about the structure of these classes.

6.5   *Exercises*

Section 6.1   Pushdown Automata

1. Formally define $\vdash$, $\vdash^*$, and $\vdash^i$ for the DPDA.

2. Trace the DPDA given in Example 6.1.5 on the following inputs: Λ, $((()$, $()))$, $(()((,$ and $((()))$.

3. Let M be a DFA. Design a DPDA M' such that $L(M) = L(M')$. Prove your answer is correct.

4. Extend the state transition diagrams used for DFAs and NFAs to represent DPDAs and PDAs.

5. In each part of this problem, assume the underlying alphabet is $\{0, 1\}$. Design DPDAs to accept the following languages:
   (a) 0^*
   (b) $\{0^i 1^i 0^j 1^j \mid i, j \geq 0\}$
   (c) $\{0^{2i} 1^i \mid i \geq 1\}$
   (d) $\{x \mid x \in \{0, 1\}^* \text{ and } \#_0(x) = \#_1(x)\}$
   (e) $\{x \Diamond x^R \mid x \in \{0, 1\}^*\}$
   (f) $\{0^m 1^n \mid m \neq n\}$

6. Trace each machine constructed in Exercise 5 on two accepted inputs of length four or more, and on two rejected inputs of length four or more.

7. Formally define the concepts of string and language acceptance for PDAs.

8. Trace the PDA given in Example 6.1.8 on the following inputs: Λ, 0011, 00111, and 0000. In each case trace all possible threads, that is, both accepting and rejecting. Which strings are accepted by M?

9. Let M be an NFA. Design a PDA M' such that $L(M) = L(M')$. Prove your answer is correct.

10. Consider the following pushdown automaton:

   $$M = (\{q_0, q_1\}, \{0, 1\}, \Delta, q_0, \{q_1\})$$

   where Δ is given in Table 6.8.
   (a) Trace all possible computations of M on input 0101.
   (b) Is $010 \in L(M)$?
   (c) Is M a DPDA? A PDA?
   (d) What language does M accept?

11. Let M be a DPDA. Design an equivalent PDA M'.

Transition Number	State	Input Symbol	Stack Pop	New State	Stack Push
1	q_0	1	Λ	q_0	1
2	q_0	0	Λ	q_0	0
3	q_0	Λ	Λ	q_1	Λ
4	q_1	0	0	q_1	Λ
5	q_1	1	1	q_1	Λ

Table 6.8

The transition table for the PDA described in Exercise 10.

12. In each part of this problem, assume the underlying alphabet is $\{0, 1\}$. Design PDAs to accept the following languages:

   (a) $\{xx \mid x \in \{0, 1\}^*\}$
   (b) $\{x \mid x \in \{0, 1\}^* \text{ and } x = x^R\}$
   (c) $\{0^m 1^n \mid n \le m \le 2n\}$
   (d) $\{0^m 1^n \mid 3n \le m \le 7n\}$

13. Trace each machine constructed in Exercise 12 on two accepted inputs of length four or more. Trace all possible threads of the machine on an input of length four or more that is rejected.

14. Can a DPDA have an infinite computation? How about a PDA?

15. Consider a PDA M with n states and m input alphabet symbols. What is the maximum possible number of rejecting computations that M could have on an input of length k?

16. Can any of the languages described in Exercise 12 be accepted by DPDAs?

17. Suppose we had defined pushdown automata as six–tuples with a separate stack alphabet Γ. Would this increase their power?

18. Suppose we did not require PDAs to accept with the empty stack condition. Would this increase their power? Prove your answer is correct.

Section 6.2   Turing Machines

19. Let $M = (Q, \Sigma, \delta, q_0, F)$ be a DTM. How many possible triples could δ be defined on?

20. Trace the DTM specified in Example 6.2.11 on the following inputs: Λ, abc, $abbc$, $aabbcc$, and $abcabc$.

21. Specify the shortest DTM program you can that goes into an infinite loop on all inputs. Assume the input alphabet is $\{0, 1\}$.

22. Extend the state transition diagrams used for DFAs and NFAs to represent DTMs and NTMs.

23. Define DTMs to accept the following languages. In each case fully specify the five–tuple. Your solution can use a multitape machine if necessary.
    (a) $\{xx \mid x \in \{0, 1\}^*\}$
    (b) $\{x \mid x \in \{0, 1\}^*$ and $x = x^R\}$
    (c) $\{x \mid x \in \{0, 1\}^*$ and $\#_0(x) > |x|/2\}$
    (d) $\{x \Diamond y \Diamond z \mid x \times y = z\}$ Encode the inputs in binary.

24. Write a DTM program (specifying its five–tuple) that generates the sequences on its work tape as required in Theorem 6.2.19. Do this for values of $p = 2$ and $p = 3$. Do not bother to erase each new value, but simply print values in successive order separated by $\Diamond$'s. For example, for $p = 2$, the sequences

    $$1 \Diamond 2 \Diamond 11 \Diamond 12 \Diamond 21 \Diamond 22 \Diamond 111 \Diamond 112 \Diamond \ldots \Diamond 222 \Diamond 1111 \Diamond 1112 \ldots$$

    should be produced. The machine will never halt.

25. Write a C program that simulates a DTM. The program takes as input a file of DTM instructions and then prompts the user to enter an input. The Turing machine's transitions should be input as a list. A transition such as

    $$\delta(q, a, b) = (q', d_1, c, d_2)$$

    should be listed in the file as a single line as follows:

    $$q \quad a \quad b \quad q' \quad d_1 \quad c \quad d_2$$

    where $d_1, d_2 \in \{-1, 0, +1\}$. The accepting states should be listed on the last line of the file and with a blank line separating them from the Turing machine transitions. The output of the program at each step of the Turing machine's computation is the current numbered step that the DTM has executed plus the current configuration of the DTM. Test your simulator on the DTMs produced in Exercise 23.

26. Formally define how a DTM with an output tape can compute a function $f : \mathbb{N} \mapsto \mathbb{N}$. For this problem consider the natural numbers to be represented in *unary*, where 1^n is the string that represents n. For example, Λ represents 0, 11111 represents 5, 111111111 represents 9, and so on.

27. Design DTMs to compute the following functions. Unless otherwise specified, the input number can be in unary; that is, n is encoded as 1^n.
    (a) The *successor function*. $f : \mathbb{N} \mapsto \mathbb{N}$, where $f(n) = n + 1$.
    (b) Let $x \Diamond y$ be an input, where $x, y \in \{1\}^*$. The *addition function*, that is, $x + y$.
    (c) The function $f : \mathbb{N} \times \mathbb{N} \mapsto \mathbb{N}$ such that $f(a, b) = \lceil a/b \rceil$.
    (d) The function $f : \mathbb{N} \mapsto \mathbb{N}$ such that $f(n) = \lceil \log_2 n \rceil$.

28. Present high–level descriptions of DTMs to accept the following languages:

    (a) $\{0^i \mid$ where i is a prime number$\}$

    (b) $\{0^i \mid$ where i is a perfect square$\}$

    (c) $\{x\diamondsuit k \mid x$ is the coding of an undirected graph and x has a clique of size $k\}$

    (d) $\{G = (V, E) \mid G$ is an undirected graph that contains a *Hamiltonian path*$\}$. A Hamiltonian path is a *simple path* that includes each node in V exactly once. A simple path is a sequence of vertices $v_1, \ldots, v_k$ such that $k \geq 1$, $v_i \neq v_j$ for $1 \leq i, j \leq k$ when $i \neq j$, and $\{v_i, v_{i+1}\} \in E$ for $1 \leq i \leq k - 1$.

    (e) $\{x\diamondsuit y\diamondsuit z \mid x \neq y \neq z$ and $x, y, z \in \{0, 1\}^*\}$

29. Formally define a k-tape DTM.

30. Formalize the argument given in Theorem 6.2.12 for the case $k = 2$ by specifying the five–tuple for the 1–tape DTM.

31. In the remarks following the proof of Theorem 6.2.12 we mentioned an alternative strategy for proving the theorem. Fill in the necessary details for such a proof.

32. Define formally what it means for an online DTM to accept a language. Show that online DTMs accept the same class of languages as offline DTMs.

33. Our DTM work tapes are infinite in both directions: you can keep writing new symbols onto either end marker and the tape will be extended. Suppose that we only allow the work tape to be semi–infinite; that is, no writing onto a $\langle$ is allowed of a symbol from $\Sigma \cup \{\}\}$. Prove that a DTM with semi–infinite work tape is equivalent to a DTM having a two–way infinite work tape.

34. Formally define a DTM that is allowed to have multidimensional tapes. Prove that a DTM with one work tape can simulate a DTM that has one two–dimensional work tape.

35. Define a *tree Turing machine* to be a DTM whose work tape is in the shape of a *binary tree*. Prove that a DTM with one work tape is equivalent to a tree Turing machine that has one work tape (in the form of a binary tree).

36. Formally define a *multiheaded Turing machine*, a model in which each tape can have k tape heads. Prove that a DTM with one work tape can simulate a two–headed Turing machine.

37. Let $M = (Q, \Sigma, \Delta, q_0, F)$ be an NTM. What is the maximum cardinality (i.e., size) of Δ?

38. Define NTMs to accept the following languages. In each case fully specify the five–tuple. Where possible provide a simpler design than used in Exercise 23.

(a) $\{xx \mid x \in \{0, 1\}^*\}$

(b) $\{x \mid x \in \{0, 1\}^* \text{ and } x = x^R\}$

(c) $\{x \mid x \in \{0, 1\}^* \text{ and } \#_0(x) > |x|/2\}$

(d) $\{x \Diamond y \Diamond z \mid x \times y = z\}$

39. Present the five–tuple for the NTM sketched in Example 6.2.17.

40. Present the five–tuple for the NTM sketched in Example 6.2.18.

41. Present high–level descriptions of NTMs to accept the following languages:

   (a) $\{0^i \mid \text{where } i \text{ is a prime number}\}$

   (b) $\{0^i \mid \text{where } i \text{ is a composite number}\}$

   (c) $\{x \Diamond k \mid x \text{ is the coding of an undirected graph and } x \text{ has a clique of size } k\}$

   (d) $\{G = (V, E) \mid G \text{ is an undirected graph that contains a } \textit{Hamiltonian path}\}$. See Exercise 28 for a definition of Hamiltonian path.

   (e) $\{x \Diamond y \Diamond z \mid x \neq y \neq z \text{ and } x, y, z \in \{0, 1\}^*\}$

42. Prove Theorem 6.2.16 by generalizing Theorem 6.2.12.

Section 6.4   *Relations among Language Classes*

43. Show explicitly that $\mathcal{L}_{\mathbf{PDA}} \subseteq \mathcal{L}_{\mathbf{NTM}}$.

44. Define a Turing machine that consists of a two–way read/write input tape plus a "guessing module." The guessing module is allowed to write down any string on the tape just to the left of the input to the machine. The computation of such a machine begins with the guessing module writing a string on the tape, leaving the head over the first character of the original input, and transferring control to the finite control of the DTM. Formalize this model. Prove that the language class accepted by this model is $\mathcal{L}_{\mathbf{NTM}}$.

CHAPTER 7

Grammars

Please pardon the grammar.
　　　　　—Rod Stewart

7.1　Introduction

So far, we have studied computation primarily from the point of view of language acceptance and enumeration (see Section 2.11). In this chapter we introduce the notion of describing a language by generation rules, that is, by a *grammar*. We begin with regular grammars in order to establish some intuition, and to demonstrate the correspondence between machines accepting a language and grammars generating a language. We then turn to context–free grammars. Although there are more general grammars, we stick to the context–free grammars because they are the most important ones in the design and implementation of programming languages. As a result, context–free grammars have been heavily studied by computer scientists. In this chapter we touch only on the basics.

7.2　Regular Grammars

Suppose you have the NFA of Figure 7.1. It accepts the language

$$L = \{x \mid x \in 10^* \text{ or } \#_1(x) \text{ is even with } x \in 1^*0(0 \cup 1)^*\}$$

How can we generate strings from L? Observe that $x \in L$ if and only if there is a path from state S to state A labeled with the symbols in x. We use capital letters for state names here as capitals are customary when discussing grammars. To generate the strings in L we need only to systematically enumerate all the paths from S to A.

We begin by writing down the possible transitions that M can make as it reads a symbol from x. If a state is an accepting state, we indicate this by $A \to \Lambda$.

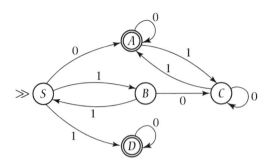

Figure 7.1

An NFA that accepts the regular language $L = \{x \mid x \in 10^*$ or $\#_1(x)$ is even with $x \in 1^*0(0 \cup 1)^*\}$.

$S \to 1D$	$A \to 0A$	
$S \to 1B$	$A \to 1C$	
$S \to 0A$	$A \to \Lambda$	
$B \to 0C$	$C \to 0C$	$D \to 0D$
$B \to 1S$	$C \to 1A$	$D \to \Lambda$

These transitions are called *productions*. A production $X \to sY$ can be interpreted as "from state X append an s to the *current working string* and move to state Y." A production $X \to \Lambda$ can be interpreted as "terminate the current working string and output it as being a member of L."

We can think of productions as editing operations that are performed on the current working string. The working string starts out as symbol S. We then apply a production as a substitution operation, where any symbol in the current working string that matches the left-hand side of the production can be replaced by the right-hand side of the production. To generate a string in L, we start with S and apply productions to the current working string, stopping only when it is impossible to apply any more productions. We indicate the application of a production with $\Rightarrow$. We identify which symbol is to be replaced by underscoring it. For example if we are applying the production to S, we mark the location by $\underline{S}$. Here is a sample derivation:

$\underline{S}$

$\Downarrow$ apply $S \to 0A$

$0\underline{A}$

$\Downarrow$ apply $A \to 1C$

$01\underline{C}$

$\Downarrow$ apply $C \to 1A$

011$\underline{A}$

$\Downarrow$ apply $A \to \Lambda$

011

Thus the string $110 \in L$. Such a sequence of production applications is called a *derivation*. In this case we have shown a derivation of the string 110. It is clear that when the set of productions comes from an NFA M, a string is in $L(M)$ if and only if it has a derivation. What happens if we simply invent a set of productions independently of some NFA? Does this define a language? How is that language related to NFAs?

To answer these questions, we have to make the previous discussion more precise by introducing the notion of a *regular grammar*. As you might expect from the name, the languages generated by regular grammars are exactly the class of regular languages.

Definition 7.2.1 A **regular grammar** *is a four-tuple* $G = (N, \Sigma, P, S)$, *where*

1. N *is an alphabet called the set of* **nonterminals**.
2. Σ *is an alphabet called the set of* **terminals**, *with* $\Sigma \cap N = \emptyset$.
3. P *is a finite set of* **productions** *or* **rules** *of the form* $A \to w$, *where* $A \in N$ *and* $w \in \Sigma^*N \cup \Sigma^*$.
4. S *is the* **start symbol**, $S \in N$.

Notice that productions in a regular grammar have at most one nonterminal on the right–hand side and that this nonterminal always occurs at the end of a production.

Some comments are in order concerning the notation used for grammars. These comments apply to the *context-free grammars*, which are introduced in the next section, as well. Typically, symbols like G, G', and H are used to represent grammars. Nonterminals are usually denoted by uppercase letters; the most frequently used letters are A, B, C, and S. Terminals are usually denoted by lowercase letters, such as a, b, and c, or by individual symbols like those occurring in tape alphabets, such as the symbols 0 and 1. The start symbol is most commonly denoted by the symbol S. Since many productions have the same left–hand nonterminal, we often factor this out and present the alternatives joined by |. For example, the productions $A \to x$ and $A \to y$ are compressed using the notation $A \to x \mid y$. When necessary, we mark the productions of a grammar G with the notation $\to_G$. Normally, we omit the subscript when it is clear from the context which grammar the productions belong to.

Definition 7.2.1 specifies the form of a regular grammar. We now need to define the semantics of a regular grammar—that is, how we determine what strings are generated by G, what the language of G is, and so on. To address these issues, we need to formally define the notion of a derivation.

Definition 7.2.2   *Let $G = (N, \Sigma, P, S)$ be a regular grammar. A* **derivation** *of regular grammar G is a finite sequence of strings $\beta_0, \beta_1, \ldots, \beta_n$ such that*

1. *For $0 \leq i \leq n$, the string $\beta_i \in \Sigma^* N \cup \Sigma^*$.*
2. *$\beta_0 = S$.*
3. *For $0 \leq i < n$, there is a production of P that when applied to β_i yields β_{i+1}. We write $\beta_i \Rightarrow \beta_{i+1}$.*
4. *$\beta_n \in \Sigma^*$. We say β_0 **derives** β_n.*

The reflexive, transitive closure of $\Rightarrow$ is denoted $\Rightarrow^*$. A sequence of the form

$$\beta_0 \Rightarrow \beta_1 \Rightarrow \cdots \Rightarrow \beta_n$$

is called an **n-step derivation** *of β_n from β_0. The number of steps in a derivation is called the* **length** *of the derivation. If β_0 derives β_n in exactly n steps, we write $\beta_0 \Rightarrow^n \beta_n$.*

The string $x = \beta_n$ is said to be **generated by** *G. The* **language generated** *by regular grammar G is*

$$L(G) = \{x \mid x \text{ is generated by } G\}$$

Let's look at a couple of examples of regular grammars before proceeding with the main theorem of this section.

Example 7.2.3   Regular grammars

1. Define the regular grammar $G = (N, \Sigma, P, S)$ with nonterminals $N = \{S\}$, terminals $\Sigma = \{0, 1\}$, and productions

   $$S \to \Lambda, \; S \to 0S, \; S \to 1S$$

   It is easy to see that $L(G) = \{0, 1\}^*$.

2. Define the regular grammar G with the following productions:

   $$S \to \Lambda, \; S \to aA, \; S \to bB, \; A \to abS, \; B \to baS$$

   From the productions we can deduce that the nonterminals are $N = \{S, A, B\}$, and the terminals are $\Sigma = \{a, b\}$. If the start symbol is S, then $L(G)$ is the regular language $(aab \cup bba)^*$. If the start symbol is B, then by inspection, we are prefixing all strings generated by S with ba, and so $L(G) = ba(aaa \cup bba)^*$.   ∎

We have already seen informally that every language accepted by an NFA can be generated by a regular grammar. It is also easy to see that every regular grammar $G = (N, \Sigma, P, S)$ has a corresponding NFA $M = (N \cup \{f\}, \Sigma, \Delta, S, \{f\})$, where Δ is formed as follows:

1. For every production of the form $A \to vB$, where $A \in N$, $v \in \Sigma^*$, and $B \in N$, the transition relation Δ contains (A, v, B).

2. For every production of the form $A \to v$, where $A \in N$, $v \in \Sigma^*$, the transition relation Δ contains (A, v, f).

Thus, although regular grammars and finite–state machines appear to be very different models of computation, in fact they have exactly the same computational power. This is embodied in the following theorem, whose formal proof is left as an exercise.

Theorem 7.2.4 *A language is regular if and only if it can be generated by a regular grammar.*

Theorem 7.2.4 provides us with yet another characterization of the regular languages. Thus a regular language can be represented by a DFA, an NFA, a regular expression, an EFA, or a regular grammar.

7.3 *Context-Free Grammars*

Consider the language $L = \{0^i 1^i \mid i \geq 0\}$. Since this language was shown to be nonregular in Section 5.5, it obviously is not generated by a regular grammar. Can we extend the notion of regular grammars so that we can generate languages like L?

First, let's list the strings in L. They are $\Lambda, 01, 0011, 0^3 1^3$, and so on. For each 0 that is generated on the left–hand side of the string being produced, a 1 needs to be generated on the right–hand side. Notice that the 0's and 1's cannot be generated independently unless we have some way of balancing the total number of each. To generate the empty string, we can think of generating zero 0's and zero 1's. So, if we relax the constraint that regular grammars place on the form of productions, and allow terminals to appear *after* the nonterminal on the right–hand side, we could have the following productions in our grammar:

$S \to \Lambda, \; S \to 0S1$

With these we can produce the string $0^3 1^3$ with the following *derivation*:

$S \Rightarrow 0\underline{S}1 \Rightarrow 00\underline{S}11 \Rightarrow 000\underline{S}111 \Rightarrow 000\Lambda 111 = 0^3 1^3$

As before, for clarity we underline the nonterminal to be replaced at each step. In the generation of the string $0^3 1^3$, we applied rule $S \to 0S1$ three times and then production $S \to \Lambda$ once. It should be clear that any other string in L can be generated by such a procedure. For example, to produce the string $0^i 1^i$, apply the rule $S \to 0S1$ i times, followed by the production $S \to \Lambda$ once.

Now consider the language L of properly nested parentheses. For example $(()(()))$ is in L, but $)($ is not. We will not be able to generate this language unless we further relax the constraints on the form of the productions to allow multiple nonterminals on the right–hand side. For example, we can generate L with these productions:

$$S \to \Lambda, \ S \to (S), \ S \to SS$$

A derivation of $(()(()))$ could look like:

$$\underline{S} \Rightarrow (\underline{S}) \Rightarrow (\underline{S}S) \Rightarrow ((\underline{S})S) \Rightarrow (()\underline{S}) \Rightarrow (()(\underline{S})) \Rightarrow (()((\underline{S}))) \Rightarrow (()(()))$$

Notice how in this derivation productions just happened to be always applied to the leftmost nonterminal in the current working string. Adopting this convention will help when we discuss parsing later.

With these examples in mind, we will now define a context–free grammar.

Definition 7.3.1   *A **context–free grammar (CFG)** is a four-tuple $G = (N, \Sigma, P, S)$, where*

1. *N is an alphabet called the set of **nonterminals**.*
2. *Σ is an alphabet called the set of **terminals**, with $\Sigma \cap N = \emptyset$.*
3. *P is a finite set of **productions** of the form $A \to w$, where $A \in N$ and $w \in (N \cup \Sigma)^*$.*
4. *S is the **start symbol**, $S \in N$.*

Definition 7.3.1 specifies the form of a CFG. We need to present the semantics for a CFG analogously to what we did for regular grammars.

Definition 7.3.2   *Let $G = (N, \Sigma, P, S)$ be a context-free grammar. A **derivation** of context-free grammar G is a finite sequence of strings $\beta_0, \beta_1, \ldots, \beta_n$ such that*

1. *For $0 \le i \le n$, the string $\beta_i \in (N \cup \Sigma)^*$.*
2. *$\beta_0 = S$.*
3. *For $0 \le i < n$, there is a production of P that when applied to β_i yields β_{i+1}.*
4. *$\beta_n \in \Sigma^*$.*

The concepts of $\Rightarrow$, derives, $\Rightarrow^*$, n-step derivation, and length of derivation are as defined for regular grammars.

*The string $x = \beta_n$ is said to be **generated by** G. The **language generated** by context-free grammar G is*

$$L(G) = \{x \mid x \text{ is generated by } G\}$$

*If there is a context-free grammar G for a given language L such that $L(G) = L$, L is called a **context–free language (CFL)**. The class of all context-free languages is denoted $\mathcal{L}_{\textbf{CFL}}$.*

All grammars are variations on a general grammar form called the *phrase structure grammar*. The different categories of grammars are defined by the structure of their productions. In Definition 7.3.2, the production $A \to w$ is always applicable to a string β of the form uAv regardless of the values of u and v—that is, regardless of the context of A. Thus such grammars are called *context-free*. Regular grammars are also context-free, but their productions are further restricted on the right-hand side to contain at most one nonterminal, which must appear at the right. There are other types of grammars that specify the circumstances that must exist around the left-hand side nonterminal of a rule before the production can be applied; that is, application of productions depends on context. These grammars are called *context-sensitive*. We will not pursue the study of context-sensitive grammars in this book.

Before addressing exactly what languages are contained in the class $\mathcal{L}_{\mathbf{CFL}}$ and how this class relates to the other language classes that we have defined, let's look at several context–free grammars.

Example 7.3.3   Context–free grammars

1. Consider the CFG G with productions

   $S \to 0S, \ S \to S1, \ S \to 0$

   $L(G) = 0^*01^*$. Note that $L(G)$ is a regular language, but G is not a regular grammar because of the production $S \to S1$.

2. Consider the CFG G with productions

   $S \to \Lambda \mid A \mid 0S1$

   $A \to 0A \mid 0$

   Sometimes in order to determine what language a specific CFG generates, it is essential to consider sample strings the CFG can generate. We usually start by considering the smallest strings the CFG can generate. In this case,

   $\underline{S} \Rightarrow \Lambda$

   $\underline{S} \Rightarrow \underline{A} \Rightarrow 0$

   $\underline{S} \Rightarrow \underline{A} \Rightarrow 0\underline{A} \Rightarrow 00$

   $\underline{S} \Rightarrow 0\underline{S}1 \Rightarrow 0\Lambda 1 = 01$

   represent derivations of the four shortest strings in $L(G)$. The derivations have lengths 1, 2, 3, and 2, respectively. It is not hard to see that

   $\{0^i1^i \mid i \geq 0\} \subseteq L(G)$

   In fact, $L(G) = \{0^i1^j \mid i \geq j\}$. So, we see that $\{0^i1^j \mid i \geq j\} \in \mathcal{L}_{\mathbf{CFG}}$.

3. The CFG specified in this example generates a portion of a typical programming language's arithmetic expressions. Let G_{exp} be defined by the following productions:

$$S \rightarrow E$$
$$E \rightarrow E + E \mid E * E \mid (E) \mid a \mid b \mid c \mid d$$

The expression $(a + b) * (a * b)$ can be generated by the following derivation:

$$\underline{S} \Rightarrow \underline{E}$$
$$\Rightarrow \underline{E} * E$$
$$\Rightarrow (\underline{E}) * E$$
$$\Rightarrow (\underline{E} + E) * E$$
$$\Rightarrow (a + \underline{E}) * E$$
$$\Rightarrow (a + b) * \underline{E}$$
$$\Rightarrow (a + b) * (\underline{E})$$
$$\Rightarrow (a + b) * (\underline{E} * E)$$
$$\Rightarrow (a + b) * (a * \underline{E})$$
$$\Rightarrow (a + b) * (a * b)$$

In this case the terminals of G_{exp} are $+$, $*$, $($, $)$, a, and b. Since

$$S \Rightarrow^* (a + b) * (a * b)$$

we see $(a + b) * (a * b) \in L(G_{exp})$. In the derivation just presented, observe that at each step we replaced the leftmost nonterminal. Such a derivation is said to be **leftmost**. Analogously, we can define a **rightmost** derivation. Because of the parentheses, the string $(a + b) * (a * b)$ only has one leftmost derivation.

On the other hand, if we have no preferred operator precedence, then the string $a + b * c + d$ has three different leftmost derivations. A CFG G for which there is a string $x \in L(G)$ having two distinct leftmost derivations of x is said to be **ambiguous**.

4. The CFG specified in this example illustrates the manner in which a CFG might be used to generate a portion of a natural language. In this example a terminal is represented by an English word and a nonterminal by a word or words enclosed in angle brackets. Define G by the following group of productions:

$$\langle sentence\rangle \to \langle noun\rangle\langle verb\rangle\langle adverb\rangle$$

$$\langle sentence\rangle \to \langle noun\rangle\langle verb\rangle$$

$$\langle noun\rangle \to \text{fish} \mid \text{birds} \mid \text{trees}$$

$$\langle verb\rangle \to \text{swim} \mid \text{eat} \mid \text{grow}$$

$$\langle adverb\rangle \to \text{fast} \mid \text{a lot} \mid \text{big}$$

In this CFG for natural language, $\langle sentence\rangle$ represents the start symbol. Some "sentences" (strings generated from the start symbol) that can be produced by the grammar are

- *fish swim*
- *birds eat a lot*
- *trees grow fast*
- *fish eat fast*

Although not high-quality prose, these simple sentences do make sense (given an appropriate context). The CFG also derives the following sentences:

- *birds grow a lot*
- *trees swim*
- *trees swim a lot*

There are obviously some difficulties in trying to model the grammar of even a basic fragment of the English language. It was, in fact, this effort that gave rise to formal grammars. The natural language processing community has made a great deal more progress than this simple example shows.   ■

The examples we have presented are useful for understanding some of the basic ideas in the definitions about CFGs and for seeing the potential applications for such CFGs in programming language specification and other related text processing. But how do you go about designing a CFG for a specific language, even a fairly simple one? Let's look at another example language to see what steps are involved in producing a CFG for it.

Consider the language

$$L = \{x \diamond x^R \mid x \in \{0, 1\}^*\}$$

The shortest string in L is $\diamond$. This occurs when x is Λ. Thus, from the start symbol in the CFG we are describing, say S, we need to be able to derive $\diamond$. Tentatively, let's define the production $S \to \diamond$. It is not essential that S go directly to $\diamond$, but in this case it will work out well. Consider a string such as $11010\diamond01011$, which is easily seen to be in L. When a 1 (or 0) is generated at the beginning on the left end of the string, a 1 (or, respectively, 0) must be generated at the right end of the string. We can view the outer symbols as being peeled off similarly to peeling an onion. This means in the productions in the CFG we have to do the reverse. That is, when we add a 1 on the left end, we need to add the corresponding 1 on the right end. This suggests adding the productions $S \rightarrow 0S0 \mid 1S1$ to our set of rules. In fact, it is not hard to see that the CFG, call it G, corresponding to the set of productions

$$\{S \rightarrow \diamond \mid 0S0 \mid 1S1\}$$

is such that $L(G) = L$. It follows that $\{x \diamond x^R \mid x \in \{0, 1\}^*\} \in \mathcal{L}_{\mathbf{CFG}}$.

The design of a CFG for a particular language is essentially a programming problem. First you are given the specification of the language, either naturally in English or mathematically in set–theoretic terms. Then you must design a grammar that satisfies the specification. Finally, if it is not obviously correct, you must prove that your grammar does indeed satisfy the specification of the language. Just like programming, there is no one generic method that always works, but the following strategy works well in practice:

Basic Strategy for CFG Design

1. Understand the specification of L. Produce examples of strings in and not in the language.

2. List the shortest strings in the language in order to determine the "base case" productions.

3. Understand the key structural properties of the language; that is, identify the rules for combining smaller sentences into larger ones. These rules will determine the constructive productions that build the long sentences in the language.

4. Test your prototype CFG on a number of carefully chosen examples. All of the base cases should be tested, along with all of the alternative productions (for a given left–hand nonterminal). Check if the grammar is consistent with your example strings from step 1.

5. Prove that your grammar is correct. This requires two arguments. One is that every string derivable in G is in L; that is, $L(G) \subseteq L$. The other is that every x in L has a derivation in G; that is, $L \subseteq L(G)$. One or both of these may be obvious. Be aware of the fact that there are often subtle flaws in a grammar that can allow you to derive strings not in the intended language.

7.4   *Closure Properties of Context-Free Languages*

Like the regular languages, the context–free languages are closed under union, concatenation, and Kleene star. The proofs of these results are remarkably similar to the versions for regular languages presented in Section 5.2. Because of this correspondence, we will present only one proof in detail and leave the others as exercises.

Unlike regular languages, CFLs are *not* closed under intersection and complement, as we will see in Section 7.8.

Theorem 7.4.1   *The context-free languages are closed under union.*

Proof: The intuitive idea of the proof is to build a new grammar from the original two, and from the start symbol of the new grammar have productions to the start symbols of the original two grammars. We now formalize the argument.

Let $G_1 = (N_1, \Sigma, P_1, S_1)$ and $G_2 = (N_2, \Sigma, P_2, S_2)$ be two context–free grammars. We can assume without loss of generality that they have a common terminal set Σ, and disjoint sets of nonterminals (i.e., $N_1 \cap N_2 = \emptyset$). Because the nonterminals are distinct, so are the production sets P_1 and P_2.

Let S be a new nonterminal not in N_1 or N_2. Construct the new grammar $G = (N, \Sigma, P, S)$, where

$$N = N_1 \cup N_2 \cup \{S\}$$

$$P = P_1 \cup P_2 \cup \{S \rightarrow S_1, \ S \rightarrow S_2\}$$

G is clearly a context–free grammar because the two new productions added are also of the correct form. We claim that $L(G) = L(G_1) \cup L(G_2)$.

Suppose that $x \in L(G_1)$. Then there is a derivation of x in G_1

$$S_1 \Rightarrow^*_{G_1} x$$

But then there is a derivation

$$S \Rightarrow_G S_1 \Rightarrow^*_G x$$

of x in G; thus $x \in L(G)$. Therefore, $L(G_1) \subseteq L(G)$. A similar argument shows $L(G_2) \subseteq L(G)$. So, we have $L(G_1) \cup L(G_2) \subseteq L(G)$.

Conversely, suppose that $x \in L(G)$. Then there is a derivation of x in G

$$S \Rightarrow_G \beta \Rightarrow^*_G x$$

Because of the way in which P is constructed, β must be either S_1 or S_2. Suppose $\beta = S_1$. Any derivation in G of the form $S_1 \Rightarrow^*_G x$ must involve only productions of G_1, and so $S_1 \Rightarrow^*_{G_1} x$ is a derivation of x in G_1. Therefore, $\beta = S_1$ implies $x \in L(G_1)$. A similar argument proves that $\beta = S_2$ implies $x \in L(G_2)$. Thus, $L(G) \subseteq L(G_1) \cup L(G_2)$.

It follows that $L(G) = L(G_1) \cup L(G_2)$.   ∎

Theorem 7.4.2   *The context-free languages are closed under concatenation.*

Theorem 7.4.3   *The context-free languages are closed under Kleene star.*

7.5   *Parsing with Nondeterministic Pushdown Automata*

Let's return to the grammar for arithmetic expressions, G_{exp}, that we introduced in the examples of Section 7.3:

$$S \to E$$
$$E \to E + E \mid E * E \mid (E)$$
$$E \to a \mid b \mid c \mid d$$

Define $L_{exp} = L(G_{exp})$.

Given a string x, how do we determine if x is in $L(G)$? If x is indeed in $L(G)$, how do we determine a derivation for x? These questions lead us to the topic of this section—*parsing*.

Suppose we already have a derivation for x. We can assume that it is a leftmost derivation, because if not, we can always convert it into one. The proof of this fact is left to the exercises.

Let $G = (N, \Sigma, P, S)$ be a context-free grammar. Let's examine the way in which a leftmost derivation proceeds. Suppose we have a derivation

$$S = \beta_0 \Rightarrow \beta_1 \Rightarrow^* \beta_i \Rightarrow \beta_{i+1} \Rightarrow^* \beta_n = x$$

The derivation begins with the start symbol S. At each step, the leftmost nonterminal is replaced by a string of terminals and nonterminals. If the derivation is finished, the resulting string is x. What happens if the derivation is not finished?

Suppose we are at step β_i. We know that $\beta_i = uVw$, where $u \in \Sigma^*$ is a (possibly empty) string of terminals, $V \in N$ is a single nonterminal (the leftmost one), and w is a string from $(\Sigma \cup N)^*$. Suppose that we move to β_{i+1} by applying the production $V \to \gamma V'z$, where V' is the leftmost nonterminal in the production, γ is the sequence of terminals before the first nonterminal, and z is the string of terminals and nonterminals to the right of the first nonterminal in the production.

After this step is taken in the derivation, $\beta_{i+1} = u\gamma V'zw$, where u and w are the same as for β_i. One effect of the step is to generate zero or more additional characters of x, in the form of the prefix $u\gamma$. Another effect is to replace the original nonterminal v with a new one V', possibly inserting a few more symbols before the w.

Thus as the derivation proceeds, the derivation string has a prefix of x that is nondecreasing in length, and a suffix starting with a nonterminal that behaves like a stack in that the first (top) symbol is the one we manipulate by applying productions. When the suffix/stack is empty, all that is left in the derivation string is x. Examine the leftmost derivation in Example 7.3.3 to see this behavior.

Now suppose that we do not have a derivation, but instead must find one. We could search through all leftmost derivations with the procedure described

begin
    push S;
    while stack nonempty **do**
        pop the top of stack into t;
        if t is a nonterminal
        then
            nondeterministically choose a production
                $t \rightarrow u$ of P;
            push the symbols of u in reverse order onto the stack;
        else
            if t matches the current input symbol
            then
                advance input head one symbol;
            else
                reject;
    if input symbol is $\rangle$ **then** accept **else** reject;
end

Figure 7.2

A high–level algorithm for parsing a CFG.

in Figure 7.2. For any given CFG G, we can use the same strategy to build the PDA transition relation. For example,

$$M = (\{q_0, f\}, \{a, b, c, d, (,), +, *, E, S\}, \Delta, q_0, \{f\})$$

where Δ is as specified in Table 7.1, is a machine for accepting the expression language we have been discussing.

The ideas presented above form the essence of the proofs of the following results that relate CFGs to PDAs. Lack of space prevents us from presenting the details of the proofs. These can be found in [26].

Theorem 7.5.1   *Let $G = (N, \Sigma, P, S)$ be a context-free grammar. Then there exists a PDA M such that $L(G) = L(M)$.*

Theorem 7.5.2   *Let $M = (Q, \Sigma, \Delta, q_0, F)$ be a PDA. Then there exists a context-free grammar G such that $L(M) = L(G)$.*

Theorems 7.5.1 and 7.5.2 combine to show the equivalence of CFGs and PDAs as models of computation.

Current State	Input Symbol	Stack Top	New State	Input Op	Stack Op
q_0	Φ	)	q_1	∘	push S
q_1	Φ	S	q_1	∘	pop; push E
q_1	Φ	E	q_1	∘	pop; push $E, +, E$
q_1	Φ	E	q_1	∘	pop; push $E, *, E$
q_1	Φ	E	q_1	∘	pop; push $(, E,)$
q_1	Φ	E	q_1	∘	pop; push a
q_1	Φ	E	q_1	∘	pop; push b
q_1	Φ	E	q_1	∘	pop; push c
q_1	Φ	E	q_1	∘	pop; push d
q_1	a	a	q_1	+	pop
q_1	b	b	q_1	+	pop
q_1	c	c	q_1	+	pop
q_1	d	d	q_1	+	pop
q_1	(	(	q_1	+	pop
q_1	)	)	q_1	+	pop
q_1	)	)	f	∘	∘

Table 7.1

The transition table Δ for a PDA to accept the language L_{exp}. The pseudosymbol Φ means "match on any symbol." Sequences of state transitions to perform a pop followed by multiple pushes have been compressed into a single stack operation entry. The accepting state f has no transitions out of it.

Theorem 7.5.3 *A language L is generated by a context-free grammar if and only if it is accepted by a PDA.*

7.6 *Parsing with Deterministic Pushdown Automata*

In practical parser construction, nondeterministic parsing is a problem, since the parser has to guess what production to apply. If the production eventually leads to failure, the parser has to backtrack to the guess and try the next production. This can result in much wasted computation.

The problem lies in being unable to determine which production to apply at any particular point in the derivation. If there were only one possible choice, the parsing process would be deterministic and would not have the backtracking overhead. Of course, any reasonable grammar must have choices of productions to apply, or the language would be uninteresting. So the trick is to design the grammar for the language so that, with a bit of look–ahead on the input stream, the parser can decide what production to apply.

Let's look at L_{exp} and see how this process works. The idea is that the next symbol in the input stream should determine the production to be applied. This means that for a given nonterminal, the right–hand side of all but one production for that terminal must begin with a unique terminal symbol, and one can begin with a nonterminal. This way a unique production can be selected on the basis of the current input symbol. If the current symbol does not match any production, then the one that begins with a nonterminal is used.

Applying this idea we arrive at the following new grammar G'_{exp} for L_{exp}:

$$S \rightarrow E$$
$$E \rightarrow (E)R \mid VR$$
$$V \rightarrow a \mid b \mid c \mid d$$
$$R \rightarrow +E \mid * E \mid A$$
$$A \rightarrow \Lambda$$

We leave the verification of the correctness of the grammar and the construction of the corresponding DPDA for G'_{exp} as an exercise.

7.7   *Parse Trees and Attribution*

When we discussed G_{exp} in the examples of Section 7.3, we indicated that an expression such as $a + b * c + d$ has more than one leftmost derivation in G_{exp}. What is the significance of this? In the following we present two different derivations. Since they are both leftmost, there is no need to indicate the active site at which a production is applied.

Derivation D_1:

$$S \Rightarrow E$$
$$\Rightarrow E + E$$
$$\Rightarrow a + E$$
$$\Rightarrow a + E * E$$
$$\Rightarrow a + b * E$$
$$\Rightarrow a + b * E + E$$
$$\Rightarrow a + b * c + E$$
$$\Rightarrow a + b * c + d$$

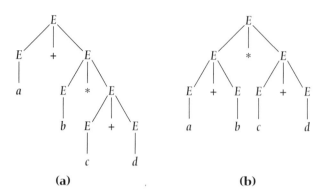

(a)   **(b)**

Figure 7.3

Alternative parse trees for $a + b * c + d \in L_{\exp}$. (a) The parse tree T_1 corresponding to D_1. (b) The parse tree T_2 corresponding to D_2.

Derivation D_2:

$$S \Rightarrow E$$
$$\Rightarrow E * E$$
$$\Rightarrow E + E * E$$
$$\Rightarrow a + E * E$$
$$\Rightarrow a + b * E$$
$$\Rightarrow a + b * E + E$$
$$\Rightarrow a + b * c + E$$
$$\Rightarrow a + b * c + d$$

The difference between these two derivations is only evident if we examine the *parse trees* associated with the two derivations. A **parse tree** is an n-ary tree constructed as follows. Initially the parse tree consists of a single root node labeled with the start symbol. The parse tree is built up by applying productions to leaf nodes until it is impossible to apply any further rules. For example, if a leaf node is labeled with nonterminal E, then any production with E on its left–hand side can be applied to the node. Applying a production creates children for the node, with one child for each symbol on the right–hand side of the production. When all leaf nodes are terminal symbols, then the tree represents a *parse* of a string x. The string is the one obtained by the sequence of leaves enumerated by a *depth-first* left-to-right traversal of the parse tree. Equivalently, we can concatenate all of the leaves together in a left-to-right order.

The parse trees T_1 and T_2 associated with the two example derivations, D_1 and D_2, are shown in Figure 7.3. Notice how the two derivations give rise to differently shaped parse trees.

To determine membership in $L(G)$, it is not a problem to have more than one parse tree for a string x. But if the language generated by the grammar is supposed to have *meaning*, then ambiguity is a problem because normally the meaning of a string x in a language L is given by a function that is applied to a parse tree of x. If there is more than one parse tree for x, there might be more than one meaning for x.

This function, called the *attribution function*, is defined inductively on the parse tree. The base case is defined by specifying the meaning of each of the terminals in G. The induction is achieved by defining the attribution function for each of the productions of G by giving the value of the left–hand side in terms of the values on the right–hand side.

Let's define a *meaning function* for grammar G_{exp}. For the sake of simplicity, we will define the meaning of the terminals a, b, c, and d to be integer constants. Then the attribution function, $\mu()$, will map a parse tree to an integer, which will correspond to the value of the expression. To make the definition precise, multiple instances of the same nonterminal in a production must be indexed by position, indicating their position as children in the parse tree.

Parse Tree Node	**Meaning**
$S \to E$	$\mu(E)$
$E \to E_1 + E_2$	$\mu(E_1) + \mu(E_2)$
$E \to E_1 * E_2$	$\mu(E_1) * \mu(E_2)$
$E \to (E_1)$	$\mu(E_1)$
$E \to a$	$\mu(a)$
$E \to b$	$\mu(b)$
$E \to c$	$\mu(c)$
$E \to d$	$\mu(d)$
a	1
b	2
c	3
d	4

Using this attribution function on the parse trees T_1 and T_2, we have $\mu(T_1) = 1 + (2 * (3 + 4)) = 15$, and $\mu(T_2) = (1 + 2) * (3 + 4) = 21$. These are different values for the same expression. This is generally accepted as not being a good thing for a programming language.

Sometimes the ambiguity in a grammar can be removed (for example, by some additional productions that introduce precedence among operators), and sometimes the grammar is inherently ambiguous and has to be completely rebuilt.

7.8   *Languages That Are Not Context-Free*

Since a grammar has a finite set of productions, there must be some repetitive or recursive structure in the productions in order to generate arbitrarily long strings. Therefore, it is not surprising that there is a *Pumping Lemma for CFLs* analogous to the Pumping Lemma for regular languages. We present a powerful version of the CFL Pumping Lemma, called *Ogden's Lemma*.

Theorem 7.8.1   (Ogden's Lemma) *Let L be a context-free language over the alphabet Σ. Suppose that L contains at least one nonempty string. Then there exists a natural number $k > 0$ such that the following holds.*

Let z be any string in L with $|z| > k$, and mark any k or more characters of z (the marking may be completely arbitrary). Then there exist strings u, v, w, x, and y in Σ^* such that

1. *$z = uvwxy$.*

2. *String vwx contains k or fewer marked characters.*

3. *Each of the strings w, uy, and vx contain at least one marked character.*

4. *For all $d \geq 0$, the string $uv^d wx^d y$ is in L.*

Proof: Let L be a context–free language that contains at least one nonempty string. Suppose that L is generated by the context–free grammar $G = (N, \Sigma, P, S)$. Define

$$n = |N|$$
$$l = \max\{|\omega| \mid A \to \omega \in P\}$$
$$k = l^{n+2}$$

The number n is the number of nonterminals in G, l is the maximum length of the right–hand side of a production, and k is the maximum length of a string that could be generated by a parse tree of depth $n + 2$.

Let z be any string of L with $|z| > k$, and mark any k or more characters of z.

First, observe that if $l = 1$, then $L(G)$ is finite, with no string longer than one symbol, so the claim is vacuously true. Thus we can assume $l > 1$.

Consider a derivation tree for $z = a_1 \cdots a_m$, with $m > k$. It will look something like Figure 7.4.

For convenience, we have drawn all the leaves of the tree at the bottom. Note that some of the leaves are Λ as we permit Λ–productions in G. The remaining leaves are terminal symbols, at least k of which are marked with a $*$.

Now consider a path ρ from S to a marked character t in the derivation of z, where we identify the variables and single terminal on the path by writing $\rho = P_0 P_1 \cdots P_m P_{m+1}$, with $S = P_0$, and $t = P_{m+1}$. We construct path ρ so that at each point P_i on the path, $0 \leq i \leq m$ (corresponding to the application of a production $A_i \to \omega_i$), the path goes in the direction of the subtree containing the maximum

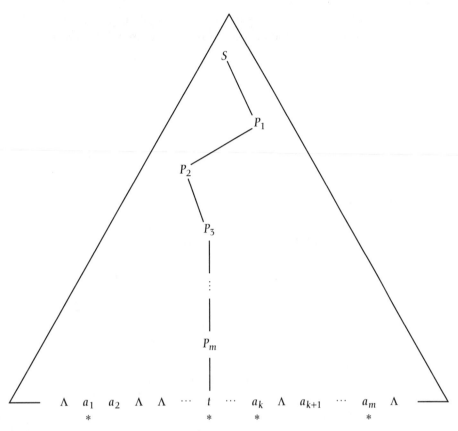

Figure 7.4

A derivation tree for the proof of Ogden's Lemma.

number of marked characters. In the event of a tie, the path follows the leftmost branch. Such a path always exists for any string of L with at least one marked character.

For each branch point P_i on ρ, define $\#(P_i)$ to be the number of *marked* characters in the subtree rooted at P_i. Note that $\#(P_0) \geq k$, $\#(P_{m+1}) = 1$, and since at most l terminal symbols are created by any production, $\#(P_m) \leq l$.

Now we consider only those branch points P_i, $0 \leq i \leq m$, for which $\#(P_i) > \#(P_{i+1})$. That is, we only consider the branch points that actually result in a difference in the number of marked characters between the subtree rooted at P_i and the subtree rooted at P_{i+1}. Call these branch points $Q_0, \ldots, Q_r$.

At each branch point Q_i, a production $A_i \to \omega_i$ is applied. Since $|\omega_i| \leq l$, the marked characters in the tree rooted at Q_i can be distributed over at most l subtrees of Q_i. So the subtree with the most marked characters must have at least

$1/l$ of the characters in the tree rooted at Q_i. Since the path ρ always selects a subtree with the maximum number of marked characters, we must have that

$$\#(Q_{i+1}) \geq \frac{\#(Q_i)}{l}$$

That is, for $0 \leq i \leq r$,

$$\#(Q_i) \geq \frac{\#(Q_0)}{l^i} \geq \frac{k}{l^i} = l^{n+2-i}$$

Similarly, each production of G can only generate at most l marked characters, so

$$\#(Q_{r-i}) \leq l^{i+1}$$

Now we ask, How many Q_i are there? From the above we have $l \geq \#(Q_r) \geq l^{n+2-r}$ and thus $r \geq n + 1$. This means that there are at least $n + 2$ branch points $Q_0, \ldots, Q_r$.

Consider the last $n + 1$ of these, that is, $Q_{r-n}, \ldots, Q_r$, where the productions $A_{r-n} \to \omega_{r-n}, \ldots, A_r \to \omega_r$ are applied at these points. Since $|N| = n$, by the Pigeonhole Principle we have that at least two of these productions must have the same variable, say A, on the left-hand side. So there are two branch points Q_i, Q_j, with $0 < i < j$, that are labeled with the same variable A. Thus we can partition the derivation tree of z as illustrated in Figure 7.5.

We can write $z = uvwxy$ and have condition 1. Now branch point Q_i is among $Q_{r-n}, \ldots, Q_r$ and so at most l^{n+1} marked characters appear in vwx, and we have condition 2.

Clearly, at least one marked character is in w. Since at least l^{n+2} marked characters appear in z, at least $l^{n+2} - \#(Q_1) \geq l^{n+2} - l^{n+1} = l^{n+1}(l - 1)$ marked characters appear in uy. Since $\#(Q_i) > \#(Q_j)$, at least one marked character appears in vx. Thus we have condition 3.

Finally, the steps in the derivation beginning with $A \to \omega_i$ (at Q_i) and ending just before $A \to \omega_j$ (at Q_j) can be removed or replicated two or more times, and the resulting tree will still be a valid derivation in G. Thus for $d \geq 0$, we have $uv^d wx^d y \in L$, and we have condition 4.   ∎

Ogden's Lemma is a very powerful tool. We now use it to show that an important language is not context-free.

Theorem 7.8.2   *The language $L = \{a^i b^i c^i \mid i \geq 0\}$ is not a context-free language.*

Proof: Assume for contradiction that L is a context-free language. Then we can apply Ogden's Lemma to obtain a natural number k for which the remainder of the lemma's properties hold. The string z is allowed to be completely arbitrary except for its length, so we can choose $z = a^k b^k c^k$. Since $k > 0$, we have $|z| > k$. We next mark all k of the b characters in z.

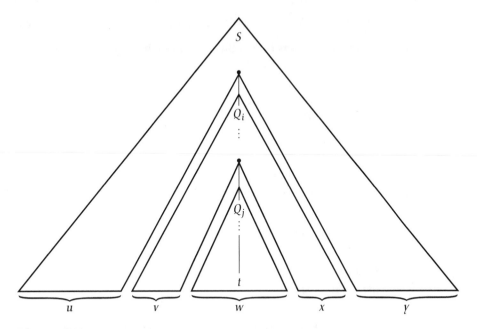

Figure 7.5

Partioning of the derivation tree of z in the proof of Ogden's Lemma.

Continuing with applying the statement of the lemma, for this particular z and associated marking, there exist u, v, w, x, and y such that

$$a^k b^k c^k = uvwxy$$

and the four conditions are satisfied.

Applying property 4, with $d = 0$, we see the string uwy is supposed to be in L. Is this really the case? According to property 3 the string vx contains at least one b. Since uwy is $uvwxy$ with vx removed, in order to preserve equal numbers of a, b, and c characters we must have $\#_a(vx) = \#_b(vx) = \#_c(vx)$.

Now by property 3, the string uy contains at least one marked character, namely, a b. If u contains a b, then neither v nor x contain an a, since all the a's must appear before the first b in u. Similarly if y contains a b, then neither v nor x contains a c. Thus $\#_a(vx) = 0$ or $\#_c(vx) = 0$, while $\#_b(vx) \geq 1$. This means that vx does not contain equal numbers of a, b, and c characters, and so uwy is not in L.

This contradiction means that L must not be context-free.   ∎

The language of Theorem 7.8.2 is especially useful for proving that other languages are *not* CFLs. We make use of it here in the next two lemmas, which show that CFLs are not closed under intersection and complementation.

Lemma 7.8.3   *The context-free languages are not closed under intersection.*

Proof: The idea is to exhibit two CFLs whose intersection results in the language $L = \{a^i b^i c^i \mid i \geq 0\}$. By Theorem 7.8.2, L is not a CFL, and therefore CFLs are not closed under intersection.

   Consider the language $L_1 = \{a^i b^i c^j \mid i, j \geq 0\}$. It is easy to see L_1 is generated by the CFG whose set of productions is given by

$$S \to S'C, \; S' \to aS'b \mid \Lambda, \; C \to cC \mid \Lambda$$

Therefore, $L_1 \in \mathcal{L}_{\mathbf{CFG}}$.

   Using a similar CFG, it is easy to show that $L_2 = \{a^i b^j c^j \mid i, j \geq 0\}$ is also a CFL. Making use of the observation that $L = L_1 \cap L_2$ completes the proof.   ■

   But by Exercise 25 we do have the following:

Lemma 7.8.4   *If L is a context-free language and R is a regular language, then $L \cap R$ is a context-free language.*

Lemma 7.8.5   *The context-free languages are not closed under complementation.*

Proof: The idea is to show that if CFLs were closed under the operation of complementation, then they would also be closed under the operation of intersection, contradicting Lemma 7.8.3. Let L_1 and L_2 be as defined in Lemma 7.8.3. Let $\Gamma = \{a, b, c\}$. Equation 2.4 tells us how to express the intersection of two languages in terms of complements. That is,

$$L_1 \cap L_2 = \overline{(\overline{L_1} \cup \overline{L_2})} = \Gamma^* - ((\Gamma^* - L_1) \cup (\Gamma^* - L_2))$$

Theorem 7.4.1 proves CFLs are closed under union, so if CFLs were closed under complementation, then they would also be closed under intersection.   ■

7.9   *Exercises*

Section 7.2   Regular Grammars

1. Specify a regular grammar (write out the entire tuple) that generates the language accepted by the DFA shown in Figure 4.8.

2. Specify regular grammars to generate the following languages:
   (a) ∅
   (b) $\{\Lambda\}$
   (c) $\{x \mid x \in \{0, 1\}^* \text{ and } \#_1(x) \geq 3\}$
   (d) $\{x \mid x \in \{0, 1\}^* \text{ and } x \text{ contains the pattern } 010\}$
   (e) $\{x \mid x \in \{0, 1\}^* \text{ and } |x| \bmod 2 = 0\}$

3. Let $G = (\{S, A, B\}, \{a, b\}, \{S \to a \mid b \mid A \mid B, A \to \Lambda \mid aB, B \to b \mid bbB\}, S)$ be a regular grammar. Which of the following strings does G derive?

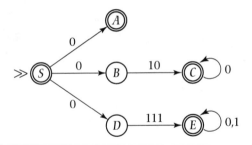

Figure 7.6

An NFA whose corresponding regular grammar is asked for in the exercises.

 (a) Λ
 (b) *aab*
 (c) *aabb*
 (d) *abbbb*

Give an eight–step derivation of some string in $L(G)$. What is the longest string in $L(G)$ that G derives in at most five steps?

4. Prove Theorem 7.2.4.

5. Using the construction of Theorem 7.2.4, produce an NFA corresponding to the following regular grammar:

$$G = (\{S, A, B\}, \{0, 1\}, \{S \rightarrow \Lambda \mid 0A \mid 0B, A \rightarrow 1S, B \rightarrow 00S\}, S)$$

6. Using the construction of Theorem 7.2.4, produce a regular grammar for the NFA shown in Figure 7.6.

7. True or false? Justify your answers.

 (a) The language represented by any regular expression can be generated by a regular grammar.

 (b) A regular grammar having only one production can generate just one string.

 (c) Any finite language can be generated by a regular grammar.

 (d) A regular grammar needs at least three rules to generate an infinite language.

Section 7.3 Context-Free Grammars

8. Consider the following CFG:

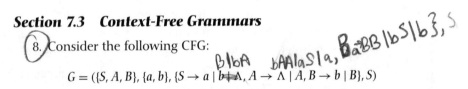

$$G = (\{S, A, B\}, \{a, b\}, \{S \rightarrow a \mid b \mp A, A \rightarrow \Lambda \mid A, B \rightarrow b \mid B\}, S)$$

Write out derivations for the shortest 10 strings in $L(G)$. What is $L(G)$?

9. Design CFGs to generate the following languages:

    (a) $\emptyset$

    (b) $\{0^i 01101^i \mid i \in \mathbb{N}\}$

    (c) $\{x \mid x \in \{0, 1\}^* \text{ and } x = x^R\}$

    (d) $\{a^m b^n \mid m, n \in \mathbb{N} \text{ and } m > 2n\}$

    (e) $\{a^m b^n \mid m, n \in \mathbb{N}, \text{ and } m = n \text{ or } m = 2n\}$

10. True or false? Justify your answers.

    (a) $\{a^m b^m c^5 \mid m \geq 5\}$ is a CFL.

    (b) If a CFG generates the empty string, it does so via a derivation of length one.

    (c) $\{a^n b^n a^m b^m \mid n, m \geq 0\}$ is not a CFL.

    (d) A two–rule CFG cannot generate an infinite language.

    (e) $|N| \geq 1$ for any CFG.

11. Write a grammar for the language L of properly nested ( ) and [ ] parentheses. For example ( ), [ ] [ ], and (( )[ ])[( )] are in L, while [( )] and]( )[are not.

12. Let L_{ww} be the language

$$L_{ww} = \{ww \mid w \in \{0, 1\}^*\}$$

    L_{ww} is not context–free. Show that $\overline{L_{ww}}$ is context–free.

13. Suppose that L is a context–free language over the one–symbol alphabet $\{1\}$. Show that L must be regular.

Section 7.4   Closure Properties of Context-Free Languages

14. Prove Theorem 7.4.2.

15. Prove Theorem 7.4.3.

16. Consider the following rules that are part of a CFG:

$$S \rightarrow aB, \ S \rightarrow aaabb, \ B \rightarrow AaB, \ B \rightarrow bb, \ A \rightarrow B, \ B \rightarrow a$$

    Give two derivations of the string *aaabb*. Is *aaabb* the shortest string that can be derived from this CFG? Explain your answer.

17. Construct and fully specify a *two*–state PDA to accept the language generated by the CFG in the previous problem. Trace an accepting computation of your machine on input *aaabb*. If your machine has a rejecting computation on this input, trace one of those as well.

18. Formally describe a CFG for generating the language $\{a^m b^n \mid m \geq n\}$ by describing all of its components.

19. Fully specify a CFG for generating the language L described below, where i and j are natural numbers:

$$L = \{a^i b^j \mid j \leq i \leq 4j\}.$$

Provide a derivation for the string *aaaaaaaabbb* using your grammar.

20. Is $\{a^n b^n c^m d^m \mid n, m \geq 0\}$ a CFL?

Section 7.5 *Parsing with Nondeterministic Pushdown Automata*

21. Prove that if x has a derivation in CFG G, then x has a leftmost derivation in G.

22. Let L be the language defined by the following context–free grammar, with start symbol $\langle expr \rangle$:

$$\langle expr \rangle \rightarrow \langle const \rangle \mid (\langle expr \rangle \langle op \rangle \langle expr \rangle)$$
$$\langle const \rangle \rightarrow 0 \mid 1$$
$$\langle op \rangle \rightarrow + \mid - \mid * \mid /$$

L consists of all fully parenthesized arithmetic expressions over the constants 0 and 1.

Write a context–free grammar for the language L_{even}, which is the subset of L in which each expression without $/$ is evenly divisible by 2. For example, $(1 + 1)$ is in L_{even}, while $(1 + (1 * (1 + 1)))$ is not.

23. Derive a CFG for generating the same language as the PDA of Table 6.2 accepts.

24. Produce a PDA for accepting the same language as the following CFG generates:

$$G = (\{S, A, B\}, \{0, 1\}, \{S \rightarrow \Lambda \mid 0A \mid 0B \mid BB1, A \rightarrow 1S \mid B1, B \rightarrow 00S\}, S)$$

25. Prove that the intersection of a CFL with a regular language is a CFL. This shows that the CFLs are closed under intersection with the regular languages.

Section 7.7 *Parse Trees and Attribution*

26. Modify CFG G_{exp} to ensure that the $*$ operator has higher precedence than the $+$ operator. That is, there should only be one possible parse for $a * b + c * d$. Is the new grammar unambiguous?

27. Write a context–free grammar for the syntax of regular expressions. What is its parse tree attribution function?

Section 7.8 Languages That Are Not Context-Free

28. Use Ogden's Lemma to show that

$$L_{ww} = \{ww \mid w \in \{0, 1\}^*\}$$

is not context-free.

29. Is the following language context-free?

$$L = \{x \in \{a, b, c\}^* \mid \#_a(x) = \#_b(x) = \#_c(x)\}$$

30. Is the following language context-free?

$$L = \{x \in \{a, b, c\}^* \mid \#_a(x) \neq \#_b(x) \text{ or } \#_b() \neq \#_c(x)\}$$

31. Is the following language context-free?

$$L = \{x \in \{a, b, c\}^* \mid \#_a(x), \#_b(x), \text{ and } \#_c(x) \text{ are distinct}\}$$

CHAPTER 8

Computational Complexity

The study of complexity measures in real computers is not pursued in theory, because it would make the results dependent on existing technology and hardware peculiarities rather than on insight and mathematical experience. Rather, through suitable machine models one attempts to provide a reasonable approximation of what one might expect if a real computer were used for one's computations.

—*Peter van Emde Boas*

8.1 *Introduction*

The goals of this chapter are

- to define asymptotic notation,
- to explain the rationale behind the asymptotic approach to studying the relative difficulties of computations,
- to study the resources time and memory,
- to define several important resource–bounded complexity classes,
- to set up a framework so that questions about resource usage can be addressed,
- to examine a number of simulation results in complexity theory, and
- to present the notion of reducibility.

Although this course of action may seem like a full plate, we really only touch on the rich subject of computational complexity theory. In the next several chapters we make use of the foundational material presented here. We begin by focusing on asymptotic notation.

8.2   *Asymptotic Notation*

Asymptotics is a concept that has been developed to help describe the growth rates of functions. In this chapter we are concerned with functions that measure the growth rates of the resources *time* and *memory* (also referred to as *space*). The concepts developed here can be applied to any type of resource, not just time and space.

Asymptotic notation allows us to focus on the dominant portions of the time and space consumption of solving a problem while avoiding being bogged down in lots of messy details. However, most useful notations can be abused, and therefore caution must be applied when employing asymptotic notation. Because the notation hides the details, it is up to the user to determine whether or not those details are pertinent to the application at hand.

Let's start by considering the most prevalent form of asymptotic notation, *big-O*. You should have already encountered big–O notation in an early algorithms course, but it is so important that it is worth reviewing in detail. At an intuitive level the idea of big–O is to indicate that one function is eventually bounded from above by another. That is, the growth rate of one function, say f, is less than a constant times that of the other function, call it g. We do not require that f always have a value bounded by g times a constant until the arguments of the functions become greater than a certain threshold value.

Figure 8.1 shows two functions $f : \mathbb{N} \mapsto \mathbb{R}^+$ and $g : \mathbb{N} \mapsto \mathbb{R}^+$. Although the domains of the functions are restricted to the natural numbers, in the figure we have illustrated f and g as continuous functions over the real numbers. We have taken this liberty to help clarify our example. Assuming that asymptotic behavior has taken over, the figure shows that g bounds f. For example, for all values of n greater than m_0, $g(n)$ is greater than $f(n)$. Also notice that the function g is bounded above by three times f for all values of n larger than n_0.

In our study of complexity theory we are interested in measuring the quantity of a given resource required to solve a problem so that we can compare the quality of different solution methods. In addition, we want to make absolute statements about the amount of resources required to solve a problem on a given computational model. As we solve larger and larger instances of the same problem, it is nearly always the case that we require additional resources.

An obvious question is, How should we measure the "size" of a problem? We can use some problem–specific feature (for example, the number of nodes and edges in a graph), but this means that we have to decide on a size measure (for example, why not just count nodes?). It is not clear how to compare solutions to the same problem that use different size measures.

Alternatively, we could use some size measure that was somewhat less de–pendent on the problem being solved. Since our computational models receive their input on an input tape, it is easy to measure the length of an input just

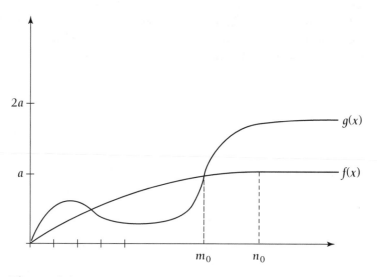

Figure 8.1

Two functions f and g, where f is bounded by g. Notice that g is bounded by $3 \cdot f$ for all values of n larger than n_0.

by counting the number of tape cells the instance to be solved occupies on the input tape. Although this is not completely independent of how we choose to represent the problem, it does have the advantage of allowing us to compare machine models independently of the problems being solved. It lets us say, for example, that if inputs of length n on machine model A take time $t(n)$, then they will take time $(t(n))^2$ on model B. Furthermore, since we usually express complexity classes in terms of languages, we prefer to talk only about the lengths of the strings being processed rather than a property of what the string represents.

Since the tape is discrete, all inputs to our computational models will have a length that is a natural number. Thus the functions we use to measure resources only need to be defined on the natural numbers. Since the resources of time and space are also discrete for our computational models, resource consumption functions need only be from naturals to naturals. But because of simplicity, and the fact that it does not affect asymptotic notation, it will sometimes be more convenient to have real-valued resource functions.

Having provided some context for our resource bounding functions, we find it convenient to assume throughout the remainder of this chapter that f, g, s, and t are functions whose domains are the natural numbers and whose ranges are the positive real numbers.

We are now ready to present the formal definition of the big-O notation.

Definition 8.2.1   *The function f is **big-O** of g, written $f(n) \in O(g(n))$ if and only if there exist constants $c > 0$ and $n_0 \in \mathbb{N}$ such that $f(n) \le cg(n)$ for all natural numbers $n \ge n_0$. The set of functions of **growth rate order** $g(n)$ is denoted $O(g(n))$.*

Rather than writing $f(n) \in O(g(n))$, it is very common for authors to express this somewhat less precisely as $f(n) = O(g(n))$. You should bear this fact in mind. For example, $f(n) = O(1)$ means that $f(n)$ is bounded above by some constant.

Let's consider an example to help illustrate the definition of big-O.

Example 8.2.2   Relating functions using the big-O notation

1. Let $f(n) = n + 3$ and $g(n) = 2n$. By choosing $c = 1$ and $n_0 = 2$, we see that

$$f(n) = n + 3 \le 1 \cdot 2n = c \cdot g(n)$$

   for all $n \ge 2$. Thus, $f(n) \in O(g(n))$, or more informally, $f(n) = O(g(n))$. Choosing $c = 2$ and $n_0 = 1$, we also see that $g(n) = O(f(n))$.

2. Let $f(n) = 100$ and $g(n) = 3.5$. By choosing $c = 100$ and $n_0 = 0$, we see that

$$f(n) = 100 \le 100 \cdot 3.5 = 350 = c \cdot g(n)$$

   for all $n \ge 0$. Thus, $f(n) = O(g(n))$. Let $h(n) = n^0 = 1$. Then choosing $c = 100$ and $n_0 = 1$, we see that $f(n) = O(h(n))$. Therefore, $f(n) = O(1)$.

3. Let $f(n) = (\lg n)^2$ and $g(n) = n + 5$. By choosing $c = 100$ and $n_0 = 1024$, we see that

$$f(n) = (\lg n)^2 \le 100 \cdot (n + 5) = c \cdot g(n)$$

   for all $n \ge 1024$. Thus, $f(n) = O(g(n))$.

4. Let $f(n) = n^3$ and $g(n) = n^2$. Since for any choice of c and any choice of n_0, we can always find an n so that $f(n) \not\le c \cdot g(n)$, we see $f(n) \ne O(g(n))$. By taking $c = 1$ and $n_0 = 0$, it is easy to see that $f(n) = O(g(n))$.   ∎

Notice in the example that we do not have to find the "tightest" c and n_0 but only two values that go together and fit the requirements of the definition. In the exercises we ask you to work with and derive some facts about the big-O notation.

The following three classes of functions are important special cases of the big-O notation.

- $n^{O(1)}$—The set of *polynomially bounded functions*. $f(n) = n^{O(1)}$ means that f is bounded above by some polynomial function.

- $f(n)^{O(1)}$—The set of functions that are *polynomial in $f(n)$*. Equivalently,

$$f(n)^{O(1)} = \bigcup_{k \ge 0} f(n)^k$$

- $(\log n)^{O(1)}$—The set of *polylogarithmic bounded functions*; that is, the set of functions that are polynomial in $\log n$. Equivalently,

$$(\lg n)^{O(1)} = \bigcup_{k \geq 0} (\lg n)^k$$

The next most commonly used asymptotic notation is that of big-Ω (pronounced "big Omega").

Definition 8.2.3   *The function f is **big-Ω** of g, written $f(n) \in \Omega(g(n))$ if and only if there exist constants $c > 0$ and $n_0 \in \mathbb{N}$ such that $f(n) \geq cg(n)$ for all natural numbers $n \geq n_0$. The set of functions of **growth rate at least order** $f(n)$ is denoted $\Omega(f(n))$.*

Again, we substitute "=" for "$\in$" as is common practice. You are asked to explore the big-Ω notation in the exercises.

A third form of asymptotic notation is Θ ("pronounced theta"). The function $f(n) = \Theta(g(n))$ if and only if $f(n) = O(g(n))$ and $g(n) = O(f(n))$. If $f(n) = \Theta(g(n))$, we say that f is tightly bounded by g. For completeness we include the definitions of two additional asymptotic notations that you may encounter.

Definition 8.2.4   *The function f is **little-o** of g, written $f(n) \in o(g(n))$ if and only if*

$$\lim_{n \to \infty} \frac{f(n)}{g(n)} = 0$$

*The set of functions whose **growth rate is asymptotically less than** $g(n)$ is denoted $o(g(n))$.*

*The function f is **little-ω** (pronounced "little omega") of g, written $f(n) \in \omega(g(n))$ if and only if*

$$\lim_{n \to \infty} \frac{f(n)}{g(n)} = \infty$$

*The set of functions whose **growth rate is asymptotically faster than** $g(n)$ is denoted $\omega(g(n))$.*

Asymptotic notation is often used in fields other than computer science, and you may encounter them in mathematics, physics, biology, economics, engineering, mathematics, and physics. We will make use of these notations in the remainder of this book.

8.3   *Time and Space Complexity*

Computations are expensive, regardless of how much computing power you have available. Eventually, either because you want to solve bigger instances of existing problems or because you want to solve new harder problems, you will begin to run short of cpu cycles (*time*) and memory (*space*). Thus it becomes important to predict what is possible with your available computing environment, or if your problem can be solved at all with available computing technology. Prediction and estimation always takes two forms. First there are high–level order–of–magnitude estimates: Does this algorithm take thousands or millions of bytes of memory? Milliseconds or years? An order–of–magnitude estimate tells you if the task is generally possible. If the high–level estimate is reasonable, then prediction moves on to the low level: Can this be done in a million bytes in 1 second on a HAL 9000?

While details of the problem representation and machine model chosen for implementation are very important to low–level prediction and estimation, they are not so important to high–level order–of–magnitude estimates. So for high–level analysis it is more important to have a model in which resource consumption is easy to measure, so long as it does not distort the details. Thus we choose the multitape Turing machine as the standard model of computation for high–level complexity theory. Space is easily counted in terms of tape cells, and time is easily counted in terms of state transitions.

Our focus on the Turing machine model is really not a limitation, at least not from a theoretical point of view. The Turing machine model, as we know from the Church-Turing Thesis, is as powerful as any yet–proposed model of computation. For all other important models of computation, such as the *random access machine* (RAM), a close (polynomial time) relationship exists between Turing machine time and the corresponding model's time. For example, if a problem can be solved on a Turing machine in time $t(n)$, then it can be solved on a RAM in time $O(t(n))$. If a problem can be solved on a RAM in time $t(n)$, then it can be solved on a multitape Turing machine in time $O((t(n))^3)$. Polynomial relationships can also be drawn between the amount of space used by a Turing machine and the amount of space used by a RAM. Analogous results hold for other models of computation as well.

The explanation just provided tells us that it is no loss of generality (at least from a theoretical angle) to use the Turing machine to study resource usage of computational models. However, what does Turing machine resource usage have to do with reality? Can we actually draw any types of realistic conclusions about practical problems by studying Turing machines?

With the remarkable advances in computing technology, it is true that the time complexity of a problem on a Turing machine may have precious little to do with whether or not a specific problem can be solved within computing resources—especially if the instances of the problem that we are required to solve are not larger than, say, one million or so. Nevertheless, the study of resource usage on Turing machines does provide us with some new insights. For example, shortly we will define several important *complexity classes* based on Turing machine resources. These classes allow us to categorize problems of the same complexity. We can then explore the structure of these problems together as a group and perhaps make statements about them on the whole. Such an approach can give us a more general perspective on the nature of computation. In the long run, having this deeper understanding of problems, their structure, and how they relate to other problems is very beneficial.

It is still reasonable to question whether the study of Turing machine resources can be of use in practice. We will develop two theories in Chapters 10 and 11. The first will allow us to classify problems that can be solved *feasibly* on a sequential computer but *not* fast on a *parallel computer*. The second will allow us to classify those problems that cannot be solved feasibly. As an example of why such theories are useful, consider the following classical scenario (made famous by Michael Garey and David Johnson).

Suppose your boss asks you to develop a fast, polynomial time algorithm for solving a problem called Π. You work hard on the problem but always come up empty–handed. Your boss is demanding an algorithm, and you are beginning to worry about your level of job security. Is it possible that no polynomial time algorithm exists for the problem? That is, did your boss give you an impossible task? If in fact the task were not possible, how would you go about obtaining evidence supporting this? The theories we develop provide you with the necessary tools. There is a large group of important problems, which arise in practical situations, for which no polynomial time algorithms are known. So indeed, when your job is at stake, this Turing–machine–based theory can play a very important role. Keep in mind that most of the problems theoreticians study are ones that were handed to them (usually because no one else could solve them) by people in the trenches working on real–world problems.

We have been using words like "time" and "space" informally up to now. We have settled on the Turing machine model for studying resources, and now it is appropriate to formalize these concepts on our way to defining complexity classes.

Definition 8.3.1   *Let M be a (multitape) deterministic Turing machine. Let $t(n)$ and $s(n)$ be functions mapping from the natural numbers to the positive real numbers.*

M is of **time complexity** *$t(n)$ if for every input of length n, M executes at most $t(n)$ steps before halting. We say the language of M, $L(M)$, has time complexity $t(n)$.*

M is of **space complexity** *$s(n)$ if for every input of length n, the sum over all work tapes of the number of tape cells between the ⟨ and ⟩ markers is at most $s(n)$. We say the language of M has space complexity $s(n)$.*

A few remarks are in order regarding Definition 8.3.1. It is customary to assume that a Turing machine reads its entire input before deciding whether or not to accept it. When this is the case, $t(n)$ is greater than or equal to n. Certainly for most languages of interest, the entire input must be processed. In the definition of space complexity, we do not include the space required to store the input, since we are more interested in knowing how much work space is needed by a computation. If nothing is ever written to any work tape, then under this definition, it is possible to use zero space. It is also important to remember that time and space bounds for a language are conservative; we are saying that there is some DTM that can accept the language within those bounds, but there may be one that is even better. We usually aim to make the bounds as tight as possible.

Let's consider an example before introducing any new concepts.

Example 8.3.2   Turing machine time and space complexities of several languages

1. Suppose the language L can be accepted by a DFA. It is clear that the time complexity of L is $O(n)$ and the space complexity of L is $O(1)$, that is, constant. The tape space used by a DFA is 0, since it has no work tape, but there is space in the sense that the DFA stores a constant amount of information in its current state.

2. Let $L = \{xcx^R \mid x \in \{0, 1\}^*\}$. It is not difficult to design a multitape DTM that accepts this language in $O(n)$, while using $O(n)$ space. Thus, for example, L has time complexity $O(n)$. Since L requires at least n steps to accept, the straightforward algorithm cannot be more than a multiplicative constant factor off from the optimal algorithm.

3. The DTM in Example 6.2.11 accepts the language $L = \{a^i b^i c^i \mid i \geq 0\}$ in $O(n^2)$ time and $O(n)$ space. This shows, for example, that L is of space complexity $O(n)$. A more clever use of space can be used to show the language is of space complexity $O(\lg n)$. We ask for this construction in the exercises.

4. Consider the language $L = \{G \Diamond s \Diamond t \mid G$ is an encoding of an undirected graph $G = (V, E)$, $s, t \in V$, and there is a path from s to t in $G\}$. A DTM that tries to enumerate all possible paths between s and t has time complexity $O(2^n)$. We ask you to improve on this in the exercises. We also ask you to prove that this language has space complexity $O((\lg n)^2)$. ∎

A set (or *family*) of languages grouped together according to their time or space complexities is called a **complexity class**. We are now in position to define our first complexity classes.

Definition 8.3.3   *The set of languages of (deterministic) time complexity $O(t(n))$ is denoted by DTIME(t(n)). The set of languages of (deterministic) space complexity $O(s(n))$ is denoted by DSPACE(s(n)).*

Based on Example 8.3.2 we can conclude, for example, that if L is a regular language, then $L \in DTIME(O(n))$ and $L \in DSPACE(O(1))$. In the exercises we ask you to draw similar conclusions based on the other three parts of the example.

Do the same notions of time and space complexity apply to NTMs as well as DTMs? Since an NTM computation could have many different threads, it is possible that each thread requires a different number of steps and consumes a different amount of space before halting. Which thread should we charge?

Consider an NTM M on an input x. The *time (or space) complexity of M on input x* is the minimum number of steps (or, respectively, work tape cells) required by any thread of M to accept x. The *time (or space) complexity* of an NTM M is $t(n)$ (or, respectively, $s(n)$) if over all inputs x of length n the maximum time (or, respectively, space) complexity of M on an input x is at most $t(n)$ (or, respectively, $s(n)$). Notice the complexity of an NTM as defined depends only on inputs that are accepted. By convention, if no input of length n is accepted, the complexity on that length input is set to one. Another way of stating the definition of resource complexity of an NTM is as follows: Consider all accepted inputs of length n, for each input take the minimum amount of resource used by an accepting thread, and finally over all possible accepted inputs x choose the maximum value.

We can now define complexity classes for NTMs as we did for DTMs.

Definition 8.3.4   *The set of languages of nondeterministic time complexity $t(n)$ is denoted by NTIME($t(n)$). The set of languages of nondeterministic space complexity $s(n)$ is denoted by NSPACE($s(n)$).*

In later chapters we make use of the complexity classes defined in this section. In the next section we examine some interesting properties about time and space complexity classes.

8.4   *Simulations*

In what follows, we examine a number of simulations from the perspective of complexity theory. This theory is very rich, and we will touch only on a few very basic theorems. The references provide you with additional places to explore. Let's begin by collecting a few simple observations about the complexity classes defined in the last section.

Observation 8.4.1   *Let $s(n)$ and $t(n)$ be functions from the natural numbers to the positive real numbers. Then*

   1. DTIME($t(n)$) $\subseteq$ NTIME($t(n)$)

   2. DSPACE($s(n)$) $\subseteq$ NSPACE($s(n)$)

   3. DTIME($t(n)$) $\subseteq$ DSPACE($t(n)$)

   4. NTIME($t(n)$) $\subseteq$ NSPACE($t(n)$)

The proof of Observation 8.4.1 is called for in the exercises. This observation is useful because it relates different resources to each other, and also determinism and nondeterminism. So, for example, if we have a $t(n)$ time algorithm for a problem, we can automatically conclude that there is an algorithm for the problem operating within a space bound of $t(n)$.

Next we present a couple of theorems about time complexity and then switch over to studying space complexity. The results will provide you with a feel for the nature of simulation proofs in complexity theory. Let's start with a classical proof showing that, when we go from a k–tape machine to a 1–tape machine, we have to, at most, square the running time. This classical result is called the *Tape Reduction Theorem*.

Theorem 8.4.2   (Tape Reduction)   *If the language $L \in DTIME(t(n))$, then L is accepted by a 1-tape deterministic Turing machine in time $O((t(n))^2)$.*

Proof: In the proof of Theorem 6.2.12, we showed how to simulate a k–tape DTM by a 1–tape DTM. We make use of that simulation to prove the theorem. First, observe that a k–tape DTM having time complexity $f(n)$ cannot have a space complexity greater than $kf(n)$ (Observation 8.4.1, part 3). Recall the simulation in Theorem 6.2.12 required the 1–tape DTM to perform six sweeps over its work tape in order to simulate one move of the k–tape machine. If the k–tape machine has time complexity $t(n)$, then each sweep requires $O(t(n))$ steps. Therefore, each move of the k–tape DTM can be simulated in $O(t(n))$ steps. Since the k–tape machine has time complexity $t(n)$, the 1–tape machine has time complexity $t(n) \cdot O(t(n)) = O((t(n))^2)$.   ■

The next theorem shows that we can always shave a constant factor off the running time of a multitape DTM, so long as its running time is nonlinear. This classical result is called the *Linear Speedup Theorem*. The proof we present is similar to that given by John Hopcroft and Jeffrey Ullman [26].

Theorem 8.4.3   (Linear Speedup)   *Suppose the language L is accepted by a deterministic Turing machine M having time complexity $t(n)$, where $t(n) \geq 1$ for all n. If $n = o(t(n))$, then for any $c > 0$, the language L is accepted by a deterministic Turing machine M' having a time complexity that for each value of n is given by $\max\{n, c \cdot t(n)\}$.*

Proof: We design M' to simulate M. The key idea is to enlarge the data alphabet of M. The new alphabet can be viewed as multitracked. Using the new data alphabet, M' can encode many symbols of M into a single symbol. By taking advantage of its enhanced alphabet, M' can carry out a large number of steps of M in a small number of steps. We now describe how to implement this intuition.

Consider an input x with $|x| = n$. If M has k work tapes, then M' has $k + 1$ work tapes. The first k of M's work tapes represent M's work tapes and the last one represents M's input tape. We encode l (where the value of l is to be chosen later) symbols of M's data alphabet into a single symbol of M''s data alphabet.

The simulation begins by encoding M's input tape contents and copying it to M''s $(k + 1)$st work tape. The input x can be encoded with $\lceil n/l \rceil$ symbols. From now on, M' uses its $(k + 1)$st work tape as its input tape. Remember the symbols in M''s data alphabet are l-tuples over M's data alphabet.

M' simulates a large number of moves of M by a series of six moves. For convenience let's call the symbols under the tape heads of M''s work tapes (we ignore M''s true input tape) the *scanned cells*. For each work tape of M, the scanned cells of M' include the tape squares currently being scanned by M.

To simulate l moves of M, M' moves its work tape heads left of the scanned cells one square, right two squares, and then returns to the original scanned cells with one left move. While doing these four moves, M' records the symbols it "saw" in its finite control. Based on the current state of M, the three input symbols scanned from the $(k + 1)$st work tape, and the symbols read off the first k work tapes, M' can simulate l moves of M. In l moves, M can move a tape head at most l squares in one direction. Because of the manner in which M' is representing M's tapes, M''s heads do not need to move out of the region of a scanned cell combined with its left and right neighboring cells. The finite control keeps track of where in this region the actual tape head is.

The l moves of M are "hard coded" into M''s finite control as one or two moves. If the direction resulting from those l moves on a given work tape is a right, for example, then M updates the "symbols" on the scanned cell of that work tape and moves the head on that work tape right, updating the necessary "symbols" in that work tape cell. Similar processes occur if the movement is left or stationary. All work tapes of M' are updated at each step.

The input head, which is really the tape head corresponding to the $(k + 1)$st work tape of M', is then moved at most one cell in the appropriate direction—that is, to the scanned cell containing M's new input head position after the execution of the l moves. If at any time before the l moves are executed M accepts, then M' accepts, too.

The simulation just described carries out l moves of M in six steps of M'. Thus, $t(n)$ moves of M require $7\lceil t(n)/l \rceil$ steps of M'. The encoding of M's input tape and resetting of the input tape head on work tape $(k + 1)$ of M' requires $n + \lceil n/l \rceil$ moves. Since $\lceil q \rceil < q + 1$ for any $q \in \mathbb{R}$, the total number of moves of M' is bounded by

$$\frac{7t(n)}{l} + \frac{n}{l} + (n + 7) \tag{8.1}$$

Since $n = o(t(n))$, for any constant r there is a natural number n_r such that for all $n \geq n_r$, $n \leq t(n)/r$. Observe that if $n \geq 7$, then $n + 7 \leq 2n$. Thus, when $n \geq n_r$ and $n \geq 7$, Equation 8.1 is bounded by

$$\left(\frac{6}{l} + \frac{2}{r} + \frac{1}{l \cdot r} \right) t(n)$$

By careful selection of the values of r and l, we can show that

$$c > \left(\frac{6}{l} + \frac{2}{r} + \frac{1}{l \cdot r} \right) \tag{8.2}$$

Choose l such that $c \cdot l \geq 16$ and $l \geq 4$. We can rewrite Equation 8.2 as

$$c \cdot l - 6 > \frac{2l}{r} + \frac{1}{r} = \frac{2l + 1}{r}$$

We want to select a value for r such that the right-hand side of this inequality is less than 10. So, rewriting we need

$$r > \frac{2l + 1}{10}$$

It is straightforward to verify that a choice of $r = l/4 + (1/10)$ suffices.

Let $q = \max\{7, n_r\}$. Then for all inputs of length $n \geq q$, the number of steps taken by M' is less than or equal to $c \cdot t(n)$.

For the fixed number of inputs of length less than q, M' can do a table lookup—that is, use its finite control to store the inputs just as a DFA would. For these inputs, only n steps are required to read them and decide on acceptance. It follows that M' has a time complexity which for each value of n is given by $\max\{n, c \cdot t(n)\}$.

■

Corollary 8.4.4   *Suppose the language L is accepted by a nondeterministic Turing machine M having time complexity $t(n)$, where $t(n) \geq 1$ for all n. If $n = o(t(n))$, then for any $c > 0$, the language L is accepted by a nondeterministic Turing machine M' having a time complexity that for each value of n is given by $\max\{n, c \cdot t(n)\}$.*

Proof: Apply the same method as used in the construction of Theorem 8.4.3.   ■

The next result relates deterministic and nondeterministic time complexity. Notice that there is a huge blowup in the time bound and that the proof is basically just a brute force approach; no better general simulation result is known.

Theorem 8.4.5   *Suppose $t(n) \geq n$ for all $n \in \mathbb{N}$, and the value of $t(n)$ can be computed by a deterministic Turing machine running in time $2^{O(t(n))}$. If the language $L \in NTIME(t(n))$, then $L \in DTIME(2^{O(t(n))})$.*

Proof: Suppose $L \in NTIME(t(n))$. Then there exists an NTM M that accepts L in time $t(n)$. The intuitive idea of the proof is to construct a DTM M' with the following conditions: it runs in time $2^{O(t(n))}$, simulates all possible threads of M, and accepts if and only if M accepts.

Recall that in Theorem 6.2.19 we simulated an NTM by a DTM. We can make wholesale use of that simulation here. All we need to do is analyze the time complexity of that simulation.

First, M' computes the value of $t(n)$ within $2^{O(t(n))}$ steps. Let p be the maximum possible number of moves that any transition of M has. The simulation of Theorem 6.2.19 requires M' (in Theorem 6.2.19 the machine doing the simulating was called N) to generate, in a breadth–first manner, M's *computation tree* comprising all the threads of M (see Figure 6.11). At each level in the computation tree, M' simulates M on every possible move sequence. The simulation begins from the root and goes forward to each node on a given level, if necessary.

On a specified input x, if M accepts, then M has at least one thread that accepts x within $t(n)$ steps. Thus, on accepted inputs, no more than $t(n)$ levels of M's computation tree will be generated. In fact, since we can easily count the number of levels generated as we produce them, the simulation can be shut off after $t(n)$ levels have been searched by comparing the current level number to the value of $t(n)$ computed. That is, if M does not accept within $t(n)$ levels, then we know it rejects or does not halt. So, the computation tree of M that M' needs to generate and search has depth $t(n)$.

As constructed in Theorem 6.2.19, the computation tree has a branching factor of p at each node. It is easy to see that such a tree has $p^{t(n)}$ leaves. The number of nonleaf nodes in such a tree is less than the number of leaves. Therefore, a tree of depth $t(n)$ with a branching factor of p has $O(p^{t(n)})$ nodes in total.

The time required to compute $t(n)$ is $2^{O(t(n))}$. To generate the next sequence of moves to simulate (by incrementing a counter), then to simulate M for at most $t(n)$ steps using this move sequence, then to clean up the second work tape, and finally to reset the input head, requires $O(t(n))$ steps in M'. In resetting the input head, we make use of the fact that $t(n)$ is greater than or equal to n. We can conclude that the running time of M' is $O(t(n)p^{t(n)}) = 2^{O(t(n))}$. Hence, $L \in DTIME(2^{O(t(n))})$. ∎

The next theorem shows that we can always shave a constant factor off the space used by a multitape DTM. This classical result is called the *Tape Compression Theorem*.

Theorem 8.4.6   (Tape Compression) *Suppose the language L is accepted by a deterministic Turing machine M having space complexity $s(n)$. Then for any $c > 0$, L is accepted by a deterministic Turing machine M' having space complexity $c \cdot s(n)$.*

Proof: The basic idea is to encode a string of symbols from M's data alphabet into a single symbol of M''s data alphabet. The construction given in the Linear Speedup Theorem can be modified to work here. The main change is that the input tape is no longer stored as a work tape, but instead M' uses its input tape to simulate M's input tape directly. The remaining details of the result, including the new specification of l, are left as an exercise. ∎

Corollary 8.4.7 *Suppose the language L is accepted by a nondeterministic Turing machine with space complexity s(n). Then for any c > 0, L is accepted by a nondeterministic Turing machine with space complexity c · s(n).*

Proof: Apply the same method as used in the construction of Theorem 8.4.6. ■

The next theorem shows how to relate nondeterministic and deterministic space complexity classes. This classical result is due to Walter Savitch.

Theorem 8.4.8 (Savitch's Theorem) *If $s(n) \geq \lg n$, then $NSPACE(s(n)) \subseteq DSPACE((s(n))^2)$.*

Proof: We provide the basic idea of the proof; the details are called for in the exercises.

Let $L \in NSPACE(s(n))$. Then there exists an NTM M that accepts L and uses space bounded by $s(n)$. Without loss of generality (which we leave as an exercise), suppose that M has a unique accepting configuration modulo the input tape contents. For example, the input tape head is reset to the beginning of the input tape, all work tapes are erased, and the machine halts in a unique final state. Attempting to simulate M deterministically, as in Theorem 6.2.19, would result in the use of far too much space. The key idea is to define a recursive procedure, which when implemented using a stack is able to reuse space over and over again, that can test whether one NTM configuration can yield another NTM configuration. That is, given two NTM configurations, C_1 and C_2, does $C_1 \vdash_M^* C_2$? We ask you to define and utilize such a recursive procedure, and then analyze its space complexity, in the exercises. ■

In this section we have tried to give you a feel for some of the classical results in complexity theory. Keep in mind that these represent only the tip of the iceberg. There are many other very interesting results that have been omitted but may be pursued via the references.

8.5   *Reducibilities*

The final goal of this chapter is to examine methods for relating problems (or languages) to one another using the concept of *reducibility*. Reducibility provides us with a mechanism for comparing the relative difficulty of two problems. The idea is to transform instances of one problem into instances of another problem. The answers to the transformed instances should allow us to answer the original instance. Once made precise, the concept of reducibility can be used to characterize the hardest problems in a complexity class.

Why is the notion of reducibility important? It is very difficult to prove *lower bounds* on a problem's resource complexity. That is, it is hard to quantify the minimum amount of a resource that must be used in order to solve a problem. Such lower bounds are tough to prove because you must show that *no* solution method can beat the lower bound, including solution methods you have not thought of! Instead of an absolute lower bound, reducibility lets us show that a problem is difficult to solve relative to another problem. As we will see later in Chapters 10 and 11, reducibility is a very powerful idea and gives us a handle on which problems are very hard to solve.

The most important form of reducibility is called *many-one reducibility*. We describe many–one reducibility and its properties in the next section. We should note that there are a number of other forms of reducibility. The references contain additional material about *Turing reducibility* and other variations of reducibility as well.

8.5.1 Many–One Reducibility

Let's begin this section by reviewing function computation on DTMs. We stated earlier that a DTM can compute a function if we equip it with a special output tape; the output tape is required to be one-way write-only. The value of the function can be written on the output tape. The domain and range of the function can be sets of strings over arbitrary alphabets. The complexity of computing a function is merely the complexity of the DTM that computes it. For the resource time we simply count the number of steps; for the resource space we charge as usual for the work tapes but do not include the space required by the output value itself.

Suppose that we have two languages L and L'. We want to determine if some string x is a member of L. Furthermore, suppose that we can transform x into a string y, using a function f, in such a way that y is a member of L' exactly when x is a member of L. That is, $x \in L$ if and only if $f(x) \in L'$. We have reduced L to L' in the sense that if we know how to test membership in L', then we can test membership in L. The function f is called a *reduction*. Observe, if we actually know how to decide membership in L', then the complexity of testing if $x \in L$ becomes the sum of the complexity of computing $f(x)$ and the complexity of testing whether $f(x) \in L'$. Naturally then, we are interested in having the complexity of the reduction be as small as possible so that it does not obscure the complexity of testing $f(x) \in L'$.

A reducibility is called *many-one* if many instances of a problem can be reduced to a single instance of another problem.

Definition 8.5.1   *A language L is* **many–one reducible** *to a language L', written $L \leq_m L'$, if there is a function f such that $x \in L$ if and only if $f(x) \in L'$.*

We say that L is **P many–one reducible** *to L', written $L \leq_m^P L'$, if and only if the function f can be computed in $DTIME(n^i)$ for some $i \in \mathbb{N}$.*

We say that L is **logarithmic space many–one reducible** *to L', written $L \leq_m^{\lg} L'$, if and only if the function f can be computed in $DSPACE(\lg n)$.*

Since reductions are usually complicated, we would like to make repeated use of them. The following notion often allows us to do this.

Definition 8.5.2   *Suppose $\leq$ is a reducibility such that whenever $L \leq L'$ and $L' \leq L''$, then $L \leq L''$. We say that the reducibility $\leq$ is* **transitive**.

Many–one reducibility is transitive. That is, suppose $x \in L$ if and only if $f(x) \in L'$, and $y \in L'$ if and only if $g(y) \in L''$, then $x \in L$ if and only if $g(f(x)) \in L''$. Therefore, the language L is also reducible to L''. Furthermore, because the following two language classes

$$\bigcup_{i=0}^{\infty} DTIME(n^i) \text{ and } DSPACE(\lg n)$$

are closed under composition (the proof is asked for in the exercises), resource-bounded reductions are also transitive.

Lemma 8.5.3   *The reducibilities $\leq_m$, $\leq_m^P$, and $\leq_m^{\lg}$ are transitive.*

Proof: The proof is left as an exercise.   ∎

The next definition is useful for equating problems of the same complexity.

Definition 8.5.4   *Let $\leq$ denote a reducibility. If $L \leq L'$ and $L' \leq L$, then L and L' are* **equivalent** *under $\leq$.*

Often when reducing a language L to a language L', the exact complexity of L' is unknown. Although this gives us no absolute information about the complexity of L, it still provides valuable information about the relative difficulties of the two languages. In particular, assuming the reduction is not too powerful, it implies that L is no more difficult to decide than L'. It is important to note that if the reduction is allowed too much power, it will mask the complexity of L', because L can then be solved directly by the reduction itself without making any use of the ability to decide L'.

Let's look at an example.

Example 8.5.5   Sample reductions

1. Let $L = \{0^i 1^i \mid i \geq 0\}$ and $L' = \{a^i b^i \mid i \geq 0\}$. Define $f : \{0, 1\}^* \mapsto \{a, b\}^*$ by $f(x) = y$, where $y(i) = a$ if $x(i) = 0$, and otherwise $y(i) = b$ for $1 \leq i \leq |x|$. It should be clear that $x \in L$ if and only if $f(x) \in L'$. This shows that $L \leq L'$. Notice that the reduction can be carried out in time n, where $|x| = n$ or in $O(1)$ space. Therefore, $L \leq_m^P L'$ and $L \leq_m^{\lg} L'$. It is apparent that the inverse of this reduction can be used to reduce L' to L.

2. An **independent set** is a set of vertices of an undirected graph that are pairwise nonadjacent. Recall that a *clique* is a set of vertices that are pairwise adjacent. Let

$$L = \left\{ G \diamond k \;\middle|\; \begin{array}{l} G \text{ is an encoding of an undirected graph, } k \in \mathbb{N}, \\ \text{and } G \text{ has an independent set of size at least } k \end{array} \right\}$$

Let
$$L' = \left\{ G \diamond k \;\middle|\; \begin{array}{l} G \text{ is an encoding of an undirected graph, } k \in \mathbb{N}, \\ \text{and } G \text{ has a clique of size at least } k \end{array} \right\}$$

Define $f(G \diamond k) = (\bar{G} \diamond k)$, where $\bar{G}$ is the *complementary* graph of G. That is, $\bar{G} = (V, E')$, where $E' = \{\{u, v\} \mid \{u, v\} \notin E$ and $u, v \in V\}$. Note that $G \diamond k \in L$ if and only if $f(G \diamond k) = (\bar{G} \diamond k) \in L'$. Furthermore, the reduction can be carried out in time $O(n)$, where $n = |G \diamond k|$, or in space $O(1)$. Therefore, $L \leq_m^P L'$ and $L \leq_m^{\lg} L'$.

3. Define the **Hamiltonian Path problem (HP)** as follows:

   Given: An undirected graph $G = (V, E)$.

   Problem: Does G contain a Hamiltonian path?

   Define the **Longest Path problem (LP)** as follows:

   Given: An undirected graph $G = (V, E)$ and $k \in \mathbb{N}$.

   Problem: Does G contain a simple path of length at least k?

   Let L be the language corresponding to HP and L' the language corresponding to LP.
   Let $G = (V, E)$. Define $f(G) = (G \diamond |V| - 1)$. The reduction f is such that $G \in$ HP if and only if $(G \diamond |V| - 1) \in$ LP. The reduction can be carried out in time $O(n)$, where $n = |G|$, or in space $O(1)$. Therefore, $L \leq_m^P L'$ and $L \leq_m^{\lg} L'$. ∎

   In Chapters 10 and 11 we will see many more examples of reductions. Here we introduced reductions to relate problems to one another. In later chapters we use reductions to relate a single problem to an entire complexity class.

8.6   Exercises

Section 8.2   Asymptotic Notation

1. In each of the following cases, if possible, prove that $g(n) = O(f(n))$ and vice versa.
   (a) $g(n) = n^2 + 2n + 7$ and $f(n) = n^3$
   (b) $g(n) = \lg n$ and $f(n) = 100$
   (c) $g(n) = n \lg n$ and $f(n) = (\lg n)^4$
   (d) $g(n) = n$ and $f(n) = n^{1.2}$
   (e) $g(n) = 2^n$ and $f(n) = n!$

2. Let $g(n)$ and $f(n)$ be functions that model the running times of two algorithms for solving the same problem. Assume that $g(n) = O(f(n))$ but not vice versa. Is it possible that the algorithm whose running time is $f(n)$ is preferable for values of n up to one million but after that the $g(n)$

bounded algorithm is better? If so, define such a $g(n)$ and $f(n)$. Propose a new algorithm that could be preferable to either of the original two.

3. Prove that if $g(n) = O(n^2)$, then $(g(n))^2 = O(n^4)$. Based on this result derive and prove a general result involving powers of n and big-O notation.

4. Prove that the big-O notation is transitive.

5. In each of the following cases, if possible, prove that $g(n) = \Omega(f(n))$ and vice versa.

   (a) $g(n) = n^2 + 2n + 7$ and $f(n) = n^3$
   (b) $g(n) = \lg n$ and $f(n) = 100$
   (c) $g(n) = n \lg n$ and $f(n) = (\lg n)^4$
   (d) $g(n) = n$ and $f(n) = n^{1.2}$
   (e) $g(n) = 2^n$ and $f(n) = n!$

6. Prove that the big-Ω notation is transitive.

7. Given two functions f and g mapping from the natural numbers to the positive real numbers, is it necessarily the case that f and g can be related in some manner using either big-O or big-Ω notation?

8. What is the relationship between big-O and big-Ω?

9. In which of the following cases is $g(n) = \Theta(f(n))$?

   (a) $g(n) = n^2 + 2n + 7$ and $f(n) = n^3$
   (b) $g(n) = \lg n$ and $f(n) = 100$
   (c) $g(n) = n \lg n$ and $f(n) = (\lg n)^4$
   (d) $g(n) = n$ and $f(n) = n^{1.2}$
   (e) $g(n) = 2^n$ and $f(n) = n!$

10. We have five types of asymptotic notation. Are there any implications among them? For example, if $f(n) = O(g(n))$, does this imply $f(n) = o(g(n))$? List and prove as many implications as possible.

Section 8.3 Time and Space Complexity

11. What are the time and space complexity of the language $\{0^i 1^i \mid i \geq 0\}$? Can the best bounds you derive be obtained simultaneously?

12. Design a DTM to show that the language $L = \{a^i b^i c^i \mid i \geq 0\}$ has space complexity $O(\lg n)$.

13. What are the time and space complexity of the DTM described in Example 6.2.13? Can you design a different DTM to reduce either the time or space complexity of the language described in this example?

14. What is the best time complexity you can prove for the language $L = \{G \Diamond s \Diamond t \mid G \text{ is an encoding of an undirected graph } G = (V, E), s, t \in V,$ and there is a path from s to t in $G\}$?

15. Prove that the space complexity of $L = \{G \Diamond s \Diamond t \mid G$ is an encoding of an undirected graph $G = (V, E)$, $s, t \in V$, and there is a path from s to t in $G\}$ is $O((\lg n)^2)$.

16. In the spirit of the remarks following Definition 8.3.3, classify the remaining languages described in Example 8.3.2.

17. Given an undirected graph $G = (V, E)$, show that the problem of determining whether G is a *tree* is in $DSPACE(\lg n)$.

18. Given an input 0^i for $i \in \mathbb{N}$, show that the problem of determining whether i is a prime number is in $DTIME(O(2^{|0^i|}))$.

19. Prove that the language $L = \{G \Diamond s \Diamond t \mid G$ is an encoding of an undirected graph $G = (V, E)$, $s, t \in V$, and there is a path from s to t in $G\}$ is in $NSPACE(\lg n)$.

Section 8.4 Simulations

20. Prove Observation 8.4.1.

21. Could the simulation described in Theorem 8.4.3 be modified to execute more than l moves of M using only six moves of M'? Elaborate.

22. Prove that the choice of r given in Theorem 8.4.3 really does work.

23. Let $c > 0$ be a constant. Prove that $DTIME(t(n)) = DTIME(c \cdot t(n))$.

24. Prove that if $g(n) = O(f(n))$ and $n = o(f(n))$, then $DTIME(g(n)) \subseteq DTIME(f(n))$ and $NTIME(g(n)) \subseteq NTIME(f(n))$.

25. Prove that $DSPACE(t(n)) \subseteq DSPACE(2^{O(t(n))})$.

26. Prove that if $g(n) = O(f(n))$, then $DSPACE(g(n)) \subseteq DSPACE(f(n))$ and $NSPACE(g(n)) \subseteq NSPACE(f(n))$.

27. Is it true that $NSPACE(s(n)) \subseteq DTIME(2^{O(s(n))})$?

28. Show that for each NTM, there is an equivalent NTM that has a unique accepting configuration for each accepted input.

29. Fill in the remaining details in the proof of Theorem 8.4.6.

30. Complete the proof of Savitch's Theorem based on the remarks given in Theorem 8.4.8.

31. Answer TRUE, FALSE, or OPEN to the following statements. Use OPEN to mean that, from the material presented in this chapter, it is not possible to derive a solution, or the answer to the question is not known. Justify your answers.

(a) $NSPACE(n) \neq DSPACE(n^2 \lg n)$

(b) $NSPACE(2^n) \subseteq DSPACE(4^n)$

(c) $DTIME(2^n) \neq DTIME(n^2 2^n)$

(d) $NTIME(n) \subseteq DSPACE(n^2)$

(e) $DSPACE(n^6) \subseteq NSPACE(n^3)$

(f) $NTIME(n^3) \subseteq DSPACE(n^7)$

Section 8.5 Reducibilities

32. Let Σ and Γ be alphabets. Let $f : \Sigma^* \mapsto \Gamma^*$ be a function. Formally define what it means for f to be computed in time $t(n)$. We say that f is in time $t(n)$.

33. Let Σ and Γ be alphabets. Let $f : \Sigma^* \mapsto \Gamma^*$ be a function. Formally define what it means for f to be computed in space $s(n)$. We say that f is in space $s(n)$.

34. Explain how reductions can be viewed as subroutine calls.

35. Suppose that f and g are functions that can be computed in time $\bigcup_{i=0}^{\infty} DTIME(n^i)$. Show that $f \circ g$, which here means f composed with g, can be computed in time n^k for some $k \in \mathbb{N}$.

36. Suppose that f and g are functions that can be computed in $DSPACE(\lg n)$. Show that $f \circ g$ can be computed within logarithmic space.

37. Prove Lemma 8.5.3.

38. Prove that if $L' \in DSPACE(\lg n)$ and $L \leq_m^{\lg} L'$, then $L \in DSPACE(\lg n)$.

39. The natural numbers $\mathbb{N}$ and integers $\mathbb{Z}$ can be considered as languages when suitably encoded as strings over $\{0, 1\}$. Show that they are equivalent under $\leq_m$.

40. Let L be the language corresponding to the Hamiltonian Path problem (see Example 8.5.5) and L' be the language corresponding to the following decision problem:

    Given: An undirected graph $G = (V, E)$ and two designated vertices $u, v \in V$.

    Problem: Is there a Hamiltonian path in G that starts at u and ends at v? Prove that $L \leq_m^P L'$.

41. Let L be the language corresponding to the Hamiltonian Path problem (see Example 8.5.5) and L' be the language corresponding to the following decision problem:

    Given: A directed graph $G = (V, E)$.

    Problem: Does G contain a *directed* Hamiltonian path? In this case all edges in the Hamiltonian path must be "pointed" in the same direction. Prove that $L \leq_m^{\lg} L'$.

CHAPTER | 9

Circuit Complexity

Does unbounded fanin refer to beer consumption at a Mariners' game?
　　—Steve Hudson

9.1　*Introduction*

The goals of this chapter are

- to explain the *Boolean circuit model*,[1]
- to define the resources of *size*, *depth*, and *width* for Boolean circuits,
- to present the concept of circuit *uniformity*,
- to give several examples of Boolean circuits and analyze their resources,
- to provide some intuition about parallel computation,
- to define the complexity class *NC*, and
- to illustrate why *NC* consists of problems that can be solved fast in parallel.

The Boolean circuit model is mathematically simple and easy to use; it is widely studied in both computer science and electrical engineering. Boolean circuits are designed to capture very fine–grained parallel computation at the resolution of a single bit; they are a formal model of the *combinational logic circuit*. Circuits are basic technology, consisting of very simple logical gates connected by bit–carrying wires. They have no memory and no notion of state. Circuits avoid almost all issues of machine organization and instruction repertoire. Their computational components correspond directly with devices that we can actually fabricate, although the Boolean circuit model remains an idealization of real electronic computing devices. Since the model ignores a host of important

---

1. Named for the mathematician George Boole.

practical considerations such as circuit area, volume, pin limitations, power dissipation, packaging, and signal propagation delay. Such issues are addressed more accurately by more complex VLSI models (see [32]). But for much of the study of parallel computation, the Boolean circuit model provides an excellent compromise between simplicity and realism. It also provides a convenient framework for addressing other important open questions in computer science, such as the *P* versus *NP* question (see Chapters 10 and 11). We begin this chapter by defining the Boolean circuit model.

9.2 *The Boolean Circuit Model of Computation*

An example of a Boolean circuit is provided in Figure 9.1. Circuit *inputs* are placed in boxes, and *gates* (excluding inputs) are represented by circles. A Boolean circuit is an acyclic, directed graph in which the edges carry unidirectional logical signals and the vertices compute elementary logical functions. The entire graph computes a Boolean function from the inputs to the outputs in the expected way (described formally below).

The Boolean circuit shown in Figure 9.1 has five types of gates: ID (I), AND (∧), OR (∨), NOT (¬), and IMPLIES (⇒). Let's examine the properties of these types of gates with the aid of *truth tables*. The most straightforward gate is the ID gate. We show its truth table in Table 9.1 with input x_1. An ID gate can be thought of as simply passing on its input unchanged.

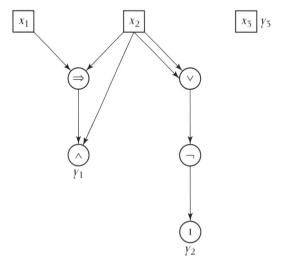

Figure 9.1

A sample Boolean circuit.

x_1	ID x_1
0	0
1	1

Table 9.1

The truth table for the ID gate with input x_1.

x_1	NOT x_1
0	1
1	0

Table 9.2

The truth table for a NOT gate with input x_1.

x_1	x_2	x_1 OR x_2
0	0	0
0	1	1
1	0	1
1	1	1

Table 9.3

The truth table for an OR gate with inputs x_1 and x_2.

The truth table for a NOT gate with input x_1 is depicted in Table 9.2. A NOT gate simply negates its input value.

The truth table for an OR gate with inputs x_1 and x_2 is depicted in Table 9.3. An OR gate evaluates to TRUE[2] if and only if at least one of its inputs is TRUE.

The truth table for an AND gate with inputs x_1 and x_2 is depicted in Table 9.4. An AND gate evaluates to TRUE if and only if both of its inputs are TRUE.

The truth table for an IMPLIES gate with inputs x_1 and x_2 is depicted in Table 9.5. IMPLIES is TRUE if and only if its antecedent is TRUE or its consequent is FALSE.

In the Boolean circuit shown in Figure 9.1, suppose $x_1 = 0$, $x_2 = 1$, and $x_3 = 1$. Under these conditions, the IMPLIES gate evaluates to 1 (see Table 9.5). The value 1

---

2. Recall that we equate the value 1 with TRUE and the value 0 with FALSE.

x_1	x_2	x_1 AND x_2
0	0	0
0	1	0
1	0	0
1	1	1

Table 9.4

The truth table for an AND gate with inputs x_1 and x_2.

x_1	x_2	x_1 IMPLIES x_2
0	0	1
0	1	1
1	0	0
1	1	1

Table 9.5

The truth table for an IMPLIES gate with inputs x_1 and x_2.

computed by the IMPLIES gate is passed on to the AND gate having label γ_1. The other input of this AND gate is $x_2 = 1$. Therefore, the AND gate evaluates to TRUE. The OR gate has two 1-inputs and so evaluates to TRUE. The NOT gate receives a 1 as input and so outputs a 0. The ID gate labeled γ_2 just passes on its input so it outputs a 0. The basic ideas of how a Boolean circuit computes should now be clear.

We have defined a number of gate types. In general, gates can be arbitrary Boolean functions of their inputs. If a gate has k inputs, it belongs to the set of **k–ary Boolean functions** $B_k = \{f \mid f : \{0, 1\}^k \to \{0, 1\}\}$. As is common practice (and in agreement with the presentation thus far), we refer informally to such functions by symbols like "1," "0," "¬," "∧," and "∨," among others. For the sake of readability and to expose you to a variety of common notations, we will also use "NOT," "AND," "OR," and other descriptive words (again as above). A list of some common gates and their corresponding symbols is provided in Table 9.6.

Let's explain how the OR function fits into the Boolean function terminology just presented. It is easy to see that OR $\in B_2$, since OR $: \{0, 1\}^2 \to \{0, 1\}$ is defined by OR$((0, 0)) = 0$, OR$((0, 1)) = 1$, OR$((1, 0)) = 1$, and OR$((1, 1)) = 1$, as is shown in Table 9.3. Other gate types fit into this scheme in an analogous manner. This notation helps us simplify the formal definition of a Boolean circuit.

Name of Gate	Symbol
AND	$\wedge$
ID	I
IMPLIES	$\Rightarrow$
NAND	$\neg\wedge$
NOR	$\neg\vee$
NOT	$\neg$
INPUT	x_i
OR	$\vee$

Table 9.6

Some common gates and their symbolic representations.

Conceptually, a Boolean circuit is simply a collection of interconnected gates, whose input values propagate towards the outputs, computing according to the functions of the gates. More precisely, we have the following definition.

Definition 9.2.1   *A **Boolean circuit** α is a labeled finite oriented directed acyclic graph. Each vertex v has a type τ,[3] where*

$$\tau(v) \in \{\text{INPUT}\} \ \cup \ B_0 \ \cup \ B_1 \ \cup \ B_2$$

*The **indegree** (or **outdegree**) of a vertex is the number of incoming (or, respectively, outgoing) edges. A vertex v with $\tau(v) = \text{INPUT}$ has indegree 0 and is called an **input**. The inputs of α are given by a tuple $(x_1, \ldots, x_n)$ of distinct vertices. A vertex v with outdegree 0 is called an **output**. The outputs of α are given by a tuple $(y_1, \ldots, y_m)$ of distinct vertices. A vertex v with $\tau(v) \in B_i$ must have indegree i. Each vertex is called a **gate**.*

Note that **fanin**, which is defined as the indegree of a gate, is less than or equal to two, but **fanout**, which is defined as the outdegree of a gate, is unrestricted. We say the fanout is *unbounded* in this case. Circuit inputs, elements of type INPUT, are also considered gates. Inputs can also be outputs, as shown in Figure 9.1. The circuit depicted there has inputs x_1, x_2, and x_3, and outputs y_1, y_2, and y_3, where $x_3 = y_3$. Input x_2 has outdegree four and thus fanout four. Gate y_2 has indegree one and thus fanin one.

Each circuit computes a function of its input bits as follows:

Definition 9.2.2   *A Boolean circuit α with inputs $(x_1, \ldots, x_n)$ and outputs $(y_1, \ldots, y_m)$ **computes a function** $f : \{0, 1\}^n \to \{0, 1\}^m$ in the following way: input x_i, $1 \le i \le n$, is*

---

3. τ (pronounced "tau") is the Greek equivalent to the letter *t*, as in "type."

assigned a value $v(x_i)$ from $\{0, 1\}$ representing the ith bit of the argument to the function.[4] *Every other vertex v is assigned a value $v(v) \in \{0, 1\}$ obtained by applying $\tau(v)$ to the value(s) of the vertices incoming to v. The value of the function is the tuple $(v(\gamma_1), \ldots, v(\gamma_m))$, in which output γ_j, $1 \le j \le m$, contributes the jth bit of the output.*

Let's apply this definition to the Boolean circuit shown in Figure 9.1. Suppose $v(x_1) = 0$, $v(x_2) = 1$, and $v(x_3) = 0$. Then $v(\gamma_1) = 1$, $v(\gamma_2) = 0$, and $v(\gamma_3) = 0$. For example, using Tables 9.5 and 9.4, $0 \Rightarrow 1 = 1$ and $1 \wedge 1 = 1$, so $v(\gamma_1) = 1$. Sometimes we will be less precise (as we were originally) and drop the v. That is, we simply say that the inputs are $x_1 = 0$, $x_2 = 1$, and $x_3 = 0$. If f is the function computed by the circuit of Figure 9.1, then $f((0, 1, 0)) = (1, 0, 0)$. In this example $n = m = 3$.

Unlike the computational models we have considered so far, individual circuits have a fixed number of input bits and so cannot handle arbitrary-length inputs (a capability even posessed by DFAs). So we need a circuit for each given length of input that we want to process. For this reason, we have to produce, communicate, and manipulate circuit descriptions. Although there are different ways of describing circuits, there are a handful of common representations, of which the most common is called the *standard encoding*.

Definition 9.2.3   *The* **standard encoding** *$\tilde{\alpha}$ of a circuit α is a string from $\{0, 1\}^*$ grouped into a sequence of four tuples (v, g, l, r), one tuple for each vertex of α, followed by two sequences of vertex numbers $\langle\langle x_1, \ldots, x_n \rangle\rangle$ and $\langle\langle \gamma_1, \ldots, \gamma_m \rangle\rangle$. Within the encoding, the vertices of α are uniquely (but arbitrarily) numbered in the range from one up to the number of gates in the circuit. The tuple (v, g, l, r) describes a vertex, numbered v, and its oriented connections to other vertices as follows. Vertex number v has gate type g, where*

$$g \in \{\text{INPUT}\} \cup B_0 \cup B_1 \cup B_2$$

The left (or right) input to v, if any, is numbered l (or, respectively, r). The vertex number of the ith input, $1 \le i \le n$, is given by x_i, and that of the jth output, $1 \le j \le m$, is given by γ_j.

The main points of this definition are that circuit descriptions are simple objects to generate and manipulate, and they are compact. Figure 10.7 in Chapter 10 shows a circuit where the gates of the circuit have been arbitrarily numbered from one to six. A standard encoding of the circuit based on this numbering at a high level is

$\langle\langle (4, \text{INPUT}, -, -), (5, \text{NAND}, 6, 3), (1, \text{NAND}, 5, 4), (6, \text{INPUT}, -, -),$

$(3, \text{INPUT}, -, -), (2, \text{NAND}, 5, 1), \langle\langle 6, 3, 4 \rangle\rangle, \langle\langle 2, 1 \rangle\rangle \rangle\rangle$

Note that this description can be converted to a binary string using the techniques of Section 2.5, although for ease of presentation we have described it as a string

---

4. The Greek letter v (pronounced "nu") is equivalent to n, but because its appearance is similar to v, it is often used to denote a "value."

over the alphabet consisting of parentheses, comma, decimal digits, and the like. As is customary we state all encodings at a high level. You can convert them into bit strings using the methods described in Section 2.5. We ask for such conversions in the exercises.

9.3 Circuit Resources

Models of computation typically have several resources that are worth investigating. For example, in the case of Turing machines, we examined time and space. For Boolean circuits the primary resources of interest are *depth* and *size*. Another interesting resource is *width*. In this section we formally define these concepts. In quantifying the amount of these resources problems take to solve on circuits, we are able to gauge how complex the problems are. It turns out that circuit resources map very nicely into the *parallel computing* domain. We will point out these connections in this section. Let's provide a bit of intuition about parallel computing before proceeding.

For the purposes of this text, view a *parallel computer* abstractly as a computer consisting of many communicating and cooperating processors. You can think of a very large number of personal computers linked together to solve problems. The important resources to study in parallel complexity are *time*, *processors*, and total *operations*. **Parallel time** is simply the time required by the longest–running processor. The **number of processors** is just the maximum number of processors ever used in a single step. The **number of operations** is the total number of steps executed by a parallel program. There are many interesting theoretical and practical issues involving parallel computation. However, our focus here is only on providing you with an intuitive sense of such models and describing how they relate to Boolean circuits.

If you have already met the electrical engineering requirement of a computer science major, you will have noticed the similarities between the Boolean circuit model and the basic building blocks of computers. This is no accident. In fact, the origins of the Boolean circuit model are exactly from the early days of logic circuits, when gates were expensive and slow compared to signal propagation times. When we draw conclusions about the Boolean circuit model, the results can be applied to address practical considerations. However, because of the simplicity of the Boolean circuit model and its level of abstraction, a certain amount of detail is lost (especially issues of signal propagation delay, power consumption, communication path bandwidth, and reliability). Nevertheless, since the Boolean circuit model is mathematically easy to work with, it is very useful for modeling parallel computation and proving *lower bounds*.

Next we present definitions for the most important circuit resources. These are usually expressed in terms of the number of circuit inputs, denoted by n.

Definition 9.3.1   *Let α be a Boolean circuit. The* **size** *of α, denoted* size(α), *is the number of gates in α.*

For example, the size of the Boolean circuit shown in Figure 9.1 is eight. Size is a measure of the amount of computation. In the parallel setting, size relates to the number of operations.

Definition 9.3.2   *Let α be a Boolean circuit. The* **depth** *of α, denoted* depth(α), *is the length of the longest path from an input gate to an output gate in α.*

For example, the depth of the Boolean circuit shown in Figure 9.1 is three. Depth is a measure of the time required by a computation. In the parallel setting, circuit depth relates directly to time, since we can view all gates as "firing" in parallel as soon as their inputs are available.

A less common resource measure for Boolean circuits is *width*. Intuitively, width corresponds to the maximum number of gate values, not counting inputs, needing to be preserved when evaluating the circuit level by level. The measure corresponds to the number of processors needed.

Definition 9.3.3   *Let α be a Boolean circuit. The* **width** *of α, denoted* width(α), *is*

$$\max_{0 < i < \text{depth}(\alpha)} \left| \left\{ v \,\middle|\, \begin{array}{l} 0 < d(v) \le i \text{ and} \\ \text{there is an edge from vertex } v \text{ to a vertex } w, d(w) > i \end{array} \right\} \right|$$

where $d(w)$, the **depth** *of w, is the length of the longest path from any input to vertex w.*

The circuit shown in Figure 9.1 has width two.

An individual circuit with n inputs and m outputs is a finite object computing a function from binary strings of length n to binary strings of length m. Consequently, different circuits are required for different length inputs. This is in contrast to our usual notion of computation for Turing machines in which one algorithm handles all possible lengths of inputs. How can the notion of circuit be generalized to functions on strings of arbitrary length? This question is the subject of the next section.

9.3.1   Uniform Circuit Families

Consider a circuit having n inputs and m outputs. Suppose the output length m is a function, possibly constant, only of the input length n. That is, we are only considering the simple case of functions f where the length of $f(x)$ is the same for all n–bit inputs x. Call this length $m(n)$. In this situation we can represent the function

$$f_\alpha : \{0, 1\}^* \rightarrow \{0, 1\}^*$$

by an infinite sequence of circuits, $\{\alpha_n\}$, where circuit α_n computes f restricted to inputs of length n. Such a sequence is called a *circuit family*.

Definition 9.3.4   *A **Boolean circuit family** $\{\alpha_n\}$ is a collection of circuits, each α_n computing a function $f^n : \{0, 1\}^n \rightarrow \{0, 1\}^{m(n)}$. The **function computed** by $\{\alpha_n\}$, denoted f_α, is the function*

$$f_\alpha : \{0, 1\}^* \rightarrow \{0, 1\}^*$$

defined by $f_\alpha(x) \equiv f^{|x|}(x)$.

The special case where the length of the output is always one is particularly important for defining language classes.

Definition 9.3.5   *Let $\{\alpha_n\}$ be a Boolean circuit family that computes the function $f_\alpha : \{0, 1\}^* \rightarrow \{0, 1\}$. The **language accepted** by $\{\alpha_n\}$, denoted L_α, is the set $L_\alpha = \{x \in \{0, 1\}^* \mid f_\alpha(x) = 1\}$. We say L_α is accepted by $\{\alpha_n\}$.*

When the output length varies with the value as well as the length of the input, some additional output bits must be computed by the circuit to indicate which of the remaining output bits are valid data. This is a technical complication that can be explored in the references.

How do we describe an infinite collection of circuits? With no constraints whatsoever, we get the so-called *nonuniform* circuit families. Nonuniform circuit families are unexpectedly powerful, in that they can "compute" noncomputable functions. For example, consider the circuit family $\{\alpha_n\}$, where circuit α_n consists of n inputs, all ignored, and a single output gate v that is a constant function. Gate v is defined to be the constant 1 function if the nth Turing machine halts on its own program description, and is defined to be a 0 gate otherwise. Thus, the circuit family $\{\alpha_n\}$ computes a function f_α that is uncomputable in the usual sense, since it can be used to solve the Halting problem.

With nonuniform circuit families, there is no method for describing the members of the family. The obvious approach to addressing this difficulty is to provide an algorithm for generating the members of the family. That is, a circuit family is defined by giving a program in some computational model that takes n as input and then outputs the encoding $\widetilde{\alpha}_n$ of the nth member. In doing so, an infinite object, the family, is effectively described by a finite object, the program. The question then becomes, How much computational power is permitted in producing the description $\widetilde{\alpha}_n$?

Guided by the intuition that the circuit constructor should have no more computational power than the object it constructs, Borodin introduced the notion of *uniformity* [5]. One example of a weak circuit constructor is a Turing machine that is limited to only $O(\lg n)$ work space on inputs of length n. It is very interesting that many problems of interest cannot actually be *solved* directly in this limited amount of space, yet this is sufficient space to produce a *description* of circuits that can solve the problems.

Definition 9.3.6 *A family $\{\alpha_n\}$ of Boolean circuits is **logarithmic space uniform** if the transformation $1^n \to \widetilde{\alpha}_n$ can be computed in $O(\lg(n + \text{size}(\alpha_n)))$ space on a deterministic Turing machine.*

Note that the complexity of producing the description of α_n is expressed in terms of the size of the resulting circuit, instead of the usual method of expressing it in terms of the input length. Encoding n in *unary* ensures that in the case of polynomial size circuits, the complexity is also logarithmic in terms of the length of the input.

Logarithmic space uniformity is sometimes called *Borodin-Cook uniformity*. This notion of uniformity has many desirable properties that may be investigated through the references. We will need the concepts of circuit family and uniformity when we define the parallel complexity class *NC* later in this chapter.

The theory of parallel computation is yet another vast region of complexity theory. There have been many parallel models proposed and many problems studied. The important point to observe here is that nearly all of the parallel models put forth have a polynomial equivalence with Boolean circuits in terms of their resource usage. That is, if a problem simultaneously requires $p(n)$ processors and $t(n)$ time to solve on some (uniform) model of parallel computation, then it simultaneously requires $p(n)^{O(1)}$ size and $t(n)^{O(1)}$ depth to solve on a (uniform) family of Boolean circuits, and vice versa. This, coupled with its other desirable features, tells us that the Boolean circuit model is a good general model of parallel computation. In the next section we investigate a couple of examples of Boolean circuits and their resources.

9.4 *Examples of Boolean Circuits*

In this section we examine two examples of Boolean circuits: one dealing with *planar* circuits and the other with computing transitive closure. Our goal is not to develop issues about circuit design but simply to reinforce the basic concepts of the Boolean circuit model. More sophisticated examples may be pursued through the references.

Let's start by looking at a *planar cross-over gadget*. A **planar circuit** is one in which no wires cross when it is drawn on a piece of paper. A **cross–over gadget** is a circuit that has as left input x_1 and as right input x_2, and has as left output y_1

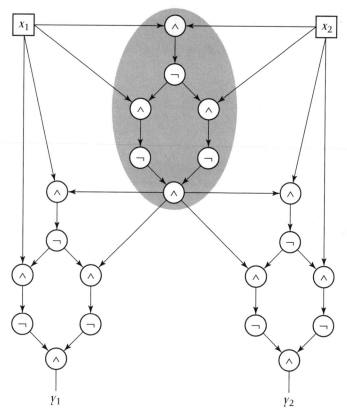

Figure 9.2

A planar cross–over gadget.

and right output y_2 with the property that $y_1 = x_2$ and $y_2 = x_1$. A **planar cross–over gadget** is a cross–over gadget that is planar. It is apparent that a planar cross–over gadget is useful for building planar circuits.

Figure 9.2 depicts the planar cross–over gadget developed by Goldschlager [19]. Notice the regularity of the circuit and that no wires cross. The same "unit" (shaded in the figure) appears three times; this unit computes *equivalence*. That is, if $x_1 = x_2$, then the unit outputs a 1. Otherwise, it outputs a 0. The circuit has size 23, depth 10, and width 8.

The second example we look at is of a circuit that computes the *transitive closure* of an $n \times n$ *Boolean matrix A*. A **Boolean matrix** is a matrix whose entries are either 0 or 1. Recall the **transitive closure** of a relation R involves closing R under the *transitive property*. That is, if $(a_1, a_2) \in R$ and $(a_2, a_3) \in R$, then $(a_1, a_3) \in R$. Once all possible pairs have been added to the relation according to the transitive

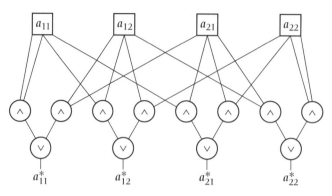

Figure 9.3

A circuit for computing the transitive closure of a 2×2 Boolean matrix.

property, and only those pairs, the transitive closure is obtained. The transitive closure of a matrix A is denoted A^*.

But how does transitive closure of relations fit into the framework of Boolean matrices? Think of the $n \times n$ Boolean matrix A as a relation on $\{1, \ldots, n\} \times \{1, \ldots, n\}$, where an ordered pair is in the relation if and only if the corresponding matrix entry is 1. In the special case where the Boolean matrix represents the adjacency matrix (see Chapter 2) of an n–node undirected graph, the transitive closure is an $n \times n$ Boolean matrix A^*. A^* has entry a_{ij}^*, $1 \leq i, j \leq n$, equal to 1 if and only if there is a path from node i to node j in the graph represented by A.

For this discussion we restrict ourselves to values of n that are a power of two, although the results presented here are easily generalized to arbitrary values of n. The key idea to compute the transitive closure is to repeatedly square the matrix— that is, compute A^2, $A^2 \cdot A^2 = A^4$, and so on. Instead of performing the usual matrix multiplication involving the operations $\times$ and $+$, we substitute AND and OR, respectively. The OR is n-way. The resulting matrix obtained from the repeated squarings is Boolean. If $n = 2^k$ for some $k \in \mathbb{N}$, then only k squarings are necessary for finding the transitive closure. We leave the proof of this fact as an exercise.

Given an $n \times n$ matrix A, there are n^2 inputs to a Boolean circuit for computing A^*. Figure 9.3 depicts a circuit for computing the transitive closure when n equals two. It does one squaring of the matrix. The construction can be generalized to produce a logarithmic space uniform family of Boolean circuits for determining the transitive closure.

The transitive closure operation is a fundamental operation in parallel computing, with many parallel algorithms using it as a subroutine in their computation. In fact, many problems (such as graph accessibility) are reducible to transitive closure. It is not hard to see that the generalized construction of Figure 9.3 results in a logarithmic space uniform circuit family of depth $O((\lg n)^2)$

and size $O(n^3 \lg n)$. The depth is $O((\lg n)^2)$ because for an arbitrary n we need to OR n values together. In Figure 9.3 the OR level was only one gate deep, $\lg 2 = 1$, but in general it will be $\lceil \lg n \rceil$ levels deep, since we only allow a fanin two for OR gates. The circuit size is $O(n^3 \lg n)$ because every $\lg n$ level contains $O(n^3)$ gates, and there are $\lg n$ of these metalevels.

9.5   *The Complexity Class NC*

Earlier in this chapter, we related the Boolean circuit model and its resources to parallel computers. In this section we define the most important complexity class in parallel computation, *NC*.

The most fundamental question in parallel computation is whether every problem having a *feasible* sequential solution (see Chapter 10) has a fast parallel solution. That is, can parallelism always be used to greatly speed up the running time of a problem? Intuitively, it seems to make sense that the maxim "many hands make light work" applies to computing as well as barn building. Perhaps the best way to illustrate the relevant issues for this discussion is via an example.

Many problems that can be solved in $DTIME(n^i)$ for some $i \in \mathbb{N}$ have truly dramatic speed improvements when solved in parallel. Here we consider a simple one, called the *Sum problem*, defined as follows:

Sum problem

Given: Natural numbers $a_1, a_2, \ldots, a_n$, and t.

Problem: Is $t = a_1 + a_2 + \cdots + a_n$?

We make several assumptions in our discussion about the Sum problem. We parameterize resources in terms of the quantity of natural numbers to be summed. This is not the same as the input size. Additionally, we treat addition as an atomic operation. You should be aware of these considerations. For the conclusions we want to draw, there is no harm done, so long as we apply the same assumptions in both the sequential and parallel settings.

Solving the Sum problem *sequentially* on a Turing machine or personal computer, we have to add numbers two at a time. Such a procedure requires $n - 1$ additions to compute the total, and the total can be checked against t to solve the problem. The Sum problem is an example of a problem that is *sequentially feasible*. Now consider solving the Sum problem using a number of processors operating in parallel.

With *limited parallelism*, which means using a fixed number of processors, we can never achieve more than a *constant factor* of improvement over the best-known sequential time. For example, with two processors we can never be more than twice as fast. However, suppose processors were so plentiful and inexpensive that we could consider using thousands or more in parallel. This introduces a qualitative change in the way we approach parallel computation. What kind of speedup could be achieved if we had essentially unlimited processing power, and could tailor the number of processors to the size of the problem?

With *polynomially bounded parallelism*, which means using a polynomial number of processors, we have the potential to achieve more than a constant factor speedup. For example, suppose that we use $p(n) = n/2$ processors to solve an instance of the Sum problem consisting of n numbers and a value t. That is, we have one processor for each pair of numbers. The computation can then be organized as a binary tree in which we add as many pairs of numbers as possible in each time step. The time to compute the addition of n numbers is the height of the tree, so the computation can be done in $O(\lg n)$ elapsed time using $n/2$ processors.

We must emphasize the importance of this example. Using only a relatively small number of processors (half the number of values to be summed), we have achieved an *exponential* improvement in the solution of the Sum problem by going from $O(n)$ sequential time to $O(\lg n)$ parallel time. Problems that exhibit this kind of speed improvement from parallelism are exactly those that belong to the complexity class *NC*, which we now define.[5]

Definition 9.5.1 *The class NC is the set of all languages L, such that L is accepted by logarithmic space uniform Boolean circuit family simultaneously having depth* $(\log n)^{O(1)}$ *and size* $n^{O(1)}$.

Sequential models generally require n steps just to process the input. It should be clear from the definition of *NC* that problems in this class are those that can be solved very quickly in parallel.

The class *NC* has been well studied; several hundred papers have been written classifying problems as being in *NC*. You may pursue the references to find out more about these results. In the next chapter we examine problems that are *unlikely* candidates for being in *NC*. That is, we study feasible problems that appear to be *inherently sequential*; such problems do not seem to have fast parallel solutions. This evidence seems to indicate that not all feasible problems can be solved in *NC* and thus do not always have a fast parallel solution.

9.6   *Exercises*

Section 9.2   The Boolean Circuit Model of Computation

1. List the Boolean functions contained in B_0, B_1, and B_2.

---

5. As an historical note, we mention that *NC* stands for "Nick's class." This complexity class was named for Nicholas Pippenger, one of the early pioneers in circuit complexity.

2. Explain how the directed graph shown in Figure 9.1 meets the requirements of the definition of Boolean circuit. What type of gates does the circuit have? What is the fanin and fanout of each gate?

3. Evaluate the Boolean circuit shown in Figure 9.1 on all possible input combinations.

4. Write out truth tables for NAND (meaning not AND) and NOR (meaning not OR) gates.

5. Construct a Boolean circuit that solves the Parity problem for an input of size 8. That is, on YES instances of Parity, it outputs a 1, and on NO instances, it outputs a 0. For an input of size 8, how many gates does your circuit have? Can your circuit be extended to a logarithmic space uniform circuit family?

6. Specify a Boolean circuit that computes the following function $g : \{0, 1\}^3 \to \{0, 1\}$, where $g(x_1, x_2, x_3) = 1$ if $x_1 + x_2 + x_3$ equals 2 and is 0 otherwise.

7. Write out the standard encoding for the Boolean circuit shown in Figure 9.1. Do this first at a high level and then as a bit string.

8. Write out the standard encoding for the Boolean circuit shown in Figure 10.3. Do this first at a high level and then as a bit string.

9. Evaluate the Boolean circuit shown in Figure 10.3 on all possible input combinations.

10. Design a logarithmic space uniform Boolean circuit family to accept the language $\{0^i \mid i \in \mathbb{N}\}$.

Section 9.3   Circuit Resources

11. Suppose circuit size were not defined as the number of gates in a circuit but instead as the number of "wires." How does this new definition of size relate to the old one? Is there a difference for unbounded fanin or unbounded fanout circuits?

12. Can you draw any relationships between circuit size, depth, and width?

13. We defined size, depth, and width for a fixed circuit. Extend these definitions to circuit families.

14. What are the size, depth, and width of the circuit shown in Figure 9.4?

15. Draw a circuit that has size 15, depth 4, and width 4.

16. Propose a parallel model of computation that has as its baseline processor the Turing machine. Describe the model in detail.

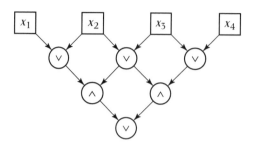

Figure 9.4

What are the values of the resources used by this Boolean circuit?

17. Design a circuit that computes the function $f : \{0, 1\}^6 \mapsto \{0, 1\}$ such that $f(x) = 1$ if and only if $\#_1(x) = 2$. What are the resources of your circuit? Are the resources minimums for this function? Can you extend your circuit to a logarithmic space uniform circuit family for the general case, where we want to see if exactly two of the inputs are 1?

Section 9.4   Examples of Boolean Circuits

18. What is the largest fanout of a gate in the circuit shown in Figure 9.2? How about fanin? How many gates have fanout at least three?

19. Prove that the planar cross–over gadget shown in Figure 9.2 actually works.

20. The planar cross–over gadget shown in Figure 9.2 has size 23. It was constructed using a *basis* consisting of NOT, OR, and AND gates. A **basis** is a set of gate types. Can you build a smaller cross–over gadget utilizing a different basis of gates?

21. Is it possible to have a planar cross–over circuit of fanout two or three?

22. Design Boolean circuit families to compute the following functions:

    (a) $f : \{0, 1\}^* \mapsto \{0, 1\}$, where $f(x) = x(1) \vee x(2) \vee \cdots \vee x(|x|)$
    (b) $f : \{0, 1\}^* \mapsto \{0, 1\}$, where $f(x) = x(1) \wedge x(2) \wedge \cdots \wedge x(|x|)$
    (c) $f : \{0, 1\}^* \mapsto \{0, 1\}$, where $f(x) = 1$ if and only if $\#_1(x) \geq |x|/2$
    (d) $f : \{0, 1\}^* \times \{0, 1\}^* \mapsto \{0, 1\}$, where $f(x, y) = 1$ if and only if $x = y$
    (e) $f : \{0, 1\}^* \times \{0, 1\}^* \mapsto \{0, 1\}$, where $f(x, y) = 1$ if and only if $|x| = |y|$ and there exists a unique i such that $x(i) \neq y(i)$

23. Let A be an $n \times n$ Boolean matrix. Prove that if $n = 2^k$, then after k repeated squarings of A, we obtain the value of the transitive closure of A, A^*.

24. Compute the transitive closure of the following adjacency matrix A:

$$\begin{pmatrix} 1 & 0 & 1 & 0 \\ 0 & 0 & 1 & 1 \\ 1 & 1 & 1 & 1 \\ 0 & 1 & 1 & 1 \end{pmatrix}$$

Assume each row represents the corresponding vertex number. That is, row 1 corresponds to vertex 1, row 2 corresponds to vertex 2, and so on. Is there a path from node 1 to node 2 in the graph represented by A?

25. Compute the transitive closure of the following matrix A using the circuit presented in Figure 9.3:

$$\begin{pmatrix} 1 & 0 \\ 1 & 1 \end{pmatrix}$$

Is it possible that this matrix represents the adjacency matrix of an undirected graph?

26. When are an $n \times n$ adjacency matrix A and its transitive closure A^* equal?

27. Generalize the construction presented in Section 9.4 for computing the transitive closure to any $n \times n$ matrix regardless of whether or not n is a power of two.

28. Draw the 4×4 transitive closure circuit.

29. Prove that the circuit family for computing the transitive closure, derived based on the techniques developed in this section, is logarithmic space uniform.

Section 9.5   The Complexity Class NC

30. Define a natural decision problem based on computing transitive closures. Is your problem in NC?

31. Prove that the Parity problem is in the class NC.

32. Is the problem of computing the OR of n bits in NC?

33. Prove that the Average problem defined in Chapter 1 is in NC.

34. Is the problem of sorting 0's and 1's in NC?

35. Formalize the discussion of the Sum problem and prove that the problem is in NC.

CHAPTER 10

Feasible Problems

Only you can know what is truly feasible.
        —*Zen master*

10.1 Introduction

The goals of this chapter are

- to introduce the complexity class *P*,
- to explain why problems in this class are said to have *feasible* solutions,
- to describe *P*-completeness theory,
- to examine a number of examples of *P*-complete problems, and
- to present several *P*-completeness reductions.

This chapter deals with those problems that have *feasible solutions*. Informally, such problems can be solved in a "reasonable" amount of time on a computer. What do we mean by "reasonable"? Although not everyone is in agreement on this point, many computer scientists feel that problems that can be solved by *polynomial time* algorithms are feasible. That is to say, if a problem Π can be solved on a DTM in time n^k, where n is the input size and k is a constant, then Π is polynomial time solvable and considered to have a feasible solution.

In practice, most useful polynomial time algorithms tend to have exponents of three or less. In Table 10.1 we show the values of several polynomials for various choices of n in order to give you a feel for how these functions grow. A quick glance at the table reveals that to solve a large problem using an algorithm having an exponent greater than three in its running time requires a very large number of steps. Whether or not this amount of computing is feasible, and exactly where the breakpoint is, are matters open to debate. We do know that the distinction between problems that can be solved in polynomial time and those for which

n	$n\lceil\log n\rceil$	$n\lceil\log n\rceil^2$	$n^{1.5}$	n^2	$n^{2.5}$	n^3	n^4	n^5
10^2	$7\cdot10^2$	$49\cdot10^2$	10^3	10^4	10^5	10^6	10^8	10^{10}
10^3	10^4	10^5	$3.2\cdot10^4$	10^6	$3.2\cdot10^7$	10^9	10^{12}	10^{15}
10^4	$14\cdot10^4$	$196\cdot10^4$	10^6	10^8	10^{10}	10^{12}	10^{16}	10^{20}
10^5	$17\cdot10^5$	$289\cdot10^5$	$3.2\cdot10^7$	10^{10}	$3.2\cdot10^{12}$	10^{15}	10^{20}	10^{25}
10^6	$2\cdot10^7$	$4\cdot10^8$	10^9	10^{12}	10^{15}	10^{18}	10^{24}	10^{30}
10^7	$24\cdot10^7$	$576\cdot10^7$	$3.2\cdot10^{10}$	10^{14}	$3.2\cdot10^{17}$	10^{21}	10^{28}	10^{35}

Table 10.1

Values of n and several polynomial functions in n.

n	n^3	2^n
2	8	4
4	64	16
8	512	256
16	4096	65,536
32	32,768	$4.3\cdot10^9$
64	262,144	$1.8\cdot10^{19}$

Table 10.2

Values of the polynomial function n^3 and the exponential function 2^n for numerous choices of n. Asymptotically, the exponential function grows much faster than the polynomial function.

the best-known algorithm runs in exponential time has proven very useful in theory and practice.

In Table 10.2 we compare values of the polynomial function n^3 with that of the exponential function 2^n for several choices of n. Even for very small values of n, the exponential function results in huge values. It is not practical to solve instances of size much more than 30 for the exponential function 2^n. For the polynomial function n^3, we could solve instances of size 1000, and for a polynomial function like $n^{1.5}$, we could solve instances of size one million or so.

In this book we view any problem having a polynomial time solution as being *feasibly solvable*. The above discussion shows there are clearly some limits to this assumption. Problems that have no polynomially bounded time algorithms are considered *intractable* (see Chapter 11). These are problems that appear to require *superpolynomial* time (usually exponential time for problems of interest in this book) to solve. Although we cannot prove that such problems require superpolynomial time to be solved, we can and do provide evidence supporting this belief.

In the next section we formally define the complexity class P using the machinery developed in Chapter 8. P contains all problems that are solvable in polynomial time. Following this, we present some background on the theory of P-completeness. This rich theory has interesting implications regarding parallel computation. The Boolean circuit model described in Chapter 9 serves as our underlying parallel model of computation. In addition to the applications in parallel computation, P-completeness theory is a good vehicle for introducing completeness theory. The subject of completeness plays an important role in complexity theory, especially in the topics of Chapter 11.

A number of examples of P-complete problems are presented in Section 10.4. The P-complete problems are the most difficult problems to solve that are in P. That is, all other problems in P can be directly reduced to them. The P-complete problems are usually deemed *inherently sequential*, meaning that they benefit very little from any parallel approach. The phrase "inherently sequential" has a precise technical meaning to be presented later on.

In Section 10.5 we examine a few additional P-complete problems and present the reductions showing their completeness. These reductions will provide you with the skills and background necessary for tackling the subject of NP-completeness addressed in Chapter 11. Although the reductions we describe are simpler than most, they nicely illustrate the ideas of reducibility and completeness.

10.2   *Polynomial Time*

The plan for this section is to formally define the complexity class P and to look at a couple of problems in this class. Recall from Chapter 8 that a complexity class is a group of problems that can all be solved within some specified resource bounds (in this case polynomial time). Nearly all complexity classes are defined in terms of language recognition questions. This is the most convenient framework to use with theoretical machines, as we have already seen. Because of the close correspondence between decision problems and language recognition questions (see Section 2.10) and the fact that it is usually easy to define a decision problem for any computational problem of interest, we will always describe an element in a complexity class as a decision problem. However, when making formal definitions, we need to refer to the corresponding language recognition questions.

The complexity class P, standing for *polynomial*, represents those problems that can be solved in polynomial time. These are problems that have feasible solutions.

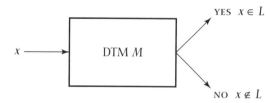

Let $|x| = n$ and $L(M) = L$. If there exists a $k \in \mathbb{N}$
    such that M runs in time n^k, then $L \in P$.

Figure 10.1

Conditions necessary for a language L to be in the complexity class P.

Definition 10.2.1   *The class P is the set of all languages L such that L is decidable by a deterministic Turing machine in time $n^{O(1)}$.*

To say that a language L is in P means there exists a polynomial time bounded DTM M such that $L(M) = L$. That is, there exists a constant k such that on any string x of length n, M runs within time $O(n^k)$ and accepts x if and only if $x \in L$. Figure 10.1 provides an illustration of this.

In Chapter 6 we showed that a number of variants of the deterministic Turing machine are equivalent in terms of their language acceptance abilities. The equivalences we described are such that if a language L can be accepted in polynomial time on one model, then it can also be accepted in polynomial time on any of the equivalent models. For example, any language that can be accepted by a k–tape DTM in polynomial time can be accepted by a 1–tape DTM in polynomial time, although with a different (larger) polynomial. What this means here is that the exact version of the Turing machine used to define P is not critical.

We can also express P in terms of the classes $DTIME(n^i)$ defined in Chapter 8. That is,

$$P = \bigcup_{i=0}^{\infty} DTIME(n^i)$$

So, any problem in P must be in $DTIME(n^i)$, for some $i \in \mathbb{N}$.

It is possible to solve many common computational problems in polynomial time. However, to place the problems in P, we sometimes need to rephrase them in terms of decision problems if they are stated as function or search problems. For example, two binary numbers can be multiplied together in polynomial time. We can define a Multiplication Decision problem to express this as follows.

Definition 10.2.2   Multiplication

Given: *Three binary numbers x, y, and i.*

Problem: *Is the ith bit (beginning from the least significant bit) of $x \times y$ a 1?*

A YES instance of Multiplication under one obvious encoding is 101◇11◇11, and a NO instance is 111◇110◇101. The former instance encodes the problem of multiplying five and three. The third bit of 15's binary representation is a 1; this is why the instance is a YES instance. A similar explanation can be given to show why 111◇110◇101 constitutes a NO instance.

Since we can multiply two binary numbers x and y on a DTM in polynomial time, it is clear that we can solve the Multiplication Decision problem in polynomial time. By solving at most $|x| + |y|$ (a polynomial in the input length) such instances of Multiplication, we could actually produce the value of the product of x and y.

Many other familiar computational problems can be easily phrased as languages that are in P. For example, breadth–first search, computing a maximum matching in a graph, computing a spanning tree in a graph, depth–first search, sorting, and so on all have natural decision problems associated with them that are in P. In the next couple of sections, more examples of problems in P will be given. We will state the problems at a high level, as discussed in Chapter 2, so the details of encodings do not detract from our main focus.

10.3   *P-Completeness Theory*

In complexity theory it is very difficult to make absolute statements about the amount of resources a given problem requires in order to be solved. This observation is true for all interesting computational resources. For example, given a specific problem Π, which is an element of a complexity class $\mathcal{C}$, it is extremely hard to prove for any nontrivial value of t that Π requires at least t steps to solve on any fixed model of computation. What do we mean here by nontrivial? For a DTM a trivial value of t would be n, since to solve a problem that depends on all of its input, as most problems of interest do, requires at least n steps. Remember that it takes $n + 1$ steps to read and detect the end of input using a DTM.

Because of the intrinsic difficulty of proving *lower bounds*, another approach is required. In this approach, called *completeness theory*, we try to show that a given problem Π is at least as tough to solve as any problem in its complexity class $\mathcal{C}$. Thus, if there are any truly difficult problems in $\mathcal{C}$, Π is one of them. P-completeness theory helps us to distinguish these problems for the class P and provides us with a measure of the relative difficulty of a problem. Next we define what it means for a problem to be P-complete.

Definition 10.3.1   *A language L is* **P-complete** *under logarithmic space reducibility if the following two conditions hold:*

1. *$L \in P$ and*
2. *for all problems $L' \in P$, $L' \leq_m^{\lg} L$.*

For a problem to be P-complete, it must be in the class P and all other problems in P must reduce to it. We recall the definition of logarithmic space reducibility from Definition 8.5.1: $L' \leq_m^{\lg} L$ if there is a function f such that $x \in L'$ if and only if $f(x) \in L$ and f can be computed by a DTM that uses only logarithmic work space. So, an instance of L' can be converted to an instance of L by a DTM that uses very little work space. Intuitively, allowing only a small amount of work space means the transformation cannot be too powerful. Another way of saying this is that L' is closely related to L.

P-complete problems capture the intrinsic difficulty of the problems in the class P. When we say a problem is P-complete, we are indicating that it is as hard to solve as any problem in P. P-completeness theory has very important implications for the subject of parallel computing. We describe some of these implications at an intuitive level in what follows. Additional details and formal definitions can be found in [23].

In Chapter 9 the complexity class NC was introduced, using Boolean circuits to model parallel computation. Circuits for solving problems that are in the class NC have only polylogarithmic depth; they also have polynomial size. NC represents those problems that can be solved very fast on a parallel computer. The following theorem indicates that no P-complete problem can be contained in NC, unless NC equals P.

Theorem 10.3.2   *Suppose L is a P-complete problem under logarithmic space reducibility. If $L \in NC$, then NC equals P.*

Proof: The proof is requested in the exercises.   ∎

A wide body of technical evidence exists supporting the belief that NC and P are different. In fact, a very important open question in computer science is, Does NC equal P? That is, do all good sequential algorithms also have good parallel algorithms?

Assuming that NC is not equal to P implies that the P-complete problems are unlikely to have fast solutions on parallel computers. Because of this, the P-complete problems are often called *inherently sequential problems*. For such problems the apparent advantage of parallelism cannot be exploited. That is, a problem that requires time n^k on a DTM for some constant k and is P-complete most likely cannot be solved by a family of Boolean circuits having polylogarithmic depth and polynomial size. Thus the problem cannot be solved by a $(\lg n)^k$-depth, polynomial size circuit family for any constant k.

The Boolean circuit model and other parallel computational models typically have an equivalence up to polylogarithmic factors in running times and polynomial factors in terms of number of "processors" simultaneously. Because of the close relationship between parallel models, *P*-complete problems cannot be solved fast in parallel on *any* parallel model of computation where only a polynomial number of processors are allowed.

10.4 *Examples of P-Complete Problems*

Several *P*-complete problems are defined in this section. In addition to serving as examples indicating the flavor of *P*-complete problems, these problems play a fundamental role in *P*-completeness theory. We will make use of several of them in the reductions given in Section 10.5. All reductions are deferred until Section 10.5.

10.4.1 Generic Machine Simulation

The first *P*-complete problem we examine is called the *Generic Machine Simulation problem*. The canonical device for performing sequential computations is the DTM, with its single processor and serial access to memory. We mentioned above that the *P*-complete problems are inherently sequential. To say that a problem is inherently sequential is to say that solving it on a parallel machine is not substantially better than solving it on a DTM. That is, its solution cannot be sped up significantly on a parallel computer. For obvious practical reasons it is important to investigate and classify problems that exhibit this type of behavior.

What could be more sequential than the problem of simulating a DTM computation? Suppose we could discover how to efficiently simulate, in parallel, every DTM that uses polynomial time. Then in view of the Church–Turing Thesis, every feasible sequential computation could be translated *automatically* into a highly parallel form. That is, each problem in *P* would be in *NC*, going against the evidence referred to in Section 10.3 supporting the contrary belief. We define a natural decision problem based on these insights.

Definition 10.4.1   Generic Machine Simulation (GMS)

Given: *A string $x \diamond \widetilde{M} \diamond 1^t$, where x is a binary string, $\widetilde{M}$ is a description of a deterministic Turing machine $M = (Q, \Sigma, \delta, q_0, F)$, and t is a natural number.*

Problem: *Does M accept x within t steps?*

$\widetilde{M}$ is a coding of M's transition function including a denotation of final states. Think of each transition as being coded depending on how states, symbols, and directions of tape head movements are encoded. Each of the encoded transitions is then delimited from other transitions. We leave a formal specification of how a DTM might be encoded as an exercise.

Let's consider an example of GMS. Suppose $\widetilde{M}$ represents the code of a DTM accepting any string that contains at least one 0. Furthermore, suppose the machine M runs in $n + 1$ steps. Then

- $1000\diamond\widetilde{M}\diamond11111$
- $101111\diamond\widetilde{M}\diamond1^{10}$
- $0\diamond\widetilde{M}\diamond11$

are three YES instances of GMS and

- $1010\diamond\widetilde{M}\diamond111$
- $111\diamond\widetilde{M}\diamond11111$
- $\diamond\widetilde{M}\diamond$
- $\diamond\diamond\diamond$

are four NO instances. Let's consider $1010\diamond\widetilde{M}\diamond111$ in detail. The string 1010 does contain a 0, so it is in the language of M. However, M takes five steps to complete its computation. The time bound specified is only three steps. Therefore, $1010\diamond\widetilde{M}\diamond111$ is a NO instance of GMS. Similar reasoning may be applied to decide the other instances listed.

An instance of GMS may be thought of as consisting of a DTM M, an input x to M, and a time bound t. We have already seen a machine that does almost what we want in Secton 6.3. This is the simulator machine, M_{sim}, used to prove the undecidability of the halting language, L_{halt}. Our machine for generic machine simulation, M_{GMS}, must also count execution steps, and it has to be able to simulate M efficiently in polynomial time in terms of the running time of M.

M_{GMS} will interpret M's program, step by step, on input x until either M accepts or t steps have been simulated, whichever comes first. Given an encoding $\widetilde{M}$ of M, and input x, the simulation of it by M_{GMS} will take time polynomial in t and the lengths of x and $\widetilde{M}$, which in turn is polynomial in the length of the input to M_{GMS}. This is why we require that t be encoded as a string of t 1's, in *unary*, instead of in binary. That is, if t were encoded in binary, the problem would no longer be in P.

Theorem 10.4.2   *The Generic Machine Simulation problem is P-complete under logarithmic space reductions.*

Proof: We argued above that the problem is in P. The proof involves reducing an arbitrary language L in P to the Generic Machine Simulation problem. The proof is straightforward, and we leave it to the exercises.   ∎

Machines M_{sim} and M_{GMS} are examples of *universal machines*. A universal machine M is one that takes a description of another machine M' in the same class of machines and a string x as input, and then simulates M''s behavior on input x. The first complete problem constructed for a class is usually some kind of general machine simulation, or universal machine construction, as this is one way of expressing the dynamic actions of machines using the rather static properties of a language. Not all complexity classes have universal machines; sometimes the class is simply not powerful enough to build a simulator.

10.4.2   The Circuit Value Problem and Some Variants

One obvious drawback of tackling the Generic Machine Simulation problem directly is its generality. It is hard to see how we could take an arbitrary DTM program and, without any hints as to what problem the machine is solving, produce a highly parallel simulation of it. Instead, it might be useful to study a very simple and structured problem that captures all the computational power of DTMs and, in addition, has some obvious parallel aspects that could potentially be exploited.

The problem that serves this role is the *Circuit Value problem* (CVP). We will see in the next chapter that the *Satisfiability problem* plays the same role in NP–completeness theory as CVP does in P–completeness theory. Both problems are valuable starting points for a wide variety of investigations in complexity theory because, in large part, of their flexibility.

The Boolean circuit model described in Chapter 9 forms the basis for defining CVP.

Definition 10.4.3   Circuit Value problem (CVP)

Given: *An encoding $\tilde{\alpha}$ of a Boolean circuit α, inputs $x_1, \ldots, x_n$, and a designated output y.*

Problem: *Is output y of α TRUE on input $x_1, \ldots, x_n$?*

Notice in the formal statement of CVP we used the *standard encoding*, as specified in Chapter 9, for describing Boolean circuits. In addition to the encoding of a circuit, the problem requires inputs $x_1, \ldots, x_n$, which are the inputs to the circuit, and a designated output gate y.

Intuitively, it is easy to see that the Circuit Value problem is solvable sequentially in polynomial time—simply make one pass through the circuit from inputs to outputs, evaluating each gate based on the values already computed by its immediate predecessors. The functions computed by the gates are very easy to implement on DTMs. Such an algorithm shows that all versions of CVP considered in this chapter are in P. We specify such an algorithm below in detail.

Topological Circuit Evaluation Algorithm

Input: A Boolean circuit α coded using the standard encoding with gates numbered in topological order $g_1, \ldots, g_{size}$ and values specified for the inputs. v is an array and *size* indicates the number of gates in α. v is used to represent gate values. τ is a function that takes a gate and returns its type.
Output: The value computed by each gate in the circuit.

begin
    if the input does not code a proper instance of CVP
        then print an error message;

    for $i \leftarrow 1$ **to** *size* **do**
        case $\tau(g_i)$
            {INPUT}: $v(i) \leftarrow$ value for input g_i;
            B_0: $v(i) \leftarrow 0$ or 1 based on the constant value of g_i;
            B_1: $v(i) \leftarrow \tau(g_i)\ v(l)$, where g_l is the input to g_i;
            B_2: $v(i) \leftarrow v(l)\ \tau(g_i)\ v(r)$, where g_l (or g_r) is the
               left (or, respectively, right) input of g_i;

    print v;
end

Figure 10.2

Topological circuit evaluation algorithm for sequentially determining the value that each gate in a Boolean circuit computes.

A *topological circuit evaluation algorithm* is shown in Figure 10.2. It assumes the underlying directed graph of the circuit α is *topologically numbered*.[1] A circuit whose vertices are topologically ordered will be such that gates receive their inputs only from lower–numbered gates. We ask you to prove that the topological circuit evaluation algorithm correctly evaluates a topologically numbered circuit. It is apparent that if $T = |\tilde{\alpha}|$, the algorithm can be implemented in a straightforward manner to run in $O(T^2)$ time on a DTM. Thus the algorithm is polynomial time.

It is easy to see at least at an intuitive level, that *any polynomial time computation* can be represented as a circuit evaluation problem. Ordinary digital computers

---

1. An acyclic, directed graph $G = (V, E)$ is **topologically ordered** or **topologically numbered** if when $(i, j) \in E$, then i is less than j. There are standard algorithms for computing topological numberings of directed graphs in polynomial time.

are built essentially from Boolean logic circuits, and a polynomial time computation can "activate" at most a polynomial number of these gates. Therefore a reduction of an arbitrary polynomial time computation to an instance of the Circuit Value problem basically involves "unrolling" the machine's "wiring diagram" to produce the circuit activated by the computation. Of course, the same thing could be done for a DTM, since its "hardware" has a particularly simple form. Thus DTMs can be simulated by Boolean circuits. As we mentioned earlier, circuits can handle inputs of only one fixed size, whereas a single DTM can handle inputs of all sizes. Thus to simulate a DTM by Boolean circuits requires a different circuit for each input size—that is, a family of circuits. But although the circuits are different, their very regular structure makes it easy to show that they are uniform (in the sense of the definitions from Section 9.3.1). In outline, we have shown the following fundamental P–completeness result.

Theorem 10.4.4   *The Circuit Value problem is P-complete under logarithmic space reductions.*

Proof: A polynomial time topological numbering algorithm combined with the topological circuit evaluation algorithm suffice to show the problem is in *P*.   ∎

The Circuit Value problem is the most useful P–complete problem. In what follows, we describe three more variants of it that are also P–complete. Proof hints or proofs of Theorems 10.4.6, 10.4.8, and 10.4.10 may be found in Greenlaw, Hoover, and Ruzzo [23].

Definition 10.4.5   Monotone Circuit Value problem (MCVP)

Given: *An encoding $\tilde{\alpha}$ of a Boolean circuit α, inputs $x_1, \ldots, x_n$, and designated output γ with the restriction that α is monotone. That is, α is constructed solely of AND and OR gates.*

Problem: *Is output γ of α TRUE on input $x_1, \ldots, x_n$?*

The word "monotone" is an abbreviation for "monotonically nondecreasing." An examination of Table 10.3 reveals that the values of AND and OR gates are monotonically nondecreasing in the following sense: If any input bit that is 0 is set to 1, the output of the gate does not decrease. Gates such as NOT or IMPLIES are not monotone. We ask for a classification of all binary gates in the exercises.

Notice MCVP is the same as CVP except for the monotone restriction on the gates. An example of a monotone circuit is shown in Figure 10.3. In the exercises, we ask you to evaluate this circuit for all possible input combinations and to produce YES and NO instances of MCVP corresponding to this circuit. Next we state a theorem about MCVP.

x_1	x_2	x_1 AND x_2	x_1 OR x_2
0	0	0	0
0	1	0	1
1	0	0	1
1	1	1	1

Table 10.3

Truth table for an AND and an OR gate with inputs x_1 and x_2.

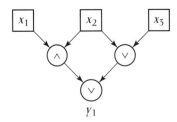

Figure 10.3

A simple example of a monotone Boolean circuit computing the value $(x_1 \wedge x_2) \vee (x_2 \vee x_3)$.

Theorem 10.4.6 *The Monotone Circuit Value problem is P-complete under logarithmic space reductions.*

This problem is often useful for demonstrating that other problems are P–complete because NOR gates are usually difficult to simulate. In the next variant of CVP we look at, the gates are assumed to have a topological numbering. Sometimes P–completeness proofs may be simplified by performing reductions from topologically ordered instances of circuits by taking advantage of the extra structure.

Definition 10.4.7 Topologically Ordered NOR Circuit Value problem (TopNORCVP)

Given: *An encoding $\widetilde{\alpha}$ of a Boolean circuit α, inputs $x_1, \ldots, x_n$, and designated output y with the additional assumptions that the vertices in the circuit are numbered in topological order and consist only of NOR gates.*

Problem: *Is output y of α TRUE on input $x_1, \ldots, x_n$?*

An example of a topologically ordered NOR circuit is shown in Figure 10.4. In the exercises, we ask you to evaluate this circuit for all possible input com–

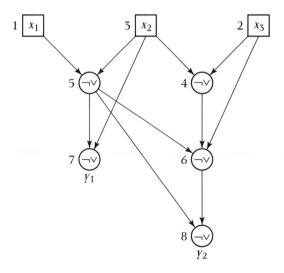

Figure 10.4

An example of a topologically ordered NOR circuit. The topological number for each vertex of the circuit is shown to its left.

binations and to provide YES and NO instances of TopNORCVP pertaining to this circuit. Next we state an important theorem regarding TopNORCVP.

Theorem 10.4.8 *The Topologically Ordered NOR Circuit Value problem is P-complete under logarithmic space reductions.*

TopNORCVP is often helpful for demonstrating that other problems are P–complete because it has only one type of gate to simulate. We will see an example of this in Section 10.5. The next variant of CVP is often useful in proving P–completeness results because of its highly restricted nature. The added structure can often be made use of in P–completeness proofs.

Definition 10.4.9 Alternating Monotone Fanin 2, Fanout 2 Circuit Value problem (AM2CVP)

Given: *An encoding $\tilde{\alpha}$ of a monotone Boolean circuit α, inputs $x_1, \ldots, x_n$, and designated output y. On any path from an input to an output, the gates are required to alternate between OR and AND gates. Inputs are required to be connected only to OR gates, and outputs must come from OR gates. The circuit is restricted to have fanout exactly two for inputs and* **internal** *(a gate that is not an input or output) gates, and to have a distinguished OR gate as output.*

Problem: *Is output y of α TRUE on input $x_1, \ldots, x_n$?*

An example of an alternating, monotone, fanin and fanout two circuit is shown in Figure 10.5. In the exercises, we ask you to evaluate this circuit

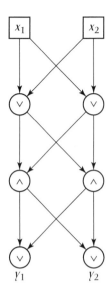

Figure 10.5

An example of an alternating, monotone, fanin and fanout two Boolean circuit.

for all possible input combinations and to provide YES and NO instances of AM2CVP corresponding to this circuit. Below we state an important theorem about AM2CVP.

Theorem 10.4.10   *The Alternating Monotone Fanin 2, Fanout 2 Circuit Value problem is P-complete under logarithmic space reductions.*

When we state a problem in this section, we assume that the input to it is in the correct form. For example, we assume that the circuits input to MCVP are in fact monotone. Why is it reasonable to assume the inputs are valid? Perhaps checking an input for correct format is as hard as, or harder than, solving the problem. Fortunately, for these circuit problems, we can check in polynomial time whether or not the encoding meets the restrictions used in this section. If the instance does not code a valid circuit, it can be rejected out of hand. Several of these verifications for different circuit properties are asked for in the exercises.

Armed with the *P*-completeness results about Boolean circuits, we can now show several other problems are *P*-complete by exploiting the transitivity of logarithmic space reductions. We carry out this plan in the next section for another problem involving Boolean circuits, a graph theory problem, and a problem in formal language theory.

P-Complete Problems and Reductions

In the previous section we defined several problems that are known to be P–complete. Because of the technical nature of the proofs, we only stated the results and provided references in the bibliography to their details. Here we examine several P-completeness proofs in detail. These results help to illustrate the steps necessary to show a problem is complete and also give you a feel for how to develop reductions. It is important to keep in mind that P-complete problems are probably inherently sequential. When you meet a new problem, it is worth thinking about how the problem might be parallelized. The difficulties you encounter can help develop a more intuitive feel for P-completeness theory.

There are several important steps in a P-completeness proof. We summarize these in Figure 10.6. Suppose you want to show a decision problem Π with corresponding language L is P-complete. The first step is to prove L is in P. A polynomial time algorithm for L must be developed, its time complexity analyzed, and its correctness established. The second step is to show that all other languages L' in P are logarithmic space reducible to L. A reduction from some existing P-complete problem is usually developed. Using the transitivity of logarithmic space reductions, you can then conclude that all problems in P reduce to L. The reduction needs to be proved correct, and its space complexity needs to be analyzed.

Developing reductions is an art. Probably the most important part of developing a reduction involves the selection of the problem to reduce from. The way to improve your ability to develop reductions is to look at as many examples as possible and to study a wide variety of problems. The more problems you have in your arsenal to select from, the more likely you are to have a problem at your disposal that can prove useful.

1. Prove L is in P.
   (a) Develop a polynomial time algorithm for solving L.
   (b) Prove the algorithm is correct.
   (c) Prove the algorithm runs in polynomial time.
2. Prove $L' \leq_m^{\lg} L$ for some P-complete language L'.
   (a) Develop a logarithmic space reduction from a known P–complete problem to L.
   (b) Prove the reduction is correct.
   (c) Prove the reduction is a logarithmic space reduction.

Figure 10.6

Key steps involved in a P-completeness proof for a language L.

x_1	x_2	x_1 NAND x_2
0	0	1
0	1	1
1	0	1
1	1	0

Table 10.4

Truth table for a NAND gate with inputs x_1 and x_2.

Our goal is to acquaint you with the notion of reduction so that you can understand and later devise your own reductions. Thus we focus on the reductions and their proofs of correctness, as opposed to the algorithmic aspects of the problems. Generally, we will focus on step 2 and skip step 1 of a P-completeness proof. The reduction is usually the most interesting and complex part of a completeness proof. The first problem we wish to show P-complete is another useful variant of CVP. Like TopNorCVP this problem can often be used to simplify other P-completeness proofs because only one type of gate is involved.

10.5.1   NAND Circuit Value Problem

We begin by formally defining the problem.

Definition 10.5.1   NAND Circuit Value problem (NANDCVP)

Given: *An encoding $\tilde{\alpha}$ of a Boolean circuit α that consists entirely of NAND gates, inputs $x_1, \ldots, x_n$, and designated output γ.*

Problem: *Is output γ of α TRUE on input $x_1, \ldots, x_n$?*

This variant of the Circuit Value problem contains only one type of gate, the NAND gate. Table 10.4 shows how NAND gates behave. Note that a NAND gate produces a 0 output only when both inputs are 1 and can be thought of as NOT AND. As mentioned, NANDCVP turns out to be a very useful problem for proving other problems are P-complete. A sample NAND circuit is shown in Figure 10.7. There we use the combination $\neg\wedge$ to denote a NAND gate. Suppose $\tilde{\alpha}$ represents the description of this NAND circuit. Then under the usual encoding, $\tilde{\alpha}\diamond 1\diamond 1\diamond 0\diamond\gamma_1$ is a YES instance and $\tilde{\alpha}\diamond 0\diamond 0\diamond 1\diamond\gamma_2$ is a NO instance of NANDCVP. Next we show that NANDCVP is P-complete.

Theorem 10.5.2   *The NAND Circuit Value problem is P-complete under logarithmic space reductions.*

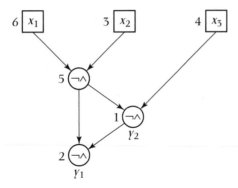

Figure 10.7

An example of a simple NAND circuit. An arbitrary numbering of the gates is shown.

Proof: A polynomial time topological numbering algorithm combined with the *topological circuit evaluation algorithm* shown in Figure 10.2 can be used to prove the problem is in P. Informally, the algorithm simply evaluates gates whose inputs are available. The reduction proving P–completeness is from AM2CVP. It proceeds as follows.

Suppose $I = \tilde{\alpha} \Diamond x_1 \ldots x_n \Diamond y$ is an instance of AM2CVP. We specify a logarithmic space reduction f such that $I \in$ AM2CVP if and only if $f(I) \in$ NANDCVP. That is, I is a YES instance of AM2CVP if and only if $f(I)$ is a YES instance of NANDCVP.

The reduction f is defined by complementing all inputs in I and individually replacing OR and AND gates in $\tilde{\alpha}$ with NAND gates. All connections in the circuit remain the same. Call the circuit produced by f, β. Then $\tilde{\beta} \Diamond \overline{x_1} \ldots \overline{x_n} \Diamond y = f(I)$ is the instance of NANDCVP produced by f.

We claim that $I \in$ AM2CVP if and only if $f(I) \in$ NANDCVP. Define the *level* of a gate in a circuit to be the length of the longest path between a circuit input and the gate. For example, the gate labeled y_2 in Figure 10.7 is at level 2. Let $v(g)$ denote the value of gate g in α on input $x_1, \ldots, x_n$. The following two items will be proved by induction:

1. If g is a gate at level k in α with corresponding NAND gate g', and g is an OR gate, then $v(g) = v(g')$.

2. If g is a gate at level k in α with corresponding NAND gate g', and g is a circuit input or AND gate, then $v(g) = \neg v(g')$.

This will show that f is a reduction from AM2CVP to NANDCVP. Since the output gate of an instance of AM2CVP must be an OR gate, the corresponding NAND gate in β computes the same value.

For the base case consider a gate g_0 at level 0 in α. Suppose g'_0 is the corresponding gate in β. By the definition of level, g_0 must be a circuit input.

Since circuit inputs are complemented by the reduction f, we have $v(g_0) = \neg v(g_0')$, so the base case is proved.

For the induction hypothesis, suppose cases 1 and 2 above hold for a value of k.

First, suppose $k + 1$ is even. Then we have an AND level. Consider an AND gate g with inputs from gates g_l and g_r in α. Let g' be the gate in β corresponding to g. The case where $k + 1$ is odd is proven below for an OR gate in α. By the definition of AM2CVP, both g_l and g_r must be OR gates. Using the induction hypothesis, we know that $v(g_l)$ and $v(g_r)$ are correctly computed by the corresponding NAND gates in β. Since $\neg(g_l \wedge g_r)$ is computed by the NAND gate corresponding to g, $v(g) = \neg v(g')$.

Now suppose $k + 1$ is odd and consider an OR gate g with inputs from gates g_l and g_r in α. Let g' be the gate in β corresponding to g. By the definition of AM2CVP, g_l and g_r must come from circuit inputs or AND gates. Let g_l' and g_r' be the corresponding gates in β. By the induction hypothesis,

$$v(g_l) = \neg v(g_l') \text{ and } v(g_r) = \neg v(g_r')$$

Using DeMorgan's Laws

$$v(g) = v(g_l) \ \vee \ v(g_r) = \neg(\neg v(g_l) \ \wedge \ \neg v(g_r))$$

we get

$$\neg(\neg v(g_l) \ \wedge \neg v(g_r)) = \neg(v(g_l') \ \wedge \ v(g_r')) = v(g_l') \text{ NAND } v(g_r')$$

by substitution. Thus

$$v(g') = v(g_l') \text{ NAND } v(g_r')$$

and we see that g' correctly simulates g as claimed. This completes the induction step.

It remains to show that f is a logarithmic space reduction. Since f simply changes all gates in α to NAND gates and complements all inputs, it is easy to see that f may be computed by a DTM that uses only constant space. ∎

It is often helpful to construct a specific instance of the reduction in order to fully understand it. We ask you to do this in the exercises.

10.5.2 Context–Free Grammar Nonempty

In this section, a problem involving context–free grammars, the focus of Chapter 7, is shown to be P–complete. There are a number of other P–complete problems involving context–free grammars; several are presented in the exercises. Remember that these results imply that solving such decision problems on a parallel com-

$G = (N, T, S, P)$ with the following:

$N = \{1, 2, 3, 4, 5, 6, 7\}$

$T = \{a\}$

$S = 7$

$P = \{3 \rightarrow a, 4 \rightarrow a, 5 \rightarrow 1 \mid 2, 6 \rightarrow 34, 7 \rightarrow 56\}$

Figure 10.8

A NO instance of the Context–Free Grammar Nonempty problem.

puter will not produce substantially faster results than on a sequential machine, unless NC equals P. We begin by formally defining the problem.

Definition 10.5.3   Context–Free Grammar Nonempty

Given: *A context-free grammar $G = (N, \Sigma, P, S)$.*

Problem: *Is $L(G)$ nonempty?*

Let's consider an example of the problem. An instance is depicted in Figure 10.8. Consider a derivation from the start symbol, 7. It will have the following form:

$$7 \Rightarrow 56 \Rightarrow 534 \Rightarrow 5a4 \Rightarrow 5aa$$

The nonterminal 5 may be replaced by either 1 or 2. However, since neither 1 nor 2 derives a string of terminals, we see $L(G) = \emptyset$. Therefore, this is a NO instance of the problem. Of course, most of the grammars described in Chapter 7 represent YES instances of the problem.

Next we show Context–Free Grammar Nonempty is P–complete by a reduction from MCVP.

Theorem 10.5.4 *The Context-Free Grammar Nonempty problem is P-complete under logarithmic space reducibility.*

Proof: The algorithm given in Section 7.3 shows that this problem can be solved in polynomial time. The reduction proving completeness is from MCVP.

Given an instance $I = \tilde{\alpha} \Diamond x_1 \ldots x_n \Diamond \gamma$ of MCVP, we define a logarithmic space reduction f that produces an instance of the Context–Free Grammar Nonempty problem. f constructs the grammar $G = (N, \Sigma, P, S)$ with nonterminals $N = \{i \mid g_i$ is a gate in $\alpha\}$, terminal set $\Sigma = \{a\}$, and start symbol $S = \gamma$. Note that we assume the gates in α are $g_1, \ldots, g_{size}$ to distinguish them from the nonterminals $1, \ldots, size$. Here $size$ represents the circuit size. As usual, let $v(g)$ denote the value of gate g and $\tau(g)$ denote the type of gate g. Recall we identify 1 with

TRUE and 0 with FALSE; for convenience we allow v to return either of these values. The productions in P have the following three different forms.

1. If $\tau(g_i) = $ INPUT and $v(g_i) = $ TRUE, then $i \to a \in P$.
2. If $\tau(g_i) = $ AND with inputs g_j and g_k, then $i \to jk \in P$.
3. If $\tau(g_i) = $ OR with inputs g_j and g_k, then $i \to j \mid k \in P$.

We claim that $v(g_i)$ is TRUE if and only if $i \Rightarrow^* \gamma$, where $\gamma \in \{a\}^+$. In particular, $v(\gamma) = $ TRUE if and only if $S \Rightarrow^* \gamma$, where $\gamma \in \{a\}^+$. So, α evaluates to TRUE if and only if the instance of Context–Free Grammar Nonempty has a YES answer.

Define the level of a gate as in Theorem 10.5.2. We establish the claim by induction on the level of a gate in α.

For the base case, consider a circuit input x_i at level 0. If $v(x_i) = $ TRUE, then $i \to a$ is a production, so $i \Rightarrow a$ is a derivation in G. If $v(x_i) = $ FALSE, then there is no production with i on the left–hand side.

For the induction hypothesis, suppose for all gates g_i at level k or less that $v(g_i) = $ TRUE if and only if $i \Rightarrow^* \gamma$, where $\gamma \in \{a\}^+$.

Consider a gate g_i at level $k + 1$. g_i is either an AND or an OR gate.

- First, suppose g_i is an AND gate with inputs g_l and g_r. $v(g_i) = $ TRUE if and only if $v(g_l)$ and $v(g_r)$ are both TRUE, which is the case if and only if $l \Rightarrow^* \gamma_l$ and $r \Rightarrow^* \gamma_r$, where γ_l and γ_r are strings from $\{a\}^+$. The second if and only if follows by the induction hypothesis. If g_i is an AND gate, then $i \to lr$ is a production in P. Therefore, $i \Rightarrow lr \Rightarrow^* \gamma_l\gamma_r \in \{a\}^+$. So, $v(g_i) = $ TRUE if and only if $i \Rightarrow^* \gamma$, where $\gamma \in \{a\}^+$ and $\gamma = \gamma_l\gamma_r$.

- Now suppose g_i is an OR gate with inputs g_l and g_r. Then $v(g_i) = $ TRUE if and only if $v(g_l)$ or $v(g_r)$ is TRUE, which is if and only if $l \Rightarrow^* \gamma_l$, where $\gamma_l \in \{a\}^+$, or $r \Rightarrow^* \gamma_r$, where $\gamma_r \in \{a\}^+$. If g_i is an OR gate, then $i \to l \mid r$ are productions in P. Therefore, $i \Rightarrow l \Rightarrow^* \gamma_l \in \{a\}^+$ or $i \Rightarrow r \Rightarrow^* \gamma_r \in \{a\}^+$. So, $v(g_i) = $ TRUE if and only if $i \Rightarrow^* \gamma$, where $\gamma \in \{a\}^+$ and γ is either γ_l or γ_r.

This completes the induction proof of the claim.

We have now shown that $I \in $ MCVP if and only if $f(I) \in $ Context–Free Grammar Nonempty. It is easy for f to generate G as it scans I. The DTM can easily compute f in constant space. ∎

Figure 10.9 depicts a monotone circuit, having inputs $x_1 = 0$, $x_2 = 0$, $x_3 = 1$, and $x_4 = 1$, that when transformed using the reduction given in Theorem 10.5.4 produces the grammar shown in Figure 10.8. Note the grammar in Figure 10.8 does not derive any strings of terminals, and the circuit shown in Figure 10.9 evaluates to FALSE on input $x_1 = 0$, $x_2 = 0$, $x_3 = 1$, and $x_4 = 1$. We ask you to carry out the reduction for another fixed instance of MCVP in the exercises.

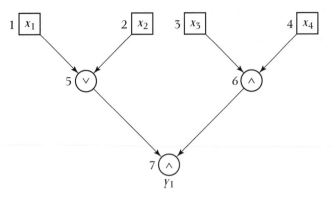

Figure 10.9

An example of a monotone Boolean circuit used to illustrate the reduction given in Theorem 10.5.4. We assume the inputs are $x_1 = 0$, $x_2 = 0$, $x_3 = 1$, and $x_4 = 1$.

10.5.3 Lexicographically First Maximal Independent Set

In this section we explore an important graph theory problem. A problem that is very closely related to this was one of the first problems shown to be P-complete. There are many other graph problems that are known to be P-complete, and this one has a similar flavor to a number of those as well. We begin with some preliminaries.

Recall an *independent set* is a set of vertices of a graph that are pairwise nonadjacent. A *maximum independent set* is such a set of largest cardinality. An independent set is *maximal* if no other vertex can be added while maintaining the independent set property. In contrast to the maximum case,[2] finding maximal independent sets is very easy. Figure 10.10 depicts a polynomial time sequential algorithm for computing a maximal independent set. The algorithm is a *greedy* algorithm: It processes the vertices in numerical order, always attempting to add the lowest numbered vertex that has not yet been tried.

Figure 10.11 depicts an undirected graph with six vertices. The lexicographically first maximal independent set of this graph consists of nodes 1, 3, and 6. This is the order in which the nodes would be added to the independent set using the algorithm in Figure 10.10. Note that this independent set is not a maximum independent. There is one independent set of cardinality four, $\{2, 3, 4, 6\}$, and this is a maximum. The smallest maximal independent set is of size two, $\{1, 5\}$. Notice that $\{1, 3, 6\}$ is lexicographically less than $\{1, 5\}$.

---

2. Given an undirected graph $G = (V, E)$ and a natural number k, the problem of determining whether G has an independent set of size at least k is intractable (see Chapter 11).

Lexicographically First Maximal Independent Set Algorithm

Input: An undirected graph $G = (V, E)$ with the vertices numbered $1, \ldots, |V|$.
Output: The lexicographically first maximal independent set of G.

begin
   $I \leftarrow \emptyset$;
   for $j \leftarrow 1$ **to** $|V|$ **do**
      if vertex j is not connected to any vertex in I
         then $I \leftarrow I \cup \{j\}$;
   print I;
end

Figure 10.10

A lexicographically first maximal independent set algorithm.

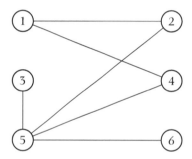

Figure 10.11

An undirected graph used to illustrate maximal independents. The lexicographically first maximal independent set is $\{1, 3, 6\}$. Another maximal independent set is $\{1, 5\}$. In this case there is only one maximum independent set, $\{2, 3, 4, 6\}$.

We can now define an important decision problem based on maximal independent sets.

Definition 10.5.5   Lexicographically First Maximal Independent Set problem (LFMIS)

Given: *An undirected graph $G = (V, E)$ with the vertices numbered from 1 to $|V|$, and a designated vertex v.*

Problem: *Is vertex v in the lexicographically first maximal independent set of G?*

An instance of the problem is shown in Figure 10.11, where, say, node 3 is the designated vertex. Since $\{1, 3, 6\}$ is the lexicographically first maximal independent set, this would be a YES instance of the problem. Of course, if the designated vertex were 2 instead, we would have a NO instance of the problem. We now prove the Lexicographically First Maximal Independent Set problem is P-complete.

Theorem 10.5.6 *The Lexicographically First Maximal Independent Set problem is P-complete under logarithmic space reducibility.*

Proof: Membership in P follows from the algorithm shown in Figure 10.10—that is, compute the lexicographically first maximal independent set and then check to see if the designated vertex is in it. The reduction proving completeness is from TopNorCVP.

Suppose $\tilde{\alpha} \Diamond x_1 \ldots x_n \Diamond \gamma$ is an instance of TopNorCVP. We describe a logarithmic space reduction f that maps YES (or NO) instances of TopNorCVP to YES (or, respectively, NO) instances of the Lexicographically First Maximal Independent Set problem.

From α, f constructs an instance of LFMIS, namely, an undirected graph G and a designated vertex v. The graph G is the same as the graph underlying the circuit α except that it is undirected, and we add a new vertex, numbered 0, that is adjacent to all FALSE inputs of α. The designated vertex v will correspond to γ, the output gate of α.

We claim that a vertex i in G is included in the lexicographically first maximal independent set (lfmis) if and only if either i equals 0 (the new vertex), or gate g_i in α has value TRUE. For clarity, we refer to gates by g_i rather than their number i. We prove the claim by induction on vertex's numbers.

For the base case, consider vertex number 0, the new vertex. Clearly, vertex 0 is in the lfmis.

Suppose for the induction hypothesis that the claim is valid for all vertices numbered k or less.

Consider the vertex numbered $k + 1$. This vertex corresponds to gate g_{k+1} in α. Note that if g_{k+1} is a circuit input, the result follows trivially. Suppose g_{k+1} is a NOR gate. That is, assume $g_{k+1} = g_l$ NOR g_r, where l and r are less than $k + 1$. By the induction hypothesis, g_l (or g_r) is TRUE if and only if l (or, respectively, r) is included in the lfmis. There are two cases to consider:

1. If either l or r is in the lfmis, then $k + 1$ is not in the lfmis. In this case, g_l or g_r is TRUE correspondingly, so g_{k+1} evaluates to FALSE.

2. If both l and r are not in the lfmis, then $k + 1$ is. In this situation, g_{k+1} evaluates to TRUE, since a NOR gate with two FALSE inputs evaluates to TRUE.

This establishes the claim.

A choice of v equal to γ completes the reduction.

You may have noticed that the instance of LFMIS we built does not quite fit the definition of the problem, since the vertex numbers begin at 0 instead of 1. We can simply add one to each vertex number to overcome this minor technical problem.

The reduction f only needs to add one to each vertex number and connect the new vertex to FALSE inputs. These tasks can be accomplished by a DTM that uses only constant space.   ■

In the exercises, we ask you to carry out the reduction given in Theorem 10.5.6 for a specific circuit.

In this chapter, we discussed the following *P*-complete problems:

- Generic Machine Simulation

- Circuit Value

- Monotone Circuit Value

- Topologically Ordered NOR Circuit Value

- Alternating Monotone Fanin 2, Fanout 2 Circuit Value

- NAND Circuit Value

- Context–Free Grammar Nonempty

- Lexicographically First Maximal Independent Set

Additional examples are provided in the exercises.

Let's conclude this chapter with a few remarks. We carefully chose reductions from the field of *P*-completeness theory that were relatively easy to explain and understand. Notice that all of the reductions used in this section can be performed in constant space. Be aware that many *P*-completeness proofs are much more complicated. Prepared with these three reductions though, you should be able to tackle many of the highly complex reductions. A number of reductions are asked for in the exercises, where several additional *P*-complete problems are defined. Chapter 11 discusses *NP*-completeness and presents several reductions that are more complicated.

10.6   *Exercises*

Section 10.1   *Introduction*

1. Construct a table comparing the functions n, $n^{1.5}$, n^2, and $(1.5)^n$ for powers of 2 from 2^5 through 2^{20}.

2. At what value of n does $(\lg n)^3$ become smaller than n? How about n^2?

Section 10.2 *Polynomial Time*

3. Prove that any language that can be accepted by a k-tape DTM in polynomial time can be accepted by a 1-tape DTM in polynomial time.

4. Define a decision problem based on addition. Give two YES and two NO instances of the problem. Prove that the Addition problem you defined is in P.

5. Define a decision problem based on sorting. Argue that your problem is in P.

6. Which of the following problems are in P?

   (a) **DFA Acceptance**
      Given: A DFA $M = (Q, \Sigma, \delta, q_0, F)$ and a string x.
      Problem: Is $x \in L(M)$?

   (b) **DFA Equivalence**
      Given: Two DFAs $M_1 = (Q_1, \Sigma_1, \delta_1, q_1, F_1)$ and $M_2 = (Q_2, \Sigma_2, \delta_2, q_2, F_2)$.
      Problem: Is $L(M_1) = L(M_2)$?

   (c) **DFA Nonempty**
      Given: A DFA $M = (Q, \Sigma, \delta, q_0, F)$.
      Problem: Is $L(M) \neq \emptyset$?

   (d) **Context–Free Grammar Membership**
      Given: A context-free grammar $G = (N, \Sigma, P, S)$.
      Problem: Is $x \in L(G)$?

   (e) **Context–Free Grammar Infinite**
      Given: A context-free grammar $G = (N, \Sigma, P, S)$.
      Problem: Is $L(G)$ infinite?

7. Let $L = \{a^i b^i c^i \mid i \geq 0\}$. Is $L \in P$?

8. Prove $NC \subseteq P$.

9. Which of the following statements are true?

   (a) $\mathcal{L}_{\textbf{DFA}} \subseteq P$
   (b) $\mathcal{L}_{\textbf{DPDA}} \subseteq P$
   (c) $\mathcal{L}_{\textbf{DTM}} = P$
   (d) $P \subseteq DTIME(2^n)$

10. Define a decision problem that you suspect is not in P. Argue informally why you believe your problem is not in P.

Section 10.3 *P-Completeness Theory*

11. Prove Theorem 10.3.2.

12. Let $L = \{0, 1\}$. Provide a logarithmic space reduction from L to Parity (see Section 1.1.3). Provide a logarithmic space reduction from Parity to L.

13. Are there any languages that can be logarithmic space reduced to the empty language?

14. Provide a logarithmic space reduction from the language $\{0^i 1^i \mid i \geq 1\}$ to the language $\{a^j b^j c^j \mid j \geq 0\}$. Can you develop a reduction in the other direction?

15. Can $\{0, 1\}^*$ be a P-complete language?

16. What is the shallowest depth Boolean circuit family that you can derive for computing Parity? Is Parity in NC?

Section 10.4   Examples of P-Complete Problems

17. Given a 1-tape DTM M with input alphabet $\Sigma = \{0, 1\}$, how could you encode M's transition function over the alphabet $\{0, 1, \diamond\}$?

18. Use the encoding developed in Exercise 17 to code a DTM for deciding the language $\{0^i 1^i \mid i \geq 0\}$. Write out two YES instances and two NO instances of the Generic Machine Simulation problem using this DTM.

19. Write out two YES instances and two NO instances of the Generic Machine Simulation problem using a DTM for solving Parity as the input machine.

20. Write out two YES instances and two NO instances of the Generic Machine Simulation problem using a DTM that decides the empty language as the input machine.

21. Prove Theorem 10.4.2. (Hint: Consider an arbitrary language in P and a polynomial time bounded DTM that accepts it.)

22. Develop a polynomial time algorithm that topologically numbers an acyclic, directed graph $G = (V, E)$.

23. Prove using induction that the topological circuit evaluation algorithm correctly evaluates a topologically ordered circuit.

24. Specify two YES instances and two NO instances of the Circuit Value problem.

25. Which of the 16 possible Boolean functions from $\{0, 1\}^2$ to $\{0, 1\}$ are monotone?

26. Specify one YES instance and one NO instance of the Circuit Value problem using the Boolean circuit shown in Figure 9.1 with y_1 as the designated output gate of the circuit. Repeat the problem with y_2 as the designated output gate.

27. Describe two YES instances and two NO instances of the Monotone Circuit Value problem using the Boolean circuit shown in Figure 10.3.

28. Write out the standard encoding for the Boolean circuit shown in Figure 10.4, first at a high level and then as a bit string.

29. Evaluate the topologically ordered NOR circuit shown in Figure 10.4 on all possible input combinations.

30. Describe one YES instance and one NO instance of the Topologically Ordered NOR Circuit Value problem using the Boolean circuit shown in Figure 10.4 with γ_1 as the designated output gate of the circuit. Repeat the problem with γ_2 as the designated output gate.

31. Write out the standard encoding for the Boolean circuit shown in Figure 10.5 at a high level.

32. Evaluate the alternating, monotone circuit shown in Figure 10.5 on all possible input combinations.

33. Describe one YES instance and one NO instance of the Alternating Monotone Fanin 2, Fanout 2 Circuit Value problem using the Boolean circuit shown in Figure 10.5 with γ_1 as the designated output gate of the circuit. Repeat the problem with γ_2 as the designated output gate.

34. Suppose you are given the standard encoding of a Boolean circuit described at a high level. Design a polynomial time test to decide whether the circuit is monotone.

35. Suppose you are given the standard encoding of a Boolean circuit described at a high level. Design a polynomial time test to determine if the circuit meets the condition of being topologically ordered.

Section 10.5 *P-Complete Problems and Reductions*

36. Describe the instance of the NAND Circuit Value problem produced by carrying out the reduction given in Theorem 10.5.2 on the Boolean circuit shown in Figure 10.5 with designated output γ_2.

37. Describe the instance of the Context–Free Grammar Empty problem produced by carrying out the reduction given in Theorem 10.5.4 on the Boolean circuit shown in Figure 10.5.

38. Describe the instance of the Lexicographically First Maximal Independent Set problem produced by carrying out the reduction given in Theorem 10.5.6 on the Boolean circuit shown in Figure 10.4.

39. Prove the following problems are *P*–complete.

    (a) **Lexicographically First Maximal Clique**
       Given: An undirected graph $G = (V, E)$ with an ordering on the vertices and a designated vertex v.

Problem: Is vertex v in the lexicographically first maximal clique of G?

(Hint: Use the Lexicographically First Maximal Independent Set problem.)

(b) **Min–Plus Circuit Value problem**

Given: An encoding $\tilde{\alpha}$ of a (min, +) circuit α and rational inputs $x_1, \ldots, x_n$.

Problem: Does α on input $x_1, \ldots, x_n$ output a nonzero value? In this problem the two gate types are minimum (min) and (+). The outputs of these gates are the minimum of the inputs and the sum of the inputs, respectively.

(Hint: Use the Monotone Circuit Value problem.)

(c) **Lexicographically First $\Delta + 1$ Vertex Coloring**

Given: An undirected graph $G = (V, E)$ with Δ equal to the maximum degree of any vertex in V, an ordering $v_1, \ldots, v_n$ on the vertices of V, a designated color c, and a vertex v.

Problem: Is vertex v colored with color c in the lexicographically least coloring of the vertices of G? A *coloring* is an assignment of colors to the vertices such that no adjacent vertices receive the same color. The coloring uses at most $\Delta + 1$ colors. If c_i is the color of v_i, where $c_i \in \{1, \ldots, \Delta + 1\}$, then each coloring corresponds to a $(\Delta + 1)$–ary number. This, combined with the ordering on the vertices, ensures that the least coloring is well–defined.

(Hint: Use the Topologically Ordered NAND Circuit Value problem.)

(d) **Context–Free Grammar Infinite**

Given: A context–free grammar $G = (N, \Sigma, P, S)$.

Problem: Is $L(G)$ infinite?

(e) **Context–Free Grammar Λ–Membership**

Given: A context–free grammar $G = (N, \Sigma, P, S)$.

Problem: Is $\Lambda \in L(G)$?

CHAPTER 11

Intractable Problems

I can't find an efficient algorithm (for this problem), but neither can all these famous people.
> —*Mike Garey and David Johnson*

11.1 Introduction

In the last chapter we examined problems that have feasible solutions. Here we analyze problems that are *intractable*. What we mean by "intractable" is that the best-known methods for solving these problems require a prohibitively large amount of time even on the fastest computers. Our goals for this chapter are

- to introduce the complexity class *NP*,
- to explain why some problems in *NP* are said to be intractable,
- to describe *NP*-completeness theory,
- to examine a number of examples of *NP*-complete problems, and
- to present several *NP*-completeness reductions.

As described in the last chapter, we consider polynomial time to be a reasonable amount of time for solving a problem. In Table 10.2 we showed that exponential functions grow too fast to be considered reasonable time bounds. Unfortunately, it turns out that many computational problems of interest appear to be intractable—they have no known polynomial time solutions. These problems, numbering in the thousands, come from many different fields, including algebra and number theory, automata theory, biology, graph theory, network design, operations research, physics, program optimization, and scheduling, among others. For these problems for which no satisfactory algorithm exists, other approaches must be tried, such as developing good *approximation algorithms*. Although our introductory text concludes with this chapter, there are many roads continuing on from the theory of *NP*-completeness. We recommend Balcázar,

Díaz, and Gabarró [4], Garey and Johnson [17], and Papadimitriou [35] as excellent starting points for further study.

In the next section we formally define the complexity class *NP* using the machinery developed in Chapter 8. The theory is analogous to the theory of *P*-completeness developed in Chapter 10. *NP* contains all problems that are solvable in nondeterministic polynomial time. Following this, we present some background on the theory of *NP*-completeness.

A number of examples of *NP*-complete problems are presented in Section 11.4. The *NP*-complete problems are the most difficult problems to solve that are in the class *NP*. That is, all other problems in *NP* can be directly reduced to them. The *NP*-complete problems are considered intractable because there is strong evidence indicating that they cannot be solved in a feasible (polynomial) amount of time. Of course, the word "intractable" has a precise technical meaning that we will present later on in the chapter.

In Section 11.5 we examine several additional *NP*-complete problems—the Traveling Salesperson problem, Vertex Cover, and Three-Dimensional Matching—and present reductions showing their completeness. These reductions will provide you with the skills and background necessary for applying the subject of *NP*-completeness to other problems. Although the reductions we describe are simpler than many, they nicely illustrate the ideas of reducibility and completeness.

11.2   *Nondeterministic Polynomial Time*

The plan for this section is to formally define the complexity class *NP* and to look at a couple of problems in this class. The complexity class *NP*, standing for *nondeterministic polynomial*, represents those problems that can be solved in nondeterministic polynomial time. These are problems whose solutions can be guessed and then verified in polynomial time.

Definition 11.2.1   *The class NP is the set of all languages L such that L is accepted by a nondeterministic Turing machine in time $n^{O(1)}$.*

To say that a language *L* is in *NP* means there exists a polynomial time bounded NTM *M* such that $L(M) = L$. That is, there exists a constant *k* such that on any string *x* of length *n*, *M* runs within time $O(n^k)$ and accepts *x* if and only if $x \in L$. Figure 11.1 provides an illustration of this.

As was done for *P* using *DTIME*, we can also express *NP* in terms of the classes $NTIME(n^i)$ defined in Chapter 8:

$$NP = \bigcup_{i=0}^{\infty} NTIME(n^i)$$

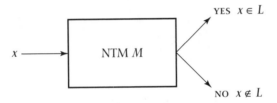

Let $|x| = n$ and $L(M) = L$. If there exists a $k \in \mathbb{N}$
such that M runs in time $O(n^k)$, then $L \in NP$.

Figure 11.1

Conditions necessary for a language L to be in the complexity class NP.

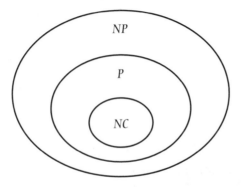

Figure 11.2

The relationships among NC, P, and NP. Note that it is possible, although considered extremely unlikely, that all three classes collapse to NC. That is, we cannot rule out the possibility that $NC = P = NP$.

Therefore, any problem in NP must be in $NTIME(n^i)$ for some $i \in \mathbb{N}$.

It should be clear that $P \subseteq NP$, since every DTM can be viewed as an NTM.

One of the most important open questions in computer science is whether P equals NP. Although we will not be able to present current research on this question, we will describe the most likely candidates (the NP-complete problems) for being in NP but not in P. Figure 11.2 shows the relationships among the classes NC, P, and NP.

The class NP contains a wide range of problems. Let's look at an example. Recall the definition of a clique from Example 6.2.13. A clique is a set of vertices that are all pairwise adjacent. Let's define a general decision problem based on cliques and show that this problem is in NP.

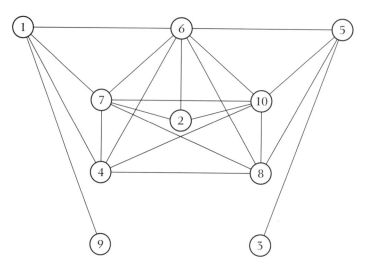

Figure 11.3

A graph used to illustrate YES and NO instances of the Clique problem. The maximum clique in this graph is size five and consists of the vertices 4, 6, 7, 8, and 10.

Definition 11.2.2   Clique

Given: *An undirected graph* $G = (V, E)$ *and a natural number k.*

Problem: *Does G contain a clique of size at least k?*

Consider the graph G shown in Figure 11.3. A YES instance of Clique would be $G \diamond 5$, where G is appropriately coded, because vertices 4, 6, 7, 8, and 10 form a 5-clique. Since there is no clique of size 6 in G, $G \diamond 6$ is a NO instance of Clique.

Even with this 10-node graph it becomes difficult to find cliques easily. Why is this the case? Clearly, there are a lot of possible combinations of vertices we need to check in order to determine if they form a clique. But just how many combinations? Is there some polynomial number, or perhaps even an exponential number, of possibilities?

Let's consider a graph $G = (V, E)$ with n nodes. Now suppose we were looking for a clique of size $n/2$ in G. How many possible subsets of nodes of size $n/2$ are there? The following observation will be useful in determining this.

Observation 11.2.3   *Suppose $m \in \mathbb{N}$ and $n = 2m$. Then*

$$\frac{n-i}{m-i} > 2 \text{ for all } i, \ 1 \le i \le m-1$$

Proof: The proof is left as a straightforward exercise.   ■

begin
    if the input is not a valid encoding of an undirected graph **then** reject;
    if $|V| < k$ **then** reject;
    guess a subset of k vertices V' from V;
    if the vertices in V' form a clique **then** accept **else** reject;
end

Figure 11.4

A nondeterministic, polynomial time algorithm for solving the Clique problem. The input consists of an undirected graph $G = (V, E)$ and a natural number k.

The number of possible subsets of size $n/2$ of a set of n elements can be written as

$$\binom{n}{\frac{n}{2}}$$

Expanding this, we get

$$\binom{n}{\frac{n}{2}} = \frac{n!}{\frac{n}{2}!(n - \frac{n}{2})!} = \frac{n(n - 1) \cdots (\frac{n}{2} + 1)}{\frac{n}{2}(\frac{n}{2} - 1) \cdots 1}$$

By applying Observation 11.2.3, we see that

$$\frac{n(n - 1) \cdots (\frac{n}{2} + 1)}{\frac{n}{2}(\frac{n}{2} - 1) \cdots 1} \geq \underbrace{2 \cdots 2}_{\frac{n}{2}} = 2^{\frac{n}{2}}$$

Thus the number of possible subsets is exponential. If we tried to use a brute force approach for finding a clique and considered all of these different subsets, an exponential time algorithm would result. Such an algorithm would not be feasible. It turns out that we know of no significantly better strategy than the brute force approach for solving the Clique problem on any deterministic model of computation such as a DTM.

Let's see how we could solve the Clique problem in polynomial time using an NTM. The algorithm sketched in Figure 11.4 shows one way of doing this. The algorithm first checks that the input correctly describes an undirected graph and that the clique size we are looking for is not larger than the total number of nodes in V. Next a subset of vertices of size k is nondeterministically guessed. The algorithm then checks to see if this subset of vertices forms a clique. That is, it tries to verify that all of the vertices are pairwise adjacent. If V' forms a clique, the algorithm accepts; otherwise, it rejects.

It is easy to see that the algorithm is correct because if a clique of size k or more exists, then there is some guess that finds a subset of k pairwise adjacent vertices. If no such subset is found, then the algorithm correctly rejects, since in this case there can be no clique of size at least k. If n is the length of the input, then the algorithm can be implemented to run in $O(n^2)$ steps on an NTM. Thus this is a nondeterministic, polynomial time algorithm for solving Clique. This shows the Clique problem is in *NP*. The advantage of nondeterminism is that we were able to guess a subset of vertices from an exponential search space and then efficiently check whether or not they form a clique.

Many other problems can be proven to be in *NP* using similar ideas. The main theme is usually the same: Guess a potential solution from the exponential size search space and then verify that it satisfies the conditions of the problem. In the next few sections, more examples of problems in *NP* will be given.

11.3   *NP-Completeness Theory*

There are many problems that computer scientists are interested in solving efficiently but for which no one has been able to develop a polynomial time algorithm. That is, no one has been able to show the underlying decision problem is in the complexity class *P*. As described in Chapter 10, it is very difficult to prove lower bounds on a problem's computational resources. For example, all attempts to show that any problem in *NP* requires at least 2^n time to solve on a DTM have failed. In view of this fact, complexity theorists try to make relative statements about the difficulty of solving particular problems. This is analogous to the strategy employed in the *P* framework.

Consider a problem Π that is in the complexity class *NP* but for which no deterministic, polynomial time algorithm is known. One possibility is to show that Π is as difficult to solve as any problem in *NP*. Thus, if there are any problems in *NP* that are not in *P*, then Π is one of them or we get a contradiction. *P*-completeness theory, as we saw, is useful for gauging the relative hardness of problems in *P*; *NP*-completeness theory serves the same role for the class *NP*. Next we define what it means for a problem to be *NP*–complete.

Definition 11.3.1   *A language L is* **NP–complete** *under logarithmic space reducibility if the following two conditions hold:*

1. *$L \in NP$.*

2. *For all problems $L' \in NP$, $L' \leq_m^{\lg} L$.*

For a problem to be *NP*-complete means it must be in the class *NP* and that all other problems in *NP* can be reduced to it. Sometimes, rather than defining *NP*-completeness using logarithmic space reducibility, *polynominal time reducibility* is used. That is, the reduction is carried out by a DTM that is allowed to run for polynomial time. This distinction is usually not important, since all problems that are known to be *NP*-complete under polynomial time reducibility are also known to be *NP*-complete under logarithmic space reducibility. You can learn about other types of reducibilities from Balcázar, Díaz, and Gabarró [3,4], and Papadimitriou [35].

NP-complete problems capture the intrinsic difficulty of the problems in NP. When we say a problem is NP-complete, we are indicating that it is as hard to solve as any problem in NP. NP-completeness theory has very important implications for many subject areas because it tells us that certain problems that we wish to solve are unlikely to be solved feasibly. Although these types of negative results can be discouraging, they at least guide us away from pursuing polynomial time algorithms that probably do not exist.

The following important theorem indicates that no NP-complete problem can be contained in P, unless P equals NP.

Theorem 11.3.2 *Suppose L is an NP-complete problem under logarithmic space reducibility. If L $\in$ P, then P equals NP.*

Proof: The proof is asked for in the exercises. ∎

A wide body of technical evidence, the details of which are beyond the scope of this book, exists supporting the belief that P and NP are different. From our perspective, this means that the NP-complete problems are very unlikely to have feasible solutions. Because of this, the NP-complete problems are called *intractable problems*. For these problems, we have to relax the requirement for solving them exactly always in polynomial time. You can try a feasible approximation algorithm for the problem, which perhaps will guarantee a certain degree of accuracy within a certain time bound. Another approach is to study subproblems in which the original problem is somehow restricted. Maybe the subproblem is in P yet still general enough to be of interest.

One logically weak form of evidence supporting the belief that P is different than NP is simply the fact that many people have tried to develop polynomial time algorithms for each of the NP-complete problems and no one has succeeded. If P does equal NP, then all of the several thousand NP-complete problems do indeed have polynomial time algorithms. Thus surely someone might have discovered one by now. As circumstantial as this evidence might seem, as time passes it becomes more compelling.

Figure 11.5 shows the relationships among NC, P, NP, the P-complete problems, and the NP-complete problems. The more difficult problems are situated higher up in the figure. Notice that we have shown the P-complete problems as being disjoint from NC, and similarly the NP-complete problems as being disjoint from P. Theorem 10.3.2 tells us that if there is overlap between NC and the P-complete problems, then NC equals P; Theorem 11.3.2 tells us that if there is overlap between the P-complete problems and NP, then P equals NP. You may have been wondering which problems are complete for NC. Complexity theorists currently do not believe that NC contains any complete problems!

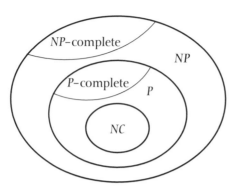

Figure 11.5

The relationships among the classes *NC*, *P*, *NP*, the *P*-complete problems, and the *NP*-complete problems. Note that it is possible, although considered extremely unlikely, that everything collapses to *NC*.

Faced with a problem for which you need to develop a polynomial time solution, what approaches can you pursue? Suppose you have been working on producing a polynomial time algorithm but have been totally unsuccessful. Perhaps you are at the point where you have convinced yourself (correctly or incorrectly) that no polynomial time algorithm exists for the problem. Your next step might be to attempt to show that the problem is *NP*-complete. For all practical purposes, this amounts to showing that no feasible algorithm exists for the problem, subject to the belief that *P* does not equal *NP*. In the remainder of this chapter we develop the tools and techniques necessary for proving that a problem is *NP*–complete.

11.4 *Examples of NP-Complete Problems*

Several *NP*–complete problems are defined in this section. In addition to serving as prototypical *NP*-complete problems, these examples play a fundamental role in *NP*-completeness theory. They form part of the basic core group of *NP*-complete problems that everyone (okay, maybe not everyone) should know. We will make use of several of these problems in the reductions given in Section 11.5.

11.4.1 **Satisfiability and Some Variants**

The most important and versatile *NP*-complete problem is called *Satisfiability*. This problem plays the same role in *NP*-completeness theory that CVP plays in *P*-completeness theory. It is involved in more *NP*-completeness proofs than any other problem. Satisfiability was the first problem proven *NP*-complete. Before defining the problem, we need to cover some background material.

Let $X = \{x_1, \ldots, x_n\}$ be a set of Boolean variables. A *truth assignment* is a total mapping

$$t : X \mapsto \{0, 1\}$$

As is customary we identify 0 with FALSE or F, and 1 with TRUE or T. So, we will view the truth assignment as being a mapping from X to $\{F, T\}$. Let x be an element of X. If $t(x) = F$, then we will say that x is FALSE. If $t(x) = T$, then we will say that x is TRUE.

If x is a variable in X, then x and $\bar{x}$ are *literals* over X. Here $\bar{x}$ denotes the negation of x. Literal x is TRUE (denoted $X = T$) under a truth assignment t if and only if x is TRUE under t; literal $\bar{x}$ is TRUE (denoted $X = F$) under a truth assignment t if and only if x is FALSE under t. For example, if $x = F$, then $\bar{x} = T$, and if $x = T$, then $\bar{x} = F$.

A *clause* over a set of variables X is a set of literals over X. A clause represents the OR or *disjunction* of its literals.

Example 11.4.1 Clauses

Let $X = \{x_1, x_2, x_3, x_4, x_5, x_6\}$.

Then $C_1 = \{x_1, x_2, x_3\}$, $C_2 = \{x_1, \overline{x_1}\}$, $C_3 = \{\overline{x_1}, \overline{x_5}, \overline{x_6}\}$, and $C_4 = \{x_1, x_4, \overline{x_6}\}$ are clauses over X.

Let $C = \{C_1, C_2, C_3, C_4\}$.

C_1 represents $x_1 \vee x_2 \vee x_3$.

C_2 represents $x_1 \vee \overline{x_1}$.

C_3 represents $\overline{x_1} \vee \overline{x_5} \vee \overline{x_6}$.

C_4 represents $x_1 \vee x_4 \vee \overline{x_6}$.

$|C_1| = |C_3| = |C_4| = 3$ and $|C_2| = 2$. ∎

A clause is *satisfied* by a truth assignment if and only if at least one literal in the clause is made TRUE by the assignment.

Example 11.4.2 Satisfied clauses

Let X and C_i for $1 \leq i \leq 4$ be given as in Example 11.4.1.

Let $t(x_i) = T$ for $1 \leq i \leq 6$.

Then C_1 is satisfied, since $t(x_1) = T$. Similar reasoning shows C_2 and C_4 are satisfied. Sometimes we will say t satisfies a clause. For example, in this case t satisfies C_1, C_2, and C_4. Notice that t does not satisfy C_3, since $\overline{x_i} = F$ for $1 \leq i \leq 6$. ∎

We usually omit the mapping t and just provide the assignment directly. For example, $x_1 = T$, $x_2 = F$, and so on.

A collection of clauses C over X is *satisfiable* if and only if there is some truth assignment that simultaneously satisfies all clauses in C. If such an assignment exists, it is called a *satisfying assignment*. Notice that what we are really doing here is taking the AND or *conjunction* of all the clauses in C.

Let X and C be as specified in Example 11.4.1. Then $x_i = T$ for $1 \leq i \leq 5$ and $x_6 = F$ is a satisfying assignment for the collection of clauses C. Thus C is satisfiable. In fact, for this particular set of clauses C, there are many different possible satisfying assignments. We can view C as the large *formula*

$$(x_1 \vee x_2 \vee x_3) \wedge (x_1 \vee \overline{x_1}) \wedge (\overline{x_1} \vee \overline{x_5} \vee \overline{x_6}) \wedge (x_1 \vee x_4 \vee \overline{x_6})$$

A conjunction of disjunctions of this type is called a *conjunctive normal form* (CNF) formula. When studying questions about satisfiability, we will always assume the formulas are in CNF. This is implicit in our definitions.

With these preliminaries on variables, clauses, and assignments, we are now ready to define the most important *NP*-complete problem.

Definition 11.4.3   Satisfiability (SAT)

Given: *A set $X = \{x_1, \ldots, x_n\}$ of variables and a collection $C = \{c_1, \ldots, c_m\}$ of clauses over X.*

Problem: *Is there a satisfying assignment for C?*

Let's consider a couple of examples of SAT.[1] Our version of SAT is sometimes called *CNFSAT* for the reasons mentioned above. Suppose X and C are as given in Example 11.4.1. As we saw above, they constitute a YES instance of SAT because the clauses can be satisfied. Suppose we have the set of clauses $C' = \{\{x_1\}, \{\overline{x_1}, x_2\}, \{\overline{x_2}\}\}$ over the variables in $\{x_1, x_2\}$. In order to satisfy the first clause in C', we must set x_1 to T. Having done this, then to satisfy the second clause we must set x_2 to T. However, now there is no way to satisfy the remaining clause. Thus $X \diamondsuit C'$ represents a NO instance of SAT.

We are now in a position to state the first theorem ever proved involving *NP*-completeness.

Theorem 11.4.4   *Satisfiability is NP-complete under logarithmic space reductions.*

Proof: Since this was the first problem ever proved *NP*-complete, the reduction had to be a generic one from an arbitrary polynomial time bounded NTM. The basic idea is very similar to the construction of the DTM for the Generic Machine Simulation of Section 10.4.1. The circuit doing the DTM simulation can be described as a collection of clauses that are satisfied if and only if the simulated machine accepts its input. The key observation is that exactly the same construction works for an NTM; you just allow more than one possible transition from the current state. Lack of space prevents us from presenting the full proof here. The proof details may be found by consulting Garey and Johnson [17].   ∎

---

1. Note that SAT is pronounced "sat" not "S–A–T." SAT is not the Scholastic Aptitude Test.

In the definition of SAT there was no restriction placed on the number of literals per clause. In many NP–completeness proofs from SAT, additional structure helps to simplify the reduction. It turns out that if we restrict SAT so that each clause contains *exactly* three literals, then the problem remains NP–complete. Thus we have added structure but not reduced the complexity of the problem. (Naturally, being complexity theorists, we would like to know what happens when there are just two literals per clause; this question is tackled in the exercises.)

Definition 11.4.5   Three Satisfiability (3SAT)

Given: *A set* $X = \{x_1, \ldots, x_n\}$ *of variables and a collection* $C = \{c_1, \ldots, c_m\}$ *of clauses over* X *with the restriction that* $|c_i| = 3$ *for* $1 \leq i \leq m$.

Problem: *Is there a satisfying assignment for C?*

This version of 3SAT is sometimes called *3CNFSAT*.

Suppose $X = \{x_1, x_2, x_3\}$ and $C = \{\{x_1, x_2, \overline{x_3}\}, \{x_1, \overline{x_2}, \overline{x_3}\}, \{x_1, x_2, x_3\}\}$. Then $X \Diamond C$ is a YES instance of 3SAT, since each clause has exactly three literals and the truth assignment $x_1 = T$ satisfies all three clauses regardless of how we set x_2 and x_3. We ask for a NO instance of 3SAT in the exercises.

Theorem 11.4.6   *Three Satisfiability is NP-complete under logarithmic space reductions.*

Proof: The idea behind the proof is to reduce SAT to 3SAT by showing how to expand clauses having only one or two literals and how to shrink clauses having four or more literals. Of course, the resulting set of clauses produced by the expanding and shrinking must be *equivalent* to the original set of clauses. That is, the new set of clauses must be satisfiable if and only if the original set of clauses was satisfiable. The proof details are left as an exercise for the problems of Section 11.5.   ■

3SAT places some uniformity on the structure of the clauses in SAT and, as a result, is often very useful in NP–completeness results. A further restriction to 3SAT that remains NP–complete and comes in handy for a number of other NP–completeness reductions is defined below.

Definition 11.4.7   Not–All–Equals Three Satisfiability (NAE3SAT)

Given: *A set* $X = \{x_1, \ldots, x_n\}$ *of variables and a collection* $C = \{c_1, \ldots, c_m\}$ *of clauses over* X *with the restriction that* $|c_i| = 3$ *for* $1 \leq i \leq m$.

Problem: *Is there a satisfying assignment for C with the property that each clause has at least one* FALSE *literal?*

In order to be a satisfying assignment, each clause must have at least one TRUE literal. Due to the requirements of the problem, we see then that each clause in a satisfying assignment has at least one FALSE literal and at least one TRUE literal. Hence, the problem is called Not–All–Equals Three SAT.

Let's consider an example of NAE3SAT (pronounced . . . oh, forget it). Suppose $X = \{x_1, x_2, x_3\}$ and $C = \{\{\overline{x_1}, \overline{x_2}, x_3\}, \{\overline{x_1}, x_2, \overline{x_3}\}, \{x_1, \overline{x_2}, \overline{x_3}\}\}$. Then $X \Diamond C$ is a YES instance of NAE3SAT, since the truth assignment $x_1 = T$, $x_2 = T$, and $x_3 = T$ satisfies all three clauses, and in the first clause $\overline{x_1} = F$ and $x_3 = T$, in the second clause $\overline{x_1} = F$ and $x_2 = T$, and in the third clause $x_1 = T$ and $\overline{x_2} = F$. Clearly, any NO instance of SAT or 3SAT is also a NO instance of NAE3SAT. If we augment C with the fourth clause $\{x_1, x_2, x_3\}$, then we end up with a NO instance of NAE3SAT.

Theorem 11.4.8 *Not-All-Equals Three Satisfiability is NP-complete under logarithmic space reductions.*

Proof: The proof is left as an exercise for the problems of Section 11.5. ■

There are several other variants of SAT that turn out to be useful in a few other NP–completeness proofs, which you may pursue through Garey and Johnson [17].

11.4.2 Hamiltonian Circuit Problem

In this section we consider another one of the most basic NP–complete problems. Unlike SAT, this problem is from graph theory. Let's begin with some terminology.

Suppose $G = (V, E)$ is an undirected graph. A *simple circuit* in G is a sequence of distinct vertices $\langle v_1, v_2, \ldots, v_k \rangle$ from V such that $\{v_i, v_{i+1}\} \in E$ for $1 \le i \le k$, $\{v_k, v_1\} \in E$, and $k > 1$. Intuitively, a circuit is just what you would naturally call a *loop* or *cycle* in the graph. The word "simple" is used to stress the requirement that no vertex is repeated (except the start and ending point) in a circuit. Note that the word "circuit" is used here in a completely different manner than in previous chapters where we talked about Boolean circuits.

Figure 11.6 depicts an undirected graph. This graph contains many simple circuits. For example, $\langle 3, 6, 5 \rangle$ is a simple circuit. Why? Because 3, 6, and 5 are three distinct vertices and $\{3, 6\}$, $\{6, 5\}$, and $\{5, 3\}$ are all edges in E. It is easy to verify that $\langle 1, 2, 3, 4, 5, 6 \rangle$ is also a simple circuit.

In this section we are interested in simple circuits that pass through every single node in the graph; this type of circuit has a special name. A *Hamiltonian circuit* of an undirected graph $G = (V, E)$ is a simple circuit that includes all the vertices of G. The graph in Figure 11.6 contains several Hamiltonian circuits—for example, $\langle 1, 4, 5, 6, 3, 2 \rangle$ and $\langle 1, 2, 3, 4, 5, 6 \rangle$. Are there others?

We are now in a position to define the Hamiltonian Circuit problem.

Definition 11.4.9 Hamiltonian Circuit problem (HC)

Given: *An undirected graph $G = (V, E)$.*

Problem: *Does G contain a Hamiltonian circuit?*

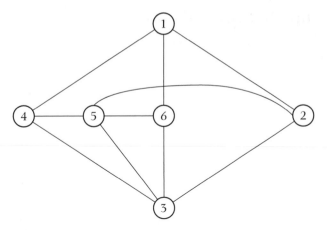

Figure 11.6

An undirected graph used to illustrate the concept of a simple circuit. The graph contains many simple circuits. Two examples are $\langle 3, 6, 5 \rangle$ and $\langle 1, 2, 3, 4, 5, 6 \rangle$. The latter is a Hamiltonian circuit.

Let's consider an example of the Hamiltonian Circuit problem using the graph in Figure 11.6. Since $\langle 1, 2, 3, 4, 5, 6 \rangle$ is a Hamiltonian circuit of this graph, G is a YES instance of HC. Consider the graph $G' = (\{1\}, \emptyset)$. Since we do not consider $\langle 1 \rangle$ to be a simple circuit (see the definition of simple circuit above; we require $k > 1$), this degenerate case is a NO instance of HC.

The main result of this section is that HC is NP-complete.

Theorem 11.4.10 *The Hamiltonian Circuit problem is NP-complete under logarithmic space reductions.*

Proof: The proof details may be found by consulting Garey and Johnson [17]. ∎

Already we see that the NP-complete problems exhibit quite a bit of variety. That is to say, there is no apparent relationship between SAT and HC. In fact, the problems look rather dissimilar and come from different areas of computer science. However, as we will soon see, it is sometimes possible to relate problems that at first appear contrasting.

With the NP-completeness results for Satisfiability and the Hamiltonian Circuit problem, we can now show several other problems are NP-complete by exploiting the transitivity of logarithmic space reductions. We carry out this plan in the next section for the Traveling Salesperson problem, Vertex Cover, and Three-Dimensional Matching. Each of these is an important NP-complete problem that is used in many other NP-completeness reductions.

►11.5 *NP-Complete Problems and Reductions*

In the previous section we defined several problems that are known to be *NP*-complete. Because of the technical nature of the proofs involved, we only stated the results and provided references to their proofs. Here we examine several *NP*-completeness proofs in detail. These results help to illustrate the steps necessary to show a problem is *NP*-complete. It is important to keep in mind that *NP*-complete problems are intractable, unless *P* equals *NP*. This means it is very unlikely that they can be solved in polynomial time. The proofs we give are slight variations of the proofs presented by Garey and Johnson [17].

Just as there are several key points in a *P*-completeness proof, there are analogous steps in an *NP*-completeness proof. We summarize these in Figure 11.7. Suppose you want to show a decision problem Π with corresponding language *L* is *NP*-complete. The first step is to prove *L* is in *NP*. A nondeterministic, polynomial time algorithm for *L* must be developed, its time complexity analyzed, and its correctness established. The second step is to show that all other languages *L'* in *NP* are logarithmic space reducible to *L*. A reduction from some existing *NP*-complete problem is usually developed. Using the transitivity of logarithmic space reductions, we can then conclude that all problems in *NP* reduce to *L*. The reduction needs to be proved correct, and its space complexity needs to be analyzed.

Our goal is to acquaint you with the subject of *NP*-completeness so that you develop a feel for which problems might be *NP*-complete and so you are capable of devising reductions. Problems whose solution comes from an exponential search space, like Clique, are potential candidates for being *NP*-complete.

In what follows, we focus on the reductions and their proofs of correctness, as opposed to the algorithmic aspects of the problems. Therefore, we generally will not include all details of an *NP*-completeness proof other than those involving the reduction. The reduction is usually the most interesting and complex part of a completeness proof.

11.5.1 Traveling Salesperson Problem

The first problem we wish to prove *NP*-complete is one that has a number of important practical applications. It is known as the *Traveling Salesperson problem*. This problem is one of the most famous *NP*-complete problems; it has made headlines in the *New York Times* on several occasions. In one experiment, using huge amounts of processing time on computers linked together from all over the world, an instance of size 300 or so was solved! At an intuitive level, the Traveling Salesperson problem is for a salesperson to visit a collection of cities using the shortest possible route. To formalize the problem, we need a few definitions.

Suppose we are given a set of cities $C = \{c_1, \ldots, c_n\}$ with n greater than 1 and a weighting or distance function $d : C \times C \mapsto \mathbb{N}$ assigning intercity costs. A **tour** is any permutation of the cities. The **cost** is the sum of the weights between adja-

1. Prove L is in NP.
   (a) Develop a nondeterministic, polynomial time algorithm for solving L.
   (b) Prove the algorithm is correct.
   (c) Prove the algorithm runs in nondeterministic polynomial time.
2. Prove $L' \leq_m^{\lg} L$ for some NP-complete language L'.
   (a) Develop a logarithmic space reduction from a known NP-complete problem to L.
   (b) Prove the reduction is correct.
   (c) Prove the reduction is a logarithmic space reduction.

Figure 11.7

Key steps involved in an NP-completeness proof for a language L.

cent cities in the permutation, including the cost of returning to the starting city. More formally, if π is a permutation, then the cost of the tour $\langle c_{\pi(1)}, \ldots, c_{\pi(n)} \rangle$ is

$$\left(\sum_{i=1}^{n-1} d(c_{\pi(i)}, c_{\pi(i+1)}) \right) + d(c_{\pi(n)}, c_{\pi(1)})$$

Next we present one of the most famous problems in computer science.

Definition 11.5.1 Traveling Salesperson problem (TSP)

Given: *A set of cities* $C = \{c_1, \ldots, c_n\}$ *with* $n > 1$, *a weighting or distance function* $d : C \times C \mapsto \mathbb{N}$ *assigning intercity costs, and a natural number* B.

Problem: *Is there a tour of the cities in* C *having total cost less than or equal to* B?

Note in the definition that we require at least two cities to constitute a tour.

Figure 11.8 illustrates an instance of TSP represented by a weighted graph. In this example the distance function is *symmetric*; that is, $d(c_i, c_j) = d(c_j, c_i)$ for $1 \leq i, j \leq n$. The "outside" tour has the least cost of $5 + 9 + 13 + 10 + 5 = 42$. Thus, with a bound $B = 35$, this would be a NO instance; for a bound $B = 45$, this would be a YES instance.

We are now ready to prove that TSP is NP-complete.

Theorem 11.5.2 *The Traveling Salesperson problem is NP-complete under logarithmic space reductions.*

Proof: The first thing we need to do is show that TSP is in NP. This is easy to see, since a nondeterministic algorithm can guess a permutation of the cities, verify that the guess is in fact a permutation, sum up the costs of the weights involved,

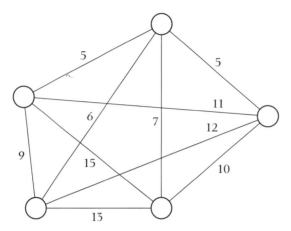

Figure 11.8

A sample instance of the Traveling Salesperson problem represented as a weighted graph. With a bound of $B = 35$, this represents a NO instance; with a bound of $B = 45$, this represents a YES instance.

and then check that the total cost is less than or equal to B, all in polynomial time. Thus, TSP is in *NP*.

The next step in an *NP*–completeness proof is to show that all problems in *NP* are logarithmic space reducible to TSP. In order to do this, we will show that HC $\leq_m^{\lg}$ TSP. By Theorem 11.4.10, HC is *NP*–complete, so using the transitivity of $\leq_m^{\lg}$ implies that all problems in *NP* are logarithmic space reducible to TSP as required.

Suppose $G = (V, E)$ is an arbitrary instance of HC. Let $n = |V|$ and $v_1, \ldots, v_n$ be the vertices in V. We will define a transformation f that produces an equivalent instance of TSP. That is, $G \in$ HC if and only if $f(G) \in$ TSP. We then argue that f can be computed in logarithmic space and is correct. Define f to produce the following instance of TSP:

Let C be the same set as V. For $1 \leq i, j \leq n$, define

$$d(v_i, v_j) = \begin{cases} 0 & \text{if } i = j \\ 1 & \text{if } \{v_i, v_j\} \in E \\ 2 & \text{otherwise} \end{cases}$$

and let $B = n$.

It is clear that f can be computed in logarithmic space by a DTM. f needs to determine the n^2 distances between the cities and to compute the value $B = n$. The distances can be computed by scanning through the input and checking if certain edges exist in E. To record an edge on the work tape requires only logarithmic space. Summing up the number of vertices requires scanning through the input and maintaining a $\lg n$ bit counter.

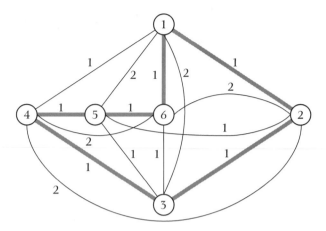

Figure 11.9

The reduction from Theorem 11.5.2 applied to the graph shown in Figure 11.6. The tour corresponding to the Hamiltonian circuit $\langle 1, 2, 3, 4, 5, 6 \rangle$ is highlighted. It has a cost of six.

To prove the reduction is valid, we need to show that G contains a Hamiltonian circuit if and only if there is a tour of all the cities in $f(G)$ that has length less than or equal to B.

($\Rightarrow$) Suppose $\langle v_1, \ldots, v_n \rangle$ is a Hamiltonian circuit for G. Note that, by the definition of Hamiltonian circuit, n is greater than one. Then clearly $\langle v_1, \ldots, v_n \rangle$ is also a tour of $f(G)$. Each intercity distance traveled in the tour corresponds to an edge in G and so has cost one. Since there are n links in the tour, the total cost of tour $\langle v_1, \ldots, v_n \rangle$ is n.

($\Leftarrow$) Suppose $\langle v_1, \ldots, v_n \rangle$ is a tour of cost less than or equal to B. By the definition of tour, n is greater than one. We will show that each link in the tour is in fact an edge in E. First observe that any two distinct cities are a distance of either one or two apart because of the definition of d. Next note that any tour must contain exactly n links. The fact that $B = n$, taken together with the two previous observations, implies that pairs of adjacent cities in the tour are a distance one apart.

From the middle case of the definition $f(G)$, it follows that for $1 \leq i \leq n - 1$ $\{v_i, v_{i+1}\}$ are edges of E. Since $d(v_n, v_1) = 1$, $\{v_n, v_1\} \in E$. This means that $\langle v_1, \ldots, v_n \rangle$ is a Hamiltonian circuit for G.

So we have shown that HC $\leq_m^{\lg}$ TSP. This completes the proof. ■

The graph shown in Figure 11.9 illustrates the result of applying the transformation of Theorem 11.5.2 to the graph of Figure 11.6. Note that $\langle 1, 2, 3, 4, 5, 6 \rangle$ is a Hamiltonian circuit in Figure 11.6, and the corresponding tour $\langle 1, 2, 3, 4, 5, 6 \rangle$ of cost six is highlighted in Figure 11.9. For each Hamiltonian circuit in Figure 11.6, there is a corresponding tour of cost six in Figure 11.9.

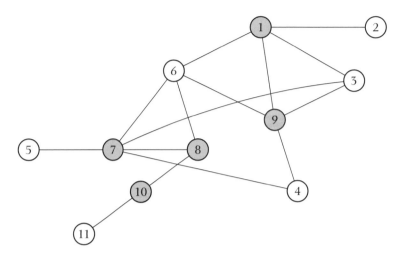

Figure 11.10

An undirected graph used to illustrate the concept of vertex cover. The shaded nodes form a vertex cover. In fact, this is a minimum vertex cover for the graph since there is no cover of size four.

There are a number of other interesting variants of TSP that are *NP*–complete. In fact, TSP is one of the most widely studied problems in all of computer science; you may pursue TSP further starting with Garey and Johnson [17].

11.5.2   Vertex Cover

There are many other *NP*–complete graph theory problems. Vertex Cover is another one. This problem is very closely related to the Clique problem and the *Independent Set problem*. In the exercises we ask you to prove a result relating these three concepts.

Let $G = (V, E)$ be an undirected graph. A *vertex cover* of G is a set $V' \subseteq V$ such that, for each edge $\{u, v\} \in E$, at least one of u and v belongs to V'. Intuitively, at least one endpoint of each edge is contained in a vertex cover.

Figure 11.10 depicts an undirected graph. A vertex cover consisting of nodes $\{1, 7, 8, 9, 10\}$ is shaded. It is not hard to check that the 15 edges in the picture each have at least one endpoint that is included in the cover (shaded). This size five cover is in fact a *minimum vertex cover*—a vertex cover of smallest possible cardinality. Clearly, the set V is always a vertex cover, but usually we are interested in finding much smaller covers if they exist.

We are now poised to define a decision problem based on the concept of vertex cover.

Definition 11.5.3   Vertex Cover (VC)

Given: *An undirected graph $G = (V, E)$ and a natural number k.*

Problem: *Does G have a vertex cover of size k or less?*

For the graph shown in Figure 11.10 with a value of $k = 5$, we get a YES instance of VC. An example of a NO instance of the problem would be the same graph in Figure 11.10 with a value of $k = 3$. If we had a feasible algorithm for deciding VC, then by using binary search (as described in Chapter 2) we could quickly determine the size of a minimum vertex cover. Unfortunately, as the next theorem shows, VC is probably intractable.

Theorem 11.5.4   *Vertex Cover is NP-complete under logarithmic space reductions.*

Proof: As a first step we need to show that VC is in *NP*. This is easy to see, since a nondeterministic, polynomial time algorithm can guess a subset of the vertices, check that the number of vertices guessed is less than or equal to k, and verify that each edge is incident to at least one of these vertices. Thus, VC is in *NP*.

The second step is to show that all problems in *NP* are logarithmic space reducible to VC. In order to do this, we will show that 3SAT $\leq_m^{\lg}$ VC. By Theorem 11.4.6, 3SAT is NP–complete, so using the transitivity of $\leq_m^{\lg}$ implies that all problems in *NP* are logarithmic space reducible to VC as required.

Suppose $X = \{x_1, \ldots, x_n\}$ and $C = \{c_1, \ldots, c_m\}$ is an arbitrary instance of 3SAT. Furthermore, suppose $c_j = \{l_{j1}, l_{j2}, l_{j3}\}$, where l_{j1}, l_{j2}, and l_{j3} are literals for $1 \leq j \leq m$. Note l_{j1}, l_{j2}, and l_{j3} are not necessarily distinct. We define a transformation f that produces an equivalent instance $(V, E)\Diamond k$ of VC. That is, $X\Diamond C \in$ 3SAT if and only if $f(X\Diamond C) \in$ VC. We then argue that f can be computed in logarithmic space and is correct.

The idea is to introduce vertices in V for each variable and its negation, form m 3-cliques made up of dummy nodes to represent each clause, and then to connect each 3-clique to the appropriate literals depending on which literals occur in the corresponding clause. More formally, f produces the following instance of VC:

$$V = \{x_i, \overline{x_i} \mid 1 \leq i \leq n\} \cup \{d_{j1}, d_{j2}, d_{j3} \mid 1 \leq j \leq m\}$$

$$E_{\text{truth}} = \{\{x_i, \overline{x_i}\} \mid 1 \leq i \leq n\}$$

$$E_{\text{triangles}} = \{\{d_{j1}, d_{j2}\}, \{d_{j2}, d_{j3}\}, \{d_{j3}, d_{j1}\} \mid 1 \leq j \leq m\}$$

$$E_{\text{connections}} = \{\{d_{jp}, l_{jp}\} \mid 1 \leq j \leq m \text{ and } 1 \leq p \leq 3\}$$

$$E = E_{\text{truth}} \cup E_{\text{triangles}} \cup E_{\text{connections}}$$

$$G = (V, E)$$

$$k = n + 2m$$

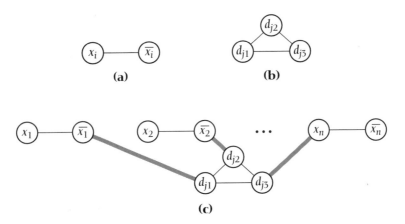

Figure 11.11

The various edge constructions needed in the proof of Theorem 11.5.4. (a) A sample edge in E_{truth}. (b) One of the m 3–cliques. (c) The edges contained in $E_{\text{connections}}$ for the example clause $c_i = \{\overline{x_1}, \overline{x_2}, x_n\}$.

Before proceeding to the proof of correctness, let us explain each component set of edges. E_{truth} includes edges connecting each variable with its negation. This is shown in Figure 11.11 (a). As we shall see, the interaction of the value of k with these edges ensures for $1 \le i \le n$ that either x_i or $\overline{x_i}$, but not both, is set to TRUE. The edges $E_{\text{triangles}}$ form m 3–cliques using dummy nodes. An example is shown in Figure 11.11 (b). The value of k and the remainder of the setup will imply that exactly two of the three dummy nodes in each 3–clique will end up in a vertex cover that corresponds to a satisfying assignment, if one exists. Sample edges from $E_{\text{connections}}$ are depicted in Figure 11.11 (c). The edges highlighted in the figure are for connecting the 3–clique corresponding to the sample clause $c_i = \{\overline{x_1}, \overline{x_2}, x_n\}$. These connections are set up so that when C is satisfied, the third dummy node in each clique, which has not yet been covered, will be covered by the vertex corresponding to a literal that was set to TRUE.

It is clear that f can be computed in logarithmic space by a DTM. A DTM M for computing f needs to output the $n + 6m$ edges that are contained in E and compute the value $k = n + 2m$. The edges are based on local structural properties of the clauses in C. Thus by scanning over the input a polynomial number of times and storing a $\lg n$ bit counter, a $\lg m$ bit counter, and the name of a vertex (again logarithmic in the instance size of 3SAT), M can output $G \diamond k$ using only log space.

To prove the reduction is valid, we need to show that C is satisfied if and only if there is a vertex cover for G of size k or less.

($\Rightarrow$) Suppose C is satisfied. We construct a set D and then argue that D is a vertex cover. Let t be a satisfying assignment for C. For $1 \leq i \leq n$, if $t(x_i) = T$, then place node x_i in D; if $t(x_i) = F$, then place $\overline{x_i}$ in D. Since C is satisfied for each c_i with $1 \leq i \leq m$, at least one of l_{ip} for $1 \leq p \leq 3$ is TRUE under t. Thus for each triangle at least one dummy node is incident to a vertex already added to the vertex cover. Select one such dummy node from each triangle and add the other two vertices to D.

We claim that D is a vertex cover of size exactly $n + 2m$. For each pair x_i and $\overline{x_i}$ with $1 \leq i \leq n$, exactly one of these is placed in D, for a total of n nodes. Thus all edges in E_{truth} are covered. Since C is satisfied, each clause has at least one TRUE literal, and this literal covers one of the connections in $E_{\text{connections}}$. We added two nodes from each triangle to D, for a total of $2m$ more nodes. These cover the remaining two edges in $E_{\text{connections}}$. It is easy to see that $|D| = n + 2m$. Finally, any two nodes in a triangle cover the three edges in a triangle; therefore the edges in E_{triangle} are covered. In conclusion D is a vertex cover of size $n + 2m$ as claimed.

($\Leftarrow$) Suppose there is a vertex cover D for G of size $k = n + 2m$ or less. In order to cover the edges in E_{truth}, it is clear that at least one of x_i or $\overline{x_i}$ must be in D. Thus we need at least n vertices to cover the edges in E_{truth}. In order to cover m triangles, we need to include at least two nodes per triangle, for a total of at least $2m$ more nodes. Since D is also a vertex cover of at most size k, D must contain exactly n vertices corresponding to literals and exactly $2m$ nodes from the triangles.

Let's construct a truth assignment t for $1 \leq i \leq n$ that sets $x_i = T$ if the node corresponding to $x_i \in D$, and $x_i = F$ if the node corresponding to $\overline{x_i} \in D$. It is clear that this is indeed a valid assignment. Because all the edges in $E_{\text{connections}}$ must be covered by D and because the two nodes from each triangle can only cover two of the three edges per clause in $E_{\text{connections}}$, the third edge must be covered by a literal. This literal is set to TRUE by t. Since each clause has at least one TRUE literal, we see t is a satisfying assignment for C.

So, we have shown that $3\text{SAT} \leq_m^{\lg} \text{VC}$. This completes the proof. ∎

In Figure 11.12 we consider an example of the reduction. The figure shows the instance of VC constructed from the formula

$$(x_1 \lor x_2 \lor x_3) \land (\overline{x_1} \lor \overline{x_2} \lor \overline{x_3}) \land (x_1 \lor x_2 \lor \overline{x_3}) \land (x_1 \lor \overline{x_2} \lor \overline{x_3})$$

In this case $n = 3$ and $m = 4$, so $n + 2m = 11$. The vertex cover corresponding to the satisfying assignment $x_1 = F$, $x_2 = T$, and $x_3 = F$ is shaded in the figure. In this case we choose to satisfy the third clause with x_2. Had we chosen $\overline{x_3}$ to satisfy this clause, then d_{32} would have been included in the vertex cover instead of d_{33}.

In the proof of Theorem 11.5.4, we heavily exploited the regular clause structure of 3SAT. In particular, this allowed us to use a uniform subgraph, namely

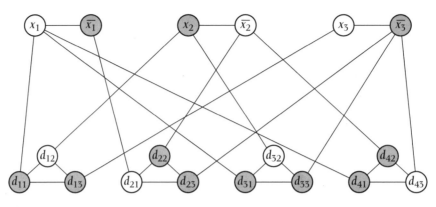

Figure 11.12

The reduction of Theorem 11.5.4 applied to the formula $(x_1 \vee x_2 \vee x_3) \wedge (\overline{x_1} \vee \overline{x_2} \vee \overline{x_3}) \wedge (x_1 \vee x_2 \vee \overline{x_3}) \wedge (x_1 \vee \overline{x_2} \vee \overline{x_3})$. The vertex cover corresponding to the satisfying assignment $x_1 = F$, $x_2 = T$, and $x_3 = F$ is shaded.

the triangle, to represent each clause. In turn, this simplified the reduction and the proof of correctness. In many NP–completeness proofs, if the right type of structure is present, then the reduction and proof of correctness fall out more easily.

11.5.3   Three–Dimensional Matching

In this section we introduce another *matching* problem. This problem is very useful for proving other problems are NP–complete. It is particularly well suited to NP–completeness proofs involving problems that contain numbers or weights. You can find many reductions utilizing this problem by consulting Garey and Johnson [17].

Let A, B, and C be three finite sets. We call A, B, and C *3-good* if they satisfy the following two properties:

1. $|A| = |B| = |C|$ and
2. $A \cap B = B \cap C = A \cap C = \emptyset$.

Suppose A, B, and C are 3–good with their cardinality equal to q. Let $M \subseteq A \times B \times C$. A *3d-matching* of M is a subset M' of M such that $|M'| = q$ and, for any two triples (a_1, b_1, c_1) and (a_2, b_2, c_2) in M, we have that $a_1 \neq a_2$, $b_1 \neq b_2$, and $c_1 \neq c_2$. That is, the triples do not match in any coordinate.

We can now define the Three–Dimensional Matching problem.

Definition 11.5.5   Three–Dimensional Matching problem (3DM)

Given: *Sets A, B, and C that are 3-good and a set $M \subseteq A \times B \times C$.*

Problem: *Does M contain a 3d-matching?*

Let's consider an example to help clarify the definition.

Example 11.5.6   Three–Dimensional Matching problem instances

1. Let $A = \{0, 1\}$, $B = \{2, 3\}$, $C = \{4, 5\}$, and $M = \{(0, 2, 4), (0, 2, 5), (0, 3, 5), (1, 2, 4),$ $(1, 3, 4), (1, 3, 5)\}$. It is easy to see that $M' = \{(0, 2, 4), (1, 3, 5)\}$ is a 3d–matching. This is true since $|A| = |B| = |C| = |M'| = 2$ and $(0, 2, 4)$ and $(1, 3, 5)$ do not agree in any component. Thus A, B, C, and M constitute a YES instance of 3DM.

2. Let $A = \{a, b\}$, $B = \{c, d\}$, $C = \{e, f\}$, and $M = \{(a, c, e), (a, c, f), (a, d, e), (a, d, f)\}$. It is not hard to see that M contains no 3d–matching, since each pair of triples agree in at least one component. Therefore, this example represents a NO instance of 3DM.

3. Let $A = \{0, 1, 2\}$, $B = \{3, 4, 5\}$, $C = \{6, 7, 8\}$, and $M = \{(0, 3, 7), (2, 5, 8), (0, 5, 8),$ $(1, 4, 8), (1, 3, 7), (0, 5, 6), (2, 5, 6)\}$. Then $M' = \{(0, 3, 7), (1, 4, 8), (2, 5, 6)\}$ forms a 3d–matching of M because $|A| = |B| = |C| = |M'| = 3$ and no two triples in M' agree in any coordinate. Thus A, B, C, and M constitute a YES instance of 3DM. ∎

We can now state the main result of this section. The proof involves the most complex reduction that we will present.

Theorem 11.5.7   *Three-Dimensional Matching is NP-complete under logarithmic space reductions.*

Proof: We need to show that 3DM is in *NP*. This is easy to see since a nondeterministic, polynomial time algorithm can guess a subset M' of M, compute the cardinality $q = |A| = |B| = |C|$, verify that $|M'|$ is of cardinality q, and then scan through the coordinates of each triple in M' to make sure that no value repeats in any position. Thus, 3DM is in *NP*.

The next step is to show that all problems in *NP* are logarithmic space reducible to 3DM. In order to do this, we will prove that 3SAT $\leq_m^{\lg}$ 3DM. By Theorem 11.4.6, 3SAT is *NP*–complete, so using the transitivity of $\leq_m^{\lg}$ implies that all problems in *NP* are logarithmic space reducible to 3DM as required.

Suppose $X = \{x_1, \ldots, x_n\}$ and $F = \{f_1, \ldots, f_m\}$ is an arbitrary instance of 3SAT; for $1 \leq j \leq m$, each f_j represents a clause containing three literals over X. Actually, we will reduce a restricted version of 3SAT to 3DM. The version of 3SAT we use is such that for each $x_i \in X$ for $1 \leq i \leq n$, x_i and $\overline{x_i}$ combined appear in at most five clauses. In the exercises we ask you to prove that this variant of 3SAT remains *NP*-complete. We define a transformation f (do not confuse this with the subscripted elements of F) that produces an equivalent instance A, B, C, and M of 3DM, with A, B, and C being 3–good and of cardinality $10n$.

There are three different types of triples that will be included in M. For each type we add a number of elements to the sets A, B, and C.

The first type of triple is used to ensure that in a 3d–matching corresponding to an assignment, each variable is either set to TRUE or FALSE. This is accomplished as follows:

- Make $10n$ elements x_{il} and $\overline{x_{il}}$, for $1 \leq i \leq n$, $1 \leq l \leq 5$, representing five "copies" each of x_i and $\overline{x_i}$, respectively, and add them to A.
- Create $5n$ elements b_{il}, with $1 \leq i \leq n$, $1 \leq l \leq 5$, and put them in B.
- Form $5n$ elements c_{il}, with $1 \leq i \leq n$, $1 \leq l \leq 5$, and place them in C.
- Define the following two sets, TRUE(i) and FALSE(i), for $1 \leq i \leq n$, containing a total of $10n$ triples to add to M:

$$\text{TRUE}(i) = \{(\overline{x_{il}}, b_{il}, c_{il}) \mid 1 \leq i \leq n, 1 \leq l \leq 5\}$$

and

$$\text{FALSE}(i) = \{(x_{il}, b_{il}, c_{i(l+1)}) \mid 1 \leq i \leq n, 1 \leq l \leq 4\} \cup \{(x_{i5}, b_{i5}, c_{i1}) \mid 1 \leq i \leq n\}$$

These $10n$ triples assure us that, in any 3d–matching for the instance of 3DM we produce, the following two properties hold:

1. Either x_i or $\overline{x_i}$ is set to TRUE, but not both.
2. The value of x_i, in the (at most five) possible clauses it occurs in, is consistent.

But exactly how are the two properties enforced by these three–tuples?

The b_{il}'s and c_{il}'s do not occur in any other triples and so in any 3d–matching must be grouped with the x_{il}'s or $\overline{x_{il}}$'s. Notice the construction implies that for each i the b_{il}'s and c_{il}'s are all matched with

1. $\overline{x_{il}}$'s from triples in TRUE(i) corresponding to $\overline{x_i}$ being set to FALSE (that is, x_i is set to TRUE)
2. x_{il}'s from triples in FALSE(i) corresponding to x_i being set to FALSE

There can be no overlap among these two sets of triples in a 3d–matching because the x_{il}'s are combined with the b_{il}'s and c_{il}'s in a pattern that is "out of phase" with how the $\overline{x_{il}}$s are hooked up with them.

Now that we have a way to mimic a truth assignment using 3DM, we need to link variables up to clauses so we can test the satisfiability of the instance $X \diamond F$ of restricted 3SAT. For this we introduce m additional elements d_j for $1 \leq j \leq m$ into B, and m new elements e_j for $1 \leq j \leq m$ into C. We add the following $3m$ triples to M, where, for $1 \leq j \leq m$ and $1 \leq l \leq 5$,

$$\text{CLAUSE}(j) = \{(x_{il}, d_j, e_j) \mid x_i \in f_j \text{ and } f_j \text{ is the } l\text{th clause that } x_i \text{ occurs in}$$

$$\cup \{(\overline{x_{il}}, d_j, e_j) \mid \overline{x_i} \in f_j \text{ and } f_j \text{ is the } l\text{th clause } \overline{x_i} \text{ occurs in}\}$$

Since the reduction is from 3SAT, CLAUSE(j) contains exactly three triples. The instance of 3SAT we are using for the reduction is restricted so that x_i or $\overline{x_i}$ can occur in at most five clauses. When such a literal occurs in fewer clauses or none at all, no triples for those higher values of l corresponding to the literal will be included. For example, if x_3 occurs in only two clauses, then there are no triples in

$$\bigcup_{j=1}^{m} \text{CLAUSE}(j)$$

whose first component is x_{33}, x_{34}, or x_{35}.

How do these triples "check" that each clause is satisfied by a given assignment? The framework we have described is such that for $1 \leq j \leq m$, d_j and e_j only appear in triples in the set CLAUSE(j). This means that for $1 \leq j \leq m$ exactly one triple from CLAUSE(j) must be contained in a 3d-matching. However, a triple having x_{il} as a first component can be used only if we include TRUE(i) in the matching. This corresponds to x_i being set to TRUE, so f_j is satisfied by the lth occurrence of x_i in this case. A similar argument can be used to show that $\overline{x_{il}}$ can be used to match d_j and e_j only if we include FALSE(i) in the matching. This corresponds to x_i being set to FALSE, so f_j is satisfied by the lth occurrence of $\overline{x_i}$ in this case.

The final stage of the construction is to introduce some additional elements into B and C so the "extra" copies of x_i and $\overline{x_i}$ can be matched. Remember we made five copies of each, although between them, they occur at most five times in total. $5n$ of the x_{il}'s and $\overline{x_{il}}$'s are matched by an "assignment" and m of them are matched in "satisfying the clauses." So, $5n - m$ of the x_{il}'s and $\overline{x_{il}}$'s are not matched. We place elements g_k with $1 \leq k \leq 5n - m$ into B, and elements h_k with $1 \leq k \leq 5n - m$ into C. To tie up the loose ends we add the following triples to M:

$$\text{UNMATCHED} = \{(x_{il}, g_k, h_k), (\overline{x_{il}}, g_k, h_k) \mid 1 \leq i \leq n, 1 \leq l \leq 5, 1 \leq k \leq 5n - m\}$$

Next we describe how these triples allow us to match up the remaining copies of x_i and $\overline{x_i}$. Suppose M' is a partial matching for the triples in FALSE(i), TRUE(i), and CLAUSE(j). Each pair of elements g_k and h_k needs to be matched up using triples from UNMATCHED that do not include any first component of those in M'. As previously mentioned, if M' "contains" an assignment and a verification that the clauses are satisfied, then there are only $5n - m$ copies of the literals that still remain to be matched. However, this is exactly the number of g's and h's. So, all unmatched copies of literals can be matched. Since we do not know in advance which literals need to be set to TRUE, the g's and h's are connected to all copies of the literals.

In summary, we have

$$A = \{x_{il}, \overline{x_{il}} \mid 1 \le i \le n, 1 \le l \le 5\}$$

$$B = \{b_{il} \mid 1 \le i \le n, 1 \le l \le 5\} \cup \{d_j \mid 1 \le j \le m\} \cup \{g_k \mid 1 \le k \le 5n - m\}$$

$$C = \{c_{il} \mid 1 \le i \le n, 1 \le l \le 5\} \cup \{e_j \mid 1 \le j \le m\} \cup \{h_k \mid 1 \le k \le 5n - m\}$$

$$M = \left(\bigcup_{i=1}^{n} \text{TRUE}(i) \right) \cup \left(\bigcup_{i=1}^{n} \text{FALSE}(i) \right) \cup \left(\bigcup_{j=1}^{m} \text{CLAUSE}(j) \right) \cup \text{UNMATCHED}$$

It is clear that A, B, and C are 3-good of cardinality $10n$ so that the instance of 3DM f produces is a "legal" one. Although we have described the relationship between satisfying assignments and matchings, we leave the formal proof that f is correct to the exercises.

Observe that at all stages in the reduction only a polynomial number in n and m of elements and triples were introduced. Thus $O(\lg n + \lg m)$ bit counters suffice for bookkeeping. Subject to the proof that f is correct, we have shown that 3SAT $\le_m^{\lg}$ 3DM. ∎

In Figure 11.13 we present an example illustrating a 3d-matching M' corresponding to the satisfying assignment $x_1 = F$, $x_2 = T$, and $x_3 = F$ for the formula

$$(x_1 \vee x_2 \vee x_3) \wedge (\overline{x_1} \vee \overline{x_2} \vee \overline{x_3}) \wedge (x_1 \vee x_2 \vee \overline{x_3}) \wedge (x_1 \vee \overline{x_2} \vee \overline{x_3})$$

In this case n equals 3 and m equals 4. Figure 11.13 (a) shows the triples in M' that are used to represent the assignment. There are $5n$, or 15, triples needed for this purpose. Figure 11.13 (b) provides the triples that are used to verify that the clauses are satisfied. Since we need one triple per clause, there are four such triples. Finally, Figure 11.13 (c) lists the remaining triples that are needed to tie up the loose ends—match the extra copies of the literals. We have paired the g's and h's with the copies of the literals using an order based on the indices of the literals. Notice the matching has $10n = 30$ triples in total.

Let us conclude this chapter with a few remarks. We carefully chose reductions from the field of NP-completeness theory that were relatively easy to explain and understand, yet still illustrate many of the key features of NP-completeness reductions. To prove another problem is NP-complete requires selecting the right problem to reduce from plus some mathematical ingenuity. In this chapter, we discussed the following NP-complete problems:

- Satisfiability
- Three Satisfiability

$(x_{11}, b_{11}, c_{12}), (x_{12}, b_{12}, c_{13}), (x_{13}, b_{13}, c_{14}), (x_{14}, b_{14}, c_{15}), (x_{15}, b_{15}, c_{11})$
$(\overline{x_{21}}, b_{21}, c_{21}), (\overline{x_{22}}, b_{22}, c_{22}), (\overline{x_{23}}, b_{23}, c_{23}), (\overline{x_{24}}, b_{24}, c_{24}), (\overline{x_{25}}, b_{25}, c_{25})$
$(x_{31}, b_{31}, c_{32}), (x_{32}, b_{32}, c_{33}), (x_{33}, b_{33}, c_{34}), (x_{34}, b_{34}, c_{35}), (x_{35}, b_{35}, c_{31})$
(a)

$(x_{21}, d_1, e_1), (\overline{x_{11}}, d_2, e_2), (x_{22}, d_3, e_3), (\overline{x_{33}}, d_4, e_4)$
(b)

$(\overline{x_{12}}, g_1, h_1), (\overline{x_{13}}, g_2, h_2), (\overline{x_{14}}, g_3, h_3), (\overline{x_{15}}, g_4, h_4)$
$(x_{23}, g_5, h_5), (x_{24}, g_6, h_6), (x_{25}, g_7, h_7)$
$(\overline{x_{31}}, g_8, h_8), (\overline{x_{32}}, g_9, h_9), (\overline{x_{34}}, g_{10}, h_{10}), (\overline{x_{35}}, g_{11}, h_{11})$
(c)

Figure 11.13

An example illustrating the reduction described in Theorem 11.5.7. The instance of restricted 3SAT we use is $(x_1 \vee x_2 \vee x_3) \wedge (\overline{x_1} \vee \overline{x_2} \vee \overline{x_3}) \wedge (x_1 \vee x_2 \vee \overline{x_3}) \wedge (x_1 \vee \overline{x_2} \vee \overline{x_3})$, with the assignment $x_1 = F$, $x_2 = T$, and $x_3 = F$. We show a 3d-matching M' corresponding to this assignment. (a) The triples in M' that correspond to the assignment. (b) The triples that are used to verify that the clauses are satisfied. (c) The remaining triples that pair up extra copies of the literals.

- Not–All–Equals Three Satisfiability
- Hamiltonian Circuit
- Traveling Salesperson
- Vertex Cover
- Restricted Three Satisfiability
- Three–Dimensional Matching

These represent some of the most useful NP-complete problems and are a good starting point for many NP-completeness proofs.

11.6   *Exercises*

Section 11.2   *Nondeterministic Polynomial Time*

1. Prove $NC \subseteq P \subseteq NP$.

2. Prove Observation 11.2.3.

3. How many different subsets of vertices are there in an n–node undirected graph?

4. Suppose you are given an undirected graph $G = (V, E)$ and two designated nodes s and t. At most how many possible different paths are there from s to t?

5. Prove the following problems are in *NP*.

   (a) **Feedback Arc Set**
       Given: A directed graph $G = (V, E)$ and a natural number k.
       Problem: Is there a subset of edges $E' \subseteq E$ with $|E'| \leq k$ such that E' contains at least one edge from every directed cycle in G?

   (b) **Chromatic Number**
       Given: An undirected graph $G = (V, E)$ and a natural number k.
       Problem: Is G *k-colorable*? That is, does there exist a function

       $$f : V \mapsto \{1, 2, \ldots, k\}$$

       such that whenever $\{u, v\} \in E$ we have $f(u) \neq f(v)$?

   (c) **Composite**
       Given: A string of 0's and 1's.
       Problem: Is the number represented by the string in binary (no leading 0's allowed) *composite*? That is, does the number have factors besides 1 and itself?
       Examples:

       - $0100 \mapsto 4$ but has a leading 0, so is a NO.
       - $111 \mapsto 7$ but this is prime, so is a NO.
       - $100 \mapsto 4 = 2 \times 2$, which is composite, so this is a YES.
       - $10 \mapsto 2$ but this is prime, so is a NO.
       - $1010 \mapsto 5 \times 2 = 10$, which is composite, so this is a YES.

   (d) **Maximum Leaf Spanning Tree**
       Given: An undirected graph $G = (V, E)$ and a natural number k.
       Problem: Is there a spanning tree of G in which at least k vertices have degree one? That is, k vertices are leaves.

   (e) **Steiner Tree in Graphs**
       Given: An undirected graph $G = (V, E)$, a subset $V' \subseteq V$, and a natural number k.
       Problem: Is there a subtree of G that includes all the vertices of V' and contains at most k edges?

6. Let Σ be an alphabet and $\diamond$ a delimiter, where $\diamond \notin \Sigma$. Let $L \subseteq \Sigma^*$ be a language. Let $R \subseteq \Sigma^* \times \Sigma^*$ be a binary relation on strings in Σ.
   R is called *polynomially decidable* if there is a DTM recognizing the language $\{x \diamond y \mid (x, y) \in R\}$ in $n^{O(1)}$ time. R is *polynomially bounded* if $(x, y) \in R$ implies $|y| \leq |x|^k$ for some $k \geq 1$.
   Prove $L \in NP$ if and only if there is a polynomially decidable and polynomially bounded relation R, such that

   $$L = \{x \mid (x, y) \in R \text{ for some } y\}$$

Section 11.3   NP-Completeness Theory

7. Prove Theorem 11.3.2.

8. You have developed a proof of NP–completeness for a problem that your boss asked you to devise a polynomial time algorithm for. Unfortunately, she is not knowledgeable about the theory of NP-completeness. Write a paragraph or two explaining why your result shows it is unlikely that the problem has a polynomial time solution.

9. A *New York Times* editor has offered you $1,000 for writing a column about the importance of NP-complete problems. He has warned you that the article must be accessible to the nonspecialist. Write the article in 500 words or less.

10. Prove that if any NP-complete problem is in NC, then $NC = P = NP$.

Section 11.4   Examples of NP-Complete Problems

11. Provide two YES and two NO instances of SAT over the variable set $X = \{x_1, x_2, x_3, x_4\}$, where each instance has four clauses containing either two or three literals per clause.

12. How many different satisfying assignments are there of the following formula?

$$(x_1 \vee x_2 \vee \overline{x_3}) \wedge (x_1 \vee \overline{x_2} \vee \overline{x_3}) \wedge (\overline{x_1} \vee \overline{x_2} \vee x_3)$$

List them.

13. Derive a formula F consisting of three variables per clause over the variable set $X = \{x_1, x_2, x_3\}$ such that F has exactly one satisfying assignment.

14. Prove SAT is in NP.

15. What is the smallest NO instance of 3SAT, which has the correct form, over the set of variables $X = \{x_1, x_2, x_3, x_4\}$?

16. Let $X = \{x_1, x_2, x_3\}$. Prove that

$$C = \{\{\overline{x_1}, \overline{x_2}, x_3\}, \{\overline{x_1}, x_2, \overline{x_3}\}, \{x_1, \overline{x_2}, \overline{x_3}\}, \{x_1, x_2, x_3\}\}$$

is a NO instance of NAE3SAT.

17. Define a Generic Machine Simulation problem for NTMs. Prove that your problem is NP-complete.

18. *Disjunctive normal form* (DNF) is OR's of AND's; contrast this with CNF. Define 3DNFSATand prove that it is NP-complete.

19. Define your own NP-complete variant of SAT.

20. Show that if only two literals are allowed per clause, then SAT, in this case called 2SAT, is in P.

21. How many different Hamiltonian circuits does the graph in Figure 11.6 have? List them in lexicographic order.

22. In a graph having n nodes, what is the minimum number of edges that it must contain in order to ensure that it has at least one Hamiltonian circuit?

Section 11.5   NP-Complete Problems and Reductions

23. Prove that Three Satisfiability is NP–complete. That is, prove Theorem 11.4.6.

24. Prove that Not–All–Equals Three Satisfiability is NP–complete. That is, prove Theorem 11.4.8.

25. Design a code for representing TSP instances and explain your scheme. Draw a picture and write down the corresponding encodings for instances where you have 0 cities, 1 city, . . . , 4 cities; you make up the instances. Tell which instances are YES and which are NO. Give nontrivial lower and upper bounds on the lengths of your encodings.

26. Define a variant of TSP as follows:

    Restricted Traveling Salesperson problem (RTSP)
    Given: A set C of m cities, a positive integer distance $d(c_i, c_j) \leq 5$ for each pair of cities $c_i, c_j \in C$, and a positive integer B.
    Problem: Is there a tour of C having length B or less?

    Note the restriction on the lengths of the distances between cities. Prove RTSP is NP–complete.

27. The *triangle inequality* is satisfied by a traveling salesperson distance function d if for any three cities $c_1, c_2,$ and c_3

    $$d(c_1, c_3) \leq d(c_1, c_2) + d(c_2, c_3)$$

    Note that the *Euclidean distance measure* obeys the triangle inequality. Define a variant of TSP called Triangle TSP. Prove that Triangle TSP is NP–complete.

28. Prove the following:

    Observation 11.6.1   *Let $G = (V, E)$ be an undirected graph and $V' \subseteq V$. Let $\overline{G}$ be the complement graph of G, i.e.,*

    $$\overline{G} = (V, \{\{u, v\} \mid u, v \in V \text{ and } \{u, v\} \notin E\})$$

    The following three statements are equivalent:

    (a) V' is a vertex cover of G.
    (b) $V - V'$ is an independent set of G.
    (c) $V - V'$ is a clique of $\overline{G}$.

29. Prove the Clique problem is NP–complete using a reduction from Vertex Cover.

30. Define the *Maximum Independent Set problem* (MIS) in the same spirit as the Clique problem was defined. Prove MIS is NP–complete.

31. Let C be a collection of subsets of a set S. A *hitting set* is a subset $S' \subseteq S$ such that S' contains at least one element from each subset in C. The *size* of the hitting set is $|S'|$. The *Hitting Set problem* is defined as follows:

    Hitting Set
    Given: A collection C of subsets of a set S, and a positive integer k.
    Problem: Does S contain a hitting set for C of size k or less?

    Prove the Hitting Set problem is NP–complete.

32. Prove that the version of 3SAT in which each literal and its negation occurs in at most five clauses is still NP–complete. See Theorem 11.5.7.

33. Prove that the transformation f defined in Theorem 11.5.7 can be computed in logarithmic space and is correct.

34. Let L and L' be arbitrary languages in P, and L'' be an arbitrary NP–complete language. Show $L \leq_m^{\lg} L''$. Prove it is not true that $L \leq_m^{\lg} L'$ for all L and L' in P.

35. Prove the following problems are NP–complete. For definitions see Exercise 5.

    (a) Feedback Arc Set
    (b) Chromatic Number
    (c) Maximum Leaf Spanning Tree
    (d) Steiner Tree in Graphs

Notation

The following table covers some of the more common notation used in this work.

Symbol	Description
$\emptyset$	The empty set. The set containing no elements. See page 29.
$|S|$	The cardinality of set S. See page 24.
2^S	The power set of S, the set of all possible subsets of S. See page 40.
$\cup$	Set union. See page 31.
$\cap$	Set intersection. See page 32.
$-$	Set difference. See page 31.
$\oplus$	Symmetric difference. See page 32.
$\bar{L}$	The complement of L. See page 31.
L^R	Language reversal. See page 34.
L^*	Kleene star. See page 34.
L^+	Kleene plus, $L \circ L^*$. See page 35.
$L^{=n}$	Set of all strings in L of length n. See page 33.
$L^{\leq n}$	Set of all strings in L of length $\leq n$. See page 33.
Σ^*	All finite strings over the alphabet Σ. See page 29.
$\Sigma^{\leq n}$	All strings over the alphabet Σ of length less than or equal to n. See page 29.
Σ^n	All strings over the alphabet Σ of length exactly n. See page 29. Use $\Sigma^{=n}$ if there would be confusion with the n-fold Cartesian product of Σ.
$\#_c(x)$	The number of occurrences of the character c in the string x. See page 25.
Λ	The empty string. See page 24.
$\langle$	Tape left end marker. See page 87.
$\rangle$	Tape right end marker. See page 87.
Σ_T	Tape alphabet associated with input alphabet Σ. See page 87.
$[p, x]$	Tape configuration with head at position p on input x. See page 88.

$\sigma[p, x]$	Current symbol under head for tape configuration $[p, x]$. See page 88.
$\rho(p, x)$	Remaining tape contents for tape configuration $[p, x]$. See page 88.
$\tau^{Initial}(x)$	Initial tape configuration for input x. See page 88.
$\tau^{Final}(x)$	Final tape configuration for input x. See page 88.
$\diamond$	A delimiter symbol used to divide an input string into fields, as in $110\diamond0011\diamond0101$.
$|x|$	The length of string x. See page 24.
$\circ$	The concatenation of strings or languages depending on context. See page 26.
x^R	String reversal. See page 28.
$\leq_{\text{lex}}$	Lexicographical ordering of strings. See page 25. Also have $<_{\text{lex}}, \geq_{\text{lex}},$ and $>_{\text{lex}}$.
$\leq_{\text{enum}}$	Enumeration ordering of strings. See page 26. Also have $<_{\text{enum}}, \geq_{\text{enum}},$ and $>_{\text{enum}}$.
(x, y)	The ordered pair consisting of x and y. If x and y are vertices in a graph, this pair represents the directed edge from x to y.
$\neg$	The NOT function. See page 243.
$\vee$	The OR function. See page 243.
$\wedge$	The AND function. See page 243.
$\leq_m$	Many–one reducibility. See page 235.
$\leq_m^{\text{lg}}$	Many–one logarithmic space reducibility. See page 235.
$O(f(n))$	The set of functions whose growth rate is order $f(n)$. See page 224.
$n^{O(1)}$	The set of polynomially bounded functions. See page 224.
$f(n)^{O(1)}$	The set of functions bounded by a polynomial in $f(n)$. See page 224.
$(\log n)^{O(1)}$	The set of polylogarithmically bounded functions. See page 225.
$\Omega(f(n))$	The set of functions whose growth rate is at least order $f(n)$. See page 225.
$o(f(n))$	The set of functions whose growth rate is asymptotically slower than $f(n)$. See page 225.
$\omega(f(n))$	The set of functions whose growth rate is asymptotically faster than $f(n)$. See page 225.
$\mathbb{N}$	The set of natural numbers, $\{0, 1, 2, \ldots\}$.
$\mathbb{Z}$	The set of integers, $\{\ldots, -2, -1, 0, 1, 2, \ldots\}$.
$\mathbb{Q}$	The set of rational numbers.
$\mathbb{R}$	The set of real numbers.
$\mathbb{R}^+$	The set of positive real numbers.
$\lceil x \rceil$	The least integer not less than x.
$\lfloor x \rfloor$	The greatest integer not exceeding x.
$\lg n$	The maximum of 1 and $\lceil \lg_2 n \rceil$. See page 36. (Note: Sometimes we include $\lceil \ \rceil$ for emphasis.)

Greek Alphabet

This appendix contains a list of the lower- and uppercase Greek letters, their spelling in English, and a comment on their most frequent usage in this text.

Symbol	Name	Usage
α, A	alpha	circuit α
β, B	beta	circuit β
γ, Γ	gamma	string γ, alphabet Γ
δ, Δ	delta	transition function δ, transition relation Δ
ϵ, E	epsilon	the empty string is also denoted ϵ in other works
ζ, Z	zeta	
η, H	eta	
θ, Θ	theta	small- and big-Theta growth rates
ι, I	iota	
κ, K	kappa	
λ, Λ	lambda	the empty string Λ, other works sometimes use λ
μ, M	mu	
ν, N	nu	gate x has value $\nu(x)$
ξ, Ξ	xi	
o, O	omicron	small- and big-O growth rates
π, Π	pi	decision problem Π
ρ, P	rho	
σ, Σ	sigma	alphabet Σ
τ, T	tau	gate type τ
υ, Υ	upsilon	
ϕ, Φ	phi	mapping ϕ
χ, X	chi	characteristic function χ
ψ, Ψ	psi	mapping ψ
ω, Ω	omega	small- and big-Omega growth rates

Bibliography

Many of the foundations of computability and complexity theory have become part of the area's folklore. This list of citations is intended to provide you with some of the original references and additionally with references that are good starting points for research exploration.

[1] Alfred V. Aho, John E. Hopcroft, and Jeffrey D. Ullman. *Data Structures and Algorithms*. Reading, MA: Addison–Wesley, 1983.

[2] Richard J. Anderson. *The Complexity of Parallel Algorithms*. PhD thesis, Stanford University, 1985. Computer Science Department Technical Report STAN–CS–86–1092.

[3] José Luis Balcázar, Josep Díaz, and Joaquim Gabarró. *Structural Complexity I*, volume 11 of *EATCS Monographs on Theoretical Computer Science*. New York: Springer–Verlag, 1988.

[4] José Luis Balcázar, Josep Díaz, and Joaquim Gabarró. *Structural Complexity II*, volume 22 of *EATCS Monographs on Theoretical Computer Science*. New York: Springer–Verlag, 1990.

[5] Allan Borodin. On relating time and space to size and depth. *SIAM Journal on Computing*, 6(4):733–744, December 1977.

[6] Gilles Brassard and P. Bratley. *Algorithmics: Theory and Practice*. Englewood Cliffs, NJ: Prentice Hall, 1988.

[7] Stephen A. Cook. Path systems and language recognition. In *Conference Record of Second Annual ACM Symposium on Theory of Computing*, pages 70–72, Northampton, MA, May 1970.

[8] Stephen A. Cook. The complexity of theorem proving procedures. In *Conference Record of Third Annual ACM Symposium on Theory of Computing*, pages 151–158, Shaker Heights, OH, May 1971.

[9] Stephen A. Cook. Deterministic CFL's are accepted simultaneously in polynomial time and log squared space. In *Conference Record*

of the Eleventh Annual ACM Symposium on Theory of Computing, pages 338–345, Atlanta, GA, April–May 1979. See also [45].

[10]   Stephen A. Cook. A taxonomy of problems with fast parallel algorithms. *Information and Control,* 64(1–3):2–22, January/February/March 1985.

[11]   Thomas H. Cormen, Charles E. Leiserson, and Ronald L. Rivest. *Introduction to Algorithms.* Cambridge, MA: MIT Press, 1990.

[12]   Martin D. Davis, Ron Sigal, and Elaine J. Weyuker. *Computability, Complexity, and Languages,* second edition. San Diego: Academic Press, 1994.

[13]   J. Edmonds. Paths, trees and flowers. *Canadian Journal of Mathematics,* 17:449–467, 1965.

[14]   Faith E. Fich. The complexity of computation on the parallel random access machine. In Reif [38], chapter 20, pages 843–899.

[15]   Robert W. Floyd and Richard Beigel. *The Language of Machines.* New York: Computer Science Press, 1994.

[16]   Merrick L. Furst, J. B. Saxe, and Michael Sipser. Parity, circuits, and the polynomial-time hierarchy. In *22nd Annual Symposium on Foundations of Computer Science,* pages 260–270, Nashville, TN, October 1981. IEEE.

[17]   Michael R. Garey and David S. Johnson. *Computers and Intractability: A Guide to the Theory of NP-Completeness.* New York: W. H. Freeman and Company, 1979.

[18]   Judith L. Gersting. *Mathematical Structures for Computer Science,* third edition. New York: Computer Science Press, 1993.

[19]   Leslie M. Goldschlager. The monotone and planar circuit value problems are log space complete for *P. SIGACT News,* 9(2):25–29, Summer 1977.

[20]   Ronald L. Graham, Donald E. Knuth, and Oren Patashnik. *Concrete Mathematics: A Foundation for Computer Science.* Reading, MA: Addison–Wesley, 1989.

[21]   Raymond Greenlaw. *The Complexity of Parallel Computations: Inherently Sequential Algorithms and P-Complete Problems.* PhD thesis, University of Washington, December 1988. Department of Computer Science Technical Report 88–12–01.

[22]   Raymond Greenlaw. Polynomial completeness and parallel computation. In Reif [38], chapter 21, pages 901–953.

[23]   Raymond Greenlaw, H. James Hoover, and Walter L. Ruzzo. *Limits to Parallel Computation: P-Completeness Theory*. Oxford: Oxford University Press, 1995.

[24]   H. James Hoover. Feasible real functions and arithmetic circuits. *SIAM Journal on Computing*, 19(1):182–204, February 1990.

[25]   H. James Hoover. Real functions, contraction mappings, and P-completeness. *Information and Computation*, 93(2):333–349, August 1991.

[26]   John E. Hopcroft and Jeffrey D. Ullman. *Introduction to Automata Theory, Languages, and Computation*. Reading, MA: Addison–Wesley, 1979.

[27]   Neil Immerman. Nondeterministic space is closed under complementation. *SIAM Journal on Computing*, 17(5):935–938, October 1988.

[28]   Joseph JáJá. *An Introduction to Parallel Algorithms*. Reading, MA: Addison–Wesley, 1992.

[29]   David S. Johnson. A catalog of complexity classes. In van Leeuwen [44], chapter 2, pages 67–161.

[30]   Neil D. Jones and William T. Laaser. Complete problems for deterministic polynomial time. *Theoretical Computer Science*, 3(1):105–117, 1976.

[31]   Richard E. Ladner. The circuit value problem is log space complete for *P*. *SIGACT News*, 7(1):18–20, January 1975.

[32]   Thomas Lengauer. VLSI theory. In van Leeuwen [44], chapter 16, pages 837–868.

[33]   Harry R. Lewis and Christos H. Papadimitriou. *Elements of the Theory of Computation*. Englewood Cliffs, NJ: Prentice Hall, 1981.

[34]   Noam Nisan and Amnon Ta–Shma. Symmetric *logspace* is closed under complement. *Chicago Journal of Theoretical Computer Science*, 1995(1), June 1995.

[35]   Christos H. Papadimitriou. *Computational Complexity*. Reading, MA: Addison–Wesley, 1994.

[36]   Nicholas J. Pippenger. On simultaneous resource bounds. In *20th Annual Symposium on Foundations of Computer Science*, pages 307–311, San Juan, Puerto Rico, October 1979. IEEE.

[37]   John H. Reif. Depth–first search is inherently sequential. *Information Processing Letters*, 20(5):229–234, 12 June 1985.

[38]   John H. Reif, editor. *Synthesis of Parallel Algorithms*. San Francisco: Morgan Kaufmann, 1993.

[39] Kenneth H. Rosen. *Discrete Mathematics and Its Applications*, second edition. New York: McGraw–Hill, 1991.

[40] Kenneth A. Ross and Charles R. B. Wright. *Discrete Mathematics*, third edition. Englewood Cliffs, NJ: Prentice Hall, 1992.

[41] Walter L. Ruzzo. On uniform circuitry complexity. *Journal of Computer and System Sciences*, 22(3):365–383, June 1981.

[42] Thomas A. Sudkamp. *Languages and Machines*, revised edition. Reading, MA: Addison–Wesley, 1991.

[43] Róbert Szelepcsényi. The method of forcing for nondeterministic automata. *Bulletin of the European Association for Theoretical Computer Science*, 33:96–100, October 1987.

[44] Jan van Leeuwen, editor. *Handbook of Theoretical Computer Science*, volume A: Algorithms and Complexity. Cambridge, MA: MIT Press/Elsevier, 1990.

[45] B. von Braunmühl, Stephen A. Cook, Kurt Mehlhorn, and Rutger Verbeek. The recognition of deterministic CFL's in small time and space. *Information and Control*, 56(1–2):34–51, January/February 1983.

[46] Derick Wood. *Theory of Computation*. New York: John Wiley & Sons, 1987.

Index

327